Praise for *Awaken the Giant Within* by Anthony Robbins

"Awaken the Giant Within *is yet another profound and powerful tool in the Robbins arsenal of self-awareness. It has been an enormous source of strength and insight for me both personally and professionally.*"

—PETER GUBER
Chairman of the Board and Chief Executive Officer
Sony Pictures Entertainment Inc.

"*Champions are those who can get themselves to constantly improve and consistently perform at peak levels. Anthony Robbins is the 'ultimate coach' for that special breed of men and women who will never settle for less than they can be.*"

—PAT RILEY
NBA "Coach of the Decade"

"*Classic Robbins vintage . . . this is the book for everyone who aspires to personal achievement and greatness, to reach a '10' in all areas of life. This is the stuff that genius is made of . . . thinking in new directions . . . restoring the ability to dream . . . bringing to life dormant courage and commitment.*"

—JIM HANSBERGER
Chairman, Director's Advisory Group, Shearson Lehman Brothers
Author, *Nice Guys Finish Rich*

"Awaken the Giant Within *should be required reading for anyone committed to increasing the quality of their life. Anthony Robbins ignites the reader with his passion as well as practical advice.*"

—DR. BARBARA DE ANGELIS
Author, #1 Bestseller *How to Make Love All the Time*
and *Secrets About Men Every Woman Should Know*

"**Awaken the Giant Within** *is a passionate call to action, challenging you to remember who you really are and to make a unique contribution with the rest of your life.*"

—MARTIN SHEEN

"*Tony Robbins has astonishing credibility. His book* Awaken the Giant Within *is packed from start to finish with scientifically sound principles and techniques. Every page bursts with well-researched and immediately practical guidelines for concentrating your thoughts and emotions on the attainment of your goals. Robbins is a powerful communicator and a true authority on the subject of personal success.*"

—SCOTT DeGARMO

Editor-in-Chief and Publisher, *Success* magazine

"*Tony Robbins is the leading thinker in the psychology of personal achievement and peak performance. Not only does* Awaken the Giant Within *give you every tool you need to achieve personal excellence, but Tony's warmth, passion and commitment will inspire you to truly master your life and to touch others in the process.*"

—KENNETH BLANCHARD, PH.D.

Coauthor, *The One-Minute Manager*

"*No one in America knows more about the subject of personal achievement and creating true success than Tony Robbins.*"

—CHARLES GIVENS

Author, *Wealth Without Risk* and *Financial Self-Defense*

"*The pages flow with the creativity of new talk and ensuing transformational awareness. Chapter 9 alone, 'The Vocabulary of Ultimate Success,' is an enrichment worth more than dollars can measure.*"

—F.J. GOULD

Professor, Applied Mathematics and Management Science
University of Chicago
President, Investment Research Co.

"Tony Robbins is one of the great influencers of this generation. Awaken the Giant Within is a fascinating, intriguing presentation of cutting-edge findings and insights across a broad spectrum of issues, including the growing consciousness that true success is first anchored to enduring values and service to others."

—STEPHEN R. COVEY

Author, *New York Times* #1 Bestseller
The 7 Habits of Highly Effective People

Also by Anthony Robbins

Unlimited Power

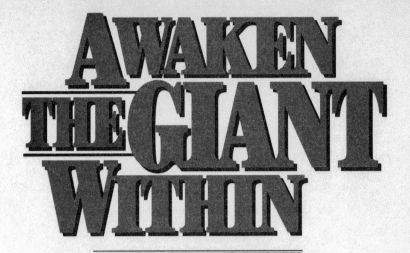

AWAKEN THE GIANT WITHIN

*How to take
immediate control
of your mental,
emotional, physical
& financial destiny!*

ANTHONY ROBBINS

A FIRESIDE BOOK
Published by Simon & Schuster
New York   London
Toronto   Sydney   Tokyo   Singapore

FIRESIDE

Rockefeller Center
1230 Avenue of the Americas
New York, New York 10020

First Fireside Edition 1992

FIRESIDE and colophon are
trademarks of Simon & Schuster Inc.

Designed by Quinn Hall
Manufactured in the United States of America

1 3 5 7 9 10 8 6 4 2
29 30 28   (pbk)

Library of Congress Cataloging-in-Publication Data
Robbins, Anthony.
Awaken the giant within : how to take immediate control of your
mental, emotional, physical & financial destiny! /Anthony Robbins.
p. cm.
Originally published: New York : Summit Books, © 1991.
"A Fireside book."
1. Success—Psychological aspects. I. Title.
[BF637.58R63 1992]
158'1—dc20   92-30041
                                                  CIP

ISBN 0-671-72734-6
ISBN 0-671-79154-0 (pbk)

ACKNOWLEDGMENTS

As I begin to reflect on the magnitude of this project, I am reminded of the celebrated quarterback who sprints onto the field in the last quarter of the game, confers in the huddle, confidently strides out to the line of scrimmage, and throws the perfect spiral pass fifty yards downfield into the end zone to score the winning touchdown! The fans cheer, the coaches are thrilled, and the quarterback gets to joyously revel in the glory of winning the game. But it was a team effort. The quarterback is the public hero; however, in any game in life there are a multitude of players who are the hidden heroes, and in this endeavor there have been many. I have never been known to have words fail me, but as I begin to put on paper the feelings I have toward so many loyal and phenomenally selfless family members, friends and co-workers, I am overwhelmed. There is difficulty in assigning a hierarchy since it has been a true team effort from the beginning.

To my wife, Becky, my mom, and my four children—Jairek, Josh, Jolie, and Tyler—your love is my strength. Nothing is more important to me.

To my assistants, Deena Tuttle and Karen Risch, two amazing dynamos, who remained devoted to the vision that what we were doing would make a difference, even when it meant staying up all night away from husbands and children, even following me all over the country, at all times remaining cheerful and supportive. This book could not have been completed without their unswerving faithfulness.

To my Field Sales Representatives and Managers, who daily work out in the field in order to bring me into a city to overflowing seminar rooms; and to my franchisees, the Personal Development Consultants, who have helped me prove that video-based seminars do make a difference, I thank you for your courage and your dedication. To the Customer Service Representatives at Robbins Research International, who inspire the customer to take action and grow to new levels, I am so grateful.

To my entire team at the Robbins Research International offices in San Diego, who work crazy hours in order to launch my brainstorms and maintain the integrity of the vision, I salute you.

To my partners and associates of all the Anthony Robbins Companies, especially my dear friends at Fortune Management, your sensitivity to my unbelievable schedule touched my heart.

To the participants who have attended my seminars, I have learned much from you and acknowledge you for your participation in this work. A special thank you to the Certification class of 1991 who supported me as I worked throughout the night for more than two weeks in order to deliver this book on time.

To Earl Strumpell, whose love, friendship, and twenty-four-hour-a-day commitment to obtain and maintain whatever resources I need has given me the peace of mind to create.

To Dr. Robert Bays, my dear friend, whose wisdom and unconditional love pulled me through the bumpy roads, and whose input I always hold valuable, I am eternally grateful. To Vicki St. George, a gem of a friend, thank you.

To Michael Hutchison, who consistently holds himself to a high standard, I feel blessed by our relationship. To my best friend, Michael Keyes, thanks, buddy, for your humor and wit, your compassion and support. To Alan, Linda, and Josh Hahn for your inspiration and friendship; I look toward a long adventurous future.

To the "castle crew," especially Theresa Lannon and Elizabeth Calfee, who are the best support system on earth, thanks for keeping this man's home his castle!

To my good friends at Guthy-Renker Corporation, Greg Renker, Bill Guthy, Lenny Lieberman, Jon Schulberg, and John Zahody, who, along with the staff of Cassette Productions, have helped me to distribute over 7 million audio tapes carrying my Personal Power philosophy to people around the world in the last two years alone, I cherish our friendship.

To Peter Guber, for your inspirational phone calls and support, I deeply value our relationship.

To Ken and Marge Blanchard, the quarterly rendezvous with Becky and me are always the source of mutual magic and ever-increasing respect.

To Martin and Janet Sheen, for being such outstanding examples of passion, integrity, and commitment, thank you for being a light.

To all of the volunteers of the Anthony Robbins Foundation, the homeless, prisoners, children, and the elderly will never be the same because of your constant commitment to selfless contribution. You truly make a difference!

To Robert Cialdini, Stu Mittleman, Phil Maffetone, Paul Pilzer, and

John Robbins, your contributions to this book will impact the quality of people's lives.

To *tae kwon do* Grand Master Jhoon Rhee, whose constant love, loyalty, and knowledge inspire me to greater accomplishment, I respectfully bow to you, sir.

To the incredible staff of our Fiji getaway, the Namale Plantation Resort, and to the members of the neighboring villages of Viville and Nadi, you have truly taught me by example that life is a gift and a joy, that happiness is the only way to live.

To Jan Miller and her competent crew, my loyal liaison in this idiosyncratic publishing business, I take off my hat. To Dick Snyder, Bob Asahina, and Sarah Bayliss, thank you for your faith in me, once again.

To the giants whose shoulders I stand upon, the teachers who have shaped so much of my philosophy, strategies, and skill, I acknowledged you in *Unlimited Power* and I salute you once again.

And finally, thank you to a whole host of behind-the-scenes folks who supported me, including: Kathy Moeller, Suzy Gonzales, Joan Meng, Nancy Minkus, Shari Wilson, Mary Kent, Valerie Felts, Leigh Lendzian, Dave Polcino, Cherrell Tarantino, Mark Lamm, Robert Mott for the art work, and the guys at Franklin Type in New York.

These people never accepted that something was impossible. We all expected and received miracles throughout this odyssey, and we have all grown and become more in the process. You are all giants in my life.

Contents

FOREWORD

As the Chief Psychologist at Bellevue Hospital in New York City, I see so much human misery, not just in the mentally ill patients we treat, but also in the "normal," "healthy" staff that treat them. I also see the same unhappiness in the high-functioning, relatively successful people I treat in my private practice. Quite often, the pain and misery are unnecessary and finally end when the people take charge of their beliefs, feelings, and actions in order to modify the process of their lives. Unfortunately, most of the time they don't. They wait, then try to alter the bad result or, often, go to a shrink wanting just to complain about their awful life or in some way be "fixed" by someone else.

Empowering people to realize that they determine the outcome of their own lives is not always easy. In fact, it's usually an overwhelming task. Consequently, I've always searched for new methods and technologies to pass along at the hospital and to my private patients. It was five years ago that I first heard about Tony Robbins's work and attended one of his seminars in New York. I expected and received a truly unusual evening. What was unexpected was Tony's genius in the realm of human behavior and communication. That night I learned that Tony shares my belief that anyone who is basically sane can take command and live life fully. Soon afterward, I attended Tony's two-week Certification course and passed on much of what I learned there to colleagues and patients. I called the course "a basic training for life." I then began recommending his tape series and his first book, *Unlimited Power*.

Although some of my colleagues are offended or surprised when I recommend the works of such a young man who doesn't have academic credentials, those who actually read or listen to Tony come to agree. In addition to comprehensive, good information, Tony has a talent and a compelling style that make his material easy to grasp.

Eventually, my wife and I took the Date With Destiny™ course which contains many of the concepts that are in Tony's latest work, *Awaken the Giant Within*. That weekend gave us the means to make alterations in our own values, rules, and controls, which, over the past two years, have allowed our lives to become much more productive and fulfilling.

I see Tony as a great coach in the game of life. His accurate insight, intelligence, passion, and commitment are always present and inspiring. Reading this book is like actually sitting across from Tony and becoming engaged in an engrossing and entertaining conversation with him. It should be referred to again and again, like a user's manual, whenever life presents a new challenge or requires a change in course. It provides an arsenal of tools for lasting change as well as lessons for enriching the quality of life. In fact, if enough people read this book and sincerely apply its teachings, it could put me and many of my colleagues out of business.

FREDERICK L. COVAN, PH.D.

"*Deep within man dwell those slumbering powers;*
powers that would astonish him,
that he never dreamed of possessing;
forces that would revolutionize his life if aroused
and put into action."
—ORISON SWETT MARDEN

PART • ONE

UNLEASH YOUR POWER

1
DREAMS
OF DESTINY

"A consistent man believes in destiny, a capricious man in chance."
—BENJAMIN DISRAELI

We all have dreams . . . We all want to believe deep down in our souls that we have a special gift, that we can make a difference, that we can touch others in a special way, and that we can make the world a better place. At one time in our lives, we all had a vision for the quality of life that we desire and deserve. Yet, for many of us, those dreams have become so shrouded in the frustrations and routines of daily life that we no longer even make an effort to accomplish them. For far too many, the dream has dissipated—and with it, so has the will to shape our destinies. Many have lost that sense of certainty that creates the winner's edge. My life's quest has been to restore the dream and to make it real, to get each of us to remember and use the unlimited power that lies sleeping within us all.

I'll never forget the day it really hit me that I was truly living my dream. I was flying my jet helicopter from a business meeting in Los Angeles, traveling to Orange County on the way to one of my seminars. As I flew over the city of Glendale, I suddenly recognized a large building, and I stopped the helicopter and hovered above it. As I looked down, I realized this was the building that I'd worked in as a janitor a mere twelve years ago!

In those days, I had been concerned whether my 1960 Volkswagen would hang together for the 30-minute trip to work. My life had been focused on how I was going to survive; I had felt fearful and alone. But that day, as I hovered there in the sky, I thought, "What a difference a decade can make!" I did have dreams back then, but at the time, it seemed they'd never be realized. Today, though, I've come to believe that all my past failure and frustration were actually laying the foundation for the understandings that have created the new level of living I now enjoy. As I continued my flight south along the coastal route, I spotted dolphins playing with the surfers in the waves below. It's a sight that my wife, Becky, and I treasure as one of life's special gifts. Finally, I reached Irvine.

Looking below, I was a little disturbed when I saw that the off ramp to my seminar was jammed with bumper-to-bumper traffic for more than a mile. I thought to myself, "Boy, I hope whatever else is going on tonight gets started soon so that the people coming to my seminar arrive on time."

But as I descended to the helipad, I began to see a new picture: thousands of people being held back by security where I was just about to land. Suddenly I began to grasp the reality. The traffic jam had been caused by people going to *my event!* Although we had expected approximately 2,000 attendees, I was facing a crowd of 7,000—in an auditorium that would hold only 5,000! When I walked into the arena from the landing pad, I was surrounded by hundreds of people who wanted to give me a hug or tell me how my work had positively impacted their lives.

The stories they shared with me were incredible. One mother introduced me to her son who had been labeled "hyperactive" and "learning disabled." Utilizing the principles of **state management** taught in this book, she was not only able to get him off the drug Ritalin, but they had also since been transferred to California where her son had been retested and evaluated at the level of genius! You should have seen his face as she shared with me his *new* label. A gentleman talked about how he had freed himself from cocaine using some of the **Success Conditioning** techniques you'll learn in this book. A couple in their mid-fifties shared with me that, after fifteen years of marriage, they had been on the brink of divorce until they learned about **personal rules**. A salesman told me how his monthly income had jumped from $2,000 to over $12,000 in a mere six months, and an entrepreneur related that he had increased corporate revenues by over $3 million in eighteen months by applying the principles of **quality questions** and **emotional management**. A lovely young woman showed me a picture of her former self, having lost fifty-two pounds by applying the principles of **leverage** that are detailed in this book.

I was touched so deeply by the emotions in that room that I got choked up, and at first I couldn't speak. As I looked out on my audience and saw 5,000 smiling, cheering, loving faces, in that moment I realized that *I am living my dream!* What a feeling to know that beyond a shadow of a doubt I had the information, strategies, philosophies, and skills that could assist any one of these people in empowering themselves to make the changes they desired most! A flood of images and emotions flowed over me. I began to remember an experience I'd had only a few years before, sitting in my 400-square-foot bachelor apartment in Venice, California, all alone and crying as I listened to the lyrics of a Neil Diamond song: "I am, I said, to no one there. And no one heard at all, not even the chair. I am, I cried. I am, said I. And I am lost, and I can't even say why, leavin' me lonely still." I remembered feeling like my life didn't matter, as if the events of the world were controlling me. I also remember the moment my life changed, the moment I finally said, "I've had it! I know I'm much more than I'm demonstrating mentally, emotionally, and physically in my life." I *made a decision* in that moment which was to alter my life forever. I decided to change virtually every aspect of my life. *I decided I would never again settle for less than I could be.* Who would have guessed that this decision would bring me to such an incredible moment?

I gave my all at the seminar that night, and when I left the auditorium, crowds of people followed me to the helicopter to see me off. To say I was deeply moved by the experience would be an understatement. A tear slid down my cheek as I thanked my Creator for these wonderful gifts. As I lifted off the grass and ascended into the moonlight, I had to pinch myself. *Could this be real?* Am I the same guy who eight years ago was struggling, frustrated, feeling alone and incapable of making my life work? Fat, broke, and wondering if I could even survive? How could a young kid like me with nothing but a high school education have created such dramatic changes?

My answer is simple: I learned to harness the principle I now call **concentration of power**. Most people have no idea of the giant capacity we can immediately command when we focus all of our resources on mastering a single area of our lives. Controlled focus is like a laser beam that can cut through anything that seems to be stopping you. When we focus consistently on improvement in any area, we develop unique distinctions on how to make that area better. One reason so few of us achieve what we truly want is that we never direct our focus; we never concentrate our power. Most people dabble their way through life, never deciding to master anything in particular. In fact, I believe most people fail in life simply because they *major in minor things.* I believe that one of life's major lessons is learning to understand what makes us do what we do. What shapes human behavior? The answers to this question provide critical keys to shaping your own destiny.

My entire life has been continually driven by a singular, compelling focus: *What makes the difference in the <u>quality</u> of people's lives?* How is it that so often people from such humble beginnings and devastating backgrounds manage in spite of it all to create lives that inspire us? Conversely, why do many of those born into privileged environments, with every resource for success at their fingertips, end up fat, frustrated, and often chemically addicted? What makes some people's lives an example and others' a warning? What is the secret that creates passionate, happy, and grateful lives in many, while for others the refrain might be, "Is that all there is?"

My own magnificent obsession began with some simple questions: "How can I take immediate control of my life? What can I do today that can make a difference—that could help me and others to shape our destinies? How can I expand, learn, grow, and share that knowledge with others in a meaningful and enjoyable way?"

At a very early age, I developed a belief that we're all here to contribute something unique, that deep within each of us lies a special gift. You see, I truly believe we all have a sleeping giant within us. Each of us has a talent, a gift, our own bit of genius just waiting to be tapped. It might be a talent for art or music. It might be a special way of relating to the ones you love. It might be a genius for selling or innovating or reaching out in your business or your career. I choose to believe that our Creator doesn't play favorites, that we've all been created unique, but with equal opportunities for experiencing life to the fullest. I decided many years ago that the most important way I could spend my life would be to invest it in something that would outlast it. *I decided that somehow I must contribute in some way that would live on long after I was gone.*

Today, I have the incredible privilege of sharing my ideas and feelings with literally millions of people through my books, tapes, and television shows. I've personally worked with over a quarter of a million people in the last few years alone. I've assisted members of Congress, CEOs, presidents of companies and countries, managers and mothers, salespeople, accountants, lawyers, doctors, psychiatrists, counselors, and professional athletes. I've worked with phobics, the clinically depressed, people with multiple personalities, and those who thought they had *no* personality. Now I have the unique good fortune of sharing the best of what I've learned with you, and for that opportunity I am truly grateful and excited.

Through it all, I've continued to recognize the power individuals have to change virtually anything and everything in their lives *in an instant.* I've learned that the resources we need to turn our dreams into reality are within us, merely waiting for the day when we decide to wake up and claim our birthright. I wrote this book for one reason: to be a wake-up call that will challenge those who are committed to living and being more to tap their God-given power. There are ideas and strategies in this book to help you produce specific, measurable, long-lasting changes in yourself and others.

You see, I believe I know who you really are. I believe you and I must be kindred souls. Your desire to expand has brought you to this book. It is the invisible hand that guided you. I know that no matter where you are in your life, you want more! No matter how well you're already doing or how challenged you now may be, deep inside of you there lies a belief that your experience of life can and will be much greater than it already is. You are destined for your own unique form of greatness, whether it is as an outstanding professional, teacher, businessperson, mother, or father. Most importantly, you not only believe this, but you've taken action. You not only bought this book, but you're also doing something right now that unfortunately is unique—you're reading it! Statistics show that less than 10 percent of people who buy a book read past the first chapter. What an unbelievable waste! This is a giant book that you can use to produce giant results in your life. Clearly, you're the kind of person who won't cheat yourself by dabbling. By consistently taking advantage of each of the chapters in this book, you'll ensure your ability to maximize your potential.

I challenge you not only to do whatever it takes to read this book in its entirety (unlike the masses who quit) but also to use what you learn in simple ways each day. This is the all-important step that's necessary for you to produce the results you're committed to.

HOW TO CREATE LASTING CHANGE

For changes to be of any true value, they've got to be lasting and consistent. We've all experienced change for a moment, only to feel let down and disappointed in the end. In fact, many people attempt change with a sense of fear and dread because unconsciously they believe the changes will only be temporary. A prime example of this is someone who needs to begin dieting, but finds himself putting it off, primarily because he unconsciously knows that whatever pain he endures in order to create the change will bring him only a short-term reward. For most of my life I've pursued what I consider to be the organizing principles of lasting change, and you'll learn many of these and how to utilize them in the pages that follow. But for now, I'd like to share with you three elementary principles of change that you and I can use immediately to change our lives. While these principles are simple, they are also extremely powerful when they are skillfully applied. These are the exact same changes that an individual must make in order to create personal change, that a company must make in order to maximize its potential, and that a country must make in order to carve out its place in the world. In fact, as a world community these are the changes that we all must make to preserve the quality of life around the globe.

STEP ONE

Raise Your Standards

Any time you sincerely want to make a change, the first thing you must do is to raise your standards. When people ask me what really changed my life eight years ago, I tell them that absolutely the most important thing was changing what I demanded of myself. I wrote down all the things I would no longer accept in my life, all the things I would no longer tolerate, and all the things that I aspired to becoming.

Think of the far-reaching consequences set in motion by men and women who raised their standards and acted in accordance with them, deciding they would tolerate no less. History chronicles the inspiring examples of people like Leonardo da Vinci, Abraham Lincoln, Helen Keller, Mahatma Gandhi, Martin Luther King, Jr., Rosa Parks, Albert Einstein, César Chávez, Soichiro Honda, and many others who took the magnificently powerful step of raising their standards. The same power that was available to them is available to you, if you have the courage to claim it. Changing an organization, a company, a country—or a world—begins with the simple step of changing yourself.

STEP TWO

Change Your Limiting Beliefs

If you raise your standards but don't really believe you can meet them, you've already sabotaged yourself. You won't even try; you'll be lacking that sense of certainty that allows you to tap the deepest capacity that's within you even as you read this. Our beliefs are like unquestioned commands, telling us how things are, what's possible and what's impossible, what we can and can not do. They shape every action, every thought, and every feeling that we experience. As a result, changing our belief systems is central to making any real and lasting change in our lives. We must develop a sense of certainty that we *can* and *will* meet the new standards before we actually *do*.

Without taking control of your belief systems, you can raise your standards as much as you like, but you'll never have the conviction to back them up. How much do you think Gandhi would have accomplished had he not *believed* with every fiber of his being in the power of nonviolent opposition? It was the congruence of his beliefs which gave him access to his inner resources and enabled him to meet challenges which would have swayed a less committed man. Empowering beliefs—this sense of certainty—is the force behind any great success throughout history.

S T E P   T H R E E

Change Your Strategy

In order to keep your commitment, you need the best strategies for achieving results. One of my core beliefs is that if you set a higher standard, and you can get yourself to believe, then you certainly can figure out the strategies. You simply *will* find a way. Ultimately, that's what this whole book is about. It shows you strategies for getting the job done, and I'll tell you now that the best strategy in almost any case is to find a role-model, someone who's already getting the results you want, and then tap into their knowledge. Learn what they're doing, what their core beliefs are, and how they think. Not only will this make you more effective, it will also save you a huge amount of time because you won't have to reinvent the wheel. You can fine-tune it, reshape it, and perhaps even make it better.

This book will provide you with the information and impetus to commit to all three of these master principles of quality change: it will help you raise your standards by discovering what they currently are and realizing what you want them to be; it will help you change the core beliefs that are keeping you from where you want to go and enhance those that already serve you; and it will assist you in developing a series of strategies for more elegantly, quickly, and efficiently producing the results you desire.

You see, in life, lots of people <u>know</u> *what to do, but few people actually do what they* <u>know</u>. Knowing is not enough! You must take action. If you will allow me the opportunity, through this book I'll be your personal coach. What do coaches do? Well, first, they care about you. They've spent years focusing on a particular area of expertise, and they've continued to make key distinctions about how to produce results more quickly. By utilizing the strategies your coach shares with you, you can immediately and dramatically change your performance. Sometimes, your coach doesn't even tell you something new, but reminds you of what you already know, and then gets you to do it. This is the role, with your permission, that I'll be playing for you.

On what, specifically, will I be coaching you? I'll offer you distinctions of power in how to create lasting improvements in the quality of your life. Together, we will concentrate on (not dabble in!) the mastery of the five areas of life that I believe impact us most. They are:

1. Emotional Mastery

Mastering this lesson alone will take you most of the way toward mastering the other four! Think about it. Why do you want to lose weight? Is it just to have less fat on your body? Or is it because of the way you think you'd *feel* if you freed yourself of those unwanted pounds, giving yourself more energy and vitality, making yourself feel more attractive to others, and boosting your confidence and self-esteem to the stratosphere? **Virtually everything we do is to change the way we feel**—yet most of us have little or no training in how to do this quickly and effectively. It's amazing how often we use the intelligence at our command to work ourselves into unresourceful emotional states, forgetting about the multitude of innate talents each of us already possesses. Too many of us leave ourselves at the mercy of outside events over which we may have no control, failing to take charge of our emotions—over which we have *all* the control—and relying instead on short-term quick fixes. How else can we explain the fact that, while less than 5 percent of the world's population lives in the United States, we consume more than 50 percent of the world's cocaine? Or that our national defense budget, which currently runs in the billions, is equaled by what we spend on alcohol consumption? Or that 15 million Americans are diagnosed every year as clinically depressed, and more than $500 million worth of prescriptions are written for the antidepressant drug Prozac?

In this book, you will discover what makes you do what you do, and the triggers for the emotions you experience most often. You will then be given a step-by-step plan to show you how to identify which emotions are empowering, which are disempowering, and how to use both kinds to your best advantage so that your emotions become not a hindrance, but instead a powerful tool in helping you achieve your highest potential.

2. Physical Mastery

Is it worth it to have everything you've ever dreamed of, yet not have the physical health to be able to enjoy it? Do you wake up every morning feeling energized, powerful, and ready to take on a new day? Or do you wake up feeling as tired as the night before, riddled with aches, and resentful at having to start all over again? Will your current lifestyle make you a statistic? One of every two Americans dies of coronary disease; one of three dies of cancer. To borrow a phrase from the seventeenth-century physician Thomas Moffett, we are "digging our graves with our teeth" as we cram our bodies with high-fat, nutritionally empty foods, poison our systems with cigarettes, alcohol, and drugs, and sit passively in front of our TV sets. This second master lesson will help you take control of your physical health so that you not only look good, but you *feel* good and know that you're *in control* of your life, in a body that radiates vitality and allows you to accomplish your outcomes.

3. Relationship Mastery

Other than mastering your own emotions and physical health, there is nothing I can think of that is more important than learning to master your relationships—romantic, family, business, and social. After all, who wants to learn, grow, and become successful and happy all by themselves? The third master lesson in this book will reveal the secrets to enable you to create quality relationships—first with yourself, then with others. You will begin by discovering what you value most highly, what your expectations are, the rules by which you play the game of life, and how it all relates to the other players. Then, as you achieve mastery of this all-important skill, you will learn how to connect with people at the deepest level and be rewarded with something we all want to experience: a sense of contribution, of knowing that we have made a difference in other people's lives. I've found that, for me, the greatest resource is a relationship because it opens the doors to every resource I need. Mastery of this lesson will give you unlimited resources for growing and contributing.

4. Financial Mastery

By the time they reach the age of sixty-five, most Americans are either dead broke—or dead! That's hardly what most people envision for themselves as they look ahead to the golden age of retirement. Yet without the conviction that you deserve financial well-being, backed up by a workable game plan, how can you turn your treasured scenario into reality? The fourth master lesson in this book will teach you how to go beyond the goal of mere survival in your autumn years of life, and even now, for that matter. Because we have the good fortune to live in a capitalist society, each of us has the capability to carry out our dreams. Yet most of us experience financial pressure on an ongoing basis, and we fantasize that having more money would relieve that pressure. This is a grand cultural delusion—let me assure you that the more money you have, the more pressure you're likely to feel. The key is not the mere pursuit of wealth, but changing your beliefs and attitudes about it so you see it as a means for contribution, not the end-all and be-all for happiness.

To forge a financial destiny of abundance, you will first learn how to change what causes scarcity in your life, and then how to experience on a consistent basis the values, beliefs, and emotions that are essential to experiencing wealth *and* holding on to it and expanding it. Then you'll define your goals and shape your dreams with an eye toward achieving the highest possible level of well-being, filling you with peace of mind and freeing you to look forward with excitement to all the possibilities that life has to offer.

5. Time Mastery

Masterpieces take time. Yet how many of us really know how to use it? I'm not talking about time management; I'm talking about actually taking time and distorting it, manipulating it so that it becomes your ally rather than your enemy. The fifth master lesson in this book will teach you, first, how short-term evaluations can lead to long-term pain. You will learn how to make a real decision and how to manage your desire for instantaneous gratification, thus allowing your ideas, your creations— even your own potential—the time to reach full fruition. Next you'll learn how to design the necessary maps and strategies for following up on your decision, making it a reality with the willingness to take massive action, the patience to experience "lag time," and the flexibility to change your approach as often as needed. Once you have mastered time, you will understand how true it is that most people overestimate what they can accomplish in a year—and underestimate what they can achieve in a decade!

I'm not sharing these lessons with you to say that I have all the answers or that my life has been perfect or smooth. I've certainly had my share of challenging times. But through it all, I've managed to learn, persist, and continually succeed throughout the years. Each time I've met a challenge, I've used what I've learned to take my life to a new level. And, like yours, my level of mastery in these five areas continues to expand.

Also, living my lifestyle may not be the answer for you. My dreams and goals may not be yours. I believe, though, that the lessons I've learned about how to turn dreams into reality, how to take the intangible and make it real, are fundamental to achieving any level of personal or professional success. **I wrote this book to be an action guide—a textbook for increasing the quality of your life and the amount of enjoyment that you can pull from it.** While I'm obviously extremely proud of my first book, *Unlimited Power,* and the impact it's had on people all over the world, I feel this book will bring you some new and unique distinctions of power that can help you move your life to the next level.

We'll be reviewing some of the fundamentals, since repetition is the mother of skill. Therefore, I hope this will be a book you'll read again and again, a book you'll come back to and utilize as a tool to trigger yourself to find the answers that already lie inside you. Even so, remember that as you read this book, you don't have to believe or use everything within it. *Grab hold of the things you think are useful; put them in action immediately.* You won't have to implement all of the strategies or use all of the tools in this book to make some major changes. All have life-changing potential individually; used together, however, they will produce explosive results.

This book is filled with the strategies for achieving the success you desire, with organizing principles that I have modeled from some of the most powerful and interesting people in our culture. I've had the unique opportunity to meet, interview, and model a huge variety of people— people with impact and unique character—from Norman Cousins to Michael Jackson, from coach John Wooden to financial wizard John Templeton, from the captains of industry to cab drivers. In the following pages, you'll find not only the benefits of my own experience, but that of the thousands of books, tapes, seminars, and interviews that I've accumulated over the last ten years of my life, as I continue the exciting, ongoing quest of learning and growing a little bit more, every single day.

The purpose of this book is not just to help you make a singular change in your life, but rather to be a **pivot point** that can assist you in taking your entire life to a new level. The focus of this book is on creating **global changes**. What do I mean by this? Well, you can learn to make changes in your life—overcome a fear or a phobia, increase the quality of a relationship, or overcome your pattern of procrastinating. All these are incredibly valuable skills, and if you've read *Unlimited Power,* you've already learned many of them. However, as you continue through the following pages, you'll find that there are key **leverage points** within your life that, if you make one small change, will literally transform every aspect of your life.

This book is designed to offer you the strategies that can help you to create, live, and enjoy the life you currently may only be dreaming of.

In this book you will learn a series of simple and specific strategies for **addressing the cause of any challenge and changing it with the least amount of effort.** For example, it might be hard for you to believe that merely by changing one word that is part of your habitual vocabulary, you could immediately change your emotional patterns for life. Or that by changing the consistent questions that you consciously or unconsciously ask yourself, you could instantly change what you focus on and therefore what actions you take every day of your life. Or that by making one belief change, you could powerfully change your level of happiness. Yet in the following chapters you'll learn to master these techniques— and many more—to effect the changes you desire.

And so it's with great respect that I begin this relationship with you as together we begin a journey of discovery and the actualization of our deepest and truest potentials. Life is a gift, and it offers us the privilege, opportunity, and responsibility to give something back by becoming more.

So let's begin our journey by exploring . . .

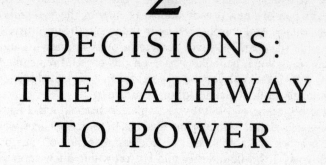

2
DECISIONS:
THE PATHWAY
TO POWER

"Man is born to live and not to prepare to live."
—BORIS PASTERNAK

Do you remember when Jimmy Carter was still the President of the United States, the Empire was striking back, Yoda and Pac Man were the rage, and nothing came between Brooke Shields and her Calvins? The Ayatollah Khomeini had come to power in Iran and held our fellow Americans hostage. In Poland, an electrician from the Gdansk shipyards named Lech Walesa did the unthinkable: he *decided* to take a stand against the Communist hold. He led his co-workers in a strike, and when they tried to lock him out of his place of work, he simply climbed over the wall. A lot of walls have come down since then, haven't they?

Do you remember hearing the news that John Lennon was murdered? Do you remember when Mount Saint Helens erupted, leveling 150 square miles? Did you cheer when the underdog U.S. hockey team beat the Soviets, and went on to win the Olympic gold medal? That was 1980, a little more than ten years ago.

Think for a moment. Where were you then? What were you like? Who were your friends? What were your hopes and dreams? If someone had asked you, "Where will you be in ten or fifteen years?" what would you have told them? Are you today where you wanted to be back then? A decade can pass quickly, can't it?

More importantly, maybe we should be asking ourselves, **"How am I going to live the *next* ten years of my life? How am I going to live *today* in order to create the tomorrow I'm committed to? What am I going to stand for *from now on*?** What's important to me *right now,* and what will be important to me in the long term? What actions can I take *today* that will shape my ultimate destiny?"

You see, ten years from now, you will surely arrive. The question is: Where? Who will you have become? How will you live? What will you contribute? *Now* is the time to design the next ten years of your life—not once they're over. We must seize the moment. We're already immersed in the early part of a new decade, and we're entering the *final years of the twentieth century!* And shortly we'll be in the twenty-first century, a new millennium. The year 2000 will be here before you know it, and in a mere ten years, you'll be looking back on this day and remembering it like you do 1980. Will you be pleased when you look back on the nineties, or perturbed? Delighted, or disturbed?

In the beginning of 1980, I was a nineteen-year-old kid. I felt alone and frustrated. I had virtually no financial resources. There were no success coaches available to me, no successful friends or mentors, no clear-cut goals. I was floundering and fat. Yet within a few short years I discovered a power that I used to transform virtually every area of my life. And once I'd mastered it, I used it to revolutionize my life in less than a year. It was the tool I used to dramatically increase my level of confidence and therefore my *ability* to take action and produce measurable results. I also used it to take back control of my physical well-being and permanently rid myself of thirty-eight pounds of fat. Through it, I attracted the woman of my dreams, married her, and created the family I desired. I used this power to change my income from subsistence level to over $1 million a year. It moved me from my tiny apartment (where I was washing my dishes in the bathtub because there was no kitchen) to my family's current home, the Del Mar Castle. *This one distinction* took me from feeling completely alone and insignificant to feeling grateful for new opportunities to contribute something to millions of people around the world. And it's a power I continue to use every single day of my life to shape my personal destiny.

In *Unlimited Power,* I made it abundantly clear that the most powerful way to shape our lives is to get ourselves to *take action.* The difference in the results that people produce comes down to what they've *done* differently from others in the same situations. **Different actions produce different results.** Why? Because any action is a cause set in motion, and its effect builds on past effects to move us in a definite direction. Every direction leads to an ultimate destination: our destiny.

In essence, if we want to direct our lives, we must take control of our consistent actions. It's not what we do once in a while that shapes our lives, but what we do consistently. The key and most important question, then, is this: What *precedes* all of our actions? What *determines* what actions we take, and therefore, who we become, and what our ultimate destination is in life? What is the father of action?

The answer, of course, is what I've been alluding to all along: **the power of decision.** Everything that happens in your life—both what you're thrilled with and what you're challenged by—began with a decision. **I believe that it's in your moments of decision that your destiny**

is shaped. The decisions that you're making right now, every day, will shape how you feel today as well as who you're going to become in the nineties and beyond.

As you look back over the last ten years, were there times when a different decision would have made your life radically different from today, either for better or for worse? Maybe, for example, you made a career decision that changed your life. Or maybe you *failed* to make one. Maybe you decided during the last ten years to get married—or divorced. You might have purchased a tape, a book, or attended a seminar and, as a result, changed your beliefs and actions. Maybe you decided to have children, or to put it off in pursuit of a career. Perhaps you decided to invest in a home or a business. Maybe you decided to start exercising, or to give it up. It could be that you decided to stop smoking. Maybe you decided to move to another part of the country, or to take a trip around the world. How have these decisions brought you to this point in your life?

Did you experience emotions of tragedy and frustration, injustice or hopelessness during the last decade of your life? I know I certainly did. If so, what did you decide to do about them? Did you push beyond your limits, or did you just give up? How have these decisions shaped your current life path?

> *"Man is not the creature of circumstances;*
> *circumstances are the creatures of men."*
> —BENJAMIN DISRAELI

More than anything else, I believe it's our *decisions,* not the *conditions* of our lives, that determine our destiny. You and I both know that there are people who were born with advantages: they've had genetic advantages, environmental advantages, family advantages, or relationship advantages. Yet you and I also know that we constantly meet, read, and hear about people who against all odds have exploded beyond the limitations of their conditions by making new decisions about what to do with their lives. They've become examples of the unlimited power of the human spirit.

If we decide to, you and I can make our lives one of these inspiring examples. How? Simply by making decisions today about how we're going to live in the nineties and beyond. If you don't make decisions about how you're going to live, then you've already made a decision, haven't you? You're making a decision to be directed by the environment instead of shaping your own destiny. My whole life changed in just one day—the day I determined not just what I'd *like* to have in my life or what I wanted to become, but when I **decided who and what I was committed to having and being in my life**. That's a simple distinction, but a critical one.

*"Wait! Wait! Listen to me! . . .
we don't have to be just sheep!"*

Think for a moment. Is there a difference between being *interested* in something, and being *committed* to it? You bet there is! Many times people say things like, "Gosh, I really would *like* to make more money," or "I'd *like* to be closer to my kids," or "You know, I'd really *like* to make a difference in the world." But that kind of statement is not a commitment at all. It's merely stating a preference, saying, "I'm *interested* in having this happen, if I don't have to *do* anything." That's not power! It's a weak prayer made without even the faith to launch it.

Not only do you have to decide what results you are committed to, but also the kind of person that you're committed to becoming. As we discussed in Chapter 1, you have to set standards for what you consider to be acceptable behavior for yourself, and decide what you should expect from those you care about. **If you don't set a baseline standard for what you'll accept in your life, you'll find it's easy to slip into behaviors and attitudes or a quality of life that's far below what you deserve.** You need to set and live by these standards no matter what happens in your life. Even if it all goes wrong, even if it rains on your parade, even if the stock market crashes, even if your lover leaves you, even if no one gives you the support that you need, you still must stay committed to your decision that you will live your life at the highest level.

Unfortunately, most people never do this because they're too busy making excuses. The reason they haven't achieved their goals or are not living the lives they desire is because of the way their parents treated them, or because of the lack of opportunities that they experienced in their youth, or because of the education they missed, or because they're too old, or because they're too young. All of these excuses are nothing but B.S. (Belief Systems)! And they're not only limiting, they're destructive.

Using the power of decision gives you the capacity to get past any excuse to change any and every part of your life *in an instant.* It can change your relationships, your working environment, your level of physical fitness, your income, and your emotional states. It can determine whether you're happy or sad, whether you're frustrated or excited, enslaved by circumstances, or expressing your freedom. It's the source of change within an individual, a family, a community, a society, our world. What's changed everything in Eastern Europe in the last few years? The people there—people like you and me—have made new decisions about what they'll stand for, what's acceptable and unacceptable to them, and what they'll no longer tolerate. Certainly Gorbachev's decisions helped pave the way, but Lech Walesa's determination and commitment to a higher standard built the road to massive economic and political change.

I often ask people who complain about their jobs, "Why did you go to work today?" Their answer usually is, "Because I had to." You and I need to remember one thing: there is virtually nothing that we *have* to do in this country. You certainly don't *have* to go to work. Not here! And you certainly don't *have* to work at a particular location on a particular day. Not in America! You don't *have* to do what you've done for the last ten years. You can decide to do something else, something new, today. **Right now you can make a decision:** to go back to school, to master dancing or singing, to take control of your finances, to learn to fly a helicopter, to turn your body into an inspiration, to begin meditating, to enroll in ballroom dancing, to attend a NASA space camp, to learn to speak French, to read more to your children, to spend more time in the flower garden, even to fly to Fiji and live on an island. **If you truly decide to, you can do almost anything.** So if you don't like the current relationship you're in, make the decision now to change it. If you don't like your current job, change it. If you don't like the way you feel about yourself, change it. If it's a higher level of physical vitality and health you want, you can change it now. In a moment you can seize the same power that has shaped history.

I've written this book to challenge you to **awaken the giant power of decision** and to **claim the birthright of unlimited power, radiant vitality, and joyous passion that is yours!** You must know that you can make a new decision right now that will immediately change your life—a decision about a habit you'll change or a skill that you'll master, or how you'll treat people, or a call that you'll now make to someone you haven't spoken to in years. Maybe there's someone you should contact to take your career to the next level. Maybe you could **make a decision right now** to enjoy and cultivate the most positive emotions that you deserve to experience daily. Is it possible you might choose more joy or more fun or more confidence or more peace of mind? Even before you turn the page, you can make use of the power that already resides within you. Make the decision now that can send you in a new, positive, and powerful direction for growth and happiness.

> *"Nothing can resist the human will that will stake even its existence on its stated purpose."*
> —BENJAMIN DISRAELI

Your life changes the moment you make a **new**, **congruent**, and **committed decision**. Who would have thought that the determination and conviction of a quiet, unassuming man—a lawyer by trade and a pacifist by principle—would have the power to topple a vast empire? Yet Mahatma Gandhi's indomitable decision to rid India of British rule was a virtual powder keg that set in motion a chain of events that would forever change the balance of world power. People didn't see how he could accomplish his aims, but he'd left himself no other choice than to act according to his conscience. He simply wouldn't accept any other possibility.

Decision was the source of John F. Kennedy's power as he faced off Nikita Khrushchev during the tense Cuban Missile Crisis and averted World War III. Decision was the source of Martin Luther King, Jr.'s power as he gave voice so eloquently to the frustrations and aspirations of a people who would no longer be denied, and forced the world to take notice. Decision was the source of Donald Trump's meteoric rise to the top of the financial world, and also the source of his devastating downfall. It's the power that allowed Pete Rose to maximize his physical abilities to Hall of Fame potential—and then ultimately to destroy his life's dream. Decisions act as the source of both problems and incredible joys and opportunities. This is the power that sparks the process of turning the invisible into the visible. True decisions are the catalyst for turning our dreams into reality.

The most exciting thing about this force, this power, is that you already possess it. The explosive impetus of decision is not something reserved for a select few with the right credentials or money or family background. It's available to the common laborer as well as the king. It's available to you now as you hold this book in your hands. In the very next moment you can use this mighty force that lies waiting within you if you merely muster the courage to claim it. Will today be the day you finally *decide* that who you are as a person is much more than you've been demonstrating? Will today be the day you *decide* once and for all to make your life consistent with the quality of your spirit? Then start by proclaiming, "This is who I am. This is what my life is about. And this is what I'm going to do. Nothing will stop me from achieving my destiny. I will not be denied!"

Consider a fiercely proud individual, a woman named Rosa Parks, who one day in 1955 stepped onto a bus in Montgomery, Alabama, and refused to give up her seat to a white person as she was legally required to do. Her one quiet act of civil disobedience sparked a firestorm of controversy and became a symbol for generations to follow. It was the beginning of the civil rights movement, a **consciousness-awakening** ground swell that we are grappling with even today as we redefine the meaning of equality, opportunity, and justice for all Americans regardless of race, creed, or sex. Was Rosa Parks thinking of the future when she refused to give up her seat in that bus? Did she have a divine plan for how she could change the structure of a society? Perhaps. But what is more likely is that her decision to hold herself to a higher standard compelled her to act. What a far-reaching effect one woman's decision has had!

If you're thinking, "I'd love to make decisions like that, but I've experienced real tragedies," let me offer you the example of Ed Roberts. He is an "ordinary" man confined to a wheelchair who became extraordinary by his decision to act beyond his apparent limitations. Ed has been paralyzed from the neck down since he was fourteen years old. He uses a breathing device that he's mastered against great odds to lead a "normal" life by day, and he spends every night in an iron lung. Having fought a battle against polio, several times almost losing his life, he certainly could have decided to focus on his own pain, but instead chose to make a difference for others.

Just what has he managed to do? For the last fifteen years, his decision to fight against a world he often found condescending has resulted in many enhancements to the quality of life for the disabled. Facing a multitude of myths about the capabilities of the physically challenged, Ed educated the public and initiated everything from wheelchair access ramps and special parking spaces to grab bars. He became the first quadriplegic to graduate from the University of California, Berkeley, and he eventually held the position of director of the California State Department of Rehabilitation, again pioneering this position for the disabled.

Ed Roberts is powerful evidence that it's not where you start out but the *decisions* you make about where you're determined to end up that matter. All of his actions were founded in a single, powerful, committed moment of decision. What could you do with your life if you really decided to?

Many people say, "Well, I'd love to make a decision like that, but I'm not sure *how* I could change my life." They're paralyzed by the fear that they don't know *exactly* how to turn their dreams into reality. And as a result, they never make the decisions that could make their lives into the masterpieces they deserve to be. I'm here to tell you that it's *not* important initially to know *how* you're going to create a result. What's important is to decide **you will find a way**, no matter what. In *Unlimited Power,* I outlined what I call "The Ultimate Success Formula," which is an elementary process for getting you where you want to go: 1) Decide what you want, 2) Take action, 3) Notice what's working or not, and 4) Change your approach until you achieve what you want. Deciding to produce a result causes events to be set in motion. If you simply decide what it is you want, get yourself to take action, learn from it, and change your approach, then you will create the momentum to achieve the result. As soon as you truly commit to making something happen, the "how" will reveal itself.

> *"Concerning all acts of initiative and creation,*
> *there is one elementary truth—that the moment*
> *one definitely commits oneself, then Providence*
> *moves, too."*
> —JOHANN WOLFGANG VON GOETHE

If making decisions is so simple and powerful, then why don't more people follow Nike's advice and "Just Do It"? I think one of the simplest reasons is that most of us don't recognize what it even means to make a real decision. We don't realize the force of change that a congruent, committed decision creates. Part of the problem is that for so long most of us have used the term "decision" so loosely that it's come to describe something like a wish list. Instead of making decisions, we keep stating preferences. Making a true decision, unlike saying, "I'd *like* to quit smoking," is cutting off any other possibility. In fact, the word "decision" comes from the Latin roots *de,* which means "from," and *caedere,* which means "to cut." **Making a true decision means committing to achieving a result, and then cutting yourself off from any other possibility.**

When you truly decide you'll never smoke cigarettes again, that's it. It's over! You no longer even *consider* the possibility of smoking. If you're one of the people who's ever exercised the power of decision this way, you know exactly what I'm talking about. An alcoholic knows that even after years of absolute sobriety, if he fools himself into thinking that he can take even one drink, he'll have to begin all over again. After making a true decision, even a tough one, most of us feel a tremendous amount of relief. We've finally gotten off the fence! And we all know how great it feels to have a clear, unquestioned objective.

This kind of clarity gives you power. With clarity, you can produce the results that you really want for your life. The challenge for most of us is that we haven't made a decision in so long we've forgotten what it feels like. We've got flabby decision-making muscles! Some people even have a hard time deciding what they're going to have for dinner.

So how do we strengthen these muscles? Give them a workout! **The way to make better decisions is to make more of them.** Then make sure you learn from each one, including those that don't seem to work out in the short term: they will provide valuable distinctions to make better evaluations and therefore decisions in the future. Realize that decision making, like any skill you focus on improving, gets better the more often you do it. The more often you make decisions, the more you'll realize that you truly are in control of your life. You'll look forward to future challenges, and you'll see them as an opportunity to make new distinctions and move your life to the next level.

I can't overemphasize the power and value of gaining even one, single distinction—a sole piece of information—that can be used to change the course of your life. **Information is power when it's acted upon,** and one of my criteria for a true decision is that action flows from it. The exciting thing is that you never know when you're going to get it! The reason I read over 700 books, listened to tapes, and went to so many seminars is that I understood the power of a single distinction. It might be on the next page or in the next chapter of this book. It might even be something you *already know.* But for some reason, this is the time it finally sinks in and you begin to *use* it. Remember that **repetition is the mother of skill.** Distinctions empower us to make better decisions and, therefore, create the results that we desire for ourselves. *Not* having certain distinctions can cause you major pain. For example, many of the most famous people in our culture have achieved their dreams but have still not found a way to enjoy them. They often turn to drugs because they feel unfulfilled. This is because they are missing the distinction between achieving one's goals and living one's values, something you will learn to master in the pages to follow. Another distinction that many people don't have causes pain in their relationships on a regular basis. It's a rules distinction, another key element we'll be examining in our journey of self-discovery. Sometimes, not having a certain distinction can cost you *everything*. People who run strenuously yet continue to eat fatty foods, clogging up their arteries, court heart attacks.

For most of my life, I've pursued what the famed business expert Dr. W. Edwards Deming calls *profound knowledge*. To me, profound knowledge is any simple distinction, strategy, belief, skill, or tool that, the minute we understand it, we can apply it to make immediate increases in the quality of our lives. This book and my life have been committed to pursuing profound knowledge that has universal application to improving our personal and professional lives. I'm constantly figuring out how to communicate this knowledge with people in ways that truly empower them to improve their mental, emotional, physical, and financial destinies.

> *"It is in your moments of decision that your destiny*
> *is shaped."*
> —ANTHONY ROBBINS

Three decisions that you make every moment of your life control your destiny. These three decisions determine what you'll notice, how you'll feel, what you'll do, and ultimately what you will contribute and who you become. If you don't control these three decisions, you simply aren't in control of your life. When you do control them, you begin to sculpt your experience.

The three decisions that control your destiny are:
1. Your decisions about **what to focus on.**
2. Your decisions about **what things mean to you.**
3. Your decisions about **what to do** to create the results you desire.

You see, it's not what's happening to you now or what has happened in your past that determines who you become. Rather, **it's your decisions about what to focus on, what things mean to you, and what you're going to do about them that will determine your ultimate destiny.** Know that if anyone is enjoying greater success than you in any area, they're making these three decisions differently from you in some context or situation. Clearly, Ed Roberts chose to focus on something different than most people in his position would. He focused on how he could make a difference. His physical difficulties meant "challenge" to him. What he decided to do, clearly, was anything that could make the quality of life for others in his position more comfortable. He absolutely committed himself to shaping the environment in a way that would improve the quality of life for all physically challenged people.

> *"I know of no more encouraging fact than the unquestionable ability of man to elevate his life by a conscious endeavor."*
> —HENRY DAVID THOREAU

Too many of us don't make the majority of our decisions consciously, especially these three absolutely crucial ones; in so doing, we pay a major price. In fact, most people live what I call **"The Niagara Syndrome."** I believe that life is like a river, and that most people jump on the river of life without ever really deciding where they want to end up. So, in a short period of time, they get caught up in the current: current events, current fears, current challenges. When they come to forks in the river, they don't consciously decide where they want to go, or which is the right direction for them. They merely "go with the flow." They become a part of the mass of people who are directed by the environment instead of by their own values. As a result, they feel out of control. They remain in this unconscious state until one day the sound of the raging water awakens them, and they discover that they're five feet from Niagara Falls in a boat with no oars. At this point, they say, "Oh, shoot!" But by then it's too late. They're going to take a fall. Sometimes it's an emotional fall. Sometimes it's a physical fall. Sometimes it's a financial fall. **It's likely that whatever challenges you have in your life currently could have been avoided by some better decisions upstream**.

How do we turn things around if we're caught up in the momentum of the raging river? Either make a decision to put both oars in the water and start paddling like crazy in a new direction, or decide to plan ahead. Set a course for where you really want to go, and have a plan or map so that you can make quality decisions along the way.

Although you may never have even thought about it, your brain has *already* constructed an internal system for making decisions. This system acts like an invisible force, directing all of your thoughts, actions, and feelings, both good and bad, every moment that you live. It controls how you evaluate everything in your life, and it's largely driven by your subconscious mind. The scary thing is that *most people never consciously set this system up.* Instead, it's been installed through the years by sources as diverse as parents, peers, teachers, television, advertisers, and the culture at large. This system is comprised of five components: 1) your **core beliefs** and **unconscious rules**, 2) your **life values**, 3) your **references**, 4) the **habitual questions** that you ask yourself, and 5) the **emotional states** you experience in each moment. The synergistic relationship of these five elements exerts a force that's responsible for prompting you to or stopping you from taking action, causing you to anticipate or worry about the future, making you feel loved or rejected, and dictating your level of success and happiness. It determines why you do what you do and why you don't do some things that you know you need to do.

By changing any one of these five elements—whether it's a core belief or rule, a value, a reference, a question, or an emotional state—you can immediately produce a powerful and measurable change in your life. Most importantly, you'll be fighting the cause instead of the effects. Remember, if you're overeating on a regular basis, the real cause is usually a values problem or a beliefs problem rather than a problem with food itself. Throughout this book, step-by-step, I'll be guiding you in discovering how *your* **master system** of decision making is set up, and you'll be making simple changes to make it consistent with your desires— rather than continue to be controlled by your past conditioning. You're about to embark on a fascinating journey of discovering who you are and what truly makes you do what you do. With these distinctions of power, you'll be able to understand the system of decision making that your business associates, spouse, and other loved ones are using. You'll finally be able to understand *their* "fascinating" behaviors, too!

The good news is that we can override this system by making conscious decisions at any moment in our lives. **We don't have to allow the programming of our past to control our present and future.** With this book, you can reinvent yourself by systematically organizing your beliefs and values in a way that pulls you in the direction of your life's design.

> *"I am not discouraged, because every wrong attempt discarded is another step forward."*
> —THOMAS EDISON

There is one final impediment to really utilizing the power of decision. That is that we must overcome our fears of making the *wrong* decisions. Without a doubt, you will make wrong decisions in your life. *You're going to screw up!* I know I certainly haven't made all the right decisions along the way. Far from it. But I didn't expect to. Nor will I always make the right decisions in the future. I have determined that no matter what decisions I make, I'll be flexible, look at the consequences, learn from them, and use those lessons to make better decisions in the future. **Remember: Success truly is the result of good judgment. Good judgment is the result of experience, and experience is often the result of bad judgment!** Those seemingly bad or painful experiences are sometimes the most important. When people succeed, they tend to party; when they fail, they tend to ponder, and they begin to make new distinctions that will enhance the quality of their lives. We must commit to learning from our mistakes, rather than beating ourselves up, or we're destined to make the same mistakes again in the future.

As important as personal experience is, think how invaluable it is to have a role model as well—someone who's navigated the rapids before you and has a good map for you to follow. You can have a role model for your finances, a model for your relationships, a model for your health, a model for your profession, or a model for any aspect of your life you're learning to master. They can save you years of pain and keep you from going over the falls.

There will be times when you're on the river solo and you'll have to make some important decisions on your own. The good news is that if you're willing to learn from your experience, then even times you might think were difficult become great because they provide valuable information—**key distinctions**—that you will use to make better decisions in the future. In fact, any extremely successful person you meet will tell you—if they're honest with you—that the reason they're more successful is that they've made more poor decisions than you have. People in my seminars often ask me, "How long do you think it will take for me to really master this particular skill?" And my immediate response is, "How long do you want it to take?" If you take action ten times a day (and have the proportionate "learning experiences") while other people act on a new skill once a month, you'll have ten months of experience in a day, you will soon master the skill, and will, ironically, probably be considered "talented and lucky."

I became an excellent public speaker because, rather than once a week, I booked myself to speak *three times a day* to anyone who would listen. While others in my organization had forty-eight speaking engagements a year, I would have a similar number within *two weeks*. Within a month, I'd have two years of experience. And within a year, I'd have a decade's worth of growth. My associates talked about how "lucky" I was to have been born with such an "innate" talent. I tried to tell them what I'm telling you now: mastery takes as long as you want it to take. By the way, were all of my speeches great? Far from it! But I did make sure that I learned from every experience and that I somehow improved until very soon I could enter a room of any size and be able to reach people from virtually all walks of life.

No matter how prepared you are, there's one thing that I can absolutely guarantee: if you're on the river of life, it's likely you're going to hit a few rocks. That's not being negative; that's being accurate. The key is that when you do run aground, instead of beating yourself up for being such a "failure," remember that **there are no failures in life**. There are only results. If you didn't get the results you wanted, learn from this experience so that you have references about how to make better decisions in the future.

> ### *"We will either find a way, or make one."*
> —HANNIBAL

One of the most important decisions you can make to ensure your long-term happiness is to decide to **use whatever life gives you in the moment.** The truth of the matter is that there's nothing you can't accomplish if: 1) You clearly decide what it is that you're absolutely committed to achieving, 2) You are willing to take massive action, 3) You notice what's working or not, and 4) You continue to change your approach until you achieve what you want, using whatever life gives you along the way.

Anyone who's succeeded on a large scale has taken these four steps and followed the Ultimate Success Formula. One of my favorite "Ultimate Success Stories" is Mr. Soichiro Honda, founder of the corporation that bears his name. Like all companies, no matter how large, Honda Corporation began with a decision and a passionate desire to produce a result.

In 1938, while he was still in school, Mr. Honda took everything he owned and invested it in a little workshop where he began to develop his concept of a piston ring. He wanted to sell his work to Toyota Corporation, so he labored day and night, up to his elbows in grease, sleeping in the machine shop, always believing he could produce the result. He even pawned his wife's jewelry to stay in business. But when he finally completed the piston rings and presented them to Toyota, he was told they didn't meet Toyota's standards. He was sent back to school for two years, where he heard the derisive laughter of his instructors and fellow students as they talked about how absurd his designs were.

But rather than focusing on the pain of the experience, he decided to continue to focus on his goal. Finally, after two more years, Toyota gave Mr. Honda the contract he'd dreamed of. His passion and belief paid off because he had known what he wanted, taken action, noticed what was working, and kept changing his approach until he got what he wanted. Then a new problem arose.

The Japanese government was gearing up for war, and they refused to give him the concrete that was necessary to build his factory. Did he quit there? No. Did he focus on how unfair this was? Did it mean to him that his dream had died? Absolutely not. Again, he decided to utilize the experience, and developed another strategy. He and his team invented a process for creating their own concrete and then built their factory. During the war, it was bombed twice, destroying major portions of the manufacturing facility. Honda's response? He immediately rallied his team, and they picked up the extra gasoline cans that the U.S. fighters had discarded. He called them "gifts from President Truman" because they provided him with the raw materials he needed for his manufacturing process—materials that were unavailable at the time in Japan. Finally, after surviving all of this, an earthquake leveled his factory. Honda decided to sell his piston operation to Toyota.

Here is a man who clearly made strong decisions to succeed. He had a passion for and belief in what he was doing. He had a great strategy. He took massive action. He kept changing his approach, but *still* he'd not produced the results that he was committed to. Yet he decided to persevere.

After the war, a tremendous gasoline shortage hit Japan, and Mr. Honda couldn't even drive his car to get food for his family. Finally, in desperation, he attached a small motor to his bicycle. The next thing he knew, his neighbors were asking if he could make one of his "motorized bikes" for them. One after another, they jumped on the bandwagon until he *ran out* of motors. He decided to build a plant that would manufacture motors for his new invention, but unfortunately he didn't have the capital.

As before, he made the decision to find a way no matter what! His solution was to appeal to the 18,000 bicycle shop owners in Japan by writing them each a personal letter. He told them how they could play a role in revitalizing Japan through the mobility that his invention could provide, and convinced 5,000 of them to advance the capital he needed. Still, his motorbike sold to only the most hard-core bicycle fans because it was too big and bulky. So he made one final adjustment, and created a much lighter, scaled-down version of his motorbike. He christened it "The Super Cub," and it became an "overnight" success, earning him the Emperor's award. Later, he began to export his motorbikes to the baby boomers of Europe and the United States, following up in the seventies with the cars that have become so popular.

Today, the Honda Corporation employs over 100,000 people in both the United States and Japan and is considered one of the biggest car-making empires in Japan, outselling all but Toyota in the United States. It succeeds because one man understood the power of a truly committed decision that is acted upon, no matter what the conditions, on a continuous basis.

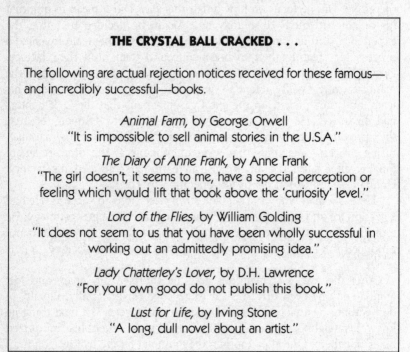

THE CRYSTAL BALL CRACKED . . .

The following are actual rejection notices received for these famous— and incredibly successful—books.

Animal Farm, by George Orwell
"It is impossible to sell animal stories in the U.S.A."

The Diary of Anne Frank, by Anne Frank
"The girl doesn't, it seems to me, have a special perception or feeling which would lift that book above the 'curiosity' level."

Lord of the Flies, by William Golding
"It does not seem to us that you have been wholly successful in working out an admittedly promising idea."

Lady Chatterley's Lover, by D.H. Lawrence
"For your own good do not publish this book."

Lust for Life, by Irving Stone
"A long, dull novel about an artist."

Honda certainly knew that sometimes when you make a decision and take action, in the short term it may look like it's not working. **In order to succeed, you must have a long-term focus.** Most of the challenges that we have in our personal lives—like indulging constantly in overeating, drinking, or smoking, to feeling overwhelmed and giving up on our dreams—come from a short-term focus. Success and failure are not overnight experiences. It's all the small decisions along the way that cause people to fail. It's failure to follow up. It's failure to take action. It's failure to persist. It's failure to manage our mental and emotional states. It's failure to control what we focus on. Conversely, success is the result of making small decisions: deciding to hold yourself to a higher standard, deciding to contribute, deciding to feed your mind rather than allowing the environment to control you—these small decisions create the life experience we call success. No individual or organization that has become successful has done so with short-term focus.

On a national scale, most of the challenges that we're currently experiencing are the result of not thinking of the potential consequences of the decisions we've made. Our crises—the S&L scandal, the challenge in our balance of trade, the budget deficit, our educational malaise, drug and alcohol problems—all are the result of short-term thinking. This is the Niagara Syndrome at its most potent. While you're raging along the river, focusing on the next rock you might hit, you don't—or can't—see far enough ahead of you to avoid the falls.

As a society, we're so focused on instantaneous gratification that our short-term solutions often become long-term problems. Our kids have trouble paying attention in school long enough to think, memorize, and learn partly because they've become addicted to instantaneous gratification from constant exposure to things like video games, TV commercials, and MTV. As a nation, we have the highest number of overweight children in history because of our unrelenting pursuit of the quick fix: fast food, instant pudding, and microwave brownies.

In business, too, this kind of short-term focus can be deadly. The whole controversy surrounding the Exxon *Valdez* disaster could have been averted by making one small decision. Exxon could have outfitted its tankers with double hulls, a proactive decision that would have prevented oil spills in the event of collision. But the oil company chose not to, looking at the immediate rather than long-range impact on its bottom line. Following the crash and resultant spill, Exxon is responsible for paying a whopping $1.1 billion* as *some* compensation for the devastating economic damage it has caused, not to mention the immeasurable ecological destruction to Alaska and surrounding areas.

Deciding to commit yourself to long-term results, rather than short-term fixes, is as important as any decision you'll make in your lifetime. Failing to do this can cause not only massive financial or societal pain, but sometimes even the ultimate personal pain.

One young man you may have heard of dropped out of high school because he decided he wasn't going to wait any longer to follow his dream of becoming a famous musician. But this dream didn't become reality quickly enough. In fact, by the time he was twenty-two, he feared that he had made the wrong decision, and that no one would *ever* love his music. He'd been playing in piano bars, and he was flat broke, sleeping in laundromats because he no longer had a home. The only thing that had been holding him together was his romantic relationship. Then his girlfriend decided to leave him, and when she did, it pushed him over the edge. He immediately focused on how he could never again find another woman as beautiful as she. What this meant to him was that

---

* At this writing, Exxon is still in court settling related legal matters which may increase this number.

his life was over, so he decided to commit suicide. Fortunately, before doing so, he reconsidered his options and decided instead to check into a mental institution. Spending time there gave him some new references about what *real* problems were. He later recalled saying, "Ohh, I'll never get *that* low again." He now declares, "It was one of the best things I ever did because I've never gotten to feel sorry for myself, no matter what's happened. Any problem since then is nothing compared with what I've seen other people go through."* By renewing his commitment and following his dream long-term, he eventually had all that he wanted. His name? Billy Joel.

Can you imagine that this man, whom millions of fans love and supermodel Christie Brinkley married, was ever worried about the quality of his music or finding a woman as beautiful as his ex-girlfriend? The key to remember is that what appeared to be impossible in the short term turned into a phenomenal example of success and happiness in the long term. Billy Joel was able to pull himself out of his depression by directing the three decisions that we all control each moment of our lives: what to focus on, what things mean, and what to do in spite of the challenges that may appear to limit us. He raised his standards, backed them up with new beliefs, and implemented the strategies he knew he must.

One belief that I've developed to carry me through extremely tough times is simply this: **God's delays are not God's denials**. Often, what seems impossible in the short term becomes very possible in the long term *if you persist*. In order to succeed, we need to discipline ourselves to consistently think long term. A metaphor that I use to remind myself of this is comparing life's ups and downs to the changing of the seasons. No season lasts forever because all of life is a cycle of planting, reaping, resting, and renewal. Winter is not infinite: even if you're having challenges today, you can never give up on the coming of spring. For some people, winter means hibernation; for others, it means bobsledding and downhill skiing! You can always just wait out the season, but why not make it into a time to remember?

HARNESS THE POWER OF DECISION

In review, let me give you six quick keys to help you harness the power of decision, the power that shapes your experience of life every moment that you live it:

1. Remember the true power of making decisions. It's a tool you can use in any moment to change your entire life. The minute you make

---

* Sheff, David and Victoria, "Playboy interview: Billy Joel," Chicago: *Playboy,* May 1982.

a new decision, you set in motion a new cause, effect, direction, and destination for your life. You literally begin to change your life the moment you make a new decision. Remember that when you start feeling overwhelmed, or when you feel like you don't have a choice, or when things are happening "*to*" you, you can change it all if you just stop and decide to do so. Remember, a real decision is measured by the fact that you've taken new action. If there's no action, you haven't truly decided.

2. Realize that the hardest step in achieving anything is making a true commitment—a true decision. Carrying out your commitment is often much easier than the decision itself, so make your decisions intelligently, but make them quickly. Don't labor forever over the question of how or if you can do it. Studies have shown that the most successful people make decisions rapidly because they are clear on their values and what they really want for their lives. The same studies show that they are slow to change their decisions, if at all. On the other hand, people who fail usually make decisions slowly and change their minds quickly, always bouncing back and forth. Just decide!

Realize that decision making is a kind of act in itself, so a good definition for a decision might be "information acted upon." You know you've truly made a decision when action flows from it. It becomes a cause set in motion. Often the effect of making a decision helps create the attainment of a larger goal. A critical rule I've made for myself is **never to leave the scene of a decision without first taking *a specific action* toward its realization**.

3. Make decisions often. The more decisions you make, the better you're going to become at making them. Muscles get stronger with use, and so it is with your decision-making muscles. Unleash your power right now by making some decisions you've been putting off. You won't believe the energy and excitement it will create in your life!

4. Learn from your decisions. There's no way around it. At times, you're going to screw up, no matter what you do. And when the inevitable happens, instead of beating yourself into the ground, **learn something**. Ask yourself, "What's good about this? What can I learn from this?" This "failure" may be an unbelievable gift in disguise if you use it to make better decisions in the future. Rather than focus on the short-term setback, choose instead to learn lessons that can save you time, money, or pain, and that will give you the ability to succeed in the future.

5. Stay committed to your decisions, but stay flexible in your approach. Once you've decided who you want to be as a person, for example, don't get stuck on the means to achieving it. It's the end you're after. Too often, in deciding what they want for their lives, people pick the best way they know at the time—they make a map—but then don't stay open to alternate routes. Don't become rigid in your approach. Cultivate the art of flexibility.

6. Enjoy making decisions. You must know that in any moment a decision you make can change the course of your life forever: the very next person you stand behind in line or sit next to on an airplane, the very next phone call you make or receive, the very next movie you see or book you read or page you turn could be the one single thing that causes the floodgates to open, and all of the things that you've been waiting for to fall into place.

If you really want your life to be passionate, you need to live with this attitude of expectancy. Years ago, I made what seemed like a small decision, and it has powerfully shaped my life. I decided to do a seminar in Denver, Colorado. That decision caused me to meet a lady named Becky. Her last name now is Robbins, and she is definitely one of the greatest gifts of my life. On that same trip, I decided to write my first book, which is now published in eleven languages around the world. A few days later, I decided to conduct a seminar in Texas, and after working for a week to fill my own program, the promoter didn't pay me for the event—he skipped town. The obvious person to talk to was the public relations agent he had hired, a woman who had similar woes. That woman became my literary agent and helped to get that first book published. As a result, I have the privilege of sharing this story with you today.

At one time, I also decided to take on a business partner. Choosing not to investigate his character in advance was a poor decision on my part. Within a year, he'd misappropriated a quarter of a million dollars and had run my corporation $758,000 in debt while I spent my life on the road doing more than 200 seminars. Fortunately, though, I learned from my poor decision and made a better one. In spite of advice from all the experts around me that the only way I could survive would be to declare bankruptcy, I decided to find a way to turn things around, and I created one of the greater successes of my life. I took my company to a whole new level, and what I learned from that experience not only created my long-term business success, but also provided many of the distinctions for the Neuro-Associative Conditioning™ and Destiny Technologies™ that you'll be learning in this book.

"Life is either a daring adventure or nothing."
—HELEN KELLER

So what is the single most important distinction to take from this chapter?

Know that it's your decisions, and not your conditions, that determine your destiny. Before we learn the technology for changing how you think and how you feel every day of your life, I want you to remember that, in the final analysis, everything you've read in this book is *worthless* . . . every other book you've read or tape you've heard or seminar you've attended is *worthless* . . . **unless you decide to use it**. Remember that a truly committed decision is the force that changes your life. It's a power available to you in any moment if you just *decide* to use it.

Prove to yourself that you've decided now. Make one or two decisions that you've been putting off: one easy decision and one that's a bit more difficult. Show yourself what you can do. Right now, *stop*. Make at least one clear-cut decision that you've been putting off—take the first action toward fulfilling it—and stick to it! By doing this, you'll be building that muscle that will give you the will to change your entire life.

You and I both know that there are going to be challenges in your future. But as Lech Walesa and the people of Eastern Europe have learned, if you've *decided* to get past the walls, you can climb over them, you can break through them, you can tunnel under them, or you can find a door. No matter how long a wall has stood, none has the power to withstand the continued force of human beings who have decided to persist until it has fallen. The human spirit truly is unconquerable. But the will to win, the will to succeed, to shape one's life, to take control, can only be harnessed when you decide what you want, and believe that no challenge, no problem, no obstacle can keep you from it. When you decide that your life will ultimately be shaped not by conditions, but by your decisions, then, in that moment, your life will change forever, and you will be empowered to take control of . . .

3
THE FORCE THAT
SHAPES YOUR LIFE

*"Men live by intervals of reason under the
sovereignty of humor and passion."*
—SIR THOMAS BROWNE

She had been been jogging for only about half an hour when it happened.
Suddenly a dozen young boys began to sprint in her direction. Before she
had time to realize what was happening, they pounced upon her, pulled
her into the bushes and began to beat her with a lead pipe. One boy
continually kicked her in the face until she was bleeding profusely. Then
they raped and sodomized her, and left her for dead.

I'm sure you've heard about this tragic, unthinkable crime that happened in Central Park several years ago. I was in New York City the night
it happened. I was appalled not only by the savagery of the attack, but
even more so to hear who the attackers were. They were children, from
the ages of 14 to 17 years old. Contrary to stereotypes, they were neither
poor nor did they come from abusive families. They were boys from
private schools, Little League players, kids who took tuba lessons. These
boys were not driven crazy by drugs, nor were they racially motivated.
They assaulted and could have killed this 28-year-old woman for one
reason and one reason only: fun. They even had a name for what they
had set out to do; they called it "wilding."

Not more than 250 miles away in our nation's capital, a jet airliner
crashed on takeoff from National Airport during a blinding snowstorm.
It hit the Potomac Bridge at the height of rush hour. As traffic snarled to
a halt, emergency rescue services were immediately dispatched to the
scene, and the bridge became a nightmare of chaos and panic. Firemen
and paramedics were overwhelmed by the destruction, and dove again
and again into the Potomac to try and save crash victims.

One man repeatedly passed the life preserver to others. He saved
many lives, but not his own. By the time the rescue helicopter finally got
to him, he had slipped beneath the icy surface of the water. This man
gave his life in order to save those of complete strangers! What drove him
to place such a high value on other people's lives—people he didn't even
know—that he was willing to give his own life in the process?

What makes a person with a "good background" behave so savagely and without remorse while another gives his own life to rescue complete strangers? What creates a hero, a heel, a criminal, a contributor? What determines the difference in human actions? Throughout my life, I have passionately sought the answer to these questions. One thing is clear to me: human beings are not random creatures; everything we do, we do for a reason. We may not be aware of the reason consciously, but there is undoubtedly a single driving force behind all human behavior. This force impacts every facet of our lives, from our relationships and finances to our bodies and brains. What is this force that is controlling you even now and will continue to do so for the rest of your life? **PAIN and PLEASURE!** *Everything you and I do, we do either out of our need to avoid pain or our desire to gain pleasure.*

So often I hear people talk about changes they want to make in their lives. But they can't get themselves to follow through. They feel frustrated, overwhelmed, even angry with themselves because they know they need to take action, but they can't get themselves to do it. There is one elementary reason: they keep trying to change their behavior, which is the *effect,* instead of dealing with the *cause* behind it.

Understanding and utilizing the forces of pain and pleasure will allow you once and for all to create the lasting changes and improvements you desire for yourself and those you care about. Failure to understand this force dooms you to a future of living in reaction, like an animal or a machine. Perhaps this sounds like a complete oversimplification, but think about it. Why don't you do some of the things you *know* you should do?

After all, what is procrastination? It's when you know you *should* do something, but you still don't *do* it. Why not? The answer is simple: at some level you believe that taking action in this moment would be more painful than just putting it off. Yet, have you ever had the experience of putting something off for so long that suddenly you felt pressure to just *do* it, to get it *done*? What happened? You changed what you linked pain and pleasure to. Suddenly, not taking action became more painful than putting it off. This is a common occurrence that many Americans experience around April 14!

> ## "A man who suffers before it is necessary, suffers more than is necessary."
> —SENECA

What keeps you from approaching that man or woman of your dreams? What keeps you from starting that new business you've been planning for years? Why do you keep putting off that diet? Why do you avoid completing your thesis? Why haven't you taken control of your financial investment portfolio? What prevents you from doing whatever it takes to make your life exactly as you've imagined it?

Even though you know that all these actions would benefit you—that they could definitely bring pleasure to your life—you fail to act simply because in that moment you associate more pain to doing what's necessary than missing the opportunity. After all, what if you approached that person, and they rejected you? What if you tried to start that new business but failed and lost the security you have in your present job? What if you started a diet and went through the pain of starving yourself, only to gain the weight back eventually anyway? What if you made an investment and lost your money? So why even try?

For most people, the fear of loss is much greater than the desire for gain. Which would drive you more: keeping someone from stealing the $100,000 you've earned over the last five years, or the potential of earning $100,000 in the next five? The fact is that most people would work much harder to hang on to what they have than they would to take the risks necessary to get what they really want from their lives.

> *"The secret of success is learning how to use pain and pleasure instead of having pain and pleasure use you. If you do that, you're in control of your life. If you don't, life controls you."*
> —ANTHONY ROBBINS

Often an interesting question comes up in discussions about these twin powers that drive us: Why is it that people can experience pain yet fail to change? They haven't experienced enough pain yet; they haven't hit what I call **emotional threshold**. If you've ever been in a destructive relationship and finally made the decision to use your personal power, take action and change your life, it was probably because you *hit a level of pain you weren't willing to settle for anymore.* We've all experienced those times in our lives when we've said, "I've had it—never again—this must change now." This is the magical moment when **pain becomes our friend**. It drives us to take new action and produce new results. We become even more powerfully compelled to act if, in that same moment, we begin to anticipate how changing will create a great deal of pleasure for our lives as well.

This process is certainly not limited to relationships. Maybe you've experienced threshold with your physical condition: you finally got fed up because you couldn't squeeze into an airline seat, you couldn't fit into your clothes, and walking up a set of stairs winded you. Finally you said, "I've had it!" and made a decision. What motivated that decision? It was the desire to remove pain from your life and establish pleasure once again: the pleasure of pride, the pleasure of comfort, the pleasure of self-esteem, the pleasure of living life the way you've designed it.

Of course, there are many levels of pain and pleasure. For example, feeling a sense of humiliation is a rather intense form of emotional pain. Feeling a sense of inconvenience is also pain. So is boredom. Obviously some of these have less intensity, but they still factor in the equation of decision-making. Likewise, pleasure weighs into this process. Much of our drive in life comes from our anticipating that our actions will lead to a more compelling future, that today's work will be well worth the effort, that the rewards of pleasure are near. Yet there are many levels of pleasure as well. For example, the pleasure of ecstasy, while most would agree is intense, may sometimes be outweighed by the pleasure of comfort. It all depends on an individual's perspective.

For example, let's say you're on your lunch break, and you're walking past a park where a Beethoven symphony is playing. Will you stop and listen? It depends, first of all, on the meaning you associate to classical music. Some people would drop anything to be able to listen to the valiant strains of the Eroica Symphony; for them, Beethoven equals pure pleasure. For others, however, listening to any kind of classical music is about as exciting as watching paint dry. Enduring the music would equal a measure of pain, and so they hurry past the park and back to work. But even some people who love classical music would not decide to stop and listen. Maybe the perceived pain of being late for work outweighs the pleasure they would get from hearing the familiar melodies. Or maybe they have a belief that stopping and enjoying music in the middle of the afternoon is wasteful of precious time, and the pain of doing something frivolous and inappropriate is greater than the pleasure the music could bring. Each day our lives are filled with these kinds of psychic negotiations. We are constantly weighing our own proposed actions and the impact they will have upon us.

LIFE'S MOST IMPORTANT LESSON

Donald Trump and Mother Teresa are driven by the exact same force. I can hear you saying, "Are you off your rocker, Tony? They couldn't be more different!" It's absolutely true that their values lie at opposite ends of the spectrum, but they're both driven by pain and pleasure. Their lives have been shaped by what they've *learned* to get pleasure from, and what they've *learned* will create pain. The most important lesson we learn in life is what creates pain for us and what creates pleasure. This lesson is different for each of us and, therefore, so are our behaviors.

What's driven Donald Trump throughout his life? He's learned to achieve pleasure by having the largest and most expensive yachts, acquiring the most extravagant buildings, making the shrewdest deals—in short, accumulating the biggest and best toys. What did he learn to link pain to? In interviews he has revealed that his ultimate pain in life is being second-best at anything—he equates it with failure. In fact, his greatest drive to achieve comes from his compulsion to avoid this pain. It's a far more powerful motivator than his desire to gain pleasure. Many competitors have taken great joy in the pain that Trump has experienced from the collapse of much of his economic empire. Rather than judge him—or anyone else, including yourself—it might be more valuable to understand what's driving him and to have some compassion for his obvious pain.

By contrast, look at Mother Teresa. Here's a woman who cares so deeply that when she sees other people in pain, she also suffers. Seeing the injustice of the caste system wounded her. She discovered that when she took action to help these people, their pain disappeared, and so did hers. For Mother Teresa, the ultimate meaning of life can be found in one of the most impoverished sections of Calcutta, the City of Joy, which is swollen past the bursting point with millions of starving and diseased refugees. For her, pleasure might mean wading through knee-deep muck, sewage and filth in order to reach a squalid hut and minister to the infants and children within, their tiny bodies ravaged by cholera and dysentery. She is powerfully driven by the sensation that helping others out of their misery helps alleviate her own pain, that in helping them experience life in a better way—giving them pleasure—*she* will feel pleasure. She learned that putting yourself on the line for others is the highest good; it gives her a sense that her life has true meaning.

While it may be a stretch for most of us to liken the sublime humility of Mother Teresa to the materialism of Donald Trump, it's critical to remember that these two individuals shaped their destinies based upon what they linked pain and pleasure to. Certainly their backgrounds and environments played a role in their choices, but ultimately they made *conscious* decisions about what to reward or punish themselves for.

WHAT YOU LINK PAIN TO AND WHAT YOU LINK PLEASURE TO SHAPES YOUR DESTINY

One decision that has made a tremendous difference in the quality of my life is that at an early age I began to link incredible pleasure to learning.

I realized that discovering ideas and strategies that could help me to shape human behavior and emotion could give me virtually everything I wanted in my life. It could get me out of pain and into pleasure. Learning to unlock the secrets behind our actions could help me to become more healthy, to feel better physically, to connect more deeply with the people I cared about. Learning provided me with something to give, the opportunity to truly contribute something of value to all those around me. It offered me a sense of joy and fulfillment. At the same time, I discovered an even more powerful form of pleasure, and that was achieved by sharing what I'd learned in a passionate way. When I began to see that what I could share helps people increase the quality of their lives, I discovered the ultimate level of pleasure! And my life's purpose began to evolve.

What are some of the experiences of pain and pleasure that have shaped your life? Whether you've linked pain or pleasure to drugs, for example, certainly has affected your destiny. So have the emotions you've learned to associate to cigarettes or alcohol, relationships, or even the concepts of giving or trusting.

If you're a doctor, isn't it true that the decision to pursue a medical career so many years ago was motivated by your belief that becoming a physician would make you feel good? Every doctor I've talked to links massive pleasure to helping people: stopping pain, healing illness, and saving lives. Often the pride of being a respected member of society was an additional motivator. Musicians have dedicated themselves to their art because few things can give them that same level of *pleasure*. And CEOs of top organizations have learned to link *pleasure* to making powerful decisions that have a huge potential to build something unique and to contribute to people's lives in a lasting way.

Think of the limiting pain and pleasure associations of John Belushi, Freddie Prinze, Jimi Hendrix, Elvis Presley, Janis Joplin, and Jim Morrison. Their associations to drugs as an escape, a quick fix, or a way out of pain and into temporary pleasure created their downfalls. They paid the ultimate price for not directing their own minds and emotions. Think of the example they set for millions of fans. I never did learn to consume drugs or alcohol. Is it because I was so brilliant? No, it's because I was very fortunate. One reason I never drank alcohol is that, as a child, there were a couple of people in my family who acted so obnoxiously when drunk that I associated extreme pain to drinking any alcohol. One especially graphic image I have is the memory of my best friend's mom. She was extremely obese, weighing close to 300 pounds, and she drank constantly. Whenever she did, she wanted to hug me and drool all over me. To this day, the smell of alcohol on anyone's breath nauseates me.

Beer, though, was another story. When I was about eleven or twelve, I didn't consider it an alcoholic drink. After all, my dad drank beer, and he didn't get that "obnoxious" or disgusting. In fact, he seemed to be a little more fun when he'd had a few beers. Plus, I linked pleasure to drinking because I wanted to be just like Dad. Would drinking beer really make me like Dad? No, but we frequently create false associations in our nervous systems (neuro-associations) as to what will create pain or pleasure in our lives.

One day I asked my mom for a "brew." She began arguing that it wasn't good for me. But trying to convince me when my mind was made up, when my observations of my father so clearly contradicted her, was not going to work. We don't believe what we hear; rather, we are certain that our perceptions are accurate—and I was certain that day that drinking beer was the next step in my personal growth. Finally, my mom realized I'd probably just go drink somewhere else if she didn't give me an experience I wouldn't forget. At some level, she must have known she had to change what I associated to beer. So she said, "Okay, you want to drink beer and be like Dad? Then you've really got to drink beer *just like* your dad." I said, "Well, what does that mean?" She said, "You've got to drink a whole six-pack." I said, *"No problem."*

She said, "You've got to drink it right here." When I took my first sip, it tasted disgusting, nothing like what I'd anticipated. Of course, I wouldn't admit it at the time because, after all, my pride was on the line. So I took a few more sips. After finishing one beer I said, "Now I'm really full, Mom." She said, "No, here's another one," and popped it open. After the third or fourth can, I started feeling sick to my stomach. I'm sure you can guess what happened next: I threw up all over myself and the kitchen table. It was disgusting, and so was cleaning up the mess! I immediately linked the smell of beer to the vomit and horrible feelings. I no longer had an intellectual association to what drinking beer meant. I now had an *emotional* association in my nervous system, a gut-level **neuro-association**—one that would clearly guide my future decisions. As a result, I've never had even a sip of beer since!

Can our pain and pleasure linkages produce a processional effect in our lives? You bet. This negative neuro-association for beer affected many of my decisions in life. It influenced whom I hung out with at school. It determined how I learned to get pleasure. I didn't use alcohol: I used learning; I used laughter; I used sports. I also learned that it felt incredible to help other people, so I became the guy in school everybody came to with their problems, and solving their problems made both them and me feel good. Some things haven't changed through the years!

I also never used drugs because of a similar experience: when I was in the third or fourth grade, the police department came to my school and showed us some films about the consequences of getting involved in the drug scene. I watched as people shot up, passed out, spaced out, and leaped out of windows. As a young boy, I associated drugs to ugliness and death, so I never tried them myself. My good fortune was that the police had helped me form painful neuro-associations to even the idea of using drugs. Therefore, I have never even considered the possibility.

What can we learn from this? Simply this: **if we link massive pain to any behavior or emotional pattern, we will avoid indulging in it at all costs. We can use this understanding to harness the force of pain and pleasure to change virtually anything in our lives**, from a pattern of procrastinating to drug use. How do we do this? Let's say, for example, you want to keep your children off drugs. The time to reach them is before they experiment and before someone else teaches them the false association that drugs equal pleasure.

My wife, Becky, and I decided that the most powerful way to make sure our kids would never use drugs was to cause them to link massive pain to drugs. We knew that unless we taught them what drugs were really about, someone else might convince them that drugs were a useful way of escaping pain.

To accomplish this task, I called upon an old friend, Captain John Rondon of the Salvation Army. For years, I've supported John in the South Bronx and Brooklyn in helping street people make changes in their lives by raising their standards, changing their limiting beliefs, and developing life skills. Becky and I are very proud of the people who've used what we've taught to get off the streets and increase the quality of their lives. I've always used my visits there as a way of giving something back and as a reminder of how fortunate I am. It keeps me feeling appreciative of the life I have the privilege to lead. It also gives me perspective and keeps my life balanced.

I explained my goals to Captain John, and he arranged to take my children on a tour they would never forget, one that would give them a clear experience of what drugs do to the human spirit. It began with a firsthand visit to a rat-infested, rotting tenement building. The minute we walked in, my children were assaulted by the stench of urine-soaked floors, the sight of addicts shooting up heedless of who was watching, child prostitutes soliciting passers-by, and the sound of neglected, crying children. Mental, emotional, and physical devastation is what my kids learned to link to drugs. That was four-and-a-half years ago. While they have all been exposed to drugs many times since, they have never touched them. These powerful neuro-associations have significantly shaped their destinies.

*"If you are distressed by anything external, the pain
is not due to the thing itself but to your own estimate
of it; and this you have the power to revoke
at any moment."*
—MARCUS AURELIUS

We are the only beings on the planet who lead such rich internal lives
that it's not the events that matter most to us, but rather, it's how we
interpret those events that will determine how we think about ourselves
and how we will act in the future. One of the things that makes us so
special is our marvelous ability to *adapt,* to transform, to manipulate
objects or ideas to produce something more pleasing or useful. And
foremost among our adaptive talents is the ability to take the raw experience of our lives, relate it to other experiences, and create from it a
kaleidoscopic tapestry of meaning that's different from everyone else's in
the world. Only human beings can, for example, change their associations so that physical pain will result in pleasure, or vice-versa.

Remember a hunger striker confined to jail. Fasting for a cause, he
survives thirty days without food. The physical pain he experiences is
considerable, but it's offset by the pleasure and validation of drawing the
world's attention to his cause. On a more personal, everyday level, individuals who follow intense physical regimens in order to sculpt their
bodies have learned to link tremendous feelings of pleasure to the "pain"
of physical exertion. They have converted the discomfort of discipline
into the satisfaction of personal growth. This is why their behavior is
consistent, as are their results!

Through the power of our wills, then, we can weigh something like
the physical pain of starvation against the psychic pain of surrendering
our ideals. We can create higher meaning; we can step out of the "Skin-
nerian box"* and take control. **But if we fail to direct our own associations to pain and pleasure, we're living no better than animals or
machines,** continually reacting to our environment, allowing whatever
comes up next to determine the direction and quality of our lives. We're
back in the box. It's as if we are a public computer, with easy access for
lots of amateur programmers!

Our behavior, both conscious and unconscious, has been rigged by
pain and pleasure from so many sources: childhood peers, moms and
dads, teachers, coaches, movie and television heroes, and the list goes on.

* B.F. Skinner, a famous behavioral science pioneer, is also infamous for the crib-size box in
which he confined his daughter for the first eleven months of her life. He did this in the name
of convenience and science, fueling his theories about stimulus-response behaviors.

You may or may not know precisely when programming and conditioning occurred. It might have been something someone said, an incident at school, an award-winning sports event, an embarrassing moment, straight A's on your report card—or maybe failing grades. All of these contributed to who you are today. I cannot emphasize strongly enough that **what you link pain and pleasure to will shape your destiny**.

As you review your own life, can you recall experiences that formed your neuro-associations and thus set in motion the chain of causes and effects that brought you to where you are today? What meaning do you attach to things? If you're single, do you look upon marriage wistfully as a joyous adventure with your life's mate, or do you dread it as a heavy ball and chain? As you sit down to dinner tonight, do you consume food matter-of-factly as an opportunity to refuel your body, or do you devour it as your sole source of pleasure?

> *"Men, as well as women, are much oftener led by their hearts than by their understandings."*
> —LORD CHESTERFIELD

Though we'd like to deny it, the fact remains that **what drives our behavior is instinctive reaction to pain and pleasure, not intellectual calculation**. Intellectually, we may believe that eating chocolate is bad for us, but we'll still reach for it. Why? Because we're not driven so much by what we intellectually know, but rather by what we've learned to link pain and pleasure to *in our nervous systems*. It's our **neuro-associations**— the associations we've established in our nervous systems—that determine what we'll do. *Although we'd like to believe it's our intellect that really drives us, in most cases our <u>emotions</u>—the sensations that we link to our thoughts—are what truly drive us.*

Many times we try to override the system. For a while we stick to a diet; we've finally pushed ourselves over the edge because we have so much pain. **We will have solved the problem for the moment—but if we haven't eliminated *the cause* of the problem, it will resurface.** Ultimately, in order for a change to last, we must link pain to our old behavior and pleasure to our new behavior, and condition it until it's consistent. Remember, we will all do more to avoid pain than we will to gain pleasure. Going on a diet and overriding our pain in the short term by pure willpower never lasts simply because we still link pain to giving up fattening foods. For this change to be long-term, we've got to link pain to eating those foods so that we no longer even desire them, and pleasure to eat more of the foods that *nourish* us. People who are fit and healthy believe that nothing tastes as good as thin feels! And they *love* foods that nourish them. In fact, they often link pleasure to pushing the plate away with food still on it. It symbolizes to them that they're in control of their lives.

The truth is that we can learn to condition our minds, bodies, and emotions to link pain or pleasure to whatever we choose. By changing what we link pain and pleasure to, we will instantly change our behaviors. With smoking, for example, all you must do is link enough pain to smoking and enough pleasure to quitting. You have the ability to do this right now, but you might not exercise this capability because you've trained your body to link pleasure to smoking, or you fear that stopping would be too painful. Yet, if you meet anyone who has stopped, you will find that this behavior changed in one day: the day they truly changed what smoking meant to them.

IF YOU DON'T HAVE A PLAN FOR YOUR LIFE, SOMEONE ELSE DOES

The mission of Madison Avenue is to influence what we link pain and pleasure to. Advertisers clearly understand that what drives us is not so much our intellect as the sensations that we link to their products. As a result, they've become experts in learning how to use exciting or soothing music, rapid or elegant imagery, bright or subdued color, and a variety of other elements to put us in certain emotional states; then, when our emotions are at their peak, when the sensations are their most intense, they flash an image of their product continuously until we link it to these desired feelings.

Pepsi employed this strategy brilliantly in carving out a bigger share of the lucrative soft-drink market from their major competitor, Coca-Cola. Pepsi observed the phenomenal success of Michael Jackson, a young man who had spent his entire life learning how to heighten people's emotions by the way he used his voice, his body, his face, and his gestures. Michael sang and danced in a way that stimulated huge numbers of people to feel incredibly good—so much so that they'd often purchase one of his albums to re-create the feelings. Pepsi asked, How can we transfer those sensations to *our* product? Their reasoning was that if people associated the same pleasurable feelings to Pepsi as they did to Michael Jackson, they'd buy Pepsi just as they bought his albums. The process of anchoring new feelings to a product or idea is the integral transference necessary to basic conditioning, something you'll learn more about in Chapter 6 as we study the science of Neuro-Associative Conditioning. But for now, consider this: **any time we're in an intense emotional state, when we're feeling strong sensations of pain or**

pleasure, anything unique that occurs consistently will become neu-rologically linked. Therefore, in the future, whenever that unique thing happens again, the emotional state will return.

You've probably heard of Ivan Pavlov, a Russian scientist who, in the late nineteenth century, conducted conditioned-response experiments. His most famous experiment was one in which he rang a bell as he offered food to a dog, thereby stimulating the dog to salivate and pairing the dog's sensations with the sound of the bell. After repeating the conditioning enough times, Pavlov found that merely ringing the bell would cause the dog to salivate—even when food was no longer being given.

What does Pavlov have to do with Pepsi? First, Pepsi used Michael Jackson to get us in a peak emotional state. Then, at that precise moment, they flashed the product. Continuous repetitions of this created an emotional linkage for millions of Jackson's fans. The truth is that Michael Jackson doesn't even drink Pepsi! And he wouldn't even hold an empty Pepsi can in his hand on camera! You might wonder, "Isn't this company crazy? They hired a guy for $15 million to represent them who doesn't even *hold* their product, and tells everybody that he won't! What kind of spokesperson is this? What a crazy idea!" Actually, it was a brilliant idea. Sales went through the roof—so high that L.A. Gear then hired Michael for $20 million to represent their product. And today, because he's able to change the way people feel (he's what I call a "state inducer") he and Sony/CBS just signed a 10-year recording contract that's reputed to be worth more than $1 billion. His ability to change people's emotional states makes him *invaluable*.

What we've got to realize is that this is all based on linking pleasurable sensations to specific behaviors. It's the idea that if we use the product, we'll live our fantasies. Advertisers have taught all of us that if you drive a BMW, then you're an extraordinary person with exceptional taste. If you drive a Hyundai, you're intelligent and frugal. If you drive a Pontiac, you'll have excitement. If you drive a Toyota, what a feeling you'll get! You're taught that if you wear Obsession cologne, you'll soon be entwined in the throes of an androgynous orgy. If you drink Pepsi, you'll be able to jam with M.C. Hammer as the epitome of hip. If you want to be a "good" mom, then you feed your children Hostess fruit pies, cupcakes and Twinkies.

Advertisers have noted that if enough pleasure can be generated, consumers are often willing to overlook the fear of pain. It is an advertising adage that "sex sells," and there's no question that the pleasurable associations created in print and on TV by using sex do the job. Take a look at the trend in selling blue jeans. What are blue jeans, anyway? They used to be work pants: functional, ugly. How are they sold today? They've become an international icon of everything that's sexy, fashionable, and youthful. Have you ever watched a Levi's 501 jeans commercial? Can you explain one to me? They make no sense, do they? They're totally confusing. But at the end, you have the distinct impression that sex took place nearby. Does this type of strategy really sell blue jeans? You bet! Levi is the number-one blue-jeans manufacturer in America today.

Is the power of conditioning to shape our associations limited to products like soft drinks, automobiles and blue jeans? Of course not. Take the lowly little raisin, for example. Do you know that in 1986, the California Raisin Advisory Board was expecting a huge harvest, yet they were beginning to panic? Year by year, they'd seen their sales dropping by 1 percent annually. In desperation they turned to their advertising agency and asked what they could do. The solution was simple: they needed to change people's *feelings* about raisins. For most people, raisins were considered wimpy, lonely, and dull, according to Robert Phinney, the former director of the raisin board.* The task was clear: pump a healthy dose of emotional appeal into the shriveled-up fruit. Link up sensations that people *wanted.* "Shriveled" and "dried" are not the sensations that most people associate with feeling good about their lives. The raisin growers kept thinking, What can we associate to raisins that would make people really want to buy them?

At the time, an old Motown hit was enjoying a national resurgence: "I Heard It Through the Grapevine." Raisin growers thought, What if we can take these sensations that make so many people feel good, and link them to raisins to make them seem hip? They hired an innovative animator named Will Vinton who then created about thirty clay raisin figurines, each with a distinct personality, to boogie to the Motown tune. In those moments, the California Raisins were born. Their first ad campaign created an instant sensation and successfully linked the sensations that the raisin growers hoped for. As people watched the hip little raisins dance, they linked strong feelings of fun, humor, and pleasure to the once boring fruit. The raisin had been reinvented as the essence of California cool, and the unspoken message of each of these ads was that if you ate them you'd be hip, too. The upshot? The raisin industry was rescued from its devastating slump in sales to a 20 percent growth factor annually. The raisin growers had succeeded in changing people's associations: instead of linking boredom to the fruit, consumers had learned to link sensations of excitement and fun!

Of course, the use of advertising as a form of conditioning is not limited to physical products. Fortunately or unfortunately, we consistently see television and radio used as tools for changing what we asso-

---

* Hillkirk, John, and Gary Jacobson, *Grit, Guts and Genius,* Boston: Houghton Mifflin Company, ©1990.

ciate to candidates in the political process. No one knows this better than the master political analyst and opinion-shaper Roger Ailes, who was responsible for key elements of Ronald Reagan's successful 1984 campaign against Walter Mondale, and who in 1988 masterminded George Bush's successful campaign against Michael Dukakis. Ailes designed a strategy to convey three specifically negative messages about Dukakis— that he was soft on defense, the environment, and crime—and cause people to link painful sensations to him. One ad portrayed Dukakis as a "kid playing war" in a tank; another seemed to blame him for pollution in the Boston Harbor. The most notorious one showed criminals being released from Massachusetts jails through a revolving door, and played on the widespread negative publicity generated around the country by the "Willie Horton incident." Convicted murderer Willie Horton, released from jail as part of a controversial furlough program in Dukakis's home state, failed to return and ten months later was arrested for terrorizing a young couple, raping the woman and assaulting the man.

Many people took issue with the negative focus of these ads. Personally, I found them highly manipulative. But it's hard to argue with their level of success, based on the fact that people do more to avoid pain than to gain pleasure. Many people didn't like the way the campaign was fought—and George Bush was one of those people—but it was hard to argue with the reality that pain was a very powerful motivator in shaping people's behavior. As Ailes says, "The negative ads cut through quicker. People tend to pay more attention to [these types of ads]. People may or may not slow down to look at a beautiful pastoral scene along the highway. But everyone looks at an auto accident."* There is no questioning the effectiveness of Ailes's strategy. Bush won a clear majority of the popular vote and soundly trounced Dukakis in one of the biggest landslides in electoral college history.

The force shaping world opinion and consumer's buying habits is also the same force that shapes *all* of our actions. It's up to you and me to take control of this force and decide on our own actions consciously, because if we don't direct our own thoughts, we'll fall under the influence of those who would condition us to behave in the way they desire. Sometimes those actions are what we would have selected anyway; sometimes not. Advertisers understand how to change what we link pain and pleasure to by changing the sensations we associate to their products. If we want to take control of our lives, we must learn to "advertise" in our own minds—and we can do this *in a moment.* How? **Simply by linking pain to the behaviors we want to stop at such a high level of emotional intensity that we won't even *consider* those behaviors any**

* Hillkirk, *Grit, Guts and Genius.*

longer. Aren't there things you would never, ever do? Think of the sensations you link to those. If you link those same feelings and sensations to the behaviors you want to avoid, you'll never do them again, either. Then, **simply link pleasure to the new behavior you desire for yourself**. Through repetition and emotional intensity, you can condition these behaviors within yourself until they are automatic.

So what's the first step in creating a change? The first step is simply *becoming aware* of the power that pain and pleasure exert over every decision, and therefore every action, that we take. The art of being aware is understanding that these linkages—between ideas, words, images, sounds, and sensations of pain and pleasure— are happening constantly.

> *"I conceive that pleasures are to be avoided if greater pains be the consequence, and pains to be coveted that will terminate in greater pleasures."*
> —MICHEL DE MONTAIGNE

The problem is that most of us base our decisions about what to do on what's going to create pain or pleasure in the *short term* instead of the long term. Yet, in order to succeed, most of the things that we value require us to be able to break through the wall of short-term pain in order to have long-term pleasure. You must put aside the passing moments of terror and temptation, and focus on what's most important in the long term: your values and personal standards. Remember, too, that **it's not actual pain that drives us, but our fear that something will lead to pain. And it's not** *actual* **pleasure that drives us, but our belief**—*our sense of certainty*—**that somehow taking a certain action will lead to pleasure.** We're not driven by the reality, but by our *perception* of reality.

Most people focus on how to avoid pain and gain pleasure *in the short term*, and thereby create *long-term* pain for themselves. Let's consider an example. Say someone wants to lose a few extra pounds. (I know this has never happened to *you*, but let's just pretend anyway!) On the one hand, this person marshals a host of excellent reasons for losing weight: they would feel healthier and more energized; they would fit into their clothes better; they would feel more confident around members of the opposite sex. On the other hand, though, there are just as many reasons to avoid losing weight: they'd have to go on a diet; they'd continually feel hungry; they'd have to deny their urge to eat fattening foods; and besides, why not wait until *after* the holidays?

With the reasons balanced in this way, many people would tip the scales in favor of the pattern of putting things off—the potential pleasure of a slimmer figure far outweighed by the short-term pain of dietary deprivation. Short term, we avoid the pain of feeling a twinge of hunger, and instead we give ourselves that immediate morsel of pleasure by indulging in a few potato chips, but it doesn't last. In the long term, we feel worse and worse about ourselves, not to mention the fact that it causes our health to deteriorate.

Remember, anything you want that's valuable requires that you break through some short-term pain in order to gain long-term pleasure. If you want a great body, you've got to sculpt that body, which requires breaking through short-term pain. Once you've done it enough times, working out becomes pleasurable. Dieting works the same way. Any type of discipline requires breaking through pain: discipline in business, relationships, personal confidence, fitness, and finances. How do you break through the discomfort and create the momentum to really accomplish your aims? Start by making the decision to overcome it. We can *always* decide to override the pain in the moment, and better yet is to follow up by conditioning ourselves, which is something we'll cover in detail in Chapter 6.

A prime example of how this short-term focus can cause us all to take a fall (as in Niagara) is reflected by the current savings-and-loan crisis— probably the single biggest financial mistake ever made in the history of our government. Estimates show it could cost taxpayers more than $500 billion, yet most Americans have no idea what *caused* it.* This problem will most certainly be one that is the source of pain—at least economic pain—for every man, woman and child in this country, probably for generations to come. In a conversation I had with L. William Seidman, chairman of the Resolution Trust Corporation and the Federal Deposit Insurance Corporation, he told me, "We are the only nation rich enough to survive such a big mistake." What did create this financial mess? It's a classic example of trying to eliminate pain by solving a problem while nurturing the cause.

It all began with savings and loan challenges that came up in the late seventies and early eighties. Banking and S&L institutions had built their business primarily on the corporate and consumer market. For a bank to profit, it has to make loans, and those loans have to be at an interest rate that's above what it pays out to depositors. In the first stages of the problem, the banks faced difficulties on several fronts. First, they were hit hard when corporations entered what had previously been the sole domain of banks: lending. Large companies found that by lending to one another, they saved significantly on interest, developing what's now

---

* If you'd like to have a greater understanding of the cause of the S&L crisis, I highly recommend my friend Paul Pilzer's book, *Other People's Money*.

known as the "commercial paper market." This was so successful that it virtually destroyed the profit centers of many banks.

Meanwhile, there were new developments on the American consumer front as well. Traditionally, consumers did not look forward to meeting with a loan officer at a bank, meekly asking for loans to purchase a car or large appliance. I think we can fairly say that this was a painful experience for most as they subjected themselves to financial scrutiny. They didn't usually feel like a "valued customer" at many banks. Car companies were smart enough to recognize this and began offering loans to their customers, creating a new source of profit for themselves. They saw that they could make as much money on the financing as they did on the car they sold, and they could give the customer a great deal of convenience and lower interest rates. Their attitude was, of course, quite different from the bankers'—they had a vested interest in seeing the customer get his loan. Soon, the customers came to prefer the in-house financing over the traditional method, appreciating the convenience, flexibility, and low financing fees. Everything was handled in one place by a courteous person who wanted their business. Consequently, General Motors Acceptance Corporation (GMAC) quickly became one of the largest car-financing companies in the country.

One of the last bastions for bank loans was the real estate market, but interest rates and inflation had soared in one year as high as 18 percent. As a result, no one could afford the monthly payments that servicing loans at this interest rate required. As you can imagine, real estate loans dropped off the map.

By this time, the banks had lost their corporate customers *en masse*, they had lost the market for a great deal of their car loans, and they had begun to lose the home loans as well. The final slap to the banks was that the depositors, in response to inflation, needed a higher rate of return while the banks were still carrying loans that would yield significantly lower interest rates. Every day, the banks were losing money; they saw their survival at stake and decided to do two things. First, they lowered their standards for qualifying customers for loans. Why? Because they believed that if they didn't lower their standards, there would be no one to loan money to. And if they didn't loan money, they couldn't profit, and they'd clearly have pain. If, however, they were able to loan money to someone who paid them back, they'd have pleasure. Plus, there was very little risk. If they loaned money and the lendee *didn't* meet the obligation, then the taxpayers, namely you and I, would bail them out anyway. So in the final analysis, there was very little fear of pain and tremendous incentive to "risk" their (our?) capital.

These banks and S&Ls also pressured Congress to help keep them from going under, and a series of changes occurred. Large banks realized that they could loan money to foreign nations that were desperately hungry for capital. The lenders realized that *over breakfast* they could commit more than $50 million to a country. They didn't have to work with millions of consumers to lend the same amount, and the profits on these larger loans were sizable. The bank managers and loan officers were also often given bonuses in relation to the size and number of loans they could produce. The banks were no longer focusing on the quality of a loan. Their focus was not on whether a country like Brazil could pay the loan back or not, and frankly, many weren't terribly concerned. Why? They did exactly what we taught them: we encouraged them to be gamblers with the Federal Deposit Insurance, promising that if they won, they won big, and if they failed, we would pick up the tab. There was simply too little pain in this scenario for the banker.

Smaller banks, who didn't have the resources to loan to foreign countries, found that the next best thing was to loan to commercial developers here in the United States. They, too, lowered their standards so that developers could borrow with no money down instead of the traditional 20 percent. What was the developers' response? Well, they had nothing on the line, they were using only other people's money, and at the same time Congress had built such high tax incentives into commercial building that the builders had absolutely nothing to lose. They no longer had to analyze whether the market was right, or whether the building was properly located or sized. The developers' only "downside" was that they would have the most incredible tax write-off of their lives.

As a result, builders built like crazy, causing a glut on the market. When the supply was so much greater than the demand, the market collapsed. Developers went back to the banks and said, "We can't pay," and the banks turned to the taxpayers and said, "We can't pay." Unfortunately, there's nobody *we* can turn to. What's worse, people have seen the abuse in this country, and the assumption now is that anyone who is wealthy must have taken advantage of somebody. This is creating negative attitudes toward many in business who are often the very people providing jobs that allow Americans' dreams to flourish. This whole mess illustrates our lack of understanding of the pain-pleasure dynamic and the inadvisability of trying to conquer long-term problems with short-term solutions.

Pain and pleasure are also the backstage directors of global drama. For years we lived through an escalating arms race with the USSR. The two nations were constantly building more weapons as the ultimate threat: "If you try to hurt us, we'll retaliate and hurt you even worse." And the standoff continued to build to the point at which we were spending $15,000 *a second* on arms. What caused Gorbachev to suddenly decide to renegotiate arms reduction? The answer is pain. He began to associate massive pain to the idea of trying to compete with our military arms buildup. Financially it just wasn't feasible; he couldn't even *feed* his people! When people can't eat, they're more concerned about their stomachs than about guns. They're more interested in filling their larders than the country's armament. They begin to believe that money is being spent frivolously, and they insist on a change. Did Gorbachev change his position because he's a great guy? Maybe. But one thing is certain: he didn't have a choice.

> *"Nature has placed mankind under the government of two sovereign masters, pain and pleasure . . . they govern us in all we do, in all we say, in all we think: every effort we can make to throw off our subjection, will serve but to demonstrate and confirm it."*
> —JEREMY BENTHAM

Why do people persist in an unsatisfying relationship, unwilling either to work toward solutions or end it and move on? It's because they know changing will lead to the unknown, and most people believe that the unknown will be much more painful than what they're already experiencing. It's like the old proverbs say: "Better the devil you know than the devil you don't know," "A bird in the hand is worth two in the bush." These core beliefs keep us from taking the actions that could change our lives.

If we want to have an intimate relationship, then we have to overcome our fears of rejection and vulnerability. If we're planning to go into business, we must be willing to overcome our fear of losing security to make that happen. In fact, most of the things that are valuable in our lives *require us to go against the basic conditioning of our nervous systems*. We must manage our fears by overriding this preconditioned set of responses and, in many cases, we must transform that fear into power. Many times, the fear that we are allowing to control us never becomes reality anyway. It's possible for people to link pain, for example, to flying in an airplane, while there's no logical reason for the phobia. They're responding to a painful experience in their past or even an imagined future. They may have read in the papers about airplane accidents, and now they avoid getting on planes: they're allowing that fear to control them. We must make sure that we live our lives in the present and respond to things that are real, not to our fears of what once was or what might someday be. The key thing to remember is that we don't move away from *real* pain; we move away from what we *believe* will lead to pain.

LET'S MAKE SOME CHANGES RIGHT NOW

First, write down four actions that you need to take that you've been putting off. Maybe you need to lose some weight. Maybe you need to stop smoking. Maybe you need to communicate with someone you've had a falling out with, or reconnect with someone who's important to you.

Second, under each of these actions, write down the answer to the following questions: Why haven't I taken action? In the past, what pain have I linked to taking this action? Answering these questions will help you understand that what has held you back is that you've associated greater pain to taking the action than to not taking it. Be honest with yourself. If you're thinking, "I have no pain associated to it," think a little harder. Maybe the pain is simple: maybe it's the pain of taking time out of your busy schedule.

Third, write down all the pleasure you've had in the past by indulging in this negative pattern. For example, if you think you should lose some weight, why have you continued to eat whole pans of brownies and bulk-size bags of chips, and to guzzle twelve-packs of soda pop? You're avoiding the pain of depriving yourself, yes, and at the same time you're really doing this because it makes you feel good right now. It gives you pleasure! Instant pleasure! No one wants to give up these feelings! In order to create a change that will last, we need to find a new way to get the same pleasure without any negative consequences. Identifying the pleasure you've been getting will help you know what your target is.

Fourth, write down what it will cost you if you *don't* change now. What will happen if you don't stop eating so much sugar and fat? If you don't stop smoking? If you don't make that phone call that you know you need to make? If you don't start consistently working out each day? Be honest with yourself. What's it going to cost you over the next two, three, four, five years? What's it going to cost you emotionally? What's it going to cost you in terms of your self-image? What will it cost you in your physical energy level? What will it cost you in your feelings of self-esteem? What will it cost you financially? What will it cost you in your relationships with the people you care about most? **How does that make you feel?** Don't just say, "It will cost me money" or "I will be fat." That's not enough. You've got to remember that what drives us is our emotions.

So get associated and use pain as your friend, one that can drive you to a new level of success.

The final step is to write down all the pleasure you'll receive by taking each of these actions *right now*. Make a huge list that will drive you emotionally, that will really get you excited: "I'll gain the feeling of really being in control of my life, of knowing that I'm in charge. I'll gain a new level of self-confidence. I'll gain physical vitality and health. I'll be able to strengthen all my relationships. I'll develop more willpower which I could use in every other area of my life. My life will be better in all these ways, now. Over the next two, three, four, five years. By taking this action, I will live my dream." Envision all the positive impacts both in the present and in the long term.

I encourage you to take the time *now* to complete this exercise, and to take advantage of the great momentum you've been building up as you've moved through this book. *Carpe diem!* Seize the day! There's no time like the present. But if you can't wait another second before pressing on to the next chapter, then by all means, do so. Just be sure to come back to this exercise later and demonstrate to yourself the control you have over the twin powers of pain and pleasure.

This chapter has shown you again and again that what we link pain to and pleasure to shapes every aspect of our lives and that we have the power to change these associations and, therefore, our actions and our destinies. But in order to do this, we must understand . . .

4

BELIEF SYSTEMS: THE POWER TO CREATE AND THE POWER TO DESTROY

"Under all that we think, lives all we believe,
like the ultimate veil of our spirits."
—ANTONIO MACHADO

He was bitter and cruel, an alcoholic and drug addict who almost killed himself several times. Today he serves a life sentence in prison for the murder of a liquor store cashier who "got in his way." He has two sons, born a mere eleven months apart, one of whom grew up to be "just like Dad": a drug addict who lived by stealing and threatening others until he, too, was put in jail for attempted murder. His brother, however, is a different story: a man who's raising three kids, enjoys his marriage, and appears to be truly happy. As regional manager for a major national concern, he finds his work both challenging and rewarding. He's physically fit, and has no alcohol or drug addictions! How could these two young men have turned out so differently, having grown up in virtually the same environment? Both were asked privately, unbeknownst to the other, "Why has your life turned out this way?" Surprisingly, they both provided the exact same answer: "What else could I have become, having grown up with a father like that?"

So often we're seduced into believing that events control our lives and that our environment has shaped who we are today. No greater lie was ever told. **It's not the events of our lives that shape us, but our beliefs as to what those events mean.**

Two men are shot down in Vietnam and imprisoned in the infamous Hoa Lo prison. They are isolated, chained to cement slabs, and continuously beaten with rusty shackles and tortured for information. Yet although these men are receiving the same abuse, they form radically different beliefs about their experience. One man decides that his life is over, and in order to avoid any additional pain, commits suicide. The other pulls from these brutalizing events a deeper belief in himself, his fellow man, and his Creator than he's ever had before. Captain Gerald Coffee uses his experience of this to remind people all over the world of the power of the human spirit to overcome virtually any level of pain, any challenge, or any problem.

Two women turn seventy years old, yet each takes a different meaning from the event. One "knows" that her life is coming to an end. To her, seven decades of living mean that her body must be breaking down and she'd better start winding up her affairs. The other woman decides that what a person is capable of at any age depends upon her belief, and sets a higher standard for herself. She decides that mountain climbing might be a good sport to begin at the age of seventy. For the next twenty five years she devotes herself to this new adventure in mastery, scaling some of the highest peaks in the world, until today, in her nineties, Hulda Crooks has become the oldest woman to ascend Mount Fuji.

You see, it's never the environment; it's never the events of our lives, but the **meaning** we attach to the events—how we *interpret them*—that shapes who we are today and who we'll become tomorrow. Beliefs are what make the difference between a lifetime of joyous contribution and one of misery and devastation. Beliefs are what separate a Mozart from a Manson. Beliefs are what cause some individuals to become heroes, while others "lead lives of quiet desperation."

What are our beliefs designed for? They're the guiding force to tell us what will lead to pain and what will lead to pleasure. Whenever something happens in your life, your brain asks two questions: 1) Will this mean pain or pleasure? 2) What must I do now to avoid pain and/or gain pleasure? The answers to these two questions are based on our **beliefs**, and our beliefs are driven by our **generalizations** about what we've learned could lead to pain and pleasure. These generalizations guide all of our actions and thus the direction and quality of our lives.

Generalizations can be very useful; they are simply the identification of similar patterns. For example, what allows you to open a door? You look down at a handle and, although you've never seen this specific one before, you can generally feel certain that this door will open if you turn the handle right or left, if you push or pull it. Why do you believe this? Simply, your experience of doors has provided enough references to create a **sense of certainty** that allows you to follow through. Without this sense of certainty, we would virtually be unable to leave the house, drive our cars, use a telephone, or do any one of the dozens of things we do in a day. Generalizations simplify our lives and allow us to function.

Unfortunately, generalizations in more complex areas of our lives can oversimplify and sometimes create limiting beliefs. Maybe you've failed to follow through on various endeavors a few times in your life, and based on that, you developed a belief that you are incompetent. Once you believe this is true, it can become a self-fulfilling prophecy. You may say, "Why even try if I'm not going to follow through anyway?" Or perhaps you've made a few poor decisions in business or in relationships, and have interpreted that to mean you will always "sabotage" yourself. Or maybe in school you didn't learn as quickly as you *thought* other kids did, and rather than considering the idea that you had a different learning strategy, you may have decided that you were "learning-disabled." On another level, isn't racial prejudice fueled by a wholesale generalization about an entire group of people?

The challenge with all these beliefs is that they become limitations for future decisions about who you are and what you're capable of. We need to remember that **most of our beliefs are generalizations about our past, based on our interpretations of painful and pleasurable experiences.** The challenge is threefold: 1) most of us do not consciously decide what we're going to believe; 2) often our beliefs are based on *misinterpretation* of past experiences; and 3) once we adopt a belief, we forget it's *merely an interpretation.* We begin to treat our beliefs as if they're realities, as if they are gospel. In fact, we rarely, if ever, question our long-held beliefs. If you ever wonder why people do what they do, again, you need to remember that human beings are not random creatures: all of our actions are the result of our beliefs. Whatever we do, it is out of our conscious or unconscious beliefs about what will lead to pleasure or away from pain. If you want to create long-term and consistent changes in your behaviors, you must change the beliefs that are holding you back.

Beliefs have the power to create and the power to destroy. Human beings have the awesome ability to take any experience of their lives and create a meaning that disempowers them or one that can literally save their lives. Some people have taken the pain of their past and said, "Because of this, I will help others. Because I was raped, no one else will be harmed again." Or, "Because I lost my son or daughter, I will make a difference in the world." It's not something they wanted to believe, but rather, adopting this type of belief was a necessity for them to be able to pick up the pieces and move on to live empowering lives. We all have the capacity to create meanings that empower us, but so many of us never tap into it, or even recognize it. If we don't adopt the faith that there is a reason for the unexplainable tragedies of life, then we begin to destroy our capacity to truly live. The need to be able to create a meaning out of life's most painful experiences was observed by psychiatrist Viktor Frankl as he and other Holocaust victims survived the horrors of Auschwitz and other concentration camps. Frankl noted that those special few who were able to make it through this "hell on earth" shared one thing in common: they were able to endure and transform their experience by finding an empowering meaning for their pain. They developed the belief that because they suffered and survived, they would be able to tell the story and make certain that no human being would ever suffer this way again.

Beliefs are not limited to impacting our emotions or actions. They can literally change our bodies in a matter of moments. I had the pleasure of interviewing Yale professor and best-selling author Dr. Bernie Siegel. As we began to speak about the power of belief, Bernie shared with me some of the research he'd done on people with Multiple Personality Disorders. Incredibly, the potency of these people's beliefs that they had become a different person resulted in an unquestioned command to their nervous system to make measurable changes in their biochemistry. The result? Their bodies would literally transform before the researchers' eyes and begin to reflect a new identity at a moment's notice. Studies document such remarkable occurrences as patients' eye color actually changing as their personality changes, or physical marks disappearing and reappearing! Even diseases such as diabetes or high blood pressure come and go depending on the person's belief as to which personality they're manifesting.

Beliefs even have the capacity to override the impact of drugs on the body. While most people believe that drugs heal, studies in the new science of psychoneuroimmunology (the mind-body relationship) have begun to bear out what many others have suspected for centuries: our beliefs about the illness and its treatment play as significant a role, maybe an even *more* significant role, than the treatment itself. Dr. Henry Beecher from Harvard University has done extensive research that clearly demonstrates that we often give credit to a drug, when in reality it's the patient's belief that makes the difference.

One demonstration of this was a groundbreaking experiment in which 100 medical students were asked to participate in testing two new drugs. One was described to them as a super-stimulant in a red capsule, the other as a super-tranquilizer in a blue capsule. Unbeknownst to the students, the contents of the capsules had been switched: the red capsule was actually a barbiturate, and the blue capsule was actually an amphetamine. Yet half of the students developed physical reactions that went along with their expectations—exactly the opposite of the chemical reaction the drugs should have produced in their bodies! These students were not just given placebos; they were given actual drugs. But their beliefs overrode the chemical impact of the drug on their bodies. As Dr.

Beecher later stated, a drug's usefulness "is a direct result of not only the chemical properties of the drug, but also the patient's belief in the usefulness and effectiveness of the drug."

"Drugs are not always necessary, [but] belief in recovery always is."
—NORMAN COUSINS

I had the privilege of knowing Norman Cousins for almost seven years, and I was fortunate enough to have the last taped interview with him just one month before he passed on. In that interview, he shared a story about how strongly our beliefs affect our physical bodies. At a football game in Monterey Park, a Los Angeles suburb, several people experienced the symptoms of food poisoning. The examining physician deduced that the cause was a certain soft drink from the dispensing machines because all of his patients had purchased some prior to becoming ill. An announcement was made over the loudspeaker requesting that no one patronize the dispensing machine, saying some people had become ill and describing the symptoms. Pandemonium immediately broke out in the stands as people retched and fainted in droves. Even a few people who had not even gone near the machine became ill! Ambulances from local hospitals did a booming business that day, as they drove back and forth to the stadium, transporting multitudes of stricken fans. When it was discovered that the dispensing machine was not the culprit, people immediately and "miraculously" recovered.

We need to realize that our beliefs have the capacity to make us sick or make us healthy *in a moment*. Beliefs have been documented to affect our immune systems. And most importantly, beliefs can either give us the resolve to take action, or weaken and destroy our drive. In this moment beliefs are shaping how you respond to what you've just read and what you're going to do with what you're learning in this book. Sometimes we develop beliefs that create limitations or strengths within a very specific context; for instance, how we feel about our ability to sing or dance, fix a car, or do calculus. Other beliefs are so generalized that they dominate virtually every aspect of our lives, either negatively or positively. I call these **global beliefs**.

Global beliefs are the giant beliefs we have about everything in our lives: beliefs about our identities, people, work, time, money, and life itself, for that matter. These giant generalizations are often phrased as *is/am/are*: "Life is . . ." "I am . . ." "People are . . ." As you can imagine, beliefs of this size and scope can shape and color every aspect of our lives. The good news about this is that making *one change* in a limiting global belief you currently hold can change virtually *every* aspect of your life in a moment! Remember: **Once accepted, our beliefs become unquestioned commands to our nervous systems, and they have the power to expand or destroy the possibilities of our present and future.**

If we want to direct our lives, then, we must take conscious control over our beliefs. And in order to do that, we first need to understand what they really are and how they are formed.

WHAT IS A BELIEF?

What is a belief, anyway? Often in life we talk about things without having a clear idea of what they really are. Most people treat a belief as if it's a thing, when really all it is is a **feeling of certainty** about something. If you say you believe that you're intelligent, all you're really saying is, "I *feel certain* that I'm intelligent." That sense of certainty allows you to tap into resources that allow you to produce intelligent results. We all have the answers inside of us for virtually anything—or at least we have access to the answers we need through others. But often our lack of belief, our lack of certainty, causes us not to be able to use the capacity that resides within us.

A simple way of understanding a belief is to think about its basic building block: an idea. There are a lot of ideas you may think about but not really believe. Let's take, for example, the idea that you're sexy. Stop for a second and say to yourself, "I'm sexy." Now, whether it's an idea or a belief will come down to the amount of certainty you feel about this phrase as you say it. If you think, "Well, I'm not really sexy," what you're really saying is, "I don't feel very certain that I'm sexy."

How do we turn an idea into a belief? Let me offer you a simple metaphor to describe the process. If you can think of an idea as being like a tabletop with no legs, you'll have a fair representation of why an idea doesn't feel as certain as a belief. Without any legs, that tabletop won't even stand up by itself. Belief, on the other hand, has *legs*. If you really believe, "I'm sexy," how do you *know* you're sexy? Isn't it true that you have some **references** to support the idea—some experiences in life to back it up? Those are the legs that make your tabletop solid, that make your belief certain.

What are some of the reference experiences you've had? Maybe men and women have *told* you that you're sexy. Or maybe you look at yourself in the mirror, compare your image to that of those whom other people consider sexy, and say, "Hey, I look like them!" Or maybe strangers on the street call out and wave to you. All these experiences mean nothing until you organize them under the idea that you're sexy. As you do this,

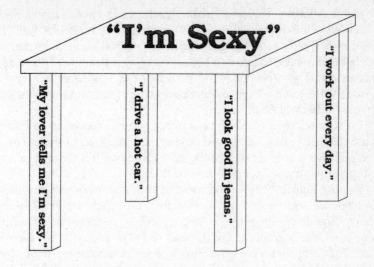

the legs make you feel solid about the idea and cause you to begin to believe it. Your idea feels certain and is now a belief.

Once you understand this metaphor, you can begin to see how your beliefs are formed, and get a hint of how you can change them as well. First, though, it's important to note that we can develop beliefs about *any-thing* if we just find enough legs—enough reference experiences—to build it up. Think about it. Isn't it true that you have enough experiences in your life, or know enough other people who have gone through tough times with other human beings, that if you really wanted to you could easily develop the belief that people are rotten and, given half a chance, would take advantage of you? Maybe you don't want to believe this, and we've already discussed that it would be disempowering, but don't you have experiences that could back up this idea and make you feel certain about it if you wanted to? Isn't it also true that you have experiences in life— references—to back up the idea that if you really care about people and treat them well, they are basically good and will want to help you too?

The question is: which one of these beliefs is the true belief? The answer is that it doesn't matter which one is true. What matters is which one is most *empowering*. We all can find someone to back up our belief and make us feel more solid about it. This is how human beings are able to rationalize. The key question, again, is whether this belief is strength-ening or weakening us, empowering or disempowering us on a daily basis. So what are the possible sources of references in our lives? Cer-tainly, we can pull from our *personal experiences*. Sometimes we gather references through *information* we get from other people, or from books, tapes, movies, and so on. And sometimes we form references based solely on our *imagination*. The emotional intensity we feel about any of these references will definitely affect the strength and width of the leg. The strongest and most solid legs are formed by personal experiences that we have a lot of *emotion* attached to because they were painful or pleasurable experiences. The other factor is the *number* of references we have— obviously, the more reference experiences supporting an idea, the stronger your belief will be in it.

Do your references have to be accurate in order for you to be willing to use them? No, they can be real or imaginary, accurate or inaccurate— even our own personal experiences, as solidly as we feel about them, are distorted by our own personal perspective.

Because human beings are capable of such distortion and invention, the reference legs we can use to assemble our beliefs are virtually un- limited. The downside of this is that, regardless of where our references come from, we begin to accept them as *real* and thus *no longer question them!* This can have very powerful negative consequences depending upon the beliefs we adopt. By the same token, we have the ability to use imagined references to propel us in the direction of our dreams. People can succeed if they imagine something vividly enough just as easily as if they had the actual experiences. That's because our brains can't tell the difference between something we've vividly imagined and something we've actually experienced. **With enough emotional intensity and rep- etition, our nervous systems experience something as real, even if it hasn't occurred yet.** Every great achiever I've ever interviewed has had the ability to get themselves to feel certain they could succeed, even though no one before them had ever accomplished it. They've been able to create references where no references existed and achieve what seemed to be impossible.

Anyone who uses a computer is likely to recognize the name "Mi- crosoft." What most people don't realize is that Bill Gates, the co-founder of that company, was not just some genius who got lucky, but a person who put himself on the line with no references to back up his belief. When he found out that an Albuquerque company was developing some- thing called a "personal computer" that needed BASIC software, he called them up and promised to deliver it, even though he had no such thing at the time. Once he had committed himself, he had to find a way. His ability to *create a sense of certainty* was his real genius. Many people were just as intelligent as he was, but he used his certainty to be able to tap into his resources, and within a few weeks he and a partner had written a language that made the personal computer a reality. By putting himself on the line and finding a way, Bill Gates set in motion that day a series of events that would change the way people do business, and became a billionaire by the time he was thirty years old. Certainty carries power!

Do you know the story of the four-minute mile? For thousands of years, people held the belief that it was impossible for a human being to run the mile in less than four minutes. But in 1954, Roger Bannister broke this imposing *belief* barrier. He got himself to achieve the "impossible" not merely by physical practice but by constantly rehearsing the event in his mind, breaking through the four-minute barrier so many times with so much emotional intensity that he created vivid references that became an unquestioned command to his nervous system to produce the result. Many people don't realize, though, that the greatest aspect of his breakthrough was what it did for others. It had seemed no one would ever be able to break a four-minute mile, yet within one year of Roger's breaking the barrier, 37 other runners also broke it. His experience provided them with references strong enough to create a sense of certainty that they, too, could "do the impossible." And the year after that, *300* other runners did the same thing!

> *"The belief that becomes truth for me . . . is that which allows me the best use of my strength, the best means of putting my virtues into action."*
> —ANDRÉ GIDE

People so often develop limiting beliefs about who they are and what they're capable of. Because they haven't succeeded in the past, they believe they won't be able to succeed in the future. As a result, out of their fear of pain, they begin to constantly focus on being "realistic." Most people who constantly say, "Let's be realistic," are really just living in fear, deathly afraid of being disappointed again. Out of that fear, they develop beliefs that cause them to hesitate, to not give their all—consequently they get limited results.

Great leaders are rarely "realistic." They are intelligent, and they are accurate, but they are not realistic by other people's standards. What is realistic for one person, though, is totally different from what is realistic for another person, based upon their references. Gandhi believed he could gain autonomy for India without violently opposing Great Britain—something that had never been done before. He wasn't being realistic, but he certainly proved to be accurate. By the same token, it certainly wasn't realistic for a man to believe he could give the world happiness by building a theme park in the middle of an orange grove and charging people not only for the rides, but even to get in! At the time, there was no such park in the world. Yet Walt Disney had a sense of certainty like few people who have ever lived, and his optimism transformed his circumstances.

If you're going to make an error in life, err on the side of overesti-mating your capabilities (obviously, as long as it doesn't jeopardize your life). By the way, this is something that's hard to do, since the human capacity is so much greater than most of us would ever dream. In fact, many studies have focused on the differences between people who are depressed and people who are extremely optimistic. After attempting to learn a new skill, the pessimists are always more accurate about how they did, while the optimists see their behavior as being more effective than it actually was. Yet this unrealistic evaluation of their own performance is the secret of their future success. Invariably the optimists eventually end up mastering the skill while the pessimists fail. Why? Optimists are those who, despite having no references for success, or even references of *failure*, manage to ignore those references, leaving unassembled such cognitive tabletops as "I failed" or "I can't succeed." Instead, optimists produce *faith* references, summoning forth their imagination to picture themselves doing something different next time and succeeding. It is this special ability, this unique focus, which allows them to *persist* until eventually they gain the distinctions that put them over the top. The reason success eludes most people is that they have insufficient refer-ences of succeeding in the past. But an optimist operates with beliefs such as, **"The past doesn't equal the future."** All great leaders, all people who have achieved success in any area of life, know the power of continuously pursuing their vision, even if all the details of how to achieve it aren't yet available. **If you develop the absolute sense of certainty that powerful beliefs provide, then you can get yourself to accomplish virtually anything, including those things that other people are certain are impossible.**

> *"Only in men's imagination does every truth find an effective and undeniable existence. Imagination, not invention, is the supreme master of art, as of life."*
> —JOSEPH CONRAD

One of the biggest challenges in anyone's life is knowing how to interpret "failures." How we deal with life's "defeats" and what we determine is the cause will shape our destinies. We need to remember that **how we deal with adversity and challenges will shape our lives more than almost anything else.** Sometimes we get so many references of pain and failure that we begin to assemble those into a belief that nothing we do can make things better. Some people begin to feel that things are pointless, that they're helpless or worthless, or that no matter what they try they'll lose anyway. These are a set of beliefs that must *never* be indulged in if we ever expect to succeed and achieve in our lives. These beliefs strip us of our personal power and destroy our ability to act. In psychology, there is a name for this destructive mindset: **learned helplessness**. When people experience enough failure at something—and you'd be surprised how few times this is for some people—they perceive their efforts as futile and develop the terminal discouragement of learned helplessness.

Encumbered with a low self-image,
Bob takes a job as a speed bump.

Dr. Martin Seligman of the University of Pennsylvania has done in-tensive research on what creates learned helplessness. In his book *Learned Optimism* he reports on three specific **patterns of beliefs** that cause us to feel helpless and can destroy virtually every aspect of our lives. He calls these three categories **permanence**, **pervasiveness**, and **personal**.

Many of our country's greatest achievers have succeeded in spite of running into huge problems and barriers. The difference between them and those who give up revolves around their beliefs about the *permanence*, or lack thereof, of their problems. Achievers rarely, if ever, see a problem as permanent, while those who fail see even the smallest problems as permanent. Once you adopt the belief that there's nothing you can do to change something, simply because nothing you've done up until now has changed it, you start to take a pernicious poison into your system. Eight years ago, when I had hit rock bottom and despaired of ever turning things around, I thought my problems were permanent. That was the closest thing to emotional death I've ever experienced. I learned to link so much pain to holding that belief that I was able to destroy it, and I've never indulged in it again. You must do the same. If you ever hear yourself or anyone you care about starting to express the belief that a problem is permanent, it's time to immediately shake that person loose. No matter what happens in your life, you've got to be able to believe, **"This, too, shall pass,"** and that if you keep persisting, you'll find a way.

The second difference between winners and losers, those who are optimistic and those who are pessimistic, is their beliefs about the *pervasiveness* of problems. An achiever never sees a problem as being pervasive, that is, that one problem controls their whole life. They always see it as, "Well, it's just a little challenge with my eating pattern." They don't see it as, "I'm the problem. Because I overeat, my whole life is destroyed." Conversely, those who are pessimistic—those who have learned helplessness—have developed a belief that because they screwed up in one area, they *are* a screw-up! They believe that because they have financial challenges, their whole life is now destroyed: their kids won't be taken care of, their spouses will leave them, and so on. Pretty soon they generalize that things are out of control and feel completely helpless. Imagine the impact of permanence and pervasiveness together! The solution to both permanence and pervasiveness is to see something you *can* take control of in your life, and begin to take action in that direction. As you do this, some of these limiting beliefs will disappear.

The final category of belief, which Seligman calls personal, I refer to as the *problem being personal*. If we don't see a failure as a challenge to modify our approach, but rather as a problem with ourselves, as a personality defect, we will immediately feel overwhelmed. After all, how do you change your entire life? Isn't that more difficult than just changing your actions in a particular area? Be wary of adopting the belief of the problem being personal. How inspired can you get by beating yourself up?

Holding these limiting beliefs is equivalent to systematically ingesting minute doses of arsenic that, over time, build up to a fatal dose. While we don't die immediately, we start dying emotionally the moment we partake of them. So we have to avoid them at all costs. Remember, as long as you believe something, your brain operates on automatic pilot, filtering any input from the environment and searching for references to validate your belief, regardless of what it is.

> *"It is the mind that maketh good of ill, that maketh wretch or happy, rich or poor."*
> —EDMUND SPENSER

HOW TO CHANGE A BELIEF

All personal breakthroughs begin with a change in beliefs. So how do we change? The most effective way is to *get your brain to associate massive pain to the old belief.* You must feel deep in your gut that not only has this belief cost you pain in the past, but it's costing you in the present and, ultimately, can only bring you pain in the future. Then you must associate tremendous pleasure to the idea of adopting a new, empowering belief. This is the basic pattern that we'll review again and again in creating change in our lives. Remember, we can never forget that everything we do, we do either out of our need to avoid pain or our desire to gain pleasure, and **if we associate enough pain to anything, we'll change**. The only reason we have a belief about something is that we've linked massive pain to not believing it or massive pleasure to keeping it alive.

Secondly, *create doubt.* If you're really honest with yourself, aren't there some beliefs that you used to defend heart and soul years ago that you'd be almost embarrassed to admit to today? What happened? Something caused you to *doubt*: maybe a new experience, maybe a counterexample to your past belief. Perhaps you met some Russians and found out that they were people just like you, not part of some "evil empire." I think that many Americans today feel a genuine compassion for Soviet citizens because they see them as people who are struggling to take care of their families. Part of what changed our perceptions was exchange programs in which we actually met Russians and saw how much they share in common with us. We got new experiences which caused us to *question,* interrupted our patterns of certainty, and began to shake our reference legs.

However, new experience in and of itself doesn't guarantee a change in belief. People can have an experience that runs directly counter to their belief, yet reinterpret it any way they want in order to bolster their conviction. Saddam Hussein demonstrated this during the Persian Gulf War, insisting that he was winning despite the destruction that surrounded him. On a personal level, a woman at one of my seminars started to experience some rather unique mental and emotional states, claiming that I was a Nazi and was poisoning the people in the room with invisible gases flowing through the air conditioning vents. As I tried to calm her down by slowing my speech patterns—a standard approach in causing someone to relax—she pointed out, "See, it's already beginning to slur your speech!" No matter what happened, she managed to use it to back up her conviction that we were all being poisoned. Eventually I was able to break her pattern. How do you do that? We'll talk about that in the next chapter.

New experiences trigger change only if they cause us to question our beliefs. Remember, **whenever we believe something, we no longer question it in any way**. The moment we begin to honestly question our beliefs, we no longer feel absolutely certain about them. We are beginning to shake the reference legs of our cognitive tables, and as a result start to lose our feeling of absolute certainty. Have you ever doubted your ability to do something? How did you do it? You probably asked yourself some poor questions like "What if I screw up?" "What if it doesn't work out?" "What if they don't like me?" But questions can obviously be tremendously empowering if we use them to examine the validity of beliefs we may have just blindly accepted. In fact, many of our beliefs are supported by information we've received from others that we failed to question at the time. If we scrutinize them, we may find that what we've unconsciously believed for years may be based on a false set of presuppositions.

If you use a typewriter or computer, I'm sure you'll appreciate this example. Why do you think the traditional arrangement of letters, numbers, and symbols on 99 percent of all typing devices is universally accepted around the world? (By the way, that arrangement of characters is known as QWERTY. If you type, you know that these are the characters on the top left row of your keyboard.) Obviously this arrangement was devised as the most efficient configuration to bolster typing speed, right? Most people never question it; after all, QWERTY has existed for 120 years. But in fact, QWERTY is about the most *inefficient* configuration you can imagine! Many programs such as the Dvorak Simplified Keyboard have been proven to cut errors and increase speed *radically*. The truth is, QWERTY was deliberately designed to *slow down the human typist* at a time when typewriter parts moved so slowly that they would jam if the operator typed too fast.

Why have we clung to the QWERTY keyboard for 120 years? In 1882, when almost everyone typed with the hunt-and-peck method, a

woman who had developed the eight-finger typing method was challenged to a typing contest by another teacher. To represent her, she hired
a professional typist, a man who had memorized the QWERTY keyboard.
With the advantage of memorization and the eight-finger method, he was
able to beat his competitor, who used the four-finger hunt-and-peck
method on a different keyboard. So from then on, QWERTY became the
standard for "speed," and no one even questioned the reference anymore
to see how valid it was. How many other beliefs do you have in daily life
about who you are, or what you can or cannot do, or how people should
act, or what capabilities your kids have that you're failing to question
also—disempowering beliefs you've begun to accept that limit your life,
and you're not even aware of it?

**If you question anything enough, eventually you'll begin to doubt
it.** This includes things that you absolutely believe "beyond the shadow
of a doubt." Years ago, I had the unique opportunity of working with the
U. S. Army, with whom I negotiated a contract to reduce certain training
times for specialized areas. My work was so successful that I also went
through top-secret clearance and had a chance to model one of the top
officials in the CIA, a man who'd worked his way up from the bottom of
the organization. Let me tell you that the skills that he and others like
him have developed for shaking another person's convictions and changing their beliefs are absolutely astounding. They create an environment
that causes people to doubt what they've always believed, and then give
them new ideas and experiences to support the adoption of new beliefs.
Watching the speed at which they can change someone's belief is almost
scary, yet it's powerfully fascinating. I've learned to use these techniques
on myself to be able to eliminate my disempowering beliefs and replace
them with empowering ones.

Our beliefs have different levels of emotional certainty and intensity,
and it's important to know just how intense they really are. In fact, I've
classified beliefs into three categories: **opinions, beliefs,** and **convictions.** An **opinion** is something we feel relatively certain about, but the
certainty is only temporary because it can be changed easily. Our cognitive tabletop is supported by wobbly, unverified reference legs that may
be based on impressions. For example, many people originally perceived
George Bush as a "wimp," based solely on his tone of voice. But when
they saw how he was able to galvanize support from leaders around the
world and effectively deal with Saddam Hussein's invasion of Kuwait,
there was a clear shift in the public opinion polls. Bush soared to one of
the highest levels of public popularity of any president in modern history. But by the time you read this paragraph, this cultural opinion may
have changed. Such is the nature of opinions: they are easily swayed, and
usually based on only a few references that a person has focused on in the

moment. A **belief**, on the other hand, is formed when we begin to develop a much larger base of reference legs, and especially reference legs about which we have strong emotion. These references give us an absolute sense of certainty about something. And again, as I've said before, these references can come in a variety of forms: anything from our personal experiences to information that we've taken in from other sources, or even things we've imagined vividly.

People with beliefs have such a strong level of certainty that they are often closed off to new input. But if you have rapport in communicating with them, it's possible to interrupt their pattern of closing off, and get them to question their references so they begin to allow for new input. This creates enough doubt to destabilize old references and make room for a new belief. A **conviction**, however, eclipses a belief, primarily because of the emotional intensity a person links to an idea. A person holding a conviction does not only feel certain, but gets angry if their conviction is even questioned. A person with a conviction is unwilling to ever question their references, even for a moment; they are totally resistant to new input, often to the point of obsession. For example, zealots through the ages have held the conviction that their view of God is the only correct one, and they will even kill to maintain those beliefs. The conviction of true believers has also been exploited by would-be saviors cloaking their murderous intent under holy guises; it's what caused that group of people living in Guyana to poison their own children, and then themselves, by drinking cyanide-laced Kool-Aid at the direction of the messianic madman Jim Jones.

Of course, fervent conviction is not the exclusive property of fanatics. It belongs to anyone with a high enough degree of commitment and dedication to an idea, principle, or cause. For example, someone who disagrees strongly with the practice of underground nuclear testing has a belief, but someone who *takes an action—even an action others do not appreciate or approve,* such as demonstrating in a protest march at the facility, has a conviction. Someone who bewails the state of public education has a belief, but someone who actually volunteers in a literacy program to try to make a difference has a conviction. Someone who fantasizes about owning an ice hockey team has an opinion about their desire, but someone who does whatever it takes to gather the necessary resources to buy a franchise has a conviction. What's the difference? Clearly, it's in the actions that one is willing to take. In fact, someone with a conviction is so passionate about their belief that they're even willing to risk rejection or make a fool of themselves for the sake of their conviction.

Probably the single biggest factor separating belief and conviction, though, is that a conviction has usually been triggered by significant emotional events, during which the brain links up, "Unless I believe this, I will suffer massive pain. *If* I were to change this belief, *then* I would be giving up my entire identity, everything my life has stood for, for years." Holding the conviction thus becomes crucial to the person's very survival. This can be dangerous because anytime we're not willing to even look at or consider the possibility that our beliefs are inaccurate, we trap ourselves in rigidity which could ultimately condemn us to long-term failure. Sometimes it may be more appropriate to have a belief about something rather than a conviction.

On the positive side, convictions—by the passion they inspire in us—can be empowering because they compel us to act. According to Dr. Robert P. Abelson, professor of psychology and political science at Yale University, "Beliefs are like possessions, and convictions are simply more valued possessions which allow an individual to passionately work toward either large-scale or individual completion of goals, projects, wishes, and desires."*

Often the best thing you can do to create mastery in any area of your life is to raise a belief to the level of conviction. Remember, conviction has the power to drive you to action, to push you through all kinds of obstacles. Beliefs can do this as well, but some areas of your life may require the added emotional intensity of conviction. For example, the conviction to never let yourself become overweight will compel you to make consistently healthy lifestyle choices, allowing you to get more enjoyment out of your life, and perhaps even saving you from a heart attack. The conviction that you are an intelligent person who can always find a way to turn things around can help steer you through some of the toughest times in your life.

So how can you create a conviction? 1) Start with the basic belief. 2) Reinforce your belief by adding new and more powerful references. For example, let's say you've decided never to eat meat again. To strengthen your resolve, talk to people who've chosen a vegetarian or vegan lifestyle: what reasons prompted them to change their diet, and what have been the consequences on their health and in other areas of their lives? In addition, begin to study the physiological impact that animal protein has. The more references you develop, and the more emotional the references are, the stronger your conviction will become. 3) Then find a triggering event, or else create one of your own. Associate yourself fully by asking, "What will it cost me if I don't?" Ask questions that create emotional intensity for you. For example, if you want to develop a conviction never

---

* Buffington, Perry W., "Say What You Mean, Mean What You Say." *Sky*, October 1990.

to abuse drugs, make the painful consequences of drug abuse feel real to you by viewing films or, better yet, visiting a shelter to see firsthand the devastation wrought by drug abuse. If you've vowed to give up smoking, visit the intensive-care wing of a hospital to observe emphysema patients confined to oxygen tents, or view an X-ray of a smoker's black lungs. These kinds of experiences have the power to push you over the edge and establish true conviction. 4) Finally, take action. Each action you take strengthens your commitment and raises the level of your emotional intensity and conviction.

One of the challenges with convictions is that they're often based on other people's enthusiasm for your beliefs. So often people believe something because everybody else believes it. This is known in psychology as **social proof**. But social proof is not always accurate. When people are not sure what to do, they look to others for guidance. In Dr. Robert Cialdini's book *Influence,* he describes a classic experiment in which someone yells "Rape!" for a subject's benefit while two people (psychological plants) ignore the cries for help and keep walking. The subject doesn't know whether to respond to the pleas or not, but when he sees the other two people act as if nothing is wrong, he decides that the cries for help are insignificant and to ignore them also.

Using social proof is a great way to limit your life—to make it just like everybody else's. Some of the strongest social proof that people use is information that they get from "experts." But are experts always right? Think about our healers throughout the years. It wasn't that long ago that the most up-to-date doctors believed absolutely in the curative properties of leeches! And in our own generation, doctors gave pregnant women a soothing-sounding medication for morning sickness—Bendectin, which sounds like "benediction"—which turned out to be linked to birth defects. Of course, these doctors were prescribing this drug because the drug companies—pharmaceutical *experts*—gave them certainty that this was the finest drug available. What's the lesson? Trusting experts blindly is not well-advised. Don't blindly accept everything I say, either! Consider things in the context of your own life; does it make sense for you?

Sometimes even the evidence of your senses can't be trusted, as the story of Copernicus illustrates. In the days of this seminal Polish astronomer, everyone *knew* that the sun moved around the earth. Why? Because anyone could walk outside, point to the sky and say, "See? The sun has moved across the sky. Obviously the earth is the center of the universe." But in 1543 Copernicus developed the first accurate model of our sun-based solar system. He, like other giants through the ages, had the courage to challenge the "wisdom" of the experts, and eventually the truth of his theories gained acceptance in the general populace, although not during his lifetime.

PAIN IS THE ULTIMATE TOOL FOR SHIFTING A BELIEF

Again, pain is still the most powerful way to change a belief. A great illustration of the power of changed beliefs occurred on the Sally Jessy Raphael show when a brave woman stood before a studio and world audience to renounce her alliance with the Ku Klux Klan. Ironically, she had been on the same show only a month before, participating in a panel of KKK women railing against all who didn't share their convictions about race, angrily shouting that racial mixing—educationally, economically, or socially—would be the downfall of the country and its people. What made her beliefs change so drastically? Three things: First, a young woman in the audience during the original show had stood up, crying, and pleaded for understanding. Her husband and child were Hispanic, and she sobbed that she couldn't believe a group of people could be so hateful.

Second, flying home, she yelled at her son (who had appeared with her, yet didn't share her views) for "embarrassing" her on national television. The rest of the women chastised him for being disrespectful, and quoted to him from the Bible: "Thou shalt honor thy mother and father." Her sixteen-year-old son responded by saying that God certainly didn't intend for him to respect the evil she was espousing, and he immediately got off the plane in Dallas, vowing never to come home again. As the woman continued her flight home, her mind raced over the day's events, and also began to think about the war that her country was fighting in the Middle East. She remembered what another member of the audience had said to her that day: "Young men and women of color are over there fighting not only for themselves, but also for *you*." She thought about her son, how much she loved him, and how spiteful she had been with him. Would she allow that brief exchange of words to be their last? Even the thought of it was too painful for her to bear. She had to make a change immediately.

As a result of this experience, she told the audience, she received a message from God which she heeded immediately: to quit the Klan and to begin to love all people equally, as her brothers and sisters. Certainly she will miss her friends—she'll be ostracized by the group—but she says that her soul is now cleansed and that she will begin her life anew with a clear conscience.

It's vital to examine our beliefs, and their consequences, to make sure that they're empowering us. How do you know what beliefs to adopt? The answer is to find someone who's producing the results you truly want in your life. These people are the role models who can give you some of the answers you seek. Invariably, behind all successful people lies a specific set of empowering beliefs.

The way to expand our lives is to model the lives of those people who are already succeeding. It's powerful, it's fun, and these people are available all around you. It's just a matter of asking questions: "What do you believe makes you different? What are the beliefs you have that separate you from others?" Years ago I read a book called *Meetings with Remarkable Men,* and used that as a theme to shape my life. Since then I've become a hunter of excellence, constantly seeking out the leading men and women in our culture to discover their beliefs, values, and strategies for achieving success. Two years ago I developed POWER-TALK!,™ my monthly audio magazine in which I interview these giants. In fact, many of the key distinctions I'm sharing with you in this book were made as a result of interviews with some of these people who are the finest in their particular areas of endeavor. By having a commitment to share these interviews, my newest thoughts, and a summary of a national best-selling book with you each month, I've developed a consistent plan not only for empowering other people but for constantly improving myself as well. I'll be happy to help you in your modeling of successful people through my program, but remember: you're not limited to me. The models that you need are surrounding you every single day.*

> *"We are what we think.*
> *All that we are arises*
> *With our thoughts.*
> *With our thoughts,*
> *We make our world."*
> —THE BUDDHA

For almost a decade now I've talked to people in my Living Health™ seminars about the direct correlation between the high percentage of animal protein in the typical American diet and the high incidence of this nation's top two killers: heart disease and cancer. By doing this, I contradicted one of the belief systems that has most significantly shaped our physical destiny for the past thirty five years: the "Four Basic Food Groups" plan that recommends generous daily servings of meat, chicken, or fish. Yet today, scientists have now established beyond the shadow of a doubt a direct relationship between eating animal protein and being at

---

* If you'd like to know more about POWERTALK! so we can have an ongoing coaching relationship, call 1-800-445-8183.

risk of developing heart disease and cancer. In fact, the 3,000-member Physicians Committee for Responsible Medicine has asked the Department of Agriculture to drop meat, fish, poultry, eggs, and milk products from the recommended daily allowances. And the government itself is considering changing the four basic food groups to six, relegating meat, chicken, and fish to just a tiny proportion of the whole. This massive shift in beliefs has caused outrage in many quarters. I believe this follows a pattern that we see throughout history and throughout our culture, and that is simply this:

As the German philosopher Arthur Schopenhauer stated, all truth goes through three steps.

> **First, it is ridiculed.**
> **Second, it is violently opposed.**
> **Finally, it is accepted as self-evident.**

These ideas about animal protein used to be ridiculed; now they're being violently opposed. Eventually they'll be accepted—but not until a lot more people become sick or even die because of their limiting beliefs about how important excessive amounts of animal protein is for their bodies.

In business, too, we have a set of false beliefs that are leading us down a road of economic frustration, and some say potential disaster. Our economy faces challenges in virtually every sector. Why? I found one clue in an article I read in the March 1991 *Forbes* magazine. This article describes two cars—the Chrysler-Plymouth Laser and the Mitsubishi Eclipse—and notes that Chrysler averaged only thirteen sales per dealership of their car while Mitsubishi averaged over 100! You may say, "What else is new? The Japanese are beating the pants off the American companies in selling cars." But the unique thing about these two cars is that they're exactly the same—they were built in partnership between these two companies. The only difference between the Laser and the Eclipse is the name and the company who's selling it. How can this be? As you may have guessed, research investigating the cause of the discrepancy in sales has shown that people want to buy Japanese cars because they believe they are of greater quality. The problem in this case is that it's a false belief. The American company's car is of the same quality because it's the very same car.

Why would consumers believe this? Obviously, it's because the Japanese have created a *reputation* for quality, providing us with numerous references to back it up—even to the point where we no longer question its validity. It may surprise you that the Japanese commitment to increasing quality is actually the result of an American export in the person of Dr. W. Edwards Deming. In 1950 this renowned quality-control ex-

pert was brought to Japan by General MacArthur, who was frustrated
with a war-ravaged Japanese industrial base where he couldn't even
count on being able to complete a phone call. At the request of the
Japanese Union of Scientists and Engineers, Deming began to train the
Japanese in his total quality-control principles. When you hear this, do
you immediately think it refers to monitoring the quality of a physical
product? Nothing could be further from the truth. Deming taught the
Japanese fourteen principles and a basic core belief that is the foundation
of virtually all decisions made in every successful, major, multinational
Japanese corporation to this day.

The core belief, simply, is this: a constant, never-ending commitment
to consistently increase the quality of their business *every single day*
would give them the power to dominate the markets of the world. Deming taught that quality was not just a matter of meeting a certain standard, but rather was a living, breathing process of never-ending
improvement. If the Japanese would live by the principles that he taught,
he promised them, within five years they would flood the world with
quality products and within a decade or two become one of the world's
dominant economic powers.

Many thought Deming's proclamations were crazy. But the Japanese
took him at his word, and today he is revered as the father of the
"Japanese miracle." In fact, each year since 1950, the highest honor a
Japanese company can receive is the National Deming Prize. This award
is given on national television and is used to acknowledge the company
that represents the highest level of increases in quality of products, service, management, and worker support throughout Japan.

In 1983 Ford Motor Company hired Dr. Deming to conduct a series
of management seminars. One of the attendees was Donald Petersen,
who would later become chairman of Ford and put Deming's principles
into practice throughout the company. Petersen decided, "We need this
man to turn our company around." At the time, Ford was losing billions
of dollars a year. Once Deming was brought in, he changed their traditional Western belief from, "How can we increase our volume and cut
our costs?" to "How can we increase the quality of what we're doing, and
do it in such a way that quality would not cost more in the long term?"
Ford reorganized its entire focus to make quality the top priority (as
reflected in their advertising slogan, "Quality is Job 1"), and by imple-
menting Deming's systems, Ford within three years moved from a staggering deficit to the dominant industry position with a *$6 billion profit!*

How did they do it? They found that Americans' perception of Japanese quality, while frustrating, had much to teach them. For example,
Ford contracted with a Japanese company to make half the transmissions
for one of their cars in order to keep the volume up. In the process, they

found that American consumers were demanding the Japanese transmission. In fact, they were willing to put their names on a waiting list, and even pay more money for them! This upset many of the executive staff at Ford, whose first reaction was, "Well, it's merely a false belief on the part of people in our culture; they're conditioned to respond this way." But under Deming's supervision the transmissions were tested, and they found that in fact the Ford transmission was much louder, broke down much more often, and was returned more often than the Japanese transmission, which had virtually no trouble, no vibration, and no sound. Deming taught the members of the Ford team that quality always costs less. This was directly the opposite of what most people believed: that you could only achieve certain levels of quality before costs got out of hand. When the experts took the Ford transmissions apart and measured all the parts, they found that all of them met the standards set forth in the Ford manual, the same standards that had been sent to the Japanese. But when they measured the Japanese transmissions, they found virtually *no* measurable differences among any of them! In fact, the transmissions had to be brought into a laboratory and measured *under a microscope* in order to detect differences.

Why did this Japanese company hold themselves to a higher standard of quality than even their contract required? They believed that *quality costs less,* that if they created a quality product they would not just have satisfied customers but loyal customers—customers who would be willing to wait in line and pay more money for their product. They were operating from the same core belief that propelled them to one of the top market positions in the world: a commitment to never-ending improvement and a constant increase in the quality of life for their customers. **This belief was an American export—one I believe we need to repatriate in order to change the direction of our economic future**.

One toxic belief that may be destroying our economic strength as a nation is what Deming calls *managing by the visible numbers,* the conventional corporate belief that profits are made by cutting costs and increasing revenues. A notable example occurred when Lynn Townsend took charge of Chrysler during an industry-wide sales slump. Townsend immediately tried to increase revenues, but more importantly, he cut costs. How? He fired two-thirds of the engineering staff. In the short term, it looked like he'd made the right decision. Profitability shot up, and he was dubbed a hero. But within a few years Chrysler was again in financial straits. What happened? Well, there certainly wasn't any one factor. But in the long term, the decisions Townsend made may have been destroying the basis of quality upon which the company's success depended. Often the very people who are injuring our companies are rewarded because they produce results in the short term. Sometimes we treat the symptoms of a problem while we nurture the cause. We've got to be careful how we interpret results. By contrast, one of the most important factors in turning Ford Motor Company around was their design staff, who came up with a new car called the Taurus. The quality of that car set a new standard for Ford, and consumers bought it in droves.

What can we learn from all this? The beliefs that we hold in business and in life control all of our decisions, and therefore our future. One of the most important global beliefs that you and I can adopt is a belief that in order to succeed and be happy, we've got to be constantly improving the quality of our lives, constantly growing and expanding.

In Japan, they understand this principle well. In fact, in Japanese businesses, as a result of Deming's influence, there is a word that is used constantly in discussions about business or relationships. That word is *kaizen*. This word literally means constant improvement, and the word is constantly used in their language. They often speak of the *kaizen* of their trade deficit, the *kaizen* of the production line, the *kaizen* of their personal relationships. As a result, they're constantly looking at how to improve. By the way, *kaizen* is based upon the principle of gradual improvement, simple improvements. But the Japanese understand that tiny refinements made *daily* begin to create compounded enhancements at a level that most people would never dream of. The Japanese have a saying: "If a man has not been seen for three days, his friends should take a good look at him, and see what changes have befallen him." Amazingly, but not surprisingly, we have no equivalent word for *kaizen* in English.

The more I began to see the impact of *kaizen* in the Japanese business culture, I realized that it was an organizing principle that made a tremendous impact in my own life. My own commitment to constantly improve, to constantly raise my own standards for a quality life is what's kept me both happy and successful. I realized that we all need a word to anchor ourselves to the focus of Constant and Never-ending Improvement. When we create a word, we encode meaning and create a way of thinking. The words that we use consistently make up the fabric of how we think and even affect our decision making.

As a result of this understanding, I created a simple mnemonic: **CANI!**™ (pronounced kuhn-EYE), which stands for Constant And Never-ending Improvement. I believe that the level of success we experience in life is in direct proportion to the level of our commitment to CANI!, to constant and never-ending improvement. CANI! is not a principle related merely to business, but to every aspect of our lives. In Japan, they often talk of company-wide quality control. I believe we have to focus on CANI! in our business, CANI! in our personal relationships, CANI! in our spiritual connection, CANI! in our health, and CANI! in our finances. How can we make constant and never-ending improvement in each of these areas? This makes life an incredible adventure in which we're always looking forward to the next level.

CANI! is a true discipline. It can't just be practiced every once in a while, when you feel like it. It must be a **constant commitment backed up by action.** The essence of CANI! is gradual, even minute, continuous improvement that *over the long term* sculpts a masterpiece of colossal proportions. If you've ever visited the Grand Canyon, you know what I'm talking about. You've witnessed the awe-inspiring beauty produced by millions of years of gradual change as the Colorado River and numerous tributaries have continually chiseled the rock to create one of the Seven Natural Wonders of the World.

Most people never feel secure because they are always worried that they will either lose their job, lose the money they already have, lose their spouse, lose their health, and so on. **The only true security in life comes from knowing that every single day you are improving yourself in some way,** that you are increasing the caliber of who you are and that you are valuable to your company, your friends, and your family. **I don't worry about** *maintaining* **the quality of my life, because every day I work on** *improving* **it.** I constantly strive to learn and to make new and more powerful distinctions about ways to add value to other people's lives. This gives me a sense of certainty that I can always learn, that I can always expand, that I can always grow.

CANI! doesn't mean you never experience challenges. In fact, you can only improve something if you realize that it's not quite right, that it's not yet at the level it should be. The purpose of CANI! is to discover problems in the making and handle them before they become crises. After all, the best time to kill a "monster" is while it's still little.

As an integral part of my personal commitment to CANI!, at the end of each day I ask myself these questions: What have I learned today? What did I contribute or improve? What did I enjoy? If every day you constantly improve your ability to enjoy your life, then you'll experience it at a level of richness most people never even dream of.

SMALL IMPROVEMENTS ARE BELIEVABLE AND THEREFORE ACHIEVABLE!

Pat Riley, formerly of the Los Angeles Lakers organization, is the winningest coach in NBA history. Some say he was fortunate because he had such incredible players. It's true that he had incredible players, but many people have had the resources to succeed and have not done so consis-

tently. Pat's ability to do this has been based on his commitment to
CANI! In fact, he said that at the beginning of the 1986 season he had a
major challenge on his hands. Many of the players had given what they
thought was their best season in the previous year but still had lost to the
Boston Celtics. In search of a believable plan to get the players to move
to the next level, he decided upon the theme of small improvements. He
convinced the players that increasing the quality of their game by a mere
1 percent over their personal best would make a major difference in their
season. This seems ridiculously small, but when you think about twelve
players increasing by 1 percent their court skills in five areas, the combined effort creates a team that's *60 percent more effective* than it was
before. A 10 percent overall difference would probably be enough to win
another championship. The real value of this philosophy, however, is
that everyone believed that it was achievable. Everyone felt certain that
they could improve at least 1 percent over their personal bests in the five
major areas of the game, and that sense of certainty in pursuit of their
goals caused them to tap even greater potentials. The result? Most of
them increased by at least 5 percent, and many of them by as much as
50 percent. According to Pat Riley, 1987 turned out to be their easiest
season ever. CANI! works if you commit to it.

Remember, the key to success is developing a sense of certainty—the
kind of belief that allows you to expand as a person and take the necessary action to make your life and the lives of those around you even
greater. You may believe something is true today, but you and I need to
remember that as the years go by and we grow, we'll be exposed to new
experiences. And we may develop even more empowering beliefs, aban-
doning things we once felt certain about. Realize that your beliefs may
change as you gather additional references. What really matters now is
whether the beliefs you have today empower or disempower you. Begin
today to develop the habit of focusing on the consequences of all your
beliefs. Are they strengthening your foundation by moving you to action
in the direction you desire, or are they holding you back?

"As he thinketh in his heart, so is he."
—PROVERBS 23:7

We've discovered so much about beliefs, but in order to truly take
control of our lives, we've got to know what beliefs *we're already using* to
guide us.

So right now, stop everything else you're doing and take the next ten
minutes to have some fun. Begin to **brainstorm all the beliefs you have,
both those that empower you and disempower you:** little beliefs that

don't seem to matter at all and global beliefs that seem to make a big difference. Make sure you cover:

- **If-then** beliefs like, "If I consistently give my all, then I will succeed," or "If I'm totally passionate with this person, then they'll leave me."

- **Global beliefs,** like beliefs about people—"People are basically good" or "People are a pain"—beliefs about yourself, beliefs about opportunity, beliefs about time, beliefs about scarcity and abundance.

Jot down as many of these as you can imagine for the next ten minutes. Please give yourself the gift of doing this right now. When you're done, I'll show you how you can strengthen your empowering beliefs and eliminate the disempowering ones. Do it right now.

DISEMPOWERING BELIEFS

Did you take enough time to make sure you wrote out both lists, both the empowering beliefs and disempowering beliefs? If not, go back and do it now!

What have you learned by doing this? Take a moment now to review your beliefs. Decide upon and **circle the three most empowering beliefs on your list**. How do they empower you? How do they strengthen your life? Think about the positive processional effects they have upon you. Years ago, I made a list like this, and I found it invaluable because I discovered that I had a belief that was underemployed. It was the belief **"There's always a way to turn things around if I'm committed."** When I read my list, I thought, "This is a belief that needs to be strengthened and turned into a conviction." I'm so glad I did because only about a year later that conviction was a life preserver that pulled me through one of the toughest times, a time when everything around me seemed to be sinking. Not only did it buoy my spirit, but it also helped me deal with one of the most difficult personal and business challenges I had yet faced. This one belief, this sense of certainty, enabled me to find ways to turn things around when everybody around me said it couldn't be done. I not only turned things around, I turned my biggest challenges into my biggest opportunities—and so can you! Review this list and strengthen your emotional intensity and sense of certainty that these beliefs are true and real so they can guide your future behaviors.

Now let's take a look at your limiting beliefs. As you review them, what are some of the consequences that these beliefs carry with them? **Circle the two most disempowering beliefs**. Decide right now, once and for all, that you're no longer willing to pay the price that these beliefs are charging your life. Remember that if you begin to doubt the beliefs and question their validity, you can shake their reference legs so they no longer impact you. Knock those legs of certainty out from under your disempowering beliefs by **asking yourself some of the following questions:**

1. How is this belief ridiculous or absurd?
2. Was the person I learned this belief from worth modeling in this area?
3. What will it ultimately cost me emotionally if I don't let go of this belief?
4. What will it ultimately cost me in my relationships if I don't let go of this belief?
5. What will it ultimately cost me physically if I don't let go of this belief?
6. What will it ultimately cost me financially if I don't let go of this belief?

7. What will it cost my family/loved ones if I don't let go of this belief?

If you've taken the time to really answer these questions, you may find
that your beliefs have been significantly weakened under the scrutiny of
these questions. Now become fully associated to what these beliefs have
been costing you and the real costs in your future if you do not change.
Link such intense pain that you'll want to rid yourself of them forever,
and then, finally, decide to do so *now*.

Finally, we can't get rid of a pattern without replacing it with a new
one. So right now, **write down the replacements for the two limiting
beliefs you've just eliminated.** What is their antithesis? For example, if
you had a belief that "I can never succeed because I'm a woman," your
new belief might be, "Because I'm a woman, I have resources available to
me that no man could ever dream of!" What are some of the references
you have to back up this idea so you begin to feel certain about it? As you
reinforce and strengthen this belief, it will begin to direct your behavior
in an entirely new and more empowering way.

If you're not getting the results you want in your life, I suggest you
ask yourself, "What would I have to believe in order to succeed here?"
Or "Who is already succeeding in this area, and what do they believe
differently than I do about what's possible?" Or "What's necessary to
believe in order to succeed?" You may very well discover the key belief
that's been eluding you. If you're experiencing pain, if you feel challenged or frustrated or angry, you may want to ask yourself, "What
would I have to believe in order to feel the way I do?" The miracle of
this simple process is that it will uncover beliefs you aren't even aware
you have. For example, if you're feeling depressed and ask yourself,
"What would I have to believe in order to feel depressed?" you'll probably come up with something that relates to the future, like, "Things
will never get better," or "There's no hope." When you hear these beliefs verbalized, you might well think, "I don't believe that! I feel bad
right now, but I know it's not going to be bad forever. This, too, shall
pass." Or you may just decide that a belief about having problems permanently is totally destructive and one you're not willing to ever consider again.

While you're examining these limiting beliefs, notice how your feelings change. Realize, believe, and trust that if you change the **meaning** of
any event in your mind, you will immediately change how you feel and
what you do, which will lead you to change your actions and thus
transform your destiny. Changing what something means will change the
decisions you make. Remember, **nothing in life has any meaning except the meaning you give it.** So make sure that you **consciously**

choose the meanings that are most in alignment with the destiny you've chosen for yourself.

Beliefs have the awesome potential to create or destroy. I believe you picked up this book because deep down you've decided you will not settle for less than the best you know you're capable of. Do you truly want to harness the power to create the vision you want rather than destroy your dreams? Then learn to choose the beliefs that empower you; create convictions that drive you in the direction of the destiny that calls to the highest within you. Your family, your business, your community, and your country deserve no less.

LEADERSHIP AND THE POWER OF BELIEF

Leaders are those individuals who live by empowering beliefs and teach others to tap their full capabilities by shifting the beliefs that have been limiting them. One great leader who impresses me is a teacher by the name of Marva Collins. You may have seen the *60 Minutes* program or the movie that was made about her. Thirty years ago, Marva utilized her personal power and decided to touch the future by making a real difference in the lives of children. Her challenge: when she got to her first teaching job in what many considered to be a ghetto of Chicago, her second-grade students had already decided that they didn't *want* to learn anything. Yet Marva's mission is to touch these children's lives. She doesn't have a mere belief that she can impact them; she has a passionate, deep-rooted conviction that she *will* influence them for good. There was no limit to the extent she would go. Faced with children labeled as dyslexics and every other kind of learning or behavioral disorder, she decided that the problem was not the children, but the way they were being taught. No one was challenging them enough. As a result, these kids had no belief in themselves. They had no references of ever being pushed to break through and find out who they really were or what they were capable of. Human beings respond to challenge, and these children, she believed, needed that more than anything else.

So she threw out all the old books that read, "See Spot run," and instead taught Shakespeare, Sophocles, and Tolstoy. All the other teachers said things like, "There's no way it can happen. There's no way these kids can understand that." And as you might guess, many of them attacked Marva personally, saying that she was going to destroy these children's lives. But Marva's students not only understood the material, they thrived on it. Why? Because she believed so fervently in the uniqueness of each child's spirit, and his or her ability to learn anything. She communicated with so much congruency and love that she literally got them to believe in themselves—some of them for the first time in their young lives. The results she has consistently produced for decades have been extraordinary.

I first met Marva and interviewed her at Westside Preparatory School, the private school she founded outside the Chicago city school system. After our meeting, I decided to interview some of her students. The first young man I met was four years old, with a smile that would knock your socks off. I shook his hand.

"Hi, I'm Tony Robbins."

"Hello, Mr. Robbins, my name is Talmadge E. Griffin. I am four years old. What would you like to know?!"

"Well, Talmadge, tell me, what are you studying these days?"

"I'm studying a lot of things, Mr. Robbins."

"Well, what books have you read recently?"

"I just finished reading *Of Mice and Men*, by John Steinbeck."

Needless to say, I was pretty impressed. I asked him what the book was about, figuring he'd say something like it was about two guys named George and Lenny.

He said, "Well, the main protagonist is . . ."

By this time I was a believer! Then I asked him what he had learned from the book.

"Mr. Robbins, I more than learned from this book. This book *permeated my soul*."

I started to laugh, and asked, "What does 'permeate' mean?"

"To diffuse through," he said, then gave me a fuller definition than I could give you.

"What touched you so much in this book, Talmadge?"

"Mr. Robbins, I noticed in the story that the children never judge anyone else by the color of their skin. Only the adults did that. What I learned from this is that although I will someday become an adult, I'll never forget the lessons of a child."

I started to get teary-eyed because I saw that Marva Collins was providing this young man and so many others like him with the kinds of powerful beliefs that will continue to shape his decisions not only today, but throughout his life. Marva increases her students' quality of life by using the three organizing principles I talked about in the beginning of this book: she gets them to hold themselves to a higher standard, she assists them in adopting new, empowering beliefs that enable them to break through their old limitations, and she backs all this up with specific skills and strategies necessary for lifelong success. The results? Her students become not only confident, but competent. The immediate results in terms of their academic excellence are striking, and the processional effects generated in their everyday lives are profound.

Finally I asked Talmadge, "What's the most important thing that Mrs. Collins has taught you?"

"The most important thing Mrs. Collins has taught me is that **SOCIETY MAY PREDICT, BUT ONLY I WILL DETERMINE MY DESTINY!**"

Maybe we all need to remember the lessons of a child. With the beliefs young Talmadge expressed so beautifully, I guarantee that he, as well as the other children in the class, will have a great opportunity to continuously interpret their lives in a way that will create the future they desire, rather than the one that most people fear.

Let's review what we've learned so far. We're clear that there's a power inside us that needs to be awakened. That power starts with the capability to make conscious decisions that shape our destiny. But there is one core belief that we must explore and resolve, and this belief can be found in your answer to the question . . .

5

CAN CHANGE HAPPEN IN AN INSTANT?

"Behold, I show you a mystery; We shall not all sleep, but we shall all be changed, in a moment, in the twinkling of an eye . . ."
—CORINTHIANS 15:51

For as long as I can remember, I've always dreamed of having the ability to help people change virtually anything in their lives. Instinctively, at an early age, I realized that to be able to help others change, I had to be able to change myself. Even in junior high school, I began to pursue knowledge through books and tapes that I thought could teach me the fundamentals of how to shift human behavior and emotion.

Of course I wanted to improve certain aspects of my own life: get myself motivated, get myself to follow through and take action, learn how to enjoy life, and learn how to connect and bond with people. I'm not sure why, but somehow I linked pleasure to learning and sharing things that could make a difference in the quality of people's lives and lead them to appreciate and maybe even love me. As a result, by the time I was in high school, I was known as the "Solutions Man." If you had a problem, I was the guy to see, and I took great pride in this identity.

The more I learned, the more addicted I became to learning even more. Understanding how to influence human emotion and behavior became an obsession for me. I took a speed-reading class and developed a voracious appetite for books. I read close to 700 books in just a few years, almost all of them in the areas of human development, psychology, influence, and physiological development. I wanted to know *anything* and *everything* there was to know about how we can increase the quality of our lives, and tried to immediately apply it to myself as well as share it with other people. But I didn't stop with books. I became a fanatic for motivational tapes and, while still in high school, saved my money to go to different types of personal development seminars. As you can imagine, it didn't take long for me to feel like I was hearing nothing but the same messages reworked over and over again. There appeared to be nothing new, and I became a bit jaded.

Just after my twenty-first birthday, though, I was exposed to a series of technologies that could make changes in people's lives with lightning-like speed: simple technologies like Gestalt therapy, and tools of influence like Ericksonian hypnosis and Neuro-Linguistic Programming. When I saw that these tools could really help people create changes *in minutes* that previously took months, years, or decades to achieve, I became an evangelist in my approach to them. I decided to commit all of my resources to mastering these technologies. And I didn't stop there: as soon as I learned something, I applied it immediately.

I'll never forget my first week of training in Neuro-Linguistic Programming. We learned things like how to eliminate a lifetime phobia in less than an hour—something that through many forms of traditional therapy could take as much as five years or more! On the fifth day, I turned to the psychologists and psychiatrists in the class and said, "Hey, guys, let's find some phobics and cure them!" They all looked at me like I was crazy. They made it very clear to me that I obviously wasn't an educated man, that we had to wait until the six-month certification program was completed, go through a testing procedure, and if we were successful, only then would we be ready to use this material!

I wasn't willing to wait. So I launched my career by appearing on radio and television programs throughout Canada and eventually the United States as well. In each of these, I talked to people about these technologies for creating change and made it clear that if we wanted to change our lives, whether it was a disempowering habit or a phobia that had been controlling us for years, that behavior or that emotional pattern could be changed in a matter of *minutes*, even though they might have tried to change it for years previously.

Was this a radical concept? You bet. But I passionately argued that **all changes are created in a moment.** It's just that most of us wait until certain things happen before we finally *decide* to make a shift. If we truly understood how the brain worked, I argued, we could stop the endless process of analyzing why things had happened to us, and if we could just simply change what we linked pain and pleasure to, we could just as easily change the way our nervous systems had been conditioned and take charge of our lives *immediately.* As you can imagine, a young kid with no Ph.D. who was making these controversial claims on the radio didn't go over very well with some traditionally trained mental-health professionals. A few psychiatrists and psychologists attacked me, some on the air.

So I learned to build my career in changing people on two principles:

technology and *challenge*. I knew I had a superior technology, a superior way of creating change based on crucial understandings of human behavior that most traditional psychologists were not trained in. And I believed that if I challenged myself and the people I worked with enough, I could find a way to turn virtually anything around.

One particular psychiatrist called me a charlatan and a liar and charged that I was making false claims. I challenged this psychiatrist to suspend his pessimism and give me an opportunity to work with one of his patients, someone he hadn't been able to change after working with her for years. It was a bold move, and at first he did not comply with my request. But after utilizing a little leverage (a technique I'll cover in the next chapter), I finally got the psychiatrist to let a patient come on her own to one of my free guest events and allow me, in front of the room, to work with her. In fifteen minutes I wiped out the woman's phobia of snakes—at the time she'd been treated for over seven years by the psychiatrist who attacked me. To say the least, he was amazed. But more importantly, can you imagine the references this created for me and the sense of certainty it gave me about what I could accomplish? I became a wild man! I stormed across the country demonstrating to people how quickly change could occur. I found that no matter where I went, people were initially skeptical. But, as I was able to demonstrate measurable results before their eyes, I was able to get not only their attention and interest but also their willingness to apply what I'd talked about to produce measurable results in their own lives.

Why is it that most people think change takes so long? One reason, obviously, is that most people have tried again and again through willpower to make changes, and failed. The assumption that they then make is that important changes must take a long time and be very difficult to make. In reality, it's only difficult because most of us don't know *how* to change! We don't have an effective strategy. Willpower by itself is not enough—not if we want to achieve lasting change.

The second reason we don't change quickly is that in our culture, we have a set of beliefs that prevents us from being able to utilize our own inherent abilities. Culturally, we link negative associations to the idea of instant change. For most, instant change means you never really had a problem at all. If you can change that easily, why didn't you change a week ago, a month ago, a year ago, and stop complaining?

For example, how quickly could a person recover from the loss of a loved one and begin to feel differently? Physically, they have the capability to do it the next morning. But they don't. Why? Because we have a set of beliefs in our culture that we need to *grieve* for a certain period of time. How long do we have to grieve? It all depends upon your own conditioning. Think about this. If the next day after you lost a loved one, you didn't grieve, wouldn't that cause a great deal of pain in your life? First, people would immediately believe you didn't care about the loved one you lost. And, based on cultural conditioning, you might begin to believe that you didn't care, either. The concept of overcoming death this easily is just too painful. We choose the pain of grieving rather than changing our emotions until we're satisfied that our rules and cultural standards about what's appropriate have been met.

There are, in fact, cultures where people *celebrate* when someone dies! Why? They believe that God always knows the right time for us to leave the earth, and that death is graduation. They also believe that if you were to grieve about someone's death, you would be indicating nothing but your own lack of understanding of life, and you would be demonstrating your own selfishness. Since this person has gone on to a better place, you're feeling sorry for no one but yourself. They link pleasure to death, and pain to grieving, so grief is not a part of their culture. I'm not saying that grief is bad or wrong. I'm just saying that we need to realize it's based upon our beliefs that pain takes a long time to recover from.

As I spoke from coast to coast, I kept encouraging people to make life-changing shifts, often in thirty minutes or less. There was no doubt I created controversy, and the more successes I had, the more assured and intense I became as well. To tell the truth, I was occasionally confrontational and more than a little cocky. I started out doing private therapy, helping people turn things around, and then began to do seminars. Within a few short years, I was traveling on the road three weeks out of four, constantly pushing myself and giving my all as I worked to extend my ability to positively impact the largest number of people I could in the shortest period of time. The results I produced became somewhat legendary. Eventually the psychiatrists and psychologists stopped attacking and actually became interested in learning my techniques for use with their own patients. At the same time, my attitudes changed and I became more balanced. But I never lost my *passion* for wanting to help as many people as I could.

One day about four and a half years ago, not long after *Unlimited Power* was first published, I was signing books after giving one of my business seminars in San Francisco. All the while I was reflecting on the incredible rewards that had come from following through on the commitments I had made to myself while still in high school: the commitments to grow, expand, contribute, and thereby make a difference. I realized as each smiling face came forward how deeply grateful I was to have developed skills that can make a difference in helping people to change virtually anything in their lives.

As the last group of people finally began to disperse, one man approached me and asked, "Do you recognize me?" Having seen literally thousands of people in that month alone, I had to admit that I didn't. He said, "Think about it for a second." After looking at him for a few moments, suddenly it clicked. I said, "New York City, right?" He said, "That's true." I said, "I did some private work with you in helping you to wipe out your smoking habit." He nodded again. I said, "Wow, that was years ago! How are you doing?" He reached in his pocket, pulled out a package of Marlboros, pointed at me with an accusing look on his face and said, *"You failed!"* Then he launched into a tirade about my inability to "program" him effectively.

I have to admit I was rattled! After all, I had built my career on my absolute willingness to put myself on the line, on my total commitment to challenging myself and other people, on my dedication to trying *anything* in order to create lasting and effective change with lightning-like speed. As this man continued to berate my ineffectiveness in "curing" his smoking habit, I wondered what could have gone wrong. Could it be that my ego had outgrown my true level of capability and skill? Gradually I began to ask myself better questions: What could I learn from this situation? What was really going on here?

"What happened after we worked together?" I asked him, expecting to hear that he had resumed smoking a week or so after the therapy. It turned out that he'd stopped smoking for two and a half *years*, after I'd worked with him for less than an hour! But one day he took a puff, and now he was back to his four-pack-a-day habit, plainly blaming me because the change had not endured.

Then it hit me: this man was not being completely unreasonable. After all, I had been teaching something called Neuro-Linguistic Programming. Think about the word "programming." It suggests that you could come to me, I would program you, and then everything would be fine. You wouldn't have to *do* anything! Out of my desire to help people at the deepest level, I'd made the very mistake that I saw other leaders in the personal development industry make: I had begun to take responsibility for other people's changes.

That day, I realized I had inadvertently placed the responsibility with the wrong person—me—and that this man, or any one of the other thousands of people I'd worked with, could easily go back to their old behaviors if they ran into a difficult enough challenge because they saw me as the person responsible for their change. If things didn't work out, they could just conveniently blame somebody else. They had no *personal responsibility,* and therefore, no *pain* if they didn't follow through on the new behavior.

As a result of this new perspective, I decided to change the metaphor for what I do. I stopped using the word "programming" because while I continue to use many NLP techniques, I believe it's inaccurate. A better metaphor for long-term change is **conditioning**. This was solidified for me when, a few days later, my wife brought in a piano tuner for our new baby grand. This man was a true craftsman. He worked on every string in that piano for literally hours and hours, stretching each one to just the right level of tension to create the perfect vibration. At the end of the day, the piano played magnificently. When I asked him how much I owed, he said, "Don't worry, I'll drop off a bill on my next visit." My response was, "Next visit? What do you mean?" He said, "I'll be back tomorrow, and then I'll come back once a week for the next month. Then I'll return every three months for the rest of the year, only because you live by the ocean."

I said, "What are you talking about? Didn't you already make all the adjustments on the piano? Isn't it set up properly?" He said, "Yes, but these strings are strong; to keep them at the perfect level of tension, we've got to *condition* them to stay at this level. I've got to come back and re-tighten them on a regular basis until the wire is trained to stay at this level." I thought, "What a business this guy has!" But I also got a great lesson that day.

This is exactly what we have to do if we're going to succeed in creating long-term change. **Once we effect a change, we should reinforce it** *immediately*. **Then, we have to** *condition our nervous systems* **to succeed not just once, but** *consistently*. You wouldn't go to an aerobics class just one time and say, "Okay, now I've got a great body and I'll be healthy for life!" The same is true of your emotions and behavior. We've got to condition ourselves for success, for love, for breaking through our fears. And through that conditioning, we can develop patterns that automatically lead us to consistent, lifelong success.

We need to remember that pain and pleasure shape all our behaviors, and that pain and pleasure can *change* our behaviors. Conditioning requires that we understand how to use pain and pleasure. What you're going to learn in the next chapter is the science that I've developed to create any change you want in your life. I call it the **Science of Neuro-Associative Conditioning™**, or **NAC**. What is it? **NAC is a step-by-step process that can condition your nervous system to associate pleasure to those things you want to continuously move toward and pain to those things you need to avoid in order to succeed consistently in your life without constant effort or willpower.** Remember, it's the feelings that we've been *conditioned* to associate in our nervous systems—our neuro-associations—that determine our emotions and our behavior.

When we take control of our neuro-associations, we take control of our lives. This chapter will show you how to condition your neuro-associations so that you are empowered to take action and produce the

results you've always dreamed of. It's designed to give you the k**NAC**k of creating consistent and lasting change.

> *"Things do not change; we change."*
> —HENRY DAVID THOREAU

What are the two changes everyone wants in life? **Isn't it true that we all want to change either 1) how we** *feel* **about things or 2) our** *behaviors?* If a person has been through a tragedy—they were abused as a child, they were raped, lost a loved one, are lacking in self-esteem—this person clearly will remain in pain until the sensations they link to themselves, these events, or situations are changed. Likewise, if a person overeats, drinks, smokes, or takes drugs, they have a set of behaviors that must change. The only way this can happen is by linking pain to the old behavior and pleasure to a new behavior.

This sounds so simple, but what I've found is that in order for us to be able to create true change—change that lasts—we need to develop a specific system for utilizing any techniques you and I learn to create change, and there are many. Every day I'm picking up new skills and new technologies from a variety of sciences. I continue to use many of the NLP and Ericksonian techniques that I began my career with; some of them are the finest available. Yet I always come back to utilizing them within the framework of the same six fundamental steps that the science of NAC represents. I created NAC as a way to use any technology for change. What NAC really provides is a specific syntax—an order and sequence—of ways to use any set of skills to create long-term change.

I'm sure you recall that in the first chapter I said that one of the key components of creating long-term change is a shift in beliefs. **The first belief we must have if we're going to create change quickly is that we can change now.** Again, most people in our society have unconsciously linked a lot of pain to the idea of being able to change quickly. On one hand, we desire to change quickly, and on the other, our cultural programming teaches us that to change quickly means that maybe we never even had a problem at all. Maybe we were just faking it or being lazy. We must adopt the belief that we can change in a moment. After all, if you can create a problem in a moment, you should be able to create a solution, too! You and I both know that when people finally do change, they do it in a moment, don't they? There's an instant when the change occurs. Why not make that instant *now*? Usually it's the *getting ready to change* that takes people time. We've all heard the joke:

Q: How many psychiatrists does it take to change a lightbulb?
A: Just one . . . but it's very expensive, it takes a long time, and the
lightbulb has to want to change.

Garbage! You and I have to get *ourselves* ready to change. You and I have
to become our own counselors and master our own lives.

**The second belief that you and I must have if we're going to
create long-term change is that we're responsible for our own change,
not anyone else.** In fact, there are three specific beliefs about responsibility that a person must have if they're going to create long-term change:

1) First, we must believe, "Something must change"—not that it
should change, not that it could or ought to, but that it absolutely *must*.
So often I hear people say, "This weight *should* come off," "Procrastinating
is a lousy habit," "My relationships *should* be better." But you know, we
can "*should*" all over ourselves, and our life still won't change! It's only
when something becomes a must that we begin the process of truly doing
what's necessary to shift the quality of our lives.

**2) Second, we must not only believe that things must change, but
we must believe, "I must change it."** We must see *ourselves* as the
source of the change. Otherwise, we'll always be looking for someone else
to make the changes for us, and we'll always have someone else to blame
when it doesn't work out. We must be the source of our change if our
change is going to last.

3) Third, we have to believe, "I can change it." Without believing
that it's possible for us to change, as we've already discussed in the last
chapter, we stand no chance of carrying through on our desires.

Without these three core beliefs, I can assure you that any change you
make stands a good chance of being only temporary. Please don't misunderstand me—it's always smart to get a great coach (an expert, a
therapist, a counselor, someone who's already produced these results for
many other people) to support you in taking the proper steps to conquer
your phobia or quit smoking or lose weight. But in the end, **you have to
be the source of your change.**

The interaction I had with the relapsed smoker that day triggered me
to ask new questions of myself about the sources of change. Why was I
so effective throughout the years? What had set me apart from others
who'd tried to help these same people who had equal intention but were
unable to produce the result? And when I'd tried to create a change in
someone and failed, what had happened then? What had prevented me
from producing the change that I was really committed to helping this
person make?

Then I began to ask larger questions, like "What really makes change
happen in any form of therapy?" All therapies work some of the time, and

all forms of therapy fail to work at other times. I also began to notice two other interesting things: some people went to therapists I didn't think were particularly skilled, and still managed to make their desired change in a very short period of time in spite of the therapist. I also saw other people who went to therapists I considered excellent, yet were not helped to produce the results they wanted in the short term.

After a few years of witnessing thousands of transformations and looking for the common denominator, finally it hit me: we can analyze our problems for years, but **nothing changes until we change the sensations we link to an experience in our nervous system,** and we have the capacity to do this quickly and powerfully if we understand . . .

THE POWER OF YOUR BRAIN

What a magnificent gift we were born with! I've learned that our brains can help us accomplish virtually anything we desire. The brain's capacity is nearly unfathomable. Most of us know little about how it works, so let's briefly focus upon this unparalleled vessel of power and how we can condition it to consistently produce the results we want in our lives.

Realize that your brain eagerly awaits your every command, ready to carry out anything you ask of it. All it requires is a small amount of fuel: the oxygen in your blood and a little glucose. In terms of its intricacy and power, the brain defies even our greatest modern computer technology. It is capable of processing up to 30 billion bits of information per second and it boasts the equivalent of 6,000 miles of wiring and cabling. Typically the human nervous system contains about 28 billion neurons (nerve cells designed to conduct impulses). Without neurons, our nervous systems would be unable to interpret the information we receive through our sense organs, unable to convey it to the brain and unable to carry out instructions from the brain as to what to do. Each of these neurons is a tiny, self-contained computer capable of processing about one million bits of information.

These neurons act independently, but they also communicate with other neurons through an amazing network of 100,000 miles of nerve fibers. The power of your brain to process information is staggering, especially when you consider that a computer—even the fastest computer—can make connections only one at a time. **By contrast, a reaction in one neuron can spread to *hundreds of thousands* of others in a span of *less than 20 milliseconds*. To give you perspective, that's about *ten times less than it takes for your eye to blink.***

A neuron takes a million times longer to send a signal than a typical computer switch, yet the brain can recognize a familiar face in less than a second—a feat beyond the ability of the most powerful computers. The brain achieves this speed because, unlike the step-by-step computer, its billions of neurons can all attack a problem *simultaneously*.

So with all this immense power at our disposal, *why can't we get ourselves to feel happy consistently?* Why can't we change a behavior like smoking or drinking, overeating or procrastinating? Why can't we immediately shake off depression, break through our frustration, and feel joyous every day of our lives? **We can!** Each of us has at our disposal the most incredible computer on the planet, but unfortunately no one gave us an owner's manual. Most of us have no idea how our brains really work, so we attempt to *think* our way into a change when, in reality, our behavior is rooted in our nervous systems in the form of physical connections—neural connections—or what I call **neuro-associations**.

NEURO-SCIENCE: YOUR TICKET TO LASTING CHANGE

Great breakthroughs in our ability to understand the human mind are now available because of a marriage between two widely different fields: neuro-biology (the study of how the brain works) and computer science. The integration of these sciences has created the discipline of **neuro-science**.

Neuro-scientists study how neuro-associations occur and have discovered that neurons are *constantly* sending electro-chemical messages back and forth across **neural pathways**, not unlike traffic on a busy thoroughfare. This communication is happening all at once, each idea or memory moving along its own path while literally billions of other impulses are traveling in individual directions. This arrangement enables us to hopscotch mentally from memories of the piney smell of an evergreen forest after a rain, to the haunting melody of a favorite Broadway musical, to painstakingly detailed plans of an evening with a loved one, to the exquisite size and texture of a newborn baby's thumb.

Not only does this complex system allow us to enjoy the beauty of our world, it also helps us to survive in it. **Each time we experience a significant amount of pain or pleasure, our brains search for the cause and record it in our nervous systems to enable us to make better decisions about what to do in the future.** For example, without a neuro-association in your brain to remind you that sticking your hand into an open flame would burn you, you could conceivably make this mistake again and again until your hand is severely burned. Thus, neuro-associations quickly provide our brains with the signals that help us to re-access our memories and safely maneuver us through our lives.

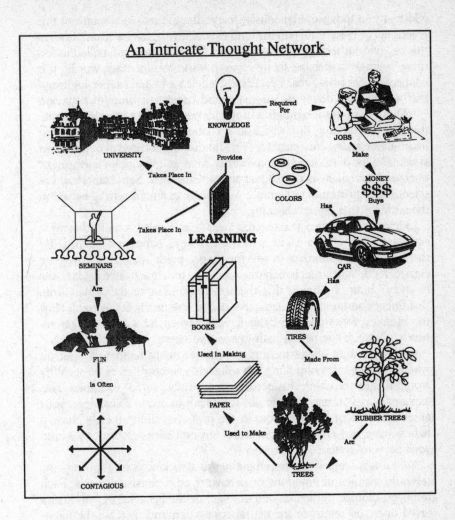

An Intricate Thought Network

"To the dull mind all nature is leaden. To the
illumined mind the whole world burns and sparkles
with light."
—RALPH WALDO EMERSON

When we do something for the first time, we *create a physical connection*,
a thin neural strand that allows us to re-access that emotion or behavior
again in the future. Think of it this way: each time we repeat the behavior, the connection strengthens. We add another strand to our neural
connection. With enough repetitions and emotional intensity, we can

add many strands simultaneously, increasing the tensile strength of this emotional or behavioral pattern until eventually we have a "trunk line" to this behavior or feeling. This is when we find ourselves compelled to feel these feelings or behave in this way *consistently.* In other words, this connection becomes what I've already labeled a neural "super-highway" that will take us down an automatic and consistent route of behavior.

This neuro-association is a biological reality—it's physical. Again, this is why thinking our way into a change is usually ineffective; our neuro-associations are a survival tool and they are secured in our nervous systems as physical connections rather than as intangible "memories." Michael Merzenich of the University of California, San Francisco, has scientifically proven that the more we indulge in any pattern of behavior, the stronger that pattern becomes.

Merzenich mapped the specific areas in a monkey's brain that were activated when a certain finger in the monkey's hand was touched. He then trained one monkey to use this finger predominantly in order to earn its food. When Merzenich remapped the touch-activated areas in the monkey's brain, he found that the area responding to the signals from that finger's additional use had expanded in size nearly *600 percent!* Now the monkey continued the behavior even when he was no longer re-warded because the neural pathway was so strongly established.

An illustration of this in human behavior might be that of a person who no longer enjoys smoking but still feels a compulsion to do so. Why would this be the case? This person is physically "wired" to smoke. This explains why you may have found it difficult to create a change in your emotional patterns or behaviors in the past. You didn't merely "have a habit"—you had created a network of strong neuro-associations within your nervous system.

We unconsciously develop these neuro-associations by allowing our-selves to indulge in emotions or behaviors on a consistent basis. Each time you indulge in the emotion of anger or the behavior of yelling at a loved one, you reinforce the neural connection and increase the likeli-hood that you'll do it again. The good news is this: research has also shown that when the monkey was forced to stop using this finger, the area of the brain where these neural connections were made actually began to *shrink in size,* and therefore the neuro-association weakened.

This is good news for those who want to change their habits! If you'll just *stop indulging* in a particular behavior or emotion long enough, if you just *interrupt your pattern* of using the old pathway for a long enough period of time, the neural connection will weaken and atrophy. Thus the disempowering emotional pattern or behavior disappears with it. We should remember this also means that if you don't use your passion it's going to dwindle. Remember: courage, unused, diminishes. Commitment, unexercised, wanes. Love, unshared, dissipates.

> *"It is not enough to have a good mind; the main*
> *thing is to use it well."*
> —RENE DESCARTES

What the science of Neuro-Associative Conditioning offers is six steps that are specifically designed to change behavior by breaking patterns that disempower you. But first, we must understand how the brain makes a neuro-association in the first place. **Any time you experience significant amounts of pain or pleasure, your brain immediately searches for the cause.** It uses the following three criteria.

1. Your brain looks for something that appears to be unique. To narrow down the likely causes, the brain tries to distinguish something that is unusual to the circumstance. It seems logical that if you're having unusual feelings, there must be an unusual cause.

2. Your brain looks for something that seems to be happening simultaneously. This is known in psychology circles as the Law of Recency. Doesn't it make sense that what occurs in the moment (or close proximity to it) of intense pleasure or pain is probably the cause of that sensation?

3. Your brain looks for consistency. If you're feeling pain or pleasure, your brain begins to immediately notice what around you is unique and is happening simultaneously. If the element that meets these two criteria also seems to occur *consistently* whenever you feel this pain or pleasure, then you can be sure that your brain will determine that it is the cause. The challenge in this, of course, is that when we feel enough pain or pleasure, we tend to generalize about consistency. I'm sure you've had someone say to you, "You *always* do that," after you've done something for the first time. Perhaps you've even said it yourself.

Because the three criteria for forming neuro-associations are so imprecise, it is very easy to fall prey to misinterpretations and create what I call **false neuro-associations.** That's why we must evaluate linkages before they become a part of our unconscious decision-making process. **So often we blame the wrong cause, and thereby close ourselves off from possible solutions.** I once knew a woman, a very successful artist, who hadn't had a relationship with a man for twelve years. Now, this woman was extremely passionate about everything she did; it's what made her such a great artist. However, when her relationship ended and she found herself in massive pain, her brain immediately searched for the cause—it searched for something that was *unique* to this relationship.

Her brain noted that the relationship had been especially passionate. Instead of identifying it as one of the beautiful parts of the relationship, she began to think that this was the *reason* that the relationship ended. Her brain also looked for something that was *simultaneous* to the pain; again it noted that there had been a great deal of passion right before it had ended. When she looked for something that was *consistent,* again passion was pinpointed as the culprit. Because passion met all three criteria, her brain decided that it must be the reason the relationship ended painfully.

Having linked this as the cause, she resolved never to feel that level of passion in a relationship again. This is a classic example of a false neuro-association. She had linked up a false cause, and this was now guiding her current behaviors and crippling the potential for a better relationship in the future. The real culprit in her relationship was that she and her partner had different values and rules. But because she linked pain to her passion, she avoided it at all costs, not only in relationships, but even in her art. The quality of her entire life began to suffer. This is a perfect example of the strange ways in which we sometimes wire ourselves; you and I must understand how our brain makes associations and question many of those connections that we've just accepted that may be limiting our lives. Otherwise, in our personal and professional lives, we are destined to feel unfulfilled and frustrated.

A SOURCE OF SELF-SABOTAGE

Even more insidious are **mixed neuro-associations**, the classic source of self-sabotage. If you've ever found yourself starting to accomplish something, and then destroying it, mixed neuro-associations are usually the culprit. Perhaps your business has been moving in fits and starts, flourishing one day and floundering the next. What is this all about? It's a case of associating both pain and pleasure to the same situation.

One example a lot of us can relate to is money. In our culture, people have incredibly mixed associations to wealth. There's no doubt that people want money. They think it would provide them with more freedom, more security, a chance to contribute, a chance to travel, to learn, to expand, to make a difference. But simultaneously, most people never climb above a certain earnings plateau because deep down they associate having "excess" money to a lot of negatives. They associate it to greed, to being judged, to stress, with immorality or a lack of spirituality.

One of the first exercises I ask people to do in my Financial Destiny™ seminars is to brainstorm all the positive associations they have to wealth, as well as all the negative ones. On the plus side they write down such things as: freedom, luxury, contribution, happiness, security, travel, opportunity, and making a difference. But on the minus side (which is usually more full) they write down such things as: fights with spouse, stress, guilt, sleepless nights, intense effort, greed, shallowness, and complacency, being judged, and taxes. Do you notice a difference in intensity between the two sets of neuro-associations? Which do you think plays a stronger role in their lives?

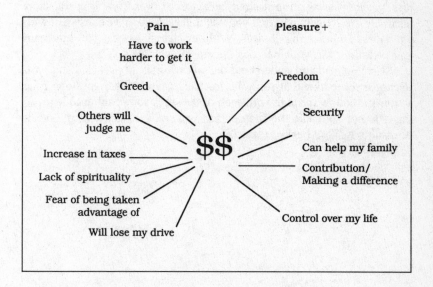

When you're deciding what to do, if your brain doesn't have a clear signal of what equals pain and what equals pleasure, it goes into overload and becomes confused. As a result, you lose momentum and the power to take the decisive actions that could give you what you want. **When you give your brain mixed messages, you're going to get mixed results.** Think of your brain's decision-making process as being like a scale: "If I were to do this, would it mean pain or pleasure?" And remember, it's not just the number of factors on each side but the weight they individually carry. It's possible that you could have more pleasurable than painful associations about money, but if just one of the negative associations is very intense, then that false neuro-association can wipe out your ability to succeed financially.

THE PAIN-PAIN BARRIER

What happens when you get to a point where you feel that you're going to have pain no matter *what* you do? I call this the **pain-pain barrier**. Often, when this occurs, we become immobilized—we don't know what to do. Usually we choose what we believe will be the least painful alternative. Some people, however, allow this pain to overwhelm them completely and they experience learned helplessness.

Using the six steps of NAC will help you to interrupt these disempowering patterns. You will create alternative pathways so that you're not just "wishing" away an undesired behavior, or overriding it in the short term, but are actually rewiring yourself to feel and behave consistent with your new, empowering choices. Without changing what you link pain and pleasure to in your nervous system, no change will last.

After you read and understand the following six steps, I challenge you to choose something that you want to change in your life right now. Take action and follow through with each of the steps you're about to learn so that you not only read the chapter, but you *produce changes* as the result of reading it. Let's begin to learn . . .

6
HOW TO CHANGE ANYTHING IN YOUR LIFE: THE SCIENCE OF NEURO-ASSOCIATIVE CONDITIONING ™

"The beginning of a habit is like an invisible thread, but every time we repeat the act we strengthen the strand, add to it another filament, until it becomes a great cable and binds us irrevocably, thought and act."
—ORISON SWETT MARDEN

If you and I want to change our behavior, there is only one effective way to do it: we must link unbearable and immediate sensations of pain to our old behavior, and incredible and immediate sensations of pleasure to a new one. Think about it this way: all of us, through the experience of life, have learned certain patterns of thinking and behaving to get ourselves out of pain and into pleasure. We all experience emotions like boredom or frustration or anger or feeling overwhelmed, and develop strategies for ending these feelings. Some people use shopping; some use food; some use sex; some use drugs; some use alcohol; some use yelling at their kids. They know, consciously or unconsciously, that this neural pathway will relieve their pain and take them to some level of pleasure in the moment.

Whatever the strategy, if you and I are going to change it, we have to go through six simple steps, the outcome of which is to find a more direct and empowering way to get out of pain and into pleasure, ways that will be more effective and elegant. These six steps of NAC will show you how to create a direct highway out of pain and into pleasure with no disempowering detours. They are:

NAC MASTER STEP 1

Decide What You Really Want and What's Preventing You From Having It Now.

You'd be surprised how many people came to me for private therapeutic work, and when I asked them what they wanted, they'd spend twenty minutes telling me what they didn't want, or what they no longer wanted to experience. We've got to remember that we get whatever we focus on in life. If we keep focusing on what we don't want, we'll have more of it. **The first step to creating any change is deciding what you _do want_ so that you have something to move toward.** The more specific you can be about what you want, the more clarity you will have, and the more power you will command to achieve what you want more rapidly.

We also must learn what's preventing us from having what we want. Invariably, what's preventing us from making the change is that we link more pain to making a change than to staying where we are. We either have a belief like, "If I change, I will have pain," or we fear the unknown that change might bring.

NAC MASTER STEP 2

Get Leverage: Associate Massive Pain to Not Changing <u>Now</u> and Massive Pleasure to the Experience of Changing <u>Now</u>!

Most people know that they really want to change, yet they just can't get themselves to do it! **But change is usually not a question of capability; it's almost always a question of motivation.** If someone put a gun to our heads and said, "You'd better get out of that depressed state and start feeling happy now," I bet any one of us could find a way to change our emotional state for the moment under these circumstances.

But the problem, as I've said, is that change is often a *should* and not a *must*. Or it's a must, but it's a must for "someday." **The only way we're**

**going to make a change now is if we create a sense of urgency that's
so intense that we're compelled to follow through.** If we want to create
change, then, we have to realize that it's not a question of whether we *can*
do it, but rather whether we *will* do it. Whether we will or not comes
down to our level of motivation, which in turn comes down to those twin
powers that shape our lives, pain and pleasure.

Every change you've accomplished in your life is the result of changing your neuro-associations about what means pain and what means
pleasure. So often, though, we have a hard time getting ourselves to
change because we have mixed emotions about changing. On the one
hand, we want to change. We don't want to get cancer from smoking. We
don't want to lose our personal relationships because our temper is out
of control. We don't want our kids to feel unloved because we're harsh
with them. We don't want to feel depressed for the rest of our lives
because of something that happened in our past. We don't want to feel
like victims anymore.

On the other hand, we fear change. We wonder, "What if I stop
smoking cigarettes, but I die of cancer anyway and I've given up the
pleasure that cigarettes used to give me?" Or "What if I let go of this
negative feeling about the rape, and it happens to me again?" We have
mixed emotions where we link both pain and pleasure to changing,
which causes our brain to be uncertain as to what to do, and keeps us
from utilizing our full resources to make the kinds of changes that can
happen literally in a moment if every ounce of our being were committed
to them.

How do we turn this around? One of the things that turns virtually
anyone around is reaching a **pain threshold.** This means experiencing
pain at such an intense level that you know you *must change now*—a
point at which your brain says, "I've had it; I can't spend another day, not
another *moment,* living or feeling this way."

Have you ever experienced this in a personal relationship, for example? You hung in there, it was painful and you really weren't happy, but
you stayed in it anyway. Why? You rationalized that it would get better,
without doing anything to *make* it better. If you were in so much pain,
why didn't you leave? Even though you were unhappy, your fear of the
unknown was a more powerful motivating force. "Yeah, I'm unhappy
now," you may have thought, "but what if I leave this person and then
I never find anyone? At least I know how to deal with the pain I have
now."

This kind of thinking is what keeps people from making changes.
Finally, though, one day the pain of being in that negative relationship
became greater than your fear of the unknown, so you hit a threshold and
made the change. Maybe you've done the same thing with your body,

when you finally decided you couldn't spend another day without doing something about your excess weight. Maybe the experience that finally pushed you over the edge was your failure to be able to squeeze into your favorite pair of jeans, or the sensations of your "thunder thighs" rubbing against each other as you waddled up a set of stairs! Or just the sight of the bulbous folds of excess flesh hanging from the side of your body!

THE ALPO DIET

Recently, a woman attending a seminar told me about her fail-safe strategy that she had developed for shedding unwanted pounds. She and a friend had committed over and over again to losing weight, but failed to keep their promise each and every time. Finally, they both reached the point where losing weight was a must. Based on what I taught them, they needed some leverage to push themselves over the edge. They needed to make not keeping their promise more *painful* than anything they could imagine.

They decided to commit to each other and a group of friends that if they welshed on their promise this time, they would each have to eat a whole can of Alpo dog food! So, to stave off any hint of a craving, these two enterprising women told everyone and kept their cans in plain view at all times as a constant reminder. She told me that when they started to feel hunger pangs, they'd pick up the can and read the label. With ingredients boasting "horsemeat chunks," they found no difficulty in sticking to their commitment. They achieved their goal without a hitch!

A lever is a device that we utilize in order to lift or move a tremendous burden we could not otherwise manage. Leverage is absolutely crucial in creating any change, in freeing yourself from behavioral burdens like smoking, drinking, overeating, cursing, or emotional patterns like feeling depressed, worried, fearful, or inadequate—you name it. Change requires more than just establishing the knowledge that you should change. It's knowing at the deepest emotional and most basic sensory level that you *must* change. If you've tried many times to make a change and you've failed to do so, this simply means that **the level of pain for failing to change is not intense enough.** You have not reached threshold, the ultimate leverage.

When I was doing private therapy, it was imperative that I find the point of greatest leverage in order to help people make changes in one session that years of therapy had failed to accomplish. I started every session by saying that I couldn't work with anyone who wasn't committed to changing now. One of the reasons was that I charged $3,000 for a session, and I didn't want them to invest their money unless they were absolutely going to get the result they were committed to *today, in this one session*. Many times these people had flown in from some other part of the country. The thought of my sending them home without handling their problem motivated my clients to spend at least half an hour convincing me that they were indeed committed and would do anything to change now. With this kind of leverage, creating change became a matter of course. To paraphrase the philosopher Nietzsche, he who has a strong enough why can bear almost any how. I've found that 20 percent of any change is knowing *how*; but 80 percent is knowing *why*. If we gather a set of strong enough reasons to change, we can change in a *minute* something we've failed to change for years.

> *"Give me a lever long enough*
> *And a prop strong enough.*
> *I can single-handedly move the world."*
> —ARCHIMEDES

The greatest leverage you can create for yourself is the pain that comes from inside, not outside. Knowing that you have failed to live up to your own standards for your life is the ultimate pain. If we fail to act in accordance with our own view of ourselves, if our behaviors are inconsistent with our standards—with the identity we hold for ourselves—then the chasm between our actions and who we are drives us to make a change.

The leverage created by pointing out an inconsistency between someone's standards and their behavior can be incredibly effective in causing them to change. It's not just pressure placed on them by the outside world, but pressure built up by themselves from within. **One of the strongest forces in the human personality is the drive to preserve the integrity of our own identity.**

The reason so many of us seem to be walking contradictions is simply that we never recognize inconsistencies for what they are. If you want to help somebody, you won't access this kind of leverage by making them wrong or pointing out that they're inconsistent, but rather by asking them questions that cause them to realize for themselves their inconsistencies. This is a much more powerful lever than attacking someone. If you try to exert only external pressure, they'll push against it, but internal pressure is next to impossible to resist.

This kind of pressure is a valuable tool to use on yourself. Complacency breeds stagnation; unless you're extremely dissatisfied with your current pattern of behavior, you won't be motivated to make the changes that are necessary. Let's face it; the human animal responds to pressure.

So why would someone not change when they feel and know that they should? **They associate more pain to making the change than to not changing**. To change someone, including ourselves, we must simply reverse this so that *not* changing is incredibly painful (painful beyond our threshold of tolerance), and the idea of changing is attractive and pleasurable!

To get true leverage, ask yourself **pain-inducing questions**: "What will this cost me if I *don't* change?" Most of us are too busy estimating the price of change. But what's the price of not changing? "Ultimately what will I miss out on in my life if I don't make the shift? What is it already costing me mentally, emotionally, physically, financially, spiritually?" Make the pain of not changing feel so real to you, so intense, so immediate that you can't put off taking that action any longer.

If that doesn't create enough leverage, then focus on how it affects your loved ones, your children, and other people you care about. Many of us will do more for others than we'll do for ourselves. So picture in graphic detail how much your failure to change will negatively impact the people who are most important to you.

The second step is to use **pleasure-associating questions** to help you link those positive sensations to the idea of changing. "If I do change, how will that make me feel about myself? What kind of momentum could I create if I change this in my life? What other things could I accomplish if I really made this change today? How will my family and friends feel? How much happier will I be now?"

The key is to get *lots of reasons*, or better yet, *strong enough reasons*, why the change should take place *immediately,* not someday in the future. If you are not driven to make the change now, then you don't really have leverage.

Now that you've linked pain in your nervous system to not changing, and pleasure to making the change, you're driven to create a change, you can proceed to the third master step of NAC. . . .

NAC MASTER STEP 3

Interrupt the Limiting Pattern.

In order for us to consistently feel a certain way, we develop characteristic patterns of thinking, focusing on the same images and ideas, asking

ourselves the same questions. The challenge is that most people want a new result, but continue to act in the same way. I once heard it said that the definition of insanity is "doing the same things over and over again and expecting a different result."

Please don't misunderstand me. There's nothing wrong with you; you don't need to be "fixed." (And I suggest you avoid anyone who uses these metaphors to describe you!) The resources you need to change anything in your life are *within you right now*. It's just that you have a set of neuro-associations that habitually cause you to not fully utilize your capability. What you must do is reorganize your neural pathways so that they consistently guide you in the direction of your desires rather than your frustrations and fears.

To get new results in our lives, we can't just know what we want and get leverage on ourselves. We can be highly motivated to change, but if we keep doing the same things, running the same inappropriate patterns, our lives are not going to change, and all we'll experience is more and more pain and frustration.

Have you ever seen a fly that's trapped in a room? It immediately searches for the light, so it heads for the window, smacking itself against the glass again and again, sometimes for hours. Have you ever noticed people do this? They're highly motivated to change: they have intense leverage. But all the motivation in the world won't help if you try to get outside through a closed window. You've *got* to change your approach. The fly stands a chance only if it backs off and looks around for another exit.

If you and I run the same old pattern, we're going to get the same old results. Record albums create the same sounds consistently because of their pattern, the continuous groove in which the sound is encoded. But what would happen if one day I picked up your record, took a needle, and scratched across it back and forth dozens of times? If I do this enough, there's a point when the pattern is so deeply interrupted that the record will never play the same way again. Likewise, just interrupting someone's limiting pattern of behavior or emotion can completely change their life because sometimes it also creates leverage, and with these two steps alone, you can change virtually anything. The additional steps of NAC are just a way to make sure the changes *last* and that you develop new choices that are enjoyable and empowering.

I created a fun pattern interrupt recently at one of my three-day Unlimited Power™ seminars in Chicago. One man claimed that he really wanted to kick his chocolate habit, yet it was clear to me that he received a great deal of pleasure from his identity as a "chocolate addict." In fact, he was even wearing a T-shirt that proclaimed "I want the world, but I'll

settle for chocolate." This provided strong evidence that this
though he may have desired to stop eating chocolate, also had
deal of "secondary gain" to maintain this habit.

Sometimes people want to create a change because a behavior
emotional pattern creates pain for them. But they may also derive bene
from the very thing they're trying to change. If a person becomes injured,
for example, and then suddenly everyone waits on them hand and foot,
giving them a great deal of attention, they may find that their injuries
don't heal quite as quickly. While they want to be over the pain, unconsciously they want more of the pleaure of knowing that people care.

You can do everything right, but if secondary gain is too strong, you
will find yourself going back to the old ways. Someone with secondary
gain has mixed emotions about changing. They say they want to change,
but often they subconsciously believe that maintaining the old behavior
or emotional pattern gives them something they couldn't get any other
way. Thus they're not willing to give up feeling depressed, even though
it's painful. Why? Because being depressed gets them attention, for example. They don't want to feel depressed, but they desperately want
attention. In the end, the need for attention wins out, and they stay
depressed. The need for attention is only one form of secondary gain. In
order to resolve this, we have to give the person enough leverage that
they must change, but also we must show them a new way to get their
needs met.

While on some level, I'm sure this man knew he needed to kick
chocolate, I'm also fairly certain that he knew he could use this opportunity to get some serious attention. Any time there is secondary gain
involved, you have to step up the leverage, so I decided that a massive
pattern interrupt would create the necessary leverage. "Sir!" I exclaimed.
"You're telling me that you're ready to give up chocolate. That's great.
There's just one thing I want you to do before we eliminate that old
pattern forever." He asked, "What's that?" I said, "To get your body in the
right condition, for the next nine days you must eat *nothing but chocolate.*
Only chocolate can pass your lips."

People in the audience started giggling, and the man looked at me
uncertainly. "Can I drink anything?" he asked. "Yes," I said, "you can
drink water. Four glasses a day—but that's all. Everything else must be
chocolate." He shrugged his shoulders and grinned. "Okay, Tony, if that's
what you want. I can do this without changing. I hate to make a fool out
of you!" I smiled and continued with the seminar.

You should have seen what happened next! As if by magic, dozens of
chocolate bars and candies materialized out of people's pockets, purses
and briefcases and were passed down to him. By the lunch break, he had
been inundated with every last morsel of chocolate in that auditorium:

Baby Ruths, Butterfingers, Snickers, Milky Ways, M & M's, Almond Joys, Fanny Farmer fudge.

He caught my eye in the lobby outside. "Thanks, Tony; this is great!" he exclaimed as he unwrapped and popped Hershey's Kisses into his mouth, determined to show that he could "beat me." But he failed to realize that he wasn't competing with me—he was competing with himself! I was merely enlisting his body as an ally in getting leverage and breaking his pattern.

Do you know how thirsty sugar makes you? By the end of the day this guy's throat was absolutely raw—and he had definitely lost his passion for chocolate as people continued to shovel Krackel bars into his pockets and press his palms with Thin Mints. By the second day he'd definitely lost his sense of humor, but he wasn't yet ready to cry uncle. "Have some more chocolate!" I insisted. He unwrapped a Three Musketeers bar and glared at me.

By the third morning, as he trailed into the auditorium, he looked like a man who had spent all night praying to the porcelain goddess. "How was breakfast?" I asked as people laughed. "Not so good," he admitted weakly. "Have some more!" I said. Feebly he accepted another piece of chocolate from someone sitting behind him, but he failed to open it or even look at it. "What's the matter?" I asked him. "Fed up?" He nodded. "Come on, you're the chocolate champion!" I goaded. "Have some more! Isn't chocolate the greatest? How about some Mounds bars? And some Peanut M & M's? And a whole box of Rocky Road fudge? Can't you just taste it? Doesn't it make your mouth water?"

The longer I talked, the greener he got. "Have some more!" I said, and finally he exploded: "YOU CAN'T MAKE ME!" The audience laughed uproariously as the man realized what he'd said. "All right, then. Throw the candy away and sit down."

Later, I came back to him, and assisted him in selecting empowering alternatives to the chocolate, laying down some new pathways to pleasure that were more empowering and didn't require him to consume something he knew wasn't good for him. Then I really got to work with him, conditioning the new associations and helping him replace his old addiction with a smorgasbord of healthful behaviors: power breathing, exercise, water-rich foods, proper food combining, and so on.*

Had I created leverage on this guy? You bet! If you can give someone pain in their body, that's undeniable leverage. They'll do anything to get out of pain and into pleasure. Simultaneously, I broke his pattern. Everybody else was trying to get him to *stop* eating chocolate. I demanded that

---

* Find out more about these principles in my Living Health seminar, or read *Unlimited Power,* Chapter 10, "Energy: The Fuel of Excellence."

he *eat* it! That was something he never expected, and it massively interrupted his pattern. He rapidly linked such painful sensations to the idea of eating chocolate that a new neural pathway was laid down overnight, and his old "Hershey Highway" was bombed beyond recognition.

When I used to conduct private therapies, people would come to see me, sit down in my office and begin to tell me what their problem was. They'd say, "My problem is . . . " and then they'd burst into tears, out of control. As soon as this happened, I would stand up and shout, "EXCUSE ME!" This would jolt them, and then I'd follow up with, "We haven't started yet!" Usually they responded, "Oh, I'm so sorry." And they'd immediately change their emotional states and regain control. It was hysterical to watch! These people who felt they had no control over their lives would immediately prove that they already knew exactly how to change how they felt!

One of the best ways to interrupt someone's pattern is to do things they don't expect, things that are radically different from what they've experienced before. Think of some of the ways you can interrupt your own patterns. Take a moment to think up some of the most enjoyable and disruptive ways you can interrupt a pattern of being frustrated, worried, or overwhelmed.

Next time you start to feel depressed, jump up, look at the sky, and yell in your most idiotic tone of voice, "H-A-L-L-E-L-U-J-A-H! My feet don't stink today!" A stupid, silly move like that will definitely shift your attention, change your state, and it will definitely change the states of everyone around you as they begin to realize that you're no longer depressed—just crazy!

If you overeat on a regular basis and want to stop, I'll give you a technique that will definitely work, if you're willing to commit to it. The next time you find yourself in a restaurant overeating, jump up in the middle of the room, point at your own chair and scream at the top of your lungs, "PIG!" I guarantee that if you do this three or four times in a public place, you won't overeat anymore! You'll link too much pain to this behavior! Just remember: the more outrageous your approach to breaking a pattern, the more effective it will be.

One of the key distinctions to interrupting a pattern is that you must do it in the moment the pattern is recurring. Pattern interrupts happen to us every day. When you say, "I just lost my train of thought," you're indicating that something or someone interrupted your pattern of concentration. Have you ever been deeply involved in a conversation with a friend, had someone interrupt you for a moment, then come back wondering, "Where were we?" Of course you have, and it's a classic example of a pattern interrupt.

Just remember, if we want to create change and we've learned in the past to get pleasure by taking a circuitous route that includes a series of negative consequences, we need to break that old pattern. We need to scramble it beyond recognition, find a new pattern (that's the next step), and condition it again and again until it becomes our consistent approach.

HOW TO BREAK LIMITING PATTERNS OF FEELING AND ACTING

Again, often it's true that interrupting a pattern enough times can change almost anyone. A simple way of breaking a pattern is by **scrambling the sensations** we link to our memories. The only reason we're upset is that we're representing things in a certain way in our minds. For example, if your boss yells at you, and you mentally rerun that experience the rest of the day, picturing him or her yelling at you over and over again, then you'll feel progressively worse. Why let the experience continue to affect you? Why not just take this record in your mind and scratch it so many times that you can't experience those feelings anymore? Maybe you can even make it funny!

Try this right now by doing the following: Think of a situation that makes you feel sad, frustrated, or angry. Now do the first two steps of NAC, which we've already covered. If you feel bad now about the situation, how do you want to be able to feel? Why do you want to feel that way? What's been preventing you from feeling that way is the sensations you've linked to this situation. Wouldn't it be wonderful if you could feel good about it? Now get some leverage on yourself. If you don't change how you feel about this situation, how will you continue to feel? Pretty lousy, I'll bet! Do you want to pay that price and continually carry around these negative sensations or upsets you have toward this person or situation? If you were to change now, wouldn't you feel better?

THE SCRAMBLE PATTERN

You've got enough leverage; now scramble the disempowering feelings until they no longer come up. After reading this, take the following steps.

1) See the situation in your mind that was bothering you so much. Picture it as a movie. Don't feel upset about it; just watch it one time, seeing everything that happened.

2) Take that same experience and turn it into a cartoon. Sit up in your chair with a big, silly grin on your face, breathing fully, and run the image backward as fast as you can so that you can see everything happening in reverse. If somebody said something, watch them swallow their words! Let the movie run backward in very fast motion, then run it forward again in even faster motion. Now change the colors of the images so that everybody's faces are rainbow-colored. If there's someone in particular who upsets you, cause their ears to grow very large like Mickey Mouse's, and their nose to grow like Pinocchio's.

Do this at least a *dozen* times, back and forth, sideways, scratching the record of your imagery with tremendous speed and humor. Create some music in your mind as you do this. Maybe it's your favorite song, or maybe some type of cartoon music. Link these weird sounds to the old image that used to upset you. This will definitely change the sensations. Key to this whole process is the speed at which you play back the imagery and the level of humor and exaggeration you can link to it.

3) Now think about the situation that was bothering you, and notice how you feel now. If done effectively, you'll easily have broken the pattern so many times you'll find it difficult or impossible to get back into those negative feelings. This can be done with things that have been bothering you *for years*. It's often a much more effective approach than trying to analyze the why's and wherefore's of a situation, which doesn't change the sensations you link to the situation.

As simplistic as it seems, effectively scrambling a situation will work in most cases, even where trauma has been involved. **Why does it work? Because all of our feelings are based on the images we focus on in our minds and the sounds and sensations we link to those specific images.** As we change the images and sounds, we change how we feel. Conditioning this again and again makes it difficult to get back into the old pattern.

One way of breaking the pattern is to *just stop* doing something, go "cold turkey." If you stop running a pattern again and again, the neural pathway will gradually dissipate. Once a neural connection is made, the brain will always have a pathway, but unless the path is used, it becomes overgrown. Like anything else, if you don't use it, you begin to lose it.

Now that you've broken the pattern that has been holding you back, you now have the open space to . . .

NAC MASTER STEP 4
———————

Create a New, Empowering Alternative.

This fourth step is *absolutely critical* to establishing long-term change. In fact, **the failure by most people to find an alternative way of getting**

out of pain and into the feelings of pleasure is the major reason most people's attempts at change are only temporary. Many people get to the point where they have to change, where change is a must, because they link so much pain to their old pattern and they link pleasure to the idea of changing. They even interrupt their patterns. But after that, they have nothing to replace the old pattern!

Remember, all of your neurological patterns are designed to help you get out of pain and into pleasure. These patterns are well established, and while they may have negative side effects, if you've learned that a habit can get you out of pain, you'll go back to it again and again since you've found no better way to get the feelings you desire.

If you've been following each one of these steps, you've gotten clear about what you wanted and what was preventing you from getting it, you've gotten leverage on yourself, you've interrupted the pattern, and now you need to fill the gap with a new set of choices that will give you the same pleasurable feelings without the negative side effects. Once you quit smoking, you must come up with a new way, or a lot of new ways, to replace whatever benefits you used to get from the old behavior; the benefits of the old feelings or behaviors must be preserved by the new behaviors or feelings while eliminating the side effects. What can you replace worry with? How about massive action on a plan you have for meeting your goals? Depression can be replaced with a focus on how to help others who are in need.

If you're not sure how to get yourself out of pain and to feel pleasure as a replacement to your smoking, drinking, worrying, or other undesirable emotion or behavior, **you can simply find the answers by modeling people who have turned things around for themselves.** Find people who have made the lasting changes; I guarantee you'll find that they had an alternative to replace the old behavior.

A good example of this is my friend Fran Tarkenton. When Fran and I first started doing my Personal Power television shows together, he had a habit that truly surprised me. He was addicted to chewing tobacco. I'd be in a meeting with Fran, and suddenly he would turn his head and spit. This did not match my picture of this powerful and elegant man. But he'd been doing it for over twenty years.

As Fran would tell me later, chewing tobacco was one of his greatest pleasures in life. It was like his best friend. If he was on the road and felt alone, he could chew tobacco, and he wouldn't feel alone anymore. In fact, he told a group of his friends one time that if he had to choose between sex and chewing tobacco, *he'd chew tobacco!* How's that for a false neuro-association? He'd wired a pathway out of pain and into pleasure via the highway of chewing tobacco. After years of continual use and reinforcement, he had created a neural trunk line from tobacco to pleasure; thus, this was his favorite route of change.

What got him to change his behavior? Finally, he got enough leverage on himself. One day, with a little help from "a friend," he began to see that chewing tobacco was massively incongruent with the quality of man he'd become. It represented a lack of control over his life, and since being in charge of his life is one of Fran's highest values, that was a standard he could not break. It was too painful to be in that position. He started to direct his mind's focus to the possibility of mouth cancer. He pictured it vividly until pretty soon he was driven away from the idea of using tobacco. The taste of it started to disgust him. These images helped him to get leverage on himself and interrupt the pattern he'd previously linked to using tobacco for pleasure.

The next most important key was that Fran found new ways to get pleasure that were even more effective than tobacco. He poured himself into his business like never before, and started producing results that have made his company, KnowledgeWare, one of the most successful computer software companies on Wall Street. Even more powerfully, now that he needed a new companion, he decided to attract a real one, and found the woman of his dreams and learned to get the kinds of emotions and feelings from his relationship with her that he could never get from any other source.

Often, if we just break our old patterns enough, our brains will automatically search for a replacement pattern to give us the feelings we desire. This is why people who finally break the pattern of smoking sometimes gain weight: their brains look for a new way to create the same kinds of pleasurable feelings, and now they eat mass quantities of food to get them. The key, then, is for us to consciously choose the new behaviors or feelings with which we're going to replace the old ones.

STUDIES IN TRANSFORMATION

A statistical study was conducted by researcher Nancy Mann to evaluate the level of rehabilitation in reformed drug abusers, and **the adoption of a replacement behavior appears to play a major role** even in this complex field of change.* The first group in the study was forced to give up their addiction through some external pressure, often applied by the legal system. As we talked about in the section on leverage, **external pressure rarely has a <u>lasting</u> impact.** Sure enough, these men and

---

* Mann, Nancy, "A Diagnostic Tool with Important Implications for Treatment of Addiction: Identification of Factors Underlying Relapse and Remission Time Distributions," *The International Journal of the Addictions* (1984).

women returned to their old habits as soon as the pressure was lifted, i.e., as soon as they were released from jail.

A second group truly wanted to quit, and tried to do so on their own. Their leverage was primarily internal. As a result, their behavioral changes lasted a great deal longer, often as much as two years after the initial commitment. What eventually caused a relapse was suffering a significant amount of stress. When this occurred, they often reverted back to their drug habit as a way of getting out of pain and into pleasure. Why? Because they had not found a *replacement* for the old neural pathway.

The third group replaced their addiction with a new alternative, something that gave them the feelings they had sought originally—or perhaps something that made them feel even better. Many found fulfilling relationships, spiritual enlightenment, a career that they could be completely passionate about. As a result, **many never returned to the old drug habits, and the majority lasted an average of over eight years** before any backsliding occurred.

The people who succeeded in kicking their drug habits followed the first four steps of NAC, and that's why they were so successful. Some of them lasted only eight years, however. Why? Because they didn't utilize the fifth and critical step of NAC.

NAC MASTER STEP 5

Condition the New Pattern Until It's Consistent.

Conditioning is the way to make sure that a change you create is consistent and lasts long-term.* The simplest way to condition something is simply to rehearse it again and again until a neurological way is created. If you find an empowering alternative, imagine doing it until you see that it can get you out of pain and into pleasure quickly. Your brain will begin to associate this as a new way of producing this result on a consistent basis. If you don't do this, you'll go back to the old pattern.

If you rehearse the new, empowering alternative again and again with tremendous **emotional intensity**, you'll carve out a pathway, and with even more repetition and emotion, it will become a highway to this new way of achieving results, and it will become a part of your habitual behavior. **Remember, your brain can't tell the difference between something you vividly imagine and something you actually experience.** Conditioning ensures that you automatically travel along the new

* See also Chapter 17 of *Unlimited Power*, "Anchoring Yourself to Success."

route, that if you spot one of the "off ramps" you used to take all the time, now you just speed past them—in fact, they'll actually become *difficult* to take.

The power of conditioning can't be overestimated. I read recently that Boston Celtics great Larry Bird was doing a soft-drink commercial in which he was supposed to miss a jump shot. He made nine baskets in a row before he could get himself to miss! That's how strongly he's conditioned himself over the years. When that ball hits his hands, he automatically goes through a pattern that is aimed at putting the ball through the hoop. I'm sure that if you examined the portion of Larry Bird's brain that is linked to that motion, you would discover a substantial neural pathway. Realize that you and I can condition <u>any</u> behavior within ourselves if we do it with enough repetition and emotional intensity.

The next step is to set up a schedule to **reinforce** your new behavior. How can you reward yourself for succeeding? Don't wait until you've gone a year without smoking. When you've gone a *day*, give yourself a reward! Don't wait until you've lost eighty pounds. Don't even wait until you've lost a pound. The *minute* you can push the plate away with food still on it, give yourself a pat on the back. Set up a series of short-term goals, or milestones, and as you reach each one, *immediately* reward yourself. If you've been depressed or worried, now each time you take action instead of worrying, or each time you smile when somebody asks how you're doing and you say, "Great," give yourself a reward for already beginning to make the changes necessary to ensure your long-term success.

In this way, your nervous system learns to link great pleasure to change. People who want to lose weight don't *always see* immediate results—usually losing a couple of pounds doesn't miraculously transform you into an Elle McPherson or a Mel Gibson. So it's important to reward yourself as soon as you take some specific actions or make any positive emotional progress, like choosing to run around the block instead of running to the nearest McDonald's. If you don't, you may find yourself saying, "Okay, I've lost a pound so far, but I'm still fat. This will take forever. I have such a long way to go . . ." Then you might use these short-term assessments as excuses to binge.

Understanding the power of **reinforcement** will speed up the process of conditioning a new pattern. Recently I had the pleasure of reading an excellent book that I highly recommend to those who really want to make a thorough study of conditioning. It's entitled *Don't Shoot the Dog!* by Karen Pryor. This book sets forth some simple distinctions about modifying animal behavior that parallel my own distinctions gained in years of shaping human behavior.

What's fascinating is how similar animals and humans are in terms of the forces that drive our actions. Knowing the fundamentals of conditioning enables us to take control of those forces and create the destiny of our choice. We can live like animals, manipulated by circumstances and those around us—or we can learn from these laws, using them to maximize our fullest potential. Pryor discusses in her book how she learned to utilize pain to train animals for years: whips and a chair for lions, the bridle for horses, the leash for dogs. But she ran into difficulty when she began to work with dolphins, because when she tried to give them pain, they just swam away! This caused her to develop a more thorough understanding of the dynamics of **positive reinforcement training.**

> *"There is nothing training cannot do. Nothing is*
> *above its reach. It can turn bad morals to good;*
> *it can destroy bad principles and recreate good ones;*
> *it can lift men to angelship."*
> —MARK TWAIN

The first organizing principle of any type of "Success Conditioning" is the power of reinforcement. You and I must know that in order to get ourselves to consistently produce any behavior or emotion, we must create a conditioned pattern. All patterns are the result of reinforcement; specifically, the key to creating consistency in our emotions and behaviors is conditioning.

THE LAW OF REINFORCEMENT

Any pattern of emotion or behavior that is continually reinforced will become an automatic and conditioned response. Anything we fail to reinforce will eventually dissipate.

We can reinforce our own behavior or someone else's through positive reinforcement, that is, every time we produce the behavior we want, we give a reward. That reward can be praise, a gift, a new freedom, etc. Or we can use negative reinforcement. This might be a frown, a loud noise, or even physical punishment. It's crucial for us to understand that reinforcement is not the same as punishment and reward. **Reinforcement is responding to a behavior *immediately* after it occurs, while punishment and reward may occur long afterward.**

TIMING IS EVERYTHING

Appropriate **timing** is absolutely critical to effective conditioning. If a coach yells, "Great!" when the basketball team executes a perfect pick-and-roll, it has a lot more impact than if he waited until they debriefed later in the locker room. Why? Because we always want to link the sensations of reinforcement in the pattern that is occurring.

One of the problems with our judicial system is that when people commit criminal acts, they are sometimes not punished until years later. Intellectually they may know the reason for their punishment, but the pattern of behavior that generated this problem in the first place is still intact—it has not been interrupted, nor does it have any pain linked to it.

This is the only way to truly change our behaviors and emotions long term. We must train our brains to do the things that are effective, not intellectually but neurologically. The challenge, of course, is that most of us don't realize that we're all conditioning each other and shaping each other's behaviors constantly. Often, we're conditioning people negatively instead of positively.

A simple example of this occurred with my daughter Jolie's ex-boyfriend. Jolie was very busy with school, dance, and a play she was in. He wanted her to call him every single day, and when she missed a few days and then called him, he gave her tremendous amounts of pain. He clearly wanted her to call more frequently, yet his strategy for reinforcement was to badger and berate her when she did call.

Have you ever been guilty of this? If you want your boyfriend, girl-friend, spouse, or significant other to call you more often, how effective do you think it would be to nag them to call? When they finally do call, do you greet them with statements like, "Oh, so you finally picked up the phone! Will wonders never cease? Why do I always have to be the one who makes the call?"

What you're doing is training him or her *not* to call you! You're giving pain right after they do the very thing you want. What will happen as a result of this? Pain will be linked to calling you; he or she will avoid it even more in the future. In Jolie's case, this pattern was continuous, going on for months until Jolie felt that she couldn't win. If she didn't call, she'd get pain. If she did call, she'd get pain. As you might guess, this pattern of negative reinforcement permeated many aspects of their rela-tionship and, eventually, the relationship ended.

If you truly want someone to call you, then when they do call, you need to respond with delight. If you tell them how much you miss them, how much you love them, how grateful you are to talk with them, do you think that they'll be more inclined to call again? Remember, link pleasure to any behavior you want someone to repeat.

In my consulting with companies across the United States, I've noted that most companies try to motivate their employees by using negative reinforcement as their primary strategy, trying to use fear of punishment as its prime motivator. This will work in the short term, but not in the long term. Sooner or later, companies run into the same problems that eastern Europe has: people will live in fear only for so long before they revolt.

The second major strategy companies use is financial incentives. While this is an excellent idea and is usually appreciated, there is a limit to its effectiveness. There is a point of diminishing return at which all the additional incentives don't really induce a greater quality of work from people. In fact, most companies find that there's a limit to what they can do in this area. If one constantly reinforces with money, people begin to expect that when they do something of great value, they must have an immediate economic return. They begin to work strictly for financial reward and won't do anything unless they get it, surpassing and stripping the capacity of the business to keep up with the economic demands of its employees.

The third and most powerful way to motivate people is through personal development. By helping your employees to grow and expand personally, they begin to feel passionate about life, people, and their jobs. This makes them want to contribute more. They do it out of a sense of personal pride rather than pressure from the outside. This doesn't mean you shouldn't have an incentive program; just make sure you have the most powerful incentive of all, which is to help people expand and grow.

> *"Good and evil, reward and punishment, are the only motives to a rational creature: these are the spur and reins whereby all mankind are set on work, and guided."*
> —JOHN LOCKE

SCHEDULE YOUR REINFORCEMENT SO CHANGE LASTS!

When you're beginning to establish a new behavior or a new emotional pattern, it's very important that you reinforce yourself or anyone else you're trying to establish these new patterns for. In the beginning, every time you perform the desired behavior (for example, pushing a plate away with food still on it), you need to give yourself acknowledgement— pleasurable reinforcement of a type that you truly will appreciate and enjoy. However, if you reinforce the behavior every time thereafter, even- tually your rewards will no longer be effective or appreciated. What at one time was a unique and enjoyable surprise will become an expected norm.

Because of my commitment to help those in need, whenever I go through airports, I invariably give to those who request money. I'll never forget one particular gentleman who had staked his claim in a particular spot in front of a terminal I frequented. Every time I came by, I gave him some money. On one morning, I was very rushed and had no money in my pocket. As I walked quickly by, I smiled and said, "Hello! I'm sorry, but I don't have any money today." He became angry because I was no longer giving him something that he once was thrilled to receive from me.

You and I need to remember that the element of pleasant surprise is one of the most enjoyable experiences that a human being can have. It's so much more important than most of us realize. This is the very reason why, if you want a behavior to last long-term, it's invaluable that you understand and utilize what's known as a **variable schedule of rein- forcement**.

Let me give you a simple example from dolphin training. In the beginning, to train a dolphin to jump, trainers wait for the dolphin to jump on its own. They catch the animals doing something right and then reward it with a fish. By doing this each time the dolphin jumps on its own, the dolphin eventually makes the neuro-association that if he jumps, he'll get a fish. This pairing of pleasure to a behavior that the trainer desires allows the trainer to condition the dolphin to jump again and again.

Eventually, though, the trainer will give the fish only when the dol- phin jumps higher. By slowly raising the standards, the trainer can shape the dolphin's behavior. Here's the key: **if the dolphin is always re- warded, he may become *habituated* and will no longer give 100 percent**. So, in the future, the dolphin is rewarded sometimes after the first jump or perhaps after the fifth, or after the second. A dolphin is never sure which jump will be rewarded. This sense of anticipation that a reward *may* be given, coupled with the uncertainty as to which try will be rewarded, causes the dolphin to consistently give its full effort. The reward is never taken for granted.

This is the identical force that drives people to gamble. Once they've gambled and been rewarded—and linked intense pleasure to the reward—that excitement and anticipation pushes them to go forward. When they haven't been rewarded in a while, often they have an even stronger sense that *this time* they'll be rewarded. What drives the gambler is the possibility of winning again. If a person were to gamble without ever receiving a reward, they would give up. However, receiving just a few small rewards, winning just a few hands, "earning" back just some of their money, keeps them in a state of anticipation that they could hit the jackpot.

This is why people who discontinue a bad habit (like smoking or gambling) for a period of months, and then decide to have "just one more hit," are actually reinforcing the very pattern that they're trying to break and making it much more difficult to be free of the habit for a lifetime. If you smoke one more cigarette, you're stimulating your nervous system to expect that in the future you'll reward yourself this way again. You're keeping that neuro-association highly active and, in fact, strengthening the very habit you're trying to break!

If you want to reinforce a person's behavior long term, you may want to utilize what's known as a **fixed schedule of reinforcement**. In her book, Karen Pryor describes training a dolphin to make ten jumps. In order to make sure that the dolphin consistently jumps ten times, you'll want to reward them on the tenth jump each and every time. You can't demand too many behaviors before reinforcement occurs, but if the dolphin is rewarded *only* on the tenth jump, the dolphin soon learns that it does not need to make as great an effort on the previous nine jumps, and quality declines.

This is the same reaction we might see in people who receive a paycheck every two weeks. Employees know there are certain things expected of them, for which they receive regular compensation. The challenge is that many people learn to do only the minimum necessary to receive the reward because there is no surprise. In the workplace, pay is expected, of course. But if it is the only reward, then workers will do only what is expected and the minimum they can do for the pay.

However, if there are occasional surprises—like recognition, bonuses, promotions, and other perks—then they will put forth the extra effort, in hopes and anticipation that they'll be rewarded and acknowledged. Remember, these surprises must not be *predictable,* or they become ineffective and taken for granted—this expectation will drive the behavior. Vary your rewards, and you'll see greater results in making change within yourself or anyone you're managing.

There is a third tool for reinforcement that can also be used: it's known as the **jackpot**. A jackpot can help you to compound the reinforcement. If, for example, once in a rare while you give a dolphin not only one fish, but *three or four*, for its behavior, it makes the dolphin anticipate even more that if it just puts out that extra effort, there might be a huge reward. This compels the dolphin to consistently give more of itself.

Human beings respond similarly. Often in companies, when people are given a reward that's much greater than anticipated, it can create great motivation to continue to give great service in the future with the anticipation that they may receive an even greater reward. This same principle can work like magic with your children!

CREATE A "JUMP-START"

The jackpot principle can also be used with someone who's not motivated to produce any results whatsoever. Again, if dolphin trainers have an animal which they seem to be unable to motivate at all, they will sometimes give it a dozen fish, even though it has done nothing to earn it. The pleasure that this creates is sometimes enough to break the dolphin's old pattern and put it into a state of such pleasure that it then becomes willing to be trained. Again, human beings are similar. If someone who seems not to have done anything right is suddenly given a reward, just out of compassion and caring, this can stimulate them to take on new levels and types of behavior and performance.

The most important thing to remember about conditioning, however, is to reinforce the desired behavior immediately. The minute you find yourself responding playfully to what used to frustrate you, reinforce yourself. Do it again and create even more pleasure. Laugh a bit. Remember, each time you create a strong emotional feeling, either positive or negative, you're creating a connection in your nervous system. If you'll repeat that pattern again and again, visualizing the same imagery that makes you feel strong or makes you laugh, you'll find it easier to be strong or to laugh in the future. The pattern will be well established.

The minute you, or anyone you want to reinforce, does something right, create an immediate reward. Reinforce it consistently with the kind of reward that you, or that individual, personally want or desire most. Give yourself the emotional reward of turning on your favorite music or smiling or seeing yourself accomplishing your goals. **Conditioning is critical. This is how we produce consistent results. Once again, remember that any pattern of emotional behavior that is reinforced or rewarded on a consistent basis will become conditioned and automatic. Any pattern that we fail to reinforce will eventually dissipate.**

Now that you've accomplished the first five steps, let's go to the final step. . . .

NAC MASTER STEP 6

Test It!

Let's review what you've accomplished: you've decided upon the new pattern of emotion or behavior that you desire; you've gotten leverage on yourself to change it; you've interrupted the old pattern; you've found a new alternative; and you've conditioned it until it's consistent. The only step left is to test it to make sure that it's going to work in the future.

One of the ways of doing this that's taught in Neuro-Linguistic Programming is "future pacing." This means that you imagine the situation that used to frustrate you, for example, and notice if in fact it still makes you feel frustrated or if your new pattern of feeling "fascinated" has replaced it. If normally you still have this urge to smoke every time you feel overwhelmed, imagine yourself in an overwhelming situation and notice if instead you have an urge to read or run or whatever new alternative you've conditioned. By imagining the same stimuli that used to trigger your old emotion or behavior and noting that you do feel certain that your new empowering alternative is automatic, you will know that this new pattern will work for you in the future.

In addition, you must test the ecology of the change you've just made. The word "ecology" implies the study of consequences. What will the impact of these changes you've made in yourself have on those around you? Will they support your business and personal relationships? Make certain that this new pattern will be appropriate, based on your current lifestyle, beliefs, and values.

On the next page is a simple checklist that you can use to help yourself be certain that your new success pattern will last and that it's appropriate.

If your attempt at creating this pattern didn't last, you need to recycle back to Step 1. **Are you really clear about what you want and why you want it?**

Review Step 2; most people who've tried unsuccessfully to make a change usually don't have enough leverage. You may need to make a public commitment in order to **get more leverage on yourself**. Make it to those people who will *not* let you off the hook!

If you feel that there's enough leverage, check Step 3: if you know what you want and you've got enough leverage, it's very possible that you're like the fly beating itself repeatedly against the window pane. You've done the same things over and over again, with more and more intensity, but you haven't changed your approach. **You must interrupt your pattern**.

If you feel that all these steps are in place, go to Step 4. If your efforts

THE ECOLOGY CHECK

1. **Make certain pain is fully associated with the old pattern.**
   When you think of your old behavior or feelings, do you picture
   and feel things that are painful now instead of pleasurable?
2. **Make certain pleasure is fully associated with the new pattern.**
   When you think of your new behavior or feelings, do you picture
   and feel things that are pleasurable now instead of painful?
3. **Align with your values, beliefs, and rules.**
   Is the new behavior or feeling consistent with the values, beliefs,
   and rules in your life? (We will discuss these in later chapters.)
4. **Make sure the benefits of the old pattern have been main-
   tained.**
   Will the new behavior or feeling still allow you to get benefits and
   feelings of pleasure that you used to get from the old pattern?
5. **Future pace—Imagine yourself behaving in this new way in
   the future.**
   Imagine the thing that would have triggered you to adopt the old
   pattern. Feel certain that you can use your new pattern instead of
   the old one.

still have not produced a change, you're clearly demonstrating that you've
left out this step. **Find a new, empowering alternative for getting
yourself out of pain and into pleasure that is as powerful and *convenient* as your old approach was.** All this means is that you now have
an opportunity to explore being a little more creative. Find a role model—
somebody else who's been able to eliminate this habit or negative set of
emotions that you want to change.

If you've started to make a change, but then not followed through,
you obviously haven't reinforced your pattern with enough pleasure. Use
Step 5, conditioning. **Utilize both variable and fixed schedules of
reinforcement to make sure that your new, empowering pattern lasts.**

The six steps of NAC can be used for anything: challenges with relationships, problems in business, being stuck in a pattern of yelling at your
children. Let's say you worry too much about things over which you have
no control. How can you use the six steps to change this disempowering
pattern?

   1) Ask yourself, "What do I want to do instead of worry?"
   2) Get leverage on yourself and realize what worry does to destroy

"Hey, bucko . . . I'm through begging."

your life. Bring it to a threshold; see what it would cost you ultimately in your life so that you're not willing to pay that price anymore. Imagine the joy of getting this monkey off your back and being truly free once and for all!

3) Interrupt the pattern! Every time you worry, break the pattern by being totally outrageous. Stick your finger up your nose, or belt out "Oh, What a Beautiful Morning!" at the top of your lungs.

4) Create an empowering alternative. What will you do instead of worry? Pull out your journal and write down a plan of what you can do immediately instead. Maybe you can go for a run, and while you're running, you can think of new solutions.

5) Condition the new pattern; vividly imagine and rehearse this new pattern with tremendous emotional intensity and repetition until this new thought, behavior or emotional pattern is automatic. Reinforce yourself by taking the first step: see yourself succeding again and again. Seeing

the results in advance can give you the pleasure you desire. Again, use repetition and emotional intensity to condition the new pattern until it's consistent.

6) Test it and see if it works. Think about the situation that used to worry you, and see that you no longer worry in this situation.

You can even use these same six master steps of NAC to negotiate a contract.

1) The first step is to lay the groundwork. Get clear about what you want and what has prevented you from getting it. What does the other person want? What's in it for both of you? How will you know you have a successful contract?

2) Get leverage by getting that person to link pain to not making the deal, and pleasure to making it.

3) Interrupt the pattern of any belief or idea that's keeping the deal from moving ahead.

4) Create an alternative that neither of you thought of before that will meet both your needs.

5) Reinforce that alternative by constantly reinforcing the pleasure and the positive impact of this alternative.

6) See if it's going to work out for everybody, a win-win situation. If so, negotiate to a successful conclusion.

The same principles can be used to get the kids to clean their rooms, improve the quality of your marriage, boost your company's level of quality, get more enjoyment out of your job, and make your country a better place to live.

By the way, sometimes our kids use these same six steps on us in abbreviated form. Remember what I said: if you get enough leverage and interrupt somebody's pattern strongly enough, they'll find a new pattern and condition it. A friend of mine tried almost everything he knew to stop smoking. Finally his pattern was broken. How? His six-year-old daughter walked in one day while he was lighting up. She knew what she wanted, she had massive leverage, and she interrupted his pattern by crying, "Daddy, please stop killing yourself!"

"Honey," he said, "what are you talking about? What's wrong?" She repeated herself. He said, "Honey, I'm not killing myself." She nodded her head, pointed to the cigarette and sobbed, "Daddy, please stop killing yourself! I want you to be there . . . *when I get m-a-r-r-i-e-d* . . ."

This was a man who'd tried to quit dozens of times, and nothing had worked—until then. The cigarettes were out the door that day, and he hasn't smoked since. With his heartstrings firmly grasped in her tiny hands, she instantly got what she wanted. Since then he's found many alternatives to smoking that give him the same pleasurable sensations.

If all you do is the first three steps of NAC, that may be enough to create tremendous change. Once you've decided what you want, gained leverage, and interrupted the pattern, life often provides you with new ways of looking at things. And if the leverage is strong enough, you'll be compelled to find a new pattern and condition it—and you can pretty much count on the world to give you the test.

Now you have the NAC of change! The key is to use it. But you won't unless you know what you're using it for. You've got to know what you truly desire; you must find . . .

7
HOW TO GET WHAT YOU REALLY WANT

*"All emotions are pure which gather you and lift you up; that emotion is impure which seizes only **one** side of your being and so distorts you."*
—RAINER MARIA RILKE

"Gimme my first attack."* Elvis Presley always called for his first hit this way, fulfilling a bizarre daily ritual designed to make sure the King of Heartbreak Hotel got to sleep after a strenuous night performing. Elvis's assistant would open the first envelope and give him "the usual": a rainbow-colored assortment of barbiturates (Amytal, Carbrital, Nembutal or Seconal), Quaaludes, Valium, and Placidyl, followed by three shots of Demerol injected just below his bare shoulder blades.

Before he went to sleep, Elvis's kitchen staff, which was on duty around the clock, would go to work. It then became a race to see how much food the King could consume before falling asleep. Typically, he'd eat three cheeseburgers and six or seven banana splits before nodding off. Often, his assistants would have to dislodge food from his windpipe to keep him from choking to death. Elvis would then sleep for about four hours before stirring.

So groggy that he had to be carried to the bathroom, he would make his second request by feebly tugging at his assistant's shirt. Elvis was unable to take the drugs himself, so the aide would pop the pills into his mouth, and carefully pour water down his throat.

Elvis was rarely able to ask for the third attack. Instead, as a matter of routine, an aide would administer the dosage and let him continue to sleep until mid-afternoon, when the bloated King would jump-start his body by popping Dexedrine and stuffing cocaine-soaked swabs up his nose before taking to the stage again.

* Goldman, Albert, "Down at the End of Lonely Street," *Life* magazine, June 1990.

On the day of his death, Elvis remained lucid and saved all of the "attacks" for one fatal dose. Why would a man, so universally adored by fans and seeming to have it all, regularly abuse his body and then take his own life in such a horrific way? According to David Stanley, Elvis's half brother, it was because he much preferred being drugged and numb to being conscious and miserable.*

Unfortunately it's not difficult to think of other famous figures —people at the top of their professions in the arts and business—who also brought about their own demise, either directly or indirectly. Think of writers like Ernest Hemingway and Sylvia Plath, actors like William Holden and Freddie Prinze, singers like Mama Cass Elliot and Janis Joplin. What do these people have in common? First, they're no longer here, and we all experienced the loss. Second, they were all sold a bill of goods that said, "Someday, someone, somehow, something . . . and then I'll be happy." But when they achieved success, when they arrived on Easy Street and got a firsthand look at the American Dream, they found that happiness still eluded them. So they continued to chase it, keeping the pain of existence at bay by drinking, smoking, overeating, until finally they got the oblivion they craved. They never discovered the true source of happiness.

What these people demonstrated is something all too familiar to so many people: 1) They didn't know what they really wanted out of life, so they distracted themselves with a variety of artificial mood alterants. 2) They developed not just neurological pathways, but *expressways* to pain. And their habits were driving them down these highways on a regular basis. Despite achieving the levels of success they'd once only dreamed of, and despite being surrounded by the love and admiration of millions of fans, they had far more references for pain. They became quite adept at generating it quickly and easily because they'd made virtual trunk lines to it. 3) They didn't know how to make themselves feel good. They had to turn to some outside force to help them deal with the present. 4) They never learned the nuts and bolts of how to consciously direct the focus of their own minds. They allowed the pain and pleasure of their environments to control them rather than taking control themselves.

Now, contrast these stories with a letter I received recently from a woman who utilized my work to utterly and completely change the quality of her life:

Dear Tony,
I had been severely abused my entire life from infancy until the death of
my second husband. As a result of the abuse and severe trauma, I devel-

* Goldman, Albert, "Down at the End of Lonely Street."

oped a mental illness known as Multiple Personality Disorder with forty-nine different personalities. None of my personalities knew about the others, or what had happened in each of their lives.

The only relief I had in forty-nine years of living as a multiple was in the form of self-destructive behavior. I know it sounds strange, but self-mutilation used to give relief. After one of my many attempts at suicide, I was sent to the hospital and put under a doctor's care. In order to integrate the personalities, I had to go back to the original trauma that created each personality. That trauma had to be remembered, relived, and felt. Each of my alters handled a specific function, a selective ability to remember, and usually a single emotional tone. I worked with an expert in the field of MPD, and he helped me to integrate all forty-nine personalities into one. What kept me going through all of the different processes we used was feeling that many of my people were very unhappy and my life had become so chaotic (one alter did not know what the other was doing, and we found ourselves in all kinds of situations and places that when I switched, I had no memory of). We thought that by becoming one we would be happy—the ultimate goal.

That was my misconception. What a shocker! I lived a year of hell. I found myself very unhappy and grieving for each of my personalities. I missed each of my people and sometimes wanted them back the way they were. This was very difficult, and I made three more attempts at suicide that year, and again was admitted to a hospital.

During the past year, I happened to see your program on TV and ordered your thirty-day tape series, Personal Power. I listened to them over and over, grasping at anything that I could use. My breakthrough came when I started to listen to your monthly POW-ERTALKs. I learned things from you as a single being that I never learned as a multiple. I learned for the first time in fifty years that happiness comes from within. As a single being I now have the memories of the horrors that each of the forty-nine endured. When these memories come up I can look at them, and if they become overbearing, I can now change my point of focus as I learned from you, and not in a dissociative way as I had done before. No longer do I have to put myself in an amnesiac trance and switch to another person.

I am learning more and more about myself, and am learning how to live as a single being. I know that I have a long way to go and a lot of exploring to do. I am sorting out my goals and planning how to get there. For now, I have begun to lose weight and plan to be at goal weight for Christmas (a nice gift to me). I also know that

I would like to have a healthy, nonabusive relationship with a man. Previous to my hospital admittance, I worked full-time for IBM and had four businesses. Today, I am running a new business and am enjoying the increased sales I have been able to realize since my release from the hospital. I am getting to know my children and grandchildren, but most importantly, I'm getting to know me."
Sincerely,
Elizabeth Pietrzak*

WHAT DO YOU WANT?

Ask yourself what you truly want in life. Do you want a loving marriage, the respect of your children? Do you want plenty of money, fast cars, a thriving business, a house on the hill? Do you want to travel the world, visit exotic ports of call, see historical landmarks firsthand? Do you want to be idolized by millions as a rock musician or as a celebrity with your star on Hollywood Boulevard? Do you want to leave your mark for posterity as the inventor of a time travel machine? Do you want to work with Mother Teresa to save the world, or take a proactive role in making a measurable impact environmentally?

Whatever you desire or crave, perhaps you should ask yourself, "Why do I want these things?" Don't you want fine cars, for example, because you really desire the feelings of accomplishment and prestige you think they would bring? Why do you want a great family life? Is it because you think it will give you feelings of love, intimacy, connection, or warmth? Do you want to save the world because of the feelings of contribution and making a difference you believe this will give you? In short, then, *isn't it true that what you really want is simply to change the way you feel?* **What it all comes down to is the fact that you want these things or results because you see them as a means to achieving certain feelings, emotions, or states that you desire.**

When somebody kisses you, what makes you feel good in that moment? Is it wet tissue touching wet tissue that really triggers the feeling? Of course not! If that's true, kissing your *dog* would turn you on! All of our emotions are nothing but a flurry of biochemical storms in our brains—and we can spark them at any moment. **But first we must learn how to take control of them consciously instead of living in reaction.** Most of our emotional responses are learned responses to the environment. We've deliberately modeled some of them, and stumbled across others.

---

* Reprinted with permission. Today, this courageous woman is not only back at work but is also a hospital volunteer.

Simply being aware of these factors is the foundation for understanding the power of **state**. Without a doubt, everything you and I do, we do to avoid pain or gain pleasure, but we can instantly change what we *believe* will lead to pain or pleasure by redirecting our focus and changing our mental-emotional-physiological states. As I said in Chapter 3 of *Unlimited Power:*

> A state can be defined as the sum of millions of neurological processes happening within us—the sum total of our experience at any moment in time. Most of our states happen without any conscious direction on our part. We see something, and we respond to it by going into a state. It may be a resourceful and useful state, or an unresourceful and limiting state, but there's not much that most of us do to control it.

Have you ever found yourself unable to remember a friend's name? Or how to spell a "difficult" word like . . . "house"? How come you weren't able to do this? You certainly knew the answer. Is it because you're stupid? No, it's because you were in a stupid *state!* **The difference between acting badly or brilliantly is not based on your ability, but on the state of your mind and/or body in any given moment.** You can be gifted with the courage and determination of Marva Collins, the grace and flair of Fred Astaire, the strength and endurance of Nolan Ryan, the compassion and intellect of Albert Einstein—but if you continually submerge yourself in negative states, you'll never fulfill that promise of excellence.

However, if you know the secret of accessing your most resourceful states, you can literally work wonders. The state that you're in at any given moment determines your perceptions of reality and thus your decisions and behavior. In other words, **your behavior is not the result of your ability, but of the state that you're in at this moment.** To change your ability, change your state. To open up the multitude of resources that lie within you, put yourself in a state of resourcefulness and active expectancy—and watch miracles happen!

So how can we change our own emotional states? Think of your states as operating a lot like a TV set. In order to have "bright, vivid color with incredible sound," you need to plug in and turn on. Turning on your physiology is like giving the set the electricity it needs to operate. If you don't have the juice, you'll have no picture, no sound, just a blank screen. Similarly, if you don't turn on by using your entire body, in other words, your **physiology**, you may indeed find yourself unable to spell "house." Have you ever woken up and stumbled around, not able to think clearly or function until you moved around enough to get your blood flowing?

Once the "static" has cleared, you're turned on, and the ideas begin to flow. If you're in the wrong state, you're not going to get any reception, even if you've got the right ideas.

Of course, once you're plugged in, you've got to be tuned to the right channel to get what you really want. Mentally, you've got to focus on what empowers you. Whatever you focus on—whatever you tune in to—you will feel more intensely. So if you don't like what you're doing, maybe it's time to change the channel.

There are unlimited sensations, unlimited ways of looking at virtually anything in life. All of the sensations that you want are available all of the time, and all you've got to do is to tune in to the right channel. There are two primary ways, then, to change your emotional state: by changing the way you use your **physical body**, or by changing your **focus**.

PHYSIOLOGY: THE POWER OF MOVEMENT

One of the most powerful distinctions that I've made in the last ten years of my life is simply this: **Emotion is created by motion.** Everything that we feel is the result of how we use our bodies. Even the most minute changes in our facial expressions or our gestures will shift the way that we're feeling in any moment, and therefore the way we evaluate our lives—the way we think and the way we act.

Try something ridiculous with me for a second. Pretend you're a rather bored and humorless symphony conductor rhythmically swinging your arms in and out. Do it very s-l-o-w-l-y. Don't get too excited; just do it as a matter of r-o-u-t-i-n-e and make sure your face reflects a state of boredom. Notice how that feels. Now take your hands, clap them together explosively, and SNAP them back out as *fast* as you can with a big, silly grin on your face! Intensify this by adding the vocal movement of an outrageously loud and explosive sound—the movement of air through your chest, throat, and mouth will change how you feel even more radically. That motion and speed you've created, both in your body and your vocal chords, will instantly change the way you feel.

Every emotion you ever feel has specific physiology linked to it: posture, breathing, patterns of movement, facial expressions. For depression, these are certainly obvious. In *Unlimited Power*, I talked about the physical attributes of depression, where your eyes are focused, how you hold yourself, and so forth. Once you learn how you use your body when in certain emotional states, you can return to those states, or avoid them, simply by changing your physiology. The challenge is that most of us limit ourselves to just a few habitual patterns of physiology. We assume them automatically, not realizing how great a role they play in shaping our behavior from moment to moment.

We each have over eighty different muscles in our faces, and if these muscles get accustomed to expressing depression, boredom, or frustration, then this habitual muscular pattern literally begins to dictate our states, not to mention our physical character. I always have people in my Date With Destiny™ seminar write down all the emotions they feel in an average week, and out of the myriad possibilities, I've found that the average is *less than a dozen.* Why? Because most people have *limited patterns of physiology* that result in *limited patterns of expression.*

TYPES OF EMOTIONS AN INDIVIDUAL MIGHT FEEL IN A WEEK

Stressed out
Frustrated
Angry
Insecure
Lonely
Bored
Miserable
Happy
Relieved
Loved
Excited
Joyous

This is such a short menu of emotional choices when you consider the thousands of enticing states available. Take care not to limit yourself to such a short list! I suggest you take advantage of the whole buffet—try new things and cultivate a refined palate. How about experiencing more enthusiasm, fascination, cheerfulness, playfulness, intrigue, sensuality, desire, gratitude, enchantment, curiosity, creativity, capability, confidence, outrageousness, boldness, consideration, kindness, gentleness, humor . . . Why not come up with a long list of your own?

You can *experience any of these* just by changing the way you use your body! You can feel strong, you can smile, you can change anything in a minute just by laughing. You've heard the old adage, "Someday you'll look back on this and laugh." If that's true, why not look back and laugh now? Why wait? Wake your body up; learn to put it in pleasurable states consistently no matter what's happened. How? Create energy by the way you think of something over and over again, and you'll change the sensations you link to that situation in the future.

If you repeatedly use your body in weak ways, if you drop your shoulders on a regular basis, if you walk around like you're tired, you will *feel* tired. How could you do otherwise? **Your body leads your emotions.** The emotional state you're in then begins to affect your body, and it becomes a sort of endless loop. Notice how you're sitting even now. Sit up right now and create more energy in your body as you continue not only to read but also to master these principles.

What are some things you can do immediately to change your state and therefore how you feel and how you perform? Take deep breaths in through your nose and exhale strongly through your mouth. Put a huge grin on your face and smile at your children. If you really want to change your life, commit for the next seven days to spending one minute five times a day, grinning from ear to ear in the mirror. This will feel incredibly stupid, but remember, by this physical act, you will be constantly triggering this part of your brain and creating a neurological pathway to pleasure that will become habitual. So do it, and make it fun!

Better yet, go out for a skip instead of a jog. Skipping is such a powerful way to change your state because it does four things: 1) It's great exercise; 2) you'll have less stress on your body than running; 3) you won't be able to keep a serious look on your face; and 4) you'll entertain everybody who's driving by! So you'll be changing other people's states, too, by making them laugh.

What a powerful thing laughter is! My son Joshua has a friend named Matt who finds it so easy to laugh that it's infectious, and everyone who hears him starts laughing, too. If you really want to improve your life, *learn to laugh.* Along with your five smiles each day, make yourself laugh for no reason at all, three times each day for seven days.

In a recent poll conducted by *Entertainment Weekly* magazine, they found that 82 percent of the people who go to movies want to laugh, 7 percent want to cry, and 3 percent want to scream. This gives you an idea how we value the sensations of laughter over so many other things. And if you've read Norman Cousins's books, or Dr. Deepak Chopra's, or Dr. Bernie Siegel's, or studied psychoneuroimmunology at all, you know what laughter can do to the physical body to stimulate the immune system.

Why not find somebody who laughs and mirror them? Have some fun. Say, "Will you do me a favor? You've got a great laugh. Let me try and duplicate it. Coach me." I guarantee you'll crack each other up in the process! Breathe the way they breathe; take on their posture and body movements; use the same facial expressions; make the same sounds. You'll feel stupid when you start, but after a while you'll get into it, and you'll both be laughing hysterically because you both look so silly. But in the process, you'll begin to lay the neurological networking to create laughter on a regular basis. As you do this again and again, you'll find it very easy to laugh and you'll certainly have fun.

> *"We know too much and feel too little. At least we feel too little of those creative emotions from which a good life springs."*
> —BERTRAND RUSSELL

Anyone can continue to feel good if they *already* feel good, or if they're "on a roll"; it doesn't take much to accomplish this. But the real key in life is to be able to make yourself feel good when you *don't* feel good, or when you don't even *want* to feel good. Know that you can do this instantaneously by using your body as a tool to change state. Once you identify the physiology attached to a state, you can use it to create the states you desire at will. Years ago, I worked with John Denver, a man who impresses me not only with his musical ability but also because his private persona is absolutely in line with his public image. The reason he's succeeded is so clear; he's such an incredibly warm and caring man.

The reason I was working with him was that he was experiencing writer's block. We identified the times when he wrote his best songs, and discovered that their inspiration had come to him when he was doing something physical. Usually an entire song would flow through him after he'd skied down a mountain, flown his jet or his biplane, or driven his sportscar at high speeds. Usually speed was involved, and the physical adrenaline rush, along with the experience of focusing on the beauty of nature, were all a major part of his creative strategy. At the time, he was experiencing a few frustrations in some areas of his life and had not been involved in the same intense outdoor activity. Just by making this change and getting back into a strong physiology, he was able to restore the certainty and flow of his creativity immediately. **You and I have the capacity to make changes like this at any time.** Just by changing our physiology, we can change our level of performance. Our capability is always there, and what we've got to do is put ourselves into states where it is accessible.

The key to success, then, is to **create patterns of movement that create confidence, a sense of strength, flexibility, a sense of personal power, and fun.** Realize that stagnation comes from lack of movement.

Can you think of an old person, someone who doesn't "get around much anymore"? Getting old is not a matter of age; it's a lack of movement. And the ultimate lack of movement is death.

If you see children walking along the sidewalk after a rain, and there's a puddle in front of them, what are they going to do when they get to that puddle? They're going to jump in! They're going to laugh, splash around, and have a good time. What does an older person do? Walk around it? No, they won't just walk around it—they'll complain the whole time! You want to live differently. You want to live with a spring in your step, a smile on your face. Why not make cheerfulness, outrageousness, playfulness a new priority for yourself? Make feeling good your expectation. You don't have to have a reason to feel good—you're alive; you can feel good *for no reason at all!*

FOCUS: THE POWER OF CONCENTRATION

If you wanted to, couldn't you get depressed at a moment's notice? You bet you could, **just by focusing** on something in your past that was horrible. We all have some experience in our past that's pretty bad, don't we? If you focus on it enough, and you picture it and think about it, pretty soon you'll start to feel it. Have you ever gone to an awful movie? Would you go back to that awful movie hundreds of times? Of course not. Why? Because it wouldn't *feel good* to do this! Then why would you go back to the awful movies *in your head* on a regular basis? Why watch yourself in your least favorite roles, playing against your least favorite leading lady or man? Why play out business disasters or bad career decisions again and again? Of course, these "B" movies are not limited only to your past experience. You can focus on something right now that you *think* you're missing out on, and feel bad. Better yet, you can focus on something that hasn't even happened yet, *and feel bad about it in advance!* Though you may laugh at this now, unfortunately that's what most of us do day to day.

If you wanted to feel like you were in ecstasy right now, could you? You could do this just as easily. Could you focus on or remember a time when you were in absolute, total ecstasy? Could you focus on how your body felt? Could you remember it with such vivid detail that you are fully associated to those feelings again? You bet you could. Or you could focus on things you're ecstatic about in your life right now, on what you feel is great in your life. And again, you could focus on things that haven't happened yet, *and feel good about them in advance*. This is the power that goals offer and why we'll be focusing on them in Chapter 12.

WHATEVER WE FOCUS ON <u>BECOMES</u> OUR IDEA OF REALITY

The truth is that very few things are absolute. Usually, how you feel about things, and the meaning of a particular experience, is all dependent upon your focus. Elizabeth, the woman with Multiple Personality Disorder, had been in pain constantly. Her escape route was to create a new personality for each incident that had to be handled emotionally. It allowed her to change her focus by seeing the problem through "somebody else's" eyes. Yet she still felt pain even after integration. It wasn't until she learned how to control her state by consciously changing her physiology and her focus that she was able to take control of her life.

Focus is not true reality, because it's one view; it's only one perception of the way things really are. Think of that view—the power of our focus—as being a camera lens. The camera lens shows only the picture and angle of what you are focused on. Because of that, photographs you take can easily distort reality, presenting only a small portion of the big picture.

Suppose you went to a party with your camera, and you sat in one corner, focused on a group of people who were arguing. How would that party be represented? It would be pictured as an unpleasant, frustrating party where no one had a good time and everyone was fighting. And it's important for us to remember that how we represent things in our minds will determine how we feel. But what if you were to focus your camera on another end of the room where people were laughing and telling jokes and having a great time? It would be shown to have been the best party of all, with everyone getting along famously!

This is why there is so much turmoil over "unauthorized" biographies: they are only one person's perception of another's life. And often, this view is offered by people whose jealousy gives them a vested interest in distorting things. The problem is, the biography's view is limited only to the author's "camera angle," and we all know that cameras distort reality, that a close-up can make things look bigger than they really are. And when manipulated expertly, a camera can minimize or blur important parts of the reality. To paraphrase Ralph Waldo Emerson, each of us sees in others what we carry in our own hearts.

MEANING IS OFTEN A MATTER OF FOCUS

If you've scheduled a business meeting, and someone is not there on time, how you feel is based strictly on what you focus on. Do you represent in your mind that the reason they are not there is that they don't care, or do you interpret it as their having great difficulties in getting to the meeting? Whichever you focus on will definitely affect your emotions. What if you were upset with them, and the real reason they were late is that they were fighting to get a better bid on the business proposal they were bringing you? Remember, whatever we focus on will determine how we feel. Maybe we shouldn't jump to conclusions; we should choose what to focus on very carefully.

Focus determines whether you perceive your reality as good or bad, whether you feel happy or sad. A fantastic metaphor for the power of focus is racing cars—a real passion for me. Driving a Formula race car can sometimes make flying a jet helicopter seem like a very relaxing experience! In a race car you cannot allow your focus to wander even for a moment from your outcome. Your attention can't be limited to where you are; neither can it be stuck in the past or fixed too far in the future. While remaining fully aware of where you are, you have to be *anticipating* what's about to happen in the near future.

This was one of the first lessons I learned when I started racing school. The instructors put me in what's called a "skid car"—an automobile that has a computer built into it with hydraulic lifts that can pull any wheel off the ground on a moment's signal from the instructor. The number-one fundamental they teach in driving is: **Focus on where you want to go,** *not* **on what you fear.**

If you start to skid out of control, the tendency, of course, is to look at the wall. But if you keep focusing on it, that's exactly where you'll end up. Drivers know that you go where you look; you travel in the direction of your focus. If you resist your fear, have faith, and focus on where you want to go, your actions will take you in that direction, and if it's possible to turn out of it, you will—but you stand no chance if you focus on what you fear. Invariably people say, "What if you're going to crash anyway?" The answer is that you *increase your chances* by focusing on what you want. Focusing on the solution is always to your benefit. If you have too much momentum in the direction of the wall, then focusing on the problem just before the crash is not going to help you anyway.

When the instructors first explained this to me, I nodded my head and thought, "Of course! I know all about this. After all, I teach this stuff." My first time out on the road I was screaming along, and all of a sudden, unbeknownst to me, they pushed the button. I started to skid out of control. Where do you think my eyes went? You bet! Right at the wall! In the final seconds, I was terrified because I knew I was going to hit it. The instructor grabbed my head and yanked it to the left, forcing me to look in the direction I needed to go. We kept skidding, and I knew we were going to crash, but I was forced to look only in the direction I wanted to go. Sure enough, as I looked in that direction, I couldn't help but turn the wheel accordingly. It caught at the last moment, and we pulled out. You can imagine my relief!

One thing that's useful to know about all of this: when you change your focus, often you don't *immediately* change direction. Isn't that true in life as well? Often there's a lag time between when you redirect your focus and when your body and your life's experience catch up. That's all the more reason to start focusing on what you want quicker and not wait any longer with the problem.

Did I learn my lesson? No. I'd had an experience, but I had not created a strong enough neuro-association. I had to condition in the new pattern. So sure enough, the next time I headed for the wall, the instructor had to loudly remind me to look at my goal. On the third time, though, I turned my head deliberately and consciously. I trusted it, and it worked. After doing it enough times, now when I go into a skid, wham! my head goes where I want it to go, the wheel turns, and my car follows. Does this guarantee I'll always succeed by controlling my focus? No. Does it increase my chances? One hundredfold!

The same thing is true in life. In later chapters, you'll learn some ways to make sure you condition your focus to be positive. For now, realize that you've got to discipline your mind. A mind out of control will play tricks on you. Directed, it's your greatest friend.

> *"Ask and you will receive. Seek and you will find;*
> *knock, and it will be opened to you."*
> —MATTHEW 7:7

The most powerful way to control focus is through the use of questions. For whatever you ask, your brain provides an answer; whatever you look for, you'll find. If you ask, "Why is this person taking advantage of me?" you're going to focus on how you're being taken advantage of, whether it's true or not. If you ask, "How can I turn this around?" you'll get a more empowering answer. Questions are such a powerful tool for changing your life, I've reserved the next chapter to talk exclusively about them. They are one of the most powerful and simple ways to change the way you're feeling about virtually anything, and thus change the direction of your life at a moment's notice. Questions provide the key to unlocking our unlimited potential.

One of the best illustrations of this is the story of a young man who grew up in Alabama. About fifteen years ago, a seventh-grade bully picked a fight with him, punched him in the nose and knocked him out. When the boy regained consciousness, he vowed to get revenge and kill the bully. He went home, grabbed his mother's .22, and set out to find his target. In a matter of moments, his destiny hung in the balance.

With the bully in his gun sight, he could simply fire and his schoolmate would be history. But at that very instant, he asked himself a question: What will happen to me if I pull the trigger? And another image came into focus: a picture as painful as any imaginable. In that split second which would take the boy's life in one of two very different directions, he visualized, with chilling clarity, what it would be like to go to jail. He pictured having to stay up all night to keep the other prisoners from raping him. That potential pain was greater than the anticipation of revenge. He reaimed his gun, and shot a tree.

This boy was Bo Jackson, and as he describes this scene in his biography, there's no question that at that pivot point in his life, the pain associated with prison was a force more powerful than the pleasure of satisfaction he thought killing the other boy would bring. One change in focus, one decision about pain and pleasure, probably made the difference between a kid with no future and one of the greatest athletic success stories of our time.

> *"As the fletcher whittles and makes straight his arrows, so the master directs his straying thoughts."*
> —THE BUDDHA

IT'S NOT ONLY WHAT YOU FOCUS ON BUT HOW . . .

Our experience of the world is created by gathering information through the use of our five senses. However, each of us tends to develop a favorite mode of focus, or a modality, as it is often called. Some people are more impacted, for example, by what they see; their visual system tends to be more dominant. For others, sounds are the trigger for the greatest of life's experiences, while for still others, feelings are the foundation.

Even within each of these modes of experience, though, there are specific elements of pictures, sounds, or other sensations that can be changed in order to increase or decrease the intensity of our experience. These foundational ingredients are called **submodalities**.* For example, you can make a picture in your mind and then take any aspect of that image (a submodality), and change it to change your feelings about it. You can brighten the picture, immediately changing the amount of intensity you feel about the experience. This is known as changing a submodality. Probably the greatest expert in submodalities is Richard Bandler, co-founder of Neuro-Linguistic Programming. The lineage of experts on this dates back to the foundational work on the five senses done by Aristotle, which categorizes perception models.

You can radically raise or lower your intensity of feeling about anything by manipulating submodalities. They affect how you feel about virtually anything, whether you feel joy, frustration, wonder, or despair. Understanding them enables you to not only change how you feel about any experience in your life, but to *change* what it means to you and thus *what you can do about it.*

One image I've found very useful is to think of submodalities as the grocery store UPC bar codes, those clusters of little black lines that have replaced price tags in just about every supermarket you patronize today. The codes look insignificant, yet when pulled across the checkout scanner, they tell the computer what the item is, how much it costs, how its sale affects the inventory, and so on. Submodalities work the same way. When pulled across the scanner of the computer we call the brain, they tell the brain what this thing is, how to feel about it, and what to do. You have your own bar codes, and there is a list of them coming up along with questions to ask to determine which of them you use.

For example, if you tend to focus upon your visual modalities, the amount of enjoyment you get from a particular memory is probably a direct consequence of the submodalities of size, color, brightness, distance, and amount of movement in the visual image you've made of it. If you represent it to yourself with auditory submodalities, then how you feel depends on the volume, tempo, pitch, tonality, and other such factors you attach to it. For example, in order for some people to feel motivated, they have to tune in a certain channel *first.* If their favorite channel is visual, then focusing on the visual elements of a situation gives them more emotional intensity about it. For other people it's the auditory or kinesthetic channels. And for some, the best strategy works like a combination lock. First the visual lock has to be aligned, then the auditory, then the kinesthetic. All three dials have to be lined up in the right place and the right order for the vault to open.

---

* For an even more detailed discussion of submodalities, see *Unlimited Power*, Chapters 6 and 8.

Once you're aware of this, you'll realize that people are constantly using words in their day-to-day language to tell you which system and which submodalities they are tuning in. Listen to the ways they describe their experience, and take it literally. (For example, in the last two sentences I used the terms "tuning in" and "listen"—clearly these are auditory examples.)

How many times have you heard someone say, "I can't picture doing that"? They're telling you what the problem is: if they *did* picture doing it, they'd go into a state where they'd feel like they could make it happen. Someone may have once said to you, "You're blowing things out of proportion." If you're really upset, they may be right. You may be taking images in your mind and making them much bigger, which tends to intensify the experience. If someone says, "This is weighing heavily upon me," you can assist them by helping them feel lighter about the situation and thereby get them in a better state to deal with it. If someone says, "I'm just tuning you guys out," you've got to get them to tune back in so they can change states. **Our ability to change the way we feel depends upon our ability to change our submodalities.** We must learn to take control of the various elements with which we represent experiences and change them in ways that support our outcomes. For example, have you ever found yourself saying you need to "get distance" from a problem? I'd like you to try something, if you would. Think of a situation that is challenging you currently. Make a picture of it in your mind, then imagine pushing that picture farther and farther away from yourself. Stand above it and look down upon the problem with a new perspective. What happens to your emotional intensity? For most people, it drops. What if the image becomes dimmer, or smaller? Now take the picture of the problem and make it bigger, brighter, and closer. For most people, this intensifies it. Push it back out and watch the sun melt it. A simple change in any one of these elements is like changing the ingredients in a recipe. They're definitely going to alter what you finally experience in your body. Although I spoke about submodalities in great depth in *Unlimited Power,* I'm reviewing the topic here because I want to make sure you grasp this distinction. It's critical to understanding much of the other work we'll be doing in this book.

Remember, how you feel about things is instantly changed by a shift in submodalities. For example, think of something that happened yesterday. Just for a moment, picture that experience. Take the image of this memory and put it behind you. Gradually push it back until it's *miles* behind you, a tiny, dim dot far off in the darkness. Does it feel like it happened yesterday, or a long time ago? If the memory is great, bring it back. Otherwise, leave it there! Who needs to focus on this memory? By contrast, you've had some incredibly wonderful experiences in your life.

COMMON EXPRESSIONS BASED ON:

Visual Submodalities—

That really brightens my day.
That puts things in a better perspective.
That's a top priority.
This guy has a checkered past.
Let's look at the big picture.
This problem keeps staring me in the face.

Auditory Submodalities—

He's constantly giving me static about that.
The problem is screaming at me.
I hear you loud and clear.
It brought everything we were doing to a screeching halt.
The guy is really offbeat.
That sounds great.

Kinesthetic Submodalities—

That guy is slimy.
The pressure's off/the pressure's on.
This thing is weighing on me.
I feel like I'm carrying this whole thing on my back.
This concert is really hot!
I'm absolutely immersed in this project.

Think of one right now, one that happened a long time ago. Recall the imagery of that experience. Bring it forward; put it in front of you. Make it big, bright, and colorful; make it three-dimensional. Step into your body as you were then and feel that experience right now as if you were there. Does it feel like it happened a long time ago, or is it something you're enjoying now? You see, even your experience of time can be changed by changing submodalities.

CREATE YOUR OWN BLUEPRINT

Discovering your submodalities is a fun process. You may want to do this on your own, although you may find it more fun to do with someone else. This will help with the accuracy, and if they're also reading this book, you'll have a lot to talk about and a partner in your commitment to personal mastery. So very quickly now, think of a time in your life when you had a very enjoyable experience, and do the following: Rate your enjoyment on a scale from 0–100, where 0 is no enjoyment at all and 100 is the peak level of enjoyment you could possibly experience. Let's say you came up with 80 on this emotional intensity scale. Now, go to the Checklist of Possible Submodalities (page 169), and let's discover which elements are apt to create more enjoyment in your life than others, more pleasure feelings than pain feelings.

Begin to evaluate each of the questions contained in the checklist against your experience. So, for example, as you remember this experience and focus on the **visual** submodalities, ask yourself, "Is it a movie or a still frame?" If it's a movie, notice how it feels. Does it feel good? Now, change it to its opposite. Make it a still frame and see what happens. Does your level of enjoyment drop? Does it drop significantly? By what percentage? As you made it a still frame, did it drop from 80 to 50, for example? Write down the impact that this change has made so you'll be able to utilize this distinction in the future.

Then, return the imagery to its initial form; that is, make it a movie again if that's what it was, so you feel like you're back at 80 again. Then go to the next question on your checklist. Is it in color or in black and white? If it was in black and white, notice how that feels. Now, again, do the opposite to it. Add color and see what happens. Does it raise your emotional intensity higher than 80? Write down the impact this has upon you emotionally. If it brings you to a 95, this might be a valuable thing to remember in the future. For example, when thinking about a task you usually avoid, if you add color to your image of it, you'll find that your positive emotional intensity grows immediately. Now drop the image back down to black and white, and again, notice what happens to your emotional intensity and what a big difference this makes. Remember to always finish by restoring the original state before going on to the next question. Put the color back into it; make it *brighter* than it was before, until you're virtually awash in vivid color.

In fact, brightness is an important submodality for most people; brightening things intensifies their emotion. If you think about the pleasurable experience right now, and make the image brighter and brighter, you probably feel better, don't you? (Of course, there are exceptions. If

CHECKLIST OF POSSIBLE SUBMODALITIES

Visual

1. Movie/still	Is it a movie or a still frame?
2. Color/black-and-white	Is it color or black-and-white?
3. Right/left/center	Is the image on the right, left, or center?
4. Up/middle/down	Is the image up, middle, or down?
5. Bright/dim/dark	Is the image bright, dim, or dark?
6. Lifesize/bigger/smaller	Is the image lifesize, bigger, or smaller?
7. Proximity	How close is the image to you?
8. Fast/medium/slow	Is the speed of the image fast, medium, or slow?
9. Specific focus?	Particular element focused on consistently?
10. In picture	Are you in the picture or watching from a distance?
11. Frame/panorama	Does the image have a frame or is it a panorama?
12. 3D/2D	Is it three-dimensional or two-dimensional?
13. Particular color	Is there a color that impacts you most?
14. Viewpoint	Are you looking down on it, up, from side, etc.?
15. Special trigger	Anything else that triggers strong feelings?

Auditory

1. Self/others	Are you saying something to yourself or hearing it from others?
2. Content	What specifically do you say or hear?
3. How it's said	How do you say or hear it?
4. Volume	How loud is it?
5. Tonality	What is the tonality?
6. Tempo	How fast is it?
7. Location	Where is the sound coming from?
8. Harmony/cacophony	Is the sound in harmony or cacophonous?
9. Regular/irregular	Is the sound regular or irregular?
10. Inflection	Is there inflection in the voice?
11. Certain words	Are certain words emphasized?
12. Duration	How long did the sound last?
13. Uniqueness	What is unique about the sound?
14. Special trigger	Anything else that triggers strong feelings?

Kinesthetic

1. Temperature change	Was there a temperature change? Hot or cold?
2. Texture change	Was there a texture change? Rough or smooth?
3. Rigid/flexible	Is it rigid or flexible?
4. Vibration	Is there vibration?
5. Pressure	Was there an increase or decrease in pressure?
6. Location of pressure	Where was the pressure located?
7. Tension/relaxation	Was there an increase in tension or relaxation?
8. Movement/direction/	Was there movement? If so, what was the direction and speed?
9. Breathing	Quality of breathing? Where did it start/end?
10. Weight	Is it heavy or light?
11. Steady/intermittent	Are the feelings steady or intermittent?
12. Size/shape change	Did it change size or shape?
13. Direction	Were feelings coming into body or going out?
14. Special trigger	Anything else that triggers strong feelings?

you're savoring the memory of a romantic moment, and suddenly turn all the lights on full blast, that may not be entirely appropriate.) What if you were to make the image dim, dark, and defocused? For most people, that makes it almost depressing. So make it brighter again; make it brilliant!

Continue down your list, noting which of these visual submodalities changes your emotional intensity the most. Then focus on the **auditory** submodalities. As you re-create the experience inside your head, how does it sound to you? What does raising the volume do to the level of pleasure you feel? How does increasing the tempo affect your enjoyment? By how much? Write it down, and shift as many other elements as you can think of. If what you're imagining is the sound of someone's voice, experiment with different inflections and accents, and notice what that does to the level of enjoyment you experience. If you change the quality of the sound from smooth and silky to rough and gravelly, what happens? Remember, finish by restoring the sounds to their original auditory form so that all the qualities continue to create pleasure for you.

Finally, focus on **kinesthetic** submodalities. As you remember this pleasurable experience, how does changing the various kinesthetic elements intensify or decrease your pleasure? Does raising the temperature make you feel more comfortable, or does it drive you up the wall? Focus on your breathing. Where are you breathing from? If you change the quality of your breaths from rapid and shallow to long and deep, how does this affect the quality of your experience? Notice what a difference this makes, and write it down. What about the texture of the image? Play around with it; change it from soft and fluffy, to wet and slimy, to gooey and sticky.

As you go through each of these changes, how does your body feel? Write it down. When you're done experimenting with the whole checklist of submodalities, go back and adjust until the most pleasurable image re-emerges; make it real enough so you can get your hands around it and squeeze the juice from it!

As you go through these exercises, you will quickly see that some of these submodalities are much more powerful for you than others. We're all made differently and have our own preferred ways of representing our experiences to ourselves. What you've just done was to create a blueprint that maps out how your brain is wired. Keep it and use it; it will come in handy some day—maybe today! By knowing which submodalities trigger you, you'll know how to increase your positive emotions and decrease your negative emotions.

For example, if you know that making something big and bright and bringing it close can tremendously intensify your emotion, you can get yourself motivated to do something by changing its imagery to match these criteria. You'll also know *not* to make your problems big, bright and close, or you'll intensify your negative emotions as well! You'll know how to instantly shake yourself out of a limiting state and into an energizing, empowering one. And you can be better equipped to continue your pathway to personal power.

Knowing the large part that submodalities play in your experience of reality is crucial in meeting challenges. For example, whether you feel confused or on track is a matter of submodalities. If you think about a time when you felt confused, remember whether you were representing the experience as a picture or a movie. Then compare it to a time when you felt that you understood something. Often when people feel confused, it's because they have a series of images in their heads that are piled up too closely together in a chaotic jumble because someone has been talking too rapidly or loudly. For other people, they get confused if things are taught to them too slowly. These individuals need to see images in movie form, to see how things relate to each other; otherwise the process is too disassociated. Do you see how understanding someone's submodalities can help you to teach them much more effectively?

The challenge is that most of us take our limiting patterns and make them big, bright, close, loud, or heavy—whichever submodalities we're most attuned to—and then wonder why we feel overwhelmed! If you've ever pulled yourself out of that state, it's probably because you or somebody else took that image and changed it, redirecting your focus. You finally said, "Oh, it's not that big a deal." Or you worked on one aspect of it, and by doing so, it didn't seem like such a big project to tackle. These are all simple strategies, many of which I laid out in *Unlimited Power*. In this chapter, I'm expecting to whet your appetite and make you aware of them.

CHANGE YOUR STATES AND YOU CHANGE YOUR LIFE

You can now change your state in so many ways, and they're all so simple. You can change your physiology immediately just by changing your breathing. You can change your focus by deciding what to focus on, or the order of things you focus on, or how you do it. You can change your submodalities. If you've been consistently focusing on the worst that could happen, there's no excuse for continuing to do that. Start now to focus on the best.

The key in life is to have so many ways to direct your life that it becomes an art. The challenge for most people is that they have only a few ways to change their state: they overeat, overdrink, oversleep, overshop, smoke, or take a drug—none of which empower us, and all of which can have disastrous and tragic consequences. The biggest problem is that many of these consequences are cumulative, so we don't even notice the danger until it's too late. That's what happened to Elvis Presley, and that, unfortunately, is also what's happening every day to so many other people. Picture an unfortunate frog in a kettle being slowly simmered to death. If he had been dropped into a fully boiling pot, the shock of the heat would have caused him to jump back out immediately—but with the heat slowly building, he never notices he's in danger until it's too late to get out.

The journey toward Niagara Falls begins when you don't control your states, because if you don't control your states, you won't be able to control your behavior. If there are things you need to accomplish but you can't get motivated, realize you're not in the appropriate state. That's not an excuse, though, that's a command! It's a command to *do whatever it takes to change your state,* whether it's changing your physiology or your focus. At one time, I put myself in a state of being *pressured* to write my book; no wonder I felt it was impossible! But then I had to find a way to change my state; otherwise, you wouldn't be reading this today. I had to be in a state of creativity, a state of excitement. If you want to go on a diet, it's not going to work if you're in a fearful state, or a worried state, or a frustrated state. **You've got to be in a *determined* state in order to succeed.** Or, if you want to perform better on your job, realize that intelligence is often a factor of state. People who supposedly have limited capability will find their talent shooting through the roof if they get into a new state. I've demonstrated this many times with dyslexic people. While dyslexia is a function of our visual faculties, it's also a function of our mental and emotional states. People who are dyslexic do not reverse letters or words every time they read something. They may do it most of the time, but they don't do it all of the time. The difference between when they're able to read clearly and when they reverse letters all comes down to state. If you change their state, you immediately change their performance. Anyone who's dyslexic or has any other state-based challenge can use these strategies to turn themselves around.

Since movement can instantly change how we feel, it makes sense for us to create lots of ways to change our state with one, singular movement in an instant. One of the things that most powerfully changed my life was something I first learned years ago. In Canada I found a man who was breaking wood karate-style. Instead of spending a year and a half to two years to learn to do it, with no martial arts training, I simply found out what he was focusing on, how he was focusing (the brightness and so on) in his head, what his beliefs were, and what his physical strategy was— how he specifically used his body to break the wood.

I practiced over and over his physical movements identically with tremendous emotional intensity, sending my brain deep sensations of certainty. And all the while, my instructor coached me on my movements. Bam! I broke through one piece of wood, then two pieces, then three pieces, then four. What had I done to accomplish this? 1) I raised my standards and made breaking the wood a must—something I previously would have accepted as a limitation; 2) I changed my limiting belief about my ability to do this by changing my emotional state into one of certainty, and 3) I modeled an effective strategy for producing the result.

This act transformed my sense of power and certainty throughout my whole body. I began to use this same "wood breaking" sense of certainty to accomplish other things I never thought I could do, breaking through my procrastination and some of my fears easily. Over the years I continued to use and reinforce these sensations, and I began to teach them to others, even children, eleven- and twelve-year-old girls, showing them how to increase their self-esteem by giving them an experience they didn't think was possible. I eventually started using this as part of my video-based Unlimited Power seminars, conducted by my franchisees, our Personal Development Consultants around the world. Often in 30 minutes or less they are able to help their participants to overcome their fears and learn how to break through anything that stops them in their lives. After breaking the wood, they learn to use this experience to give themselves the sense of certainty that is necessary in pursuing anything they want to achieve in life. It's always fascinating to see a huge man who thinks he can do it with just brute force get up there and miss, and then watch a woman half his size and muscular tone break through in a heartbeat because she's developed the certainty in her physiology.

> *"Experience is not what happens to a man; it is what a man does with what happens to him."*
> —ALDOUS HUXLEY

You've got to realize that you must take conscious control of running your own mind. You've got to do it deliberately; otherwise, you're going to be at the mercy of whatever happens around you. The first skill you must master is to be able to change your state *instantly* no matter what the environment, no matter how scared or frustrated you are. This is one of the foundational skills people develop in my seminars. They learn how to quickly change their state from being afraid and "knowing" they can't do something, to knowing they can do it and being able to take effective action. Developing experiences like this in which you change quickly gives you tremendous power in your life—something you can't fully appreciate until you really try it for yourself.

The second skill is that you should be able to change state consistently *in any environment*—maybe in an environment that used to make you uncomfortable, but in which you can now change your state time and again, conditioning yourself until you feel *good* no matter where you are. The third skill, of course, is to establish a set of habitual patterns of using your physiology and focus so that you *consistently* feel good without any conscious effort whatsoever. My definition of success is to **live your life in a way that causes you to feel tons of pleasure and very little pain**—and because of your lifestyle, have the people around you feel a lot more pleasure than they do pain. Someone who's achieved a lot but is living in emotional pain all the time, or is surrounded by people in pain all the time, isn't truly successful. The fourth goal is to enable *others* to change their state instantly, to change their state in any environment, and to change their state for their whole life. This is what my franchisees learn to be able to do in their seminars and in their one-on-one work with people.

So, what do you need to remember from this chapter? **All that you really want in life is to change how you feel**. Again, *all your emotions are nothing but biochemical storms in your brain,* and you are in control of them at any moment in time. You can feel ecstasy *right now,* or you can feel pain or depression or overwhelmed—it's all up to you. You don't need drugs or anything else to do it. There are much more effective ways and, as you learned in the chapter on beliefs, drugs can be overpowered by the chemicals you create in *your own body,* by changing your focus and the way you're using your physiology. These chemicals are much more powerful than virtually any outside substance.

> *"Every great and commanding moment in the annals of the world is the triumph of some enthusiasm."*
> —RALPH WALDO EMERSON

DO YOU KNOW HOW TO MAKE YOURSELF FEEL GOOD?

On a business trip to Toronto, I felt physically stressed because of intense back pain. As the plane descended, I began to think about what I needed to do when I got to my hotel. It would already be 10:30 P.M., and I had to be up early the next morning to conduct my seminar. I could eat something—after all, I'd had nothing all day—but it was awfully late. I could do my paperwork and watch the news. In that moment I realized all of these actions were merely strategies for getting out of pain and into some level of pleasure. Yet none of them were all that compelling. I needed to expand my list of ways to experience pleasure, regardless of the time or place.

So do you know how to make yourself feel good? This sounds like a stupid question, doesn't it? But really, do you have a set of specific and empowering ways to make yourself feel good at a moment's notice? Can you accomplish this without the use of food, alcohol, drugs, cigarettes, or other addictive sources? I'm sure you have a few, but let's expand the list. Right now, let's identify some of the positive choices you already have for making yourself feel good. **Sit down right now and write down a list of things that you currently do to change how you feel**. As long as you're making a list, why not add some new things you may not have tried before that could positively change your state as well?

Don't stop until you have a minimum of fifteen ways to instantly feel good, and the ideal would be at least twenty-five. This is an exercise you may want to come back to again until you have hundreds of ways!

When I made a list for myself, I realized that playing music was one of the most powerful ways I could change my state quickly. Reading was another way to feel good because it changed my focus, and I love to learn—especially reading something instructional and informational, something I can immediately apply to my life. Changing my body movements is something I can do instantly to break out of a limiting state and into a resourceful one: exercising on my StairMaster™ with the music cranking full tilt, jumping up and down on my rebounder unit, running five miles uphill, swimming laps.

Here are some others: dancing, singing along with my favorite CDs, watching a comedy film, going to a concert, listening to informational audio tapes. Taking a Jacuzzi, a warm bath. Making love with my wife. Having a family dinner where we all sit down at the table and chat about what's most important to us. Hugging and kissing my children, hugging and kissing Becky. Taking Becky to a movie like *Ghost* where we sit in our seats, in puddles of tears. Creating a new idea, a new company, a new concept. Refining or improving anything that I'm currently doing. Creating anything. Telling jokes to friends. Doing anything that makes me feel like I'm contributing. Conducting any of my seminars, especially *huge* ones (one of my favorite submodalities). Polishing up my memories, vividly remembering a wonderful experience I've had recently or in the past within my journal.

LIST OF WAYS TO CHANGE HOW I FEEL, TO GO FROM PAIN TO PLEASURE, AND TO FEEL GOOD IMMEDIATELY

1. MAKING ART
2. WRITING
3. READING
4. LISTENING TO MUSIC
5. MAKING LOVE
6. PLAYING BASKETBALL
7. PLAYING W/ ALEX
8. WATCHING A GOOD MOVIE
9. ORGANIZING
10. RUNNING
11. PHOTOGRAPHY
12. A REFRESHING SHOWER
13. THE RANCHO
14. SITTING IN THE BACKYARD
15. COOKING
16. TALKING W/ ALEX
17. HUGGING & KISSING ALEX
18. HELPING PEOPLE
19. DRIVING IN THE COUNTRY
20. _____
21. _____
22. _____
23. _____
24. _____
25. _____

IF YOU DON'T HAVE A PLAN FOR PLEASURE, YOU WILL HAVE PAIN

The whole key here is to create a *huge* list of ways to make yourself feel good so you don't need to turn to those other ways that are destructive. If you link pain to the destructive habits and more and more pleasure to these new empowering ones, you'll find that most of them are accessible most of the time. Make this list a reality; develop a **plan for pleasure for each and every day**. Don't just randomly hope that pleasure will somehow show up; set yourself up for ecstasy. *Make room for it!*

What we're talking about, again, is conditioning your nervous system, your body, and your mental focus so that it searches constantly to see how everything in your life benefits you. Just remember that if you continue to have a limiting emotional pattern, it's because you are using your body in a habitual way, or are continuing to focus in a certain disempowering way. If it's your focus that needs to be shifted, there is one incredible tool that can change it instantly. You must know that . . .

that had been shoveled into the back of a truck—men, women, and children who had been gassed. The gold fillings had been pulled from their teeth; everything that they owned—any jewelry—even their clothing, had been taken. Instead of asking, "How could the Nazis be so despicable, so destructive? How could God make something so evil? Why has God done this to me?," Stanislavsky Lech asked a different question. He asked, **"How can I use this to escape?"** And instantly he got his answer.

As the end of the day neared and the work party headed back into the barracks, Lech ducked behind the truck. In a heartbeat, he ripped off his clothes and dove naked into the pile of bodies while no one was looking. He pretended that he was dead, remaining totally still even though later he was almost crushed as more and more bodies were heaped on top of him.

The fetid smell of rotting flesh, the rigid remains of the dead surrounded him everywhere. He waited and waited, hoping that no one would notice the one living body in that pile of death, hoping that sooner or later the truck would drive off.

Finally, he heard the sound of the engine starting. He felt the truck shudder. And in that moment, he felt a stirring of hope as he lay among the dead. Eventually, he felt the truck lurch to a stop, and then it dumped its ghastly cargo—dozens of the dead and one man pretending to be one of them—in a giant open grave outside the camp. Lech remained there for hours until nightfall. When he finally felt certain no one was there, he extracted himself from the mountain of cadavers, and he ran naked twenty-five miles to freedom.

What was the difference between Stanislavsky Lech and so many others who perished in the concentration camps? **While, of course, there were many factors, one critical difference was that he asked a different question.** He asked persistently, he asked with expectation of receiving an answer, and his brain came up with a solution that saved his life. The questions he asked himself that day in Krakow caused him to make split-second decisions that led to actions that significantly impacted his destiny. But before he could get the answer, make the decisions, and take those actions, he had to ask himself the right *questions*.

Throughout this book you've learned how our beliefs affect our decisions, our actions, the direction of our lives, and therefore our ultimate destiny. But all these influences are a product of *thinking*—of the way your brain has *evaluated* and *created meaning* throughout your entire life. So to get to the bottom of how we create our reality on a daily basis **we need to answer the question,** *"Just how do we* <u>*think*</u>*?"*

8
QUESTIONS
ARE THE ANSWER

"He who asks questions cannot avoid the answers."
—CAMEROON PROVERB

They needed no reason. They came simply because he was of Jewish descent. The Nazis stormed into his home, arresting him and his entire family. Soon they were herded like cattle, packed into a train and then sent to a death camp in Krakow. His most disturbing nightmares could never have prepared him for seeing his family shot before his very eyes. How could he live through the horror of seeing his child's clothing on another because his son was now dead as the result of a "shower"?

Somehow he continued. One day he looked at the nightmare around him and confronted an inescapable truth: if he stayed there even one more day, he would surely die. He made a *decision* that he must escape and that escape must happen immediately! He knew not how, he simply knew he must. For weeks he'd asked the other prisoners, "How can we escape this horrible place?" The answers he received seemed always to be the same: "Don't be a fool," they said, "there is no escape! Asking such questions will only torture your soul. Just work hard and pray you survive." But he couldn't accept this—*he wouldn't accept it.* He became obsessed with escape, and even when his answers didn't make any sense, he kept asking over and over again, "How can I do it? There must be a way. How can I get out of here healthy, alive, *today?*"

It is said that if you ask, you shall receive. And for some reason, on this day he got his answer. Perhaps it was the intensity with which he asked his question, or maybe it was his sense of certainty that "now is the time." Or possibly it was just the impact of continually focusing on the answer to one burning question. For whatever reason, the giant power of the human mind and spirit awakened in this man. The answer came to him through an unlikely source: the sickening smell of decaying human flesh. There, only a few feet from his work, he saw a huge pile of bodies

OUR QUESTIONS DETERMINE OUR THOUGHTS

One day, I was thinking about important events in my own life and in the lives of people I had encountered along the way. I had met so many people, fortunate and unfortunate, successful and unsuccessful; I really wanted to know what allowed successful people to achieve great things, while others with similar or better backgrounds disappeared over the falls of Niagara. So I asked myself, *"What really makes the biggest difference in my life, in who I become, in who I am as a person, and in where I am going?"* The answer I came up with was one I've already shared with you. **"It's not the events that shape my life that determine how I feel and act, but, rather, it's the way I *interpret* and *evaluate* my life experiences**. The *meaning* I attach to an event will determine the *decisions* I make, the *actions* I take, and therefore my ultimate *destiny*. But," I asked myself, "how do I go about evaluating? What exactly *is* an evaluation?"

I thought, "Well, right now I'm evaluating, aren't I? I'm trying to *evaluate* how to describe what an evaluation is. What am I doing right now?" And then I realized I had just been asking myself a series of **questions**, and obviously those questions were:

> **How do I go about evaluating?**
> **What exactly *is* an evaluation?**
> **Right now I'm evaluating, aren't I?**
> **What am I doing right now?**

Then I thought, "Is it possible that **evaluations are nothing but questions?**" And I started laughing and thought, "Well, isn't *that* a question?"

I began to realize that thinking itself is nothing but the process of asking and answering questions. If after reading this you're thinking, "That's true," or "That's not true," you had to ask yourself—either consciously or unconsciously—a question, and that question was, "Is this true?" Or even if you thought, "I need to think about that," what you're really saying is, "I need to ask myself some questions about that. I need to consider that for a moment." As you consider it, you'll begin to question it. We need to realize that most of what we do, day in and day out, is ask and answer questions. So if we want to change the quality of our lives, we should change our **habitual questions**. These questions direct our focus, and therefore how we think and how we feel.

The masters of question asking, of course, are kids. How many millions of questions do they constantly bombard us with as they're growing up? Why do you think that is? Is it just to drive us crazy? We need to realize that they're constantly making evaluations as to what things mean and what they should do. They're starting to create neuro-associations that will guide their futures. They're learning machines, and the way to learn, to think, to make new connections, is initiated by questions—either questions we ask of ourselves or others.

This entire book and my life's work is the result of my asking questions about what makes us all do what we do and how we can produce change more quickly and easily than it has been done before. Questions are the primary way that we learn virtually anything. In fact, the entire Socratic method (a way of teaching that dates back to the ancient Greek philosopher Socrates) is based upon the teacher doing nothing but *asking questions,* directing the students' focus, and getting them to come up with their own answers.

When I realized the incredible power of questions to shape our thoughts and literally our every response to our experiences, I went on a "quest for questions." I began to notice how often questions appeared in our culture. Games like Trivial Pursuit, Jeopardy!, and Scruples were all the rage. *The Book of Questions*—an entire book of nothing but questions to make you think about your life and your values, was a bestseller. Ads on TV and in print asked, "What becomes a legend most?" "How do you spell relief?" "Is it soup yet?" Spike Lee asks Michael Jordan "Is it the shoes?" in a TV ad for Nike's Air Jordan basketball shoes.

I not only wanted to know what questions we were asking as a society, but I also wanted to discover the questions that made a difference in people's lives. I asked people in my seminars, in airplanes, in meetings; I asked everyone I met, from CEOs in high-rises to homeless people on the street, trying to discover the questions that created their experience of day-to-day life. I realized that the main difference between the people who seemed to be successful—in any area!—and those who weren't was that **successful people asked better questions, and as a result, they got better answers**. They got answers that empowered them to know exactly what to do in any situation to produce the results they desired.

Quality questions create a quality life. You need to burn this idea into your brain, because it's as important as anything else you'll learn in this book. Businesses succeed when those who make the decisions that control their destiny ask the right questions about markets or strategies or product lines. Relationships flourish when people ask the right questions about where potential conflicts exist and how to support each other instead of tearing each other down. Politicians win elections when the questions they raise—whether explicitly or implicitly—provide answers that work for them *and their community*.

When the automobile was in its infancy, hundreds of people tinkered with building them, but Henry Ford asked, "How can I mass-produce it?" Millions chafed under communism, but Lech Walesa asked, "How can I raise the standard of living for all working men and women?" **Questions set off a processional effect that has an impact beyond our imagination. Questioning our limitations is what tears down the walls in life—in business, in relationships, between countries. *I believe all human progress is preceded by new questions.***

THE POWER OF QUESTIONS

"Some men see things as they are, and say, 'Why?'
I dream of things that never were, and say,
'Why not?' "
—GEORGE BERNARD SHAW

Most of us, when we see someone of extraordinary capability or someone who seems to have a superhuman capacity to deal with life's challenges, think things like, "They're so lucky! They're so talented! They must have been born that way." But in reality, the human brain has the capacity to produce answers faster than the "smartest" computer on earth, even considering today's microtechnology with computers that calculate in nanoseconds (*billionths* of a second). It would take two buildings the size of the World Trade Center to house the storage capacity of your brain! Yet this three-pound lump of gray matter can give you more firepower *instantly* for coming up with solutions to challenges and creating powerful emotional sensations than anything in man's vast arsenal of technology.

Just like a computer boasting tremendous capacity, without an understanding of how to retrieve and utilize all that's been stored, the brain's capacity means nothing. I'm sure you've known someone (maybe even yourself) who has purchased a new computer system and never used it simply because he or she didn't figure out how. If you want access to the files of valuable information in a computer, you must understand how to retrieve the data by asking for it with the proper commands. Likewise, what enables you to get anything you want from your own personal databanks is the commanding power of asking questions.

"Always the beautiful answer who asks a more beautiful question."
—E. E. CUMMINGS

I'm here to tell you that **the difference between people is the difference in the questions they ask consistently.** Some people are depressed on a regular basis. Why? As we revealed in the last chapter, part of the problem is their limited states. They conduct their lives with limited movements and hamstrung physiology, but more importantly, they focus on things that make them feel overloaded and overwhelmed. Their pattern of focus and evaluation seriously limits their emotional experience of life. Could this person change how they feel in a moment? You bet—just by changing mental focus.

So what's the quickest way to change focus? Simply by *asking a new question.* When people are depressed, it is more than likely due to asking themselves disempowering questions on a regular basis, questions like: "What's the use? Why even try, since things never seem to work out anyway? Why me, Lord?" **Remember, ask and you shall receive. If you ask a terrible question, you'll get a terrible answer. Your mental computer is ever ready to serve you, and whatever question you give it, it will surely come up with an answer.** So if you ask, "Why can't I ever succeed?," it will tell you—even if it has to make something up! It might come up with an answer like, "Because you're stupid," or "Because you don't deserve to do well anyway."

Now, what's an example of brilliant questions? How about my good friend, W. Mitchell? If you read *Unlimited Power,* you know his story. How do you think he was able to survive having two-thirds of his body burned and still feel good about his life? How could he then endure an airplane accident years later, lose the use of his legs, and be confined to a wheelchair—and *still* find a way to enjoy contributing to others? *He learned to control his focus by asking the right questions.*

When he found himself in the hospital, with his body burned beyond recognition, and surrounded by a large number of other patients in the ward who were feeling sorry for themselves, patients who were asking themselves, "Why me? How could God do this to me? Why is life so unfair? What's the use of living as a 'cripple'?," Mitchell chose instead to ask himself, **"How can I use this? Because of this, what will I be able to contribute to others?"** These questions are what created the difference in destinies: "Why me?" rarely produces a positive result, while "How can I use this?" usually leads us in the direction of turning our difficulties into a driving force to make ourselves and the world better. Mitchell realized that being hurt, angry, and frustrated wouldn't change his life, so instead of looking at what he didn't have, he said to himself, *"What do I still have? Who am I really? Am I really only my body, or am I something more? What am I capable of now, even more so than before?"*

After his airplane accident, while in the hospital and paralyzed from the waist down, he met an incredibly attractive woman, a nurse named

Annie. With his entire face burned off, his body paralyzed from the waist down, he had the audacity to ask: "How could I get a date with her?" His buddies said, "You're insane. You're deluding yourself." But a year and a half later, he and Annie were in a relationship, and today she's his wife. That's the beauty of asking empowering questions: they bring us an irreplaceable resource: answers and solutions.

Questions determine everything you do in life, from your abilities to your relationships to your income. For example, many people fail to commit to a relationship simply because they keep asking questions that create doubt: "What if there's somebody better out there? What if I commit myself now and miss out?" What terribly disempowering questions! This fuels the fear that the grass will always be greener on the other side of the fence, and it keeps you from being able to enjoy what you already have in your own life. Sometimes these same people destroy the relationships they do eventually have with more terrible questions: "How come you *always* do this to me? Why don't you appreciate me? What if I were to leave right now—how would that make you feel?" Compare this with "How did I get so lucky to have you in my life? What do I love the most about my husband/wife? How much richer will our lives be as a result of our relationship?"

Think of the questions you habitually ask yourself in the area of finances. Invariably, if a person isn't doing well financially, it's because they're creating a great deal of fear in their life—fear that keeps them from investing or mastering their finances in the first place. They ask questions like "What toys do I want right now?" instead of "What plan do I need in order to achieve my ultimate financial goals?" The questions you ask will determine where you focus, how you think, how you feel, and what you do. If we want to change our finances, we've got to hold ourselves to higher standards, change our beliefs about what's possible, and develop a better strategy. One of the things that I've noticed in modeling some of today's financial giants is that they consistently ask different questions than the masses—questions that often run counter to even the most widely accepted financial "wisdom."

Currently, there is no denying that Donald Trump is experiencing financial challenges. For almost a decade, though, he was clearly an economic kingpin. How did he do it? There were many factors, but one that virtually everybody agrees on is that in the mid-seventies, when New York City faced bankruptcy and most developers fretted over questions like "How will we survive if this city goes under?," Trump asked a unique question: "How can I get rich while everyone else is afraid?" This one question helped to shape many of his business decisions and clearly led him to the position of economic dominance he enjoyed.

Trump didn't stop there. He also asked another great question, one which would be good to emulate before making any financial investments. Once he was convinced that a project had tremendous potential for economic gain, he would then ask, "What's the downside? What's the worst that can happen, and can I handle it?" His belief was that if he knew he could handle the worst-case scenario, then he should do the deal because the upside would take care of itself. So if he asked such shrewd questions, what happened?

Trump had put deals together that no one else would have considered during those economically stressful times. He had taken over the old Commodore building and turned it into the Grand Hyatt (his first major economic success). And when the tide turned, he had won big. However, he eventually ran into major economic trouble. Why? Many say he changed what he focused on in making investments. He began to ask questions like "What can I enjoy owning?" instead of "What is the most profitable deal?" Worse, some say Trump began to believe he was invincible, and as a result he stopped asking his "downside" questions. This single change in his evaluation procedure—in the questions he was asking himself—may have cost him a good part of his fortune. **Remember, it's not only the questions you ask, but the questions you *fail* to ask, that shape your destiny.**

If there's one thing I've learned in seeking out the core beliefs and strategies of today's leading minds, it's that **superior evaluations create a superior life.** We *all* have the capacity to evaluate life at a level that produces outstanding results. What do you think of when you hear the word "genius"? If you're like me, what immediately comes to mind is a picture of Albert Einstein. But how did Einstein move beyond his failed high school education into the realm of truly great thinkers? Undoubtedly, it was because he asked supremely formulated questions.

As Einstein was first exploring the idea of time and space relativity, he asked, "Is it possible that things that seem simultaneous are not really so?" For example, if you are a few miles away from a sonic boom, do you hear it at the exact moment it occurs in space? Einstein conjectured that you do not, that what you experience as happening in that moment is not *really* happening then, but rather occurred only a moment ago. In day-to-day life, he reasoned, time is relative depending on how you occupy your mind.

Einstein once said, "When a man sits with a pretty girl for an hour, it seems like a minute. But let him sit on a hot stove for a minute and it's longer than any hour. That's relativity." He conjectured further into the realm of physics, and believing that the speed of light is fixed, he found himself asking the question, "What if you could put light aboard a rocket? Would its speed be increased then?" In the process of answering these fascinating questions, and others like them, Einstein postulated his renowned theory of relativity.

> *"The important thing is not to stop questioning.*
> *Curiosity has its own reason for existing. One cannot*
> *help but be in awe when he contemplates the*
> *mysteries of eternity, of life, of the marvelous*
> *structure of reality. It is enough if one tries merely*
> *to comprehend a little of this mystery every day.*
> *Never lose a holy curiosity."*
> —ALBERT EINSTEIN

The powerful distinctions that Einstein made resulted from a series of questions. Were they simple? Yes. Were they powerful? Absolutely. **What power could *you* unleash by asking some equally simple but powerful questions?** Questions are undeniably a magic tool that allows the genie in our minds to meet our wishes; they are the wake-up call to our giant capacities. They allow us to achieve our desires if only we present them in the form of a specific and well-thought-out request. **A genuine quality of life comes from consistent, quality questions.** Remember, your brain, like the genie, will give you whatever you ask of it. So be careful what you ask for—whatever you look for you'll find.

So with all this power between our ears, why aren't more people "happy, healthy, wealthy, and wise"? Why are so many frustrated, feeling like there are no answers in their lives? One answer is that when they ask questions, they lack the certainty that causes the answers to come to them, and most importantly, they fail to consciously ask empowering questions of themselves. They run roughshod over this critical process with no forethought or sensitivity to the power they are abusing or failing to ignite by their lack of faith.

A classic example of this is a person who wants to lose weight and "can't." It's not that they can't: it's that their present plan of evaluating what to eat is not supporting them. They ask questions like "What would make me feel most full?" and "What is the sweetest, richest food I can get away with?" This leads them to select foods filled with fat and sugar—a guarantee of more unhappiness. What if instead they asked questions like "What would really nourish me?," "What's something light that I can eat that would give me energy?," or "Will this cleanse or clog me?" Better yet, they could ask, "If I eat this, what will I have to give up in order to still achieve my goals? What's the ultimate price I'll pay if I don't stop this indulgence now?" By asking questions like this, they'll associate pain to overeating, and their behavior will change immediately.

To change your life for the better, you must change your habitual questions. Remember, the patterns of questions you consistently ask will create either enervation or enjoyment, indignation or inspiration, misery or magic. Ask the questions that will uplift your spirit and push you along the path of human excellence.

HOW QUESTIONS WORK

Questions accomplish three specific things:

1. **Questions immediately change what we're focusing on and therefore how we feel.** If you keep asking questions like "How come I'm so depressed?" or "Why doesn't anybody like me?" you will focus on, look for, and find references to back up the idea that there is a reason for you to feel depressed and unloved. As a result, you'll stay in those unresourceful states. If instead you ask, "How can I change my state so that I am feeling happy and am being more lovable?," you'll focus on solutions. Even if your brain initially responds, "There's nothing I can do," but like Stanislavsky Lech or W. Mitchell you persist with a sense of certainty and expectation in spite of it all, then eventually you will get the answers you need and deserve. You will come up with authentic reasons for feeling better, and as you focus on them, your emotional state will immediately follow suit.

There's a big difference between an affirmation and a question. When you say to yourself, "I'm happy; I'm happy; I'm happy," this might cause you to feel happy if you produce enough emotional intensity, change your physiology and therefore your state. But in reality, you can make affirmations all day long and not really change how you feel. What will really change the way you feel is *asking,* "What am I happy about now? What *could* I be happy about if I wanted to be? How would that make me feel?" If you keep asking questions like this, you'll come up with real references that will make you begin to focus on reasons that do in fact exist for you to feel happy. You'll feel certain that you're happy.

Instead of just "pumping you up," questions provide you with actual *reasons to feel* the emotion. **You and I can change how we feel in an instant, just by changing our focus.** Most of us don't realize the power of memory management. Isn't it true that you have treasured moments in your life that if all you did was focus on them and think about them you'd immediately feel wonderful again in this moment now? Perhaps it was the birth of a child, your wedding day, or your first date. Questions are the guide to those moments. If you ask yourself questions like "What are my most treasured memories?" or "What's really great in my life right now?" and you can seriously consider the question, you'll start thinking of experiences that make you feel absolutely phenomenal. And in that phenomenal emotional state, you'll not only feel better, but you'll be able to contribute more to those around you.

The challenge, as you may have guessed, is that most of us are on automatic pilot. By failing to consciously control the habitual questions we ask, we severely limit our emotional range and thus our ability to utilize the resources at hand. The solution? As we covered in Chapter 6, the first step is to become aware of what you want and discover your old limiting pattern. Get leverage: ask yourself, "If I don't change this, what is the ultimate price? What will this cost me in the long run?" and "How will my whole life be transformed if I did this right now?"; interrupt the pattern (if you've ever felt pain, then been distracted and not felt it, you know how effective this is); create a new, empowering alternative with a set of better questions; and then condition them by rehearsing them until they become a consistent part of your life.

A SKILL OF POWER

Learning to ask empowering questions in moments of crisis is a critical skill that has pulled me through some of the toughest times in my life. I'll never forget the moment I discovered a former associate doing a seminar and claiming credit for material I had developed, word for word. My first impulse was to ask things like "How dare he! How could he have the nerve to do this?," but I soon realized that getting involved in these kinds of unanswerable questions would only whip me into a frenzy, creating an endless loop out of which there seemed no escape. The guy did what he did—I realized I should simply allow my attorneys to apply the pain-pleasure principle to straighten him out—so why should I have stayed in an angry state in the meantime? I decided to move on and enjoy my life, but as long as I kept asking, "How could he do this to me?," I'd remain in this negative state. The fastest way to change my state would be to ask a series of new questions. So I asked myself, "What do I respect about this guy?" At first my brain screamed, "Nothing!" but then I asked, "What *could* I respect about him if I wanted to?," and finally I came up with an answer: "Well, I've got to admit that he's not sitting around passively; *at least* he's using what I taught him!" This made me laugh and definitely broke my pattern, enabling me to change my state, reassess my options, and feel good about their pursuit.

One of the ways that I've discovered to increase the quality of my life is to **model the habitual questions of people I really respect.** If you find someone who's extremely happy, I can guarantee you that there is a reason. It is that this person focuses consistently on things that make them happy, and this means that they're asking questions about happiness. Find out their questions, use them, and you'll begin to feel the way they do.

Some questions we will simply not consider. Walt Disney, for instance, refused to entertain any questions about whether his organizations could succeed or not. But that doesn't mean that the creator of the Magic Kingdom did not use questions in more resourceful ways. My grandfather, Charles Shows, was a writer with Disney before he went on to work with Hanna-Barbera developing such cartoon characters as Yogi Bear and Huckleberry Hound. One of the things he shared with me was that anytime they were working on a new project or script, Disney had a unique way of requesting input. He designated a whole wall on which he would display the project, script, or idea, and everyone in the company would come by and write down the answers to the question: "How can we improve this?" They'd write solution after solution, covering the wall with suggestions. Then Disney would review everyone's answers to the question he'd asked. In this way, Walt Disney accessed the resources of every person in his company, and then produced results commensurate with that quality of input.

The answers we receive depend upon the questions we're willing to ask. For example, if you're feeling really angry, and somebody says, "What's great about this?," you may not be willing to respond. But if you value learning highly, you might be willing to answer your own questions of, "What can I learn from this situation? How can I use this situation?" Your desire for new distinctions will cause you to take the time to answer your questions, and in so doing, you'll change your focus, your state, and the results you're getting.

Ask yourself some empowering questions right now. **What are you truly happy about in your life right now?** What's really great in your life today? **What are you truly grateful for?** Take a moment to think about the answers and notice how good it feels to know that you have legitimate reasons for you to feel great now.

2. Questions change what we delete. Human beings are marvelous "deletion creatures." You and I have so many millions of things going on around us that we can focus on right now, from the blood flowing through our ears to the wind that may be brushing against our arms. However, we can consciously focus on only a small number of things simultaneously. *Unconsciously*, the mind can do all sorts of things, but consciously we're limited in terms of the number of things we can focus on simultaneously. So the brain spends a good deal of its time trying to prioritize what to pay attention to, and more importantly, what *not* to pay attention to, or what to "delete."

If you're feeling really sad, there is only one reason: it's because *you're deleting all the reasons you could be feeling good.* And if you're feeling good, it's because you're deleting all the bad things you could be focusing on. So when you ask someone a question, you change what they're focusing on and what they're deleting. If someone asks you, "Are you as frustrated as I am with this project?," even if you weren't frustrated before, you may begin to focus on what you were deleting previously, and you may start to feel bad, too. If someone asks you, "What's really lousy in your life?," *then you may be compelled to answer, regardless of how ridiculous the question is.* If you don't answer it consciously, then the question can stick in your mind unconsciously.

Conversely, if you're asked, "What's really great in your life?," and you keep focusing on the answer, you might find yourself feeling excellent immediately. If someone says, "You know this project really is great. Have you ever thought about the impact we're going to have because of what we've created here?," you might become inspired by a project that seemed laborious. **Questions are the laser of human consciousness. They concentrate our focus and determine what we feel and do.** Stop for a moment and as you look around the room, ask yourself a question: "What in this room is brown?" Look around and see it: brown, brown, brown. Now, look down at this page. Blocking off your peripheral vision, think of everything that's . . . green. If you're in a room you know very well, you can probably do this easily, but if you're in a strange room, chances are that you'll remember a lot more brown than green. So now look around and notice what's green: green, green, green. Do you see more green this time? Again, if you're in an unfamiliar environment, I'm sure your answer is yes. What does this teach us? Whatever we look for we'll find.

So, if you're angry, one of the best things you could ask yourself is, *"How can I learn from this problem so that this never happens again?"* This is an example of a quality question, in that it will lead you from your current challenge to finding resources that can keep you from having this pain in the future. Until you ask this question you're deleting the possibility that this problem is really an opportunity.

THE POWER OF PRESUPPOSITION

Questions have the power to affect our beliefs and thus what we consider possible or impossible. As we learned in Chapter 4, asking penetrating questions can weaken the reference legs of disempowering beliefs, enabling us to dismantle them and replace them with more empowering ones. But did you realize that the specific words we select and the very order of the words that we use in a question can cause us to not even consider certain things while taking others for granted? This is known as the power of **presupposition**, something of which you should be very aware.

Presuppositions program us to accept things that may or may not be true, and they can be used on us by others, or even, subconsciously, by ourselves. For example, if you ask yourself a question like "Why do I always sabotage myself?" after something ends disappointingly, you set yourself up for more of the same and set in motion a self-fulfilling prophecy. Why? Because, as we've already said, your brain will obediently come up with an answer for anything you ask of it. You'll take for granted that you've sabotaged things because you're focusing on *why* you do it, not on *whether* you do it.

One example occurred during the 1988 presidential election, just after George Bush had announced Dan Quayle as his running mate. A television news organization conducted a nationwide poll, asking people to call a 900 number to answer the question, "Does it bother you that Dan Quayle used his family's influence to go into the National Guard and stay out of Vietnam?" The glaring presupposition built into this question, of course, was that Quayle had indeed used his family's influence to unfair advantage—something that had never been proven. Yet people responded to it as if it were a given. They never *questioned* it, and just automatically accepted it. Worse, many people called to say that they were extremely upset about this fact. No such fact was ever substantiated! Unfortunately, this process happens all too often; we do it to ourselves and to others all the time. Don't fall into the trap of accepting someone else's or your own disempowering presuppositions. Find references to back up new beliefs that empower you.

3. Questions change the resources available to us. I arrived at a critical juncture in my life about five years ago when I came home from a grueling schedule on the road to discover that one of my business associates had embezzled a quarter of a million dollars and run my company $758,000 into debt. The questions I failed to ask when I first hired this man had brought me to this point, and now my destiny hinged on the new questions I would ask. All of my advisors informed me that I had only one choice: I'd have to declare bankruptcy.

They immediately started asking questions like "What should we sell off first? Who will tell the employees?" But I refused to accept defeat. I resolved that, whatever it took, I would *find a way* to keep my company going. I'm still in business today not because of the great advice I got from those around me, but because I asked a better question: **"How can I turn this around?"**

Then I asked an even more inspirational question: "How can I turn my company around, take it to the next level and cause it to have even more impact than it ever has in the past?" I knew that if I asked a better question, I'd get a better answer.

At first, I didn't get the answer I wanted. Initially, it was, "There is no way to turn it around," but I kept asking with intensity and expectation. I expanded my question to "How can I add even more value, and help more people even while I sleep? How can I reach people in a way that is not limited to my physical presence?" With these questions came the idea of my franchise operation in which more people could represent me across the country. Out of these same questions, a year later I came up with the idea of producing a television infomercial, an answer that I received from that same burning question.

Since that time, we have created and distributed over 7 million tapes worldwide. Because I asked a question with intensity, I got an answer that's helped me develop relationships with people all over the world whom I would never have otherwise had a chance to meet, know, or touch in any way.

In the realm of business, especially, questions do open up new worlds and give us access to resources we might not otherwise realize we have available. At Ford Motor Company, retired president Donald Petersen was known for his persistent questions: "What do you think? How can your job be improved?" On one occasion, Petersen asked a question that undoubtedly steered Ford's profitability up the road of success. He asked designer Jack Telnack, "Do you like the cars you are designing?" Telnack replied, "Actually, no, I don't." And then Petersen asked him the critical question: "Why don't you ignore management and design a car you'd love to own?"

The designer took the president at his word and went to work on the 1983 Ford Thunderbird, a car that inspired the later models of Taurus and Sable. By 1987, under the direction of master questioner Petersen, Ford had surpassed General Motors in profitability, and today Taurus ranks as one of the finest cars made.

Donald Petersen is a great example of someone who really utilized the incredible power of questions. With one simple question, he completely changed the destiny of Ford Motor Company. **You and I have that same power at our disposal every moment of the day. At any moment, the questions that we ask ourselves can shape our perception of who we are, what we're capable of, and what we're willing to do to achieve our dreams.** Learning to consciously control the questions you ask will take you further to achieving your ultimate destiny than almost anything

I know. Often our resources are limited only by the questions we ask ourselves.

One important thing to remember is that our beliefs affect the questions we'll even consider. Many people would never have asked the question "How can I turn things around?" simply because everyone around them had told them it was impossible. They would feel it was a waste of their time and energy. Be careful not to ask limited questions, or you'll receive limited answers. The only thing that limits your questions is your belief about what's possible. A core belief that has shaped my personal and professional destiny is that if I continue to ask any question, I will receive an answer. All we need to do is to create a better question, and we'll get a better answer. A metaphor I sometimes use is that life is just a *Jeopardy!* game; all the answers are there—all you have to do is come up with the right questions to win.

PROBLEM-SOLVING QUESTIONS

The key, then, is to develop a pattern of consistent questions that empower you. You and I both know that no matter what we're involved with in our lives, there are going to be times when we come up against these things we call "problems": the roadblocks to personal and professional progress. Every person, no matter what station of life they've achieved, has to deal with these special "gifts."

The question is not whether you're going to have problems, but how you're going to deal with them when they come up. We all need a systematic way to deal with challenges. So, realizing the power of questions to immediately change my state and give me access to resources and solutions, I began to interview people and ask them how they got themselves out of problems. I found out that there are certain questions that seem to be somewhat consistent. Here is a list of the five questions I use for any type of problem that comes up, and I can tell you that these have absolutely changed the quality of my life. If you choose to use them, they can do the same for you as well.

I'll never forget one of the first times I used these questions to change my state. It was after I'd been on the road almost 100 days out of 120. I was utterly exhausted. I found a stack of "urgent" memos that had to be responded to from executives of a variety of my companies, and a list of over 100 phone calls that I had to return personally. These were not calls from people wanting to visit with me, but important calls to some of my closest friends, business associates, and family members. I lost it right then and there! I began to ask myself some incredibly disempowering questions: "How come I have no time? Why don't they leave me alone?

THE PROBLEM-SOLVING QUESTIONS

1. What is great about this problem?
2. What is not perfect yet?
3. What am I willing to do to make it the way I want it?
4. What am I willing to no longer do in order to make it the way I want it?
5. How can I enjoy the process while I do what is necessary to make it the way I want it?

Don't they understand I'm not a machine? Why don't I ever get a break?" You can imagine what kind of emotional state I was in at this point.

Fortunately, in the midst of it I caught myself. I broke my pattern and realized that getting angrier wasn't going to make it any better; it was going to make it worse. My state was making me ask terrible questions. I needed to change my state by asking some better questions. I turned to my checklist of problem-solving questions and began with,

1. **"What is great about this problem?"** My first response, like so many other times, was "Absolutely nothing!" But I thought about it for a moment and realized that just eight years ago I would have given anything to have twenty business associates and friends who wanted to visit with me, much less 100 people of such national impact and caliber that this list of friends and business associates represented. As I realized this, I started to laugh at myself, it broke my pattern, and I began to feel grateful that there were so many people whom I respect and love who wanted to spend time with me.

2. **"What is not perfect yet?"** My schedule obviously needed more than a little fine-tuning. I felt like I had no time to myself, and that my life was out of balance. Note the presupposition of this question: asking "What is not perfect yet?" clearly implies that things *will* be perfect. This question not only gives you new answers, but reassures you simultaneously.

3. **"What am I willing to do to make it the way I want it?"** I decided then that I was willing to organize my life and my schedule so that they were more balanced, and I was willing to take control and learn to say no to certain things. I also realized that I needed to hire a new CEO for one of my companies, someone who could handle some of my workload. This would give me more special time at home and with my family.

4. **"What am I willing to no longer do in order to make it the way I want it?"** I knew that I could no longer whine and complain about how

unfair it all was or feel abused when people were really trying to support me.

5. **"How can I enjoy the process while I do what is necessary to make it the way I want it?"** When I asked this last, most important question, I looked around for a way to make it fun. I thought, "How can I enjoy making 100 calls?" Sitting there at my desk did not turn up the mental and emotional juice. Then I got an idea: I'd not been in my Jacuzzi in six months. I quickly slipped on my swim trunks, grabbed my portable computer and speaker phone, and headed for the Jacuzzi. I set up shop out in my back yard, and started making the calls. I called a few of my business associates in New York and teased them, saying, "Really, it's that cold? Hmmm. Well, it's really tough out here in California, you know. I'm sitting here in my Jacuzzi!" We all had fun with it and I managed to turn the whole "chore" into a game. (But I was so wrinkled that I looked about 400 years old by the time I got to the bottom of my list!)

That Jacuzzi is always in my back yard, but you'll notice that it took the right *question* to uncover it as a resource. By having the list of these five questions in front of you on a regular basis, you have a pattern of how to deal with problems that will instantly change your focus and give you access to the resources you need.

> ### *"He that cannot ask cannot live."*
> —OLD PROVERB

Every morning when we wake up, we ask ourselves questions. When the alarm goes off, what question do you ask yourself? Is it, "How come I have to get up right now?," "Why aren't there more hours in the day?," "What if I hit the snooze alarm *just one more time?*" And as you get in the shower, what are you asking yourself? "Why do I have to go to work?," "How bad is the traffic going to be today?," "What kind of stuff is going to be dumped on my desk today?" What if every day you consciously started asking a pattern of questions that would put you in the right frame of mind and that caused you to remember how grateful, happy, and excited you are? What kind of day do you think you'd have, with those positive emotional states as your filter? Obviously it would affect how you feel about virtually everything.

Realizing this, I decided I needed a "success ritual," and I created a series of questions that I ask myself every morning. The wonderful thing about asking yourself questions in the morning is that you can do it in the shower, while you're shaving or drying your hair, and so on. You're already asking questions anyway, so why not ask the right ones? I realized that there are certain emotions we all need to cultivate

THE MORNING POWER QUESTIONS

Our life experience is based on what we focus on. The following questions are designed to cause you to experience more happiness, excitement, pride, gratitude, joy, commitment, and love every day of your life. Remember, quality questions create a quality life.

Come up with two or three answers to all of these questions and feel fully associated. If you have difficulty discovering an answer simply add the word "could." Example: "What *could* I be most happy about in my life now?"

1. **What am I happy about in my life now?**
   What about that makes me happy? How does that make me feel?
2. **What am I excited about in my life now?**
   What about that makes me excited? How does that make me feel?
3. **What am I proud about in my life now?**
   What about that makes me proud? How does that make me feel?
4. **What am I grateful about in my life now?**
   What about that makes me grateful? How does that make me feel?
5. **What am I enjoying most in my life right now?**
   What about that do I enjoy? How does that make me feel?
6. **What am I committed to in my life right now?**
   What about that makes me committed? How does that make me feel?
7. **Who do I love? Who loves me?**
   What about that makes me loving? How does that make me feel?

In the evening, sometimes I ask the Morning Questions, and sometimes I ask an additional three questions. Here they are:

THE EVENING POWER QUESTIONS

1. **What have I given today?**
   In what ways have I been a giver today?
2. **What did I learn today?**
3. **How has today added to the quality of my life or how can I use today as an investment in my future?**
   Repeat the Morning Questions (optional).

in order to be happy and successful individuals. Otherwise, you could be winning and feel like you're losing, if you don't keep score or take the time to feel how fortunate you are. So take the time now to review the following questions. Take a moment to deeply experience the feelings of each one.

If you really want to create a shift in your life, make this a part of your daily ritual for personal success. By consistently asking these questions, you'll find that you access your most empowering emotional states on a regular basis, and you'll begin to create the highways to these emotions of happiness, excitement, pride, gratitude, joy, commitment, and love. Pretty soon, you'll find that when you open your eyes, these questions will fire off automatically just out of habit, and you will have trained yourself to ask the kinds of questions that will empower you to experience greater richness in life.

GIVE THE GIFT OF QUESTIONS

Once you know how to ask empowering questions, you not only can help yourself, but others as well. You can give these as a gift to other people. Once in New York City, I met a friend and business associate of mine for lunch. A prominent literary attorney, I admired him for his business acumen and for the practice he'd built since he was a young man. But on that day, he had suffered what he perceived as a devastating blow—his partner had left the firm, leaving him with tremendous overhead and not many ideas as to how to turn it around.

Remember that what he was focusing on was determining the meaning. In any situation, you can focus on what is disempowering, or on what is empowering, and if you look for it that's what you'll find. The problem was that he was asking all the wrong questions: "How could my partner abandon me this way? Doesn't he care? Doesn't he realize that this is destroying my life? Doesn't he realize that I can't do this without him? How will I explain to my clients that I can't stay in business any longer?" All of these questions were riddled with presuppositions about how his life was destroyed.

I had many ways in which I could intervene, but I decided that I could just ask him a few questions. I said, "Recently I've created this simple questions technology, and when I've applied it to myself, I've found it to have incredible impact. It's pulled me out of some pretty tough spots. Do you mind if I ask you a couple questions and see if it works for you?" He said, "Yeah, but I don't think anything's going to help me right now." So I started out by asking him the Morning Questions, and then the Problem-Solving Questions.

I started with, "What are you happy about? I know that sounds stupid and ridiculous and Pollyanna, but what are you really happy about?" His first response was, "Nothing." So I said, "What could you be happy about right now if you wanted to be?" He said, "I'm really happy about my wife because she's doing really well right now, and our relationship is very close." I asked him, "How does that make you feel when you think of how close you are with her?" He said, "It's one of the most incredible gifts in my life." I said, "She's a special lady, isn't she?" He started focusing on her and feeling phenomenal.

You might say that I was just distracting him. No, I was helping him to get into a better state, and in a better state, you can come up with better ways of dealing with challenges. First we had to break the pattern and put him in a positive emotional environment.

I asked him what else he was happy about. He started talking about how he *should* be happy about how he'd just helped a writer to close his first book deal, and the writer was delighted. He told me that he should feel proud, but he didn't. So I asked him, "If you did feel proud, how would that feel?" He began to think about how great that would be, and his state began to change immediately. I said, "What are you proud of?" He said, "I'm really proud of my kids. They're such special people. They're not just successful in business; they really care about people. I'm proud of who they've become as men and women and that they're my children. They're part of my legacy." I said, "How does it make you feel to know that you've had that impact?"

All of a sudden, a man who had earlier believed that his life was over came alive. I asked him what he was really grateful for. He said that he was really grateful that he'd made it through the tough times when he was a young and struggling lawyer, that he'd built his career from the bottom up, that he'd lived the American Dream. Then I asked, "What are you really excited about?" He said, "Actually, I'm excited that I have an opportunity right now to make a change." And it was the first time he'd thought about that, and it was because he'd changed his state so radically. I asked him, "Who do you love, and who loves you?" He started talking about his family and how incredibly close they were.

So I asked him, "What's great about your partner's leaving?" He said, "You know, what could be great about this is that I hate coming to New York City. I love being at my home in Connecticut." He continued, "What's great about this is that I get to look at everything in a new way." This started a whole string of possibilities and he resolved to set up a new office in Connecticut not five minutes from his home, bring his son into the business, and have an answering service pick up his calls in Manhattan. He got so excited, he decided to immediately go and look for a new office.

In a matter of minutes, the power of questions had worked their magic. He always had the resources to be able to deal with this, but the disempowering questions he'd asked had rendered his power inaccessible, and had caused him to see himself as an old man who'd lost everything he'd built. In reality, life had given him a tremendous gift, but the truth had been deleted until he started asking quality questions.

A QUESTION OF DESTINY

One of my favorite people—and one of the most impassioned men I've ever met—is Leo Buscaglia, author of *Love* and many other outstanding books in the area of human relations. One of the things that is great about Leo is his continued persistence in asking himself a question that his father instilled in him from the time he was a little boy. Each day at the dinner table, his father would ask, *"Leo, what have you learned today?"* Leo had to have an answer, and a quality one. If he hadn't learned something really interesting in school that day, he would run and get the encyclopedia to study something that he could share. He says that to this day he won't go to bed until he's learned something new that's of value. As a result he's constantly stimulating his mind, and a great deal of his passion and love for learning has come from this question, asked repeatedly, begun decades ago.

What are some questions that would be useful for you to ask of yourself on a regular basis? I know two of my favorite are the most simple. They help me to turn around any challenges that may come up in my life. They are simply, "What's great about this?" and "How can I use this?" By asking what's great about any situation, I usually find some powerful, positive meaning, and by asking how I can use it, I can take any challenge and turn it into a benefit. So what are two questions that you can use to change your emotional states or give you the resources you truly desire? Add two to the standard morning questions I've already given you, and customize them so that they meet your personal and emotional needs.

Some of the most important questions we'll ask in our lives are "What is my life really about?," "What am I really committed to?," "Why am I here?," and "Who am I?" These are incredibly powerful questions, but if you wait to get the perfect answer, you're going to be in deep trouble. Often, the first emotional, gut-level response you get to any question is the one you should trust and act upon. This is the final point I want to make with you. **There's a point at which you must stop asking questions in order to make progress.** If you keep asking questions, you're going to be uncertain, and only certain actions will produce certain results. **At some point, you've got to stop evaluating and start doing.** How? You finally decide what's most important to you, at least in the moment, and you use your personal power to follow through and begin to change the quality of your life.

So let me ask you a question. If there was one action that you could take immediately to instantly change the quality of your emotions and feelings each and every day of your life, would you want to know about it? Then go on quickly to . . .

9
THE VOCABULARY
OF ULTIMATE
SUCCESS

*"A powerful agent is the right word. Whenever we
come upon one of those intensely right words . . .
the resulting effect is physical as well as spiritual,
and electrically prompt."*
—MARK TWAIN

Words . . . They've been used to make us laugh and cry. They can wound
or heal. They offer us hope or devastation. With words we can make our
noblest intentions felt and our deepest desires known.

Throughout human history, our greatest leaders and thinkers have
used the power of words to transform our emotions, to enlist us in their
causes, and to shape the course of destiny. Words can not only create
emotions, they create actions. And from our actions flow the results of
our lives. When Patrick Henry stood before his fellow delegates and
proclaimed, "I know not what course others may take; but as for me, give
me liberty, or give me death!," his words ignited a firestorm that unleashed our forefathers' unbridled commitment to extinguish the tyranny
that had suppressed them for so long.

The privileged heritage that you and I share, the choices that we have
today because we live in this nation, were created by men who chose
words that would shape the actions of generations to come:

> When in the Course of human Events, it becomes necessary for
> one People to dissolve the Political Bands which have con-
> nected them with another . . .

This simple Declaration of Independence, this assemblage of words,
became the vessel of change for a nation.

Certainly, the impact of words is not limited to the United States of

America. During World War II, when the very survival of Great Britain was in question, one man's words helped to mobilize the will of the English people. It was once said that Winston Churchill had the unique ability to send the English language into battle. His famous call to all Britons to make this their "finest hour" resulted in courage beyond compare, and crushed Hitler's delusion about the invincibility of his war machine.

Most beliefs are formed by words—and they can be changed by words as well. Our nation's view of racial equality was certainly shaped by actions, but those actions were inspired by impassioned words. Who can forget the moving invocation of Martin Luther King, Jr., as he shared his vision, "I have a dream that one day this nation will rise up and live the true meaning of its creed . . ."?

Many of us are well aware of the powerful part that words have played in our history, of the power that great speakers have to move us, but few of us are aware of our *own* power to use these same words to move ourselves emotionally, to challenge, embolden, and strengthen our spirits, to move ourselves to action, to seek greater richness from this gift we call life.

An effective selection of words to describe the experience of our lives can heighten our most empowering emotions. A poor selection of words can devastate us just as surely and just as swiftly. Most of us make unconscious choices in the words that we use; we sleepwalk our way through the maze of possibilities available to us. **Realize now the power that your words command if you simply choose them wisely.**

What a gift these simple symbols are! We transform these unique shapes we call letters (or sounds, in the case of the spoken word) into a unique and rich tapestry of human experience. They provide us with a vehicle for expressing and sharing our experience with others; however, most of us don't realize that **the words you habitually choose also affect how you communicate with yourself and therefore what _you_ experience.**

Words can injure our egos or inflame our hearts—we can instantly change any emotional experience simply by choosing new words to describe to ourselves what we're feeling. If, however, we fail to master words, and if we allow their selection to be determined strictly by unconscious habit, we may be denigrating our entire experience of life. If you describe a magnificent experience as being "pretty good," the rich texture of it will be smoothed and made flat by your limited use of vocabulary. **People with an impoverished vocabulary live an impoverished emotional life; people with rich vocabularies have a multihued palette of colors with which to paint their experience, not only for others, but for themselves as well.**

Most people are not challenged, though, by the *size* of the vocabulary they consciously understand, but rather by the words they *choose* to use. Many times, we use words as "short cuts," but often these short cuts *shortchange* us emotionally. To consciously control our lives, we need to consciously evaluate and improve our consistent vocabulary to make sure that it is pulling us in the direction we desire instead of that which we wish to avoid. You and I must realize that the English language is filled with words that, in addition to their literal meanings, convey distinct emotional intensity. For example, if you develop a habit of saying you "hate" things—you "hate" your hair; you "hate" your job; you "hate" having to do something—do you think this raises the intensity of your negative emotional states more than if you were to use a phrase like "I *prefer* something else"?

Using emotionally charged words can magically transform your own state or someone else's. Think of the word "chivalry." Does it conjure up different images and have more emotional impact than words like "politeness" or "gentlemanliness"? I know that for me it does. Chivalry makes me think of a valiant knight seated on a white steed, championing his raven-haired damsel; it conveys nobility of spirit, a great round table about which are seated men of honor, the whole Arthurian ethic—in short, the wonder of Camelot. Or how do the words "impeccable" or "integrity" compare to "well done" and "honesty"? The words "pursuit of excellence" certainly create more intensity than "trying to make things better."

For years I've observed firsthand the power of changing just one key word in communicating with someone, and noted how it instantly changes the way people feel—and often the way they subsequently behaved. After working with hundreds of thousands of people, I can tell you something I know beyond a shadow of a doubt, something that at first glance may be hard to believe: **Simply by changing your habitual vocabulary—the words you consistently use to describe the emotions of your life—you can instantaneously change how you think, how you feel, and how you live.**

The experience that first triggered this insight for me occurred several years ago in a business meeting. I was with two men, one who used to be the CEO of one of my companies and the other a mutual associate and good friend, and in the midst of the meeting we received some rather upsetting news. Someone with whom we were negotiating was obviously "trying to take unfair advantage," had violated the integrity of our understanding, and it appeared he had the upper hand. To say the least, this angered and upset me, but although I was caught up in the situation, I couldn't help but notice how differently the two people sitting next to me responded to the same information.

My CEO was out of control with rage and fury while my associate was hardly moved by the situation. How could all three of us hear of these actions that should have impacted us all equally (we all had the same stake in the negotiation), yet respond in such radically different ways? Quite honestly, the intensity of my CEO's response to the situation seemed even to me to be disproportionate to what had occurred. He kept talking about how "furious" and "enraged" he was, as his face turned beet-red and the veins in his forehead and neck visibly protruded.

He clearly linked acting on his rage with either eliminating pain or gaining pleasure. When I asked him what being enraged meant to him, why he was allowing himself to be so intense about this, through clenched teeth he said, "If you're in a rage, you get stronger, and when you're strong, you can make things happen—you can turn anything around!" He regarded the emotion of rage as a resource for getting himself out of the experience of pain and into the pleasure of feeling like he was in control of the business.

I then turned to the next question in my mind: Why was my friend responding to the situation with almost no emotion at all? I said to him, "You don't seem to be upset by this. Aren't you angry?" And my CEO said, "Doesn't it make you *FURIOUS?*" My friend simply said, "No, it's not worth being upset over." As he said this, I realized that in the several years I had known him, I'd never seen him become very upset about *anything*. I asked him what being upset meant to him, and he responded, "If you get upset, then you lose control." "Interesting," I thought. "What happens if you lose control?" He said matter-of-factly, "Then the other guy wins."

I couldn't have asked for a greater contrast: one person clearly linked the pleasure of taking control to becoming angry, while the other linked the pain of losing control to the same emotion. **Their behavior obviously reflected their beliefs**. I began to examine my own feelings. What did I believe about this? For years I've believed that I can handle anything if I'm angry, but I also believe that I don't have to be angry to do so. I can be equally effective in a peak state of happiness. As a result, I don't avoid anger—I use it if I get in that state—nor do I pursue it, since I can access my strength without being "furious." *What really interested me was the difference in the words that we all used to describe this experience.* I had used the words "angry" and "upset," my CEO had used the words "furious" and "enraged," and my friend had said that he was "a bit annoyed" by the experience. I couldn't believe it! *Annoyed?*

I turned to him and said, "That's all you feel, just a little bit annoyed? You must get really angry or upset some of the time." He said, "Not really. It takes a lot to make that happen, and it almost never occurs." I asked him, "Do you remember the time the IRS took a quarter of a million dollars of your money, and it was *their mistake?* Didn't it take you two and a half years to get the money back? Didn't that make you unbelievably angry?" My CEO chimed in, "Didn't that make you *LIVID?*" He said, "No, it didn't upset me. Maybe I was a little bit peeved." *Peeved?* I thought this was the stupidest word I'd ever heard! I would never have used a word like that to describe my emotional intensity. How could this wealthy and successful businessman go around using a word like "peeved" and still keep a straight face? The answer is, he *didn't* keep a straight face! He seemed almost to enjoy talking about things that would have driven me crazy.

I began to wonder, "If I did use that word to describe my emotions, how would I begin to feel? Would I find myself smiling where I used to be stressed? Hmmm," I thought, "maybe this warrants some looking into." For days after that, I continued to be intrigued by the idea of using my friend's language patterns and seeing what it would do to my emotional intensity. What might happen if, when I was feeling really angry, I could turn to somebody and say, "This really *peeves* me!"? Just the thought of it made me laugh—it was so ridiculous. For fun, I decided to give it a shot.

I got my first opportunity to use it after a long night flight when I arrived at my hotel. Because one of my staff had neglected to handle the check-in for me, I had the privilege of standing at the front desk for an extra fifteen or twenty minutes, physically exhausted and at my emotional threshold. The clerk dragged himself to the check-in counter and began to hunt-and-peck my name into the computer at a pace that would make a snail impatient. I felt "a bit of anger" welling up inside of me, so I turned to the clerk and said, "You know, I know this isn't your fault, but right now I'm exhausted and I need to get to my room quickly because the longer I stand here the more I fear I will become a bit *PEEVED.*"

The clerk glanced up at me with a somewhat perplexed look, and then broke a smile. I smiled back; my pattern was broken. The emotional volcano that had been building up inside of me instantly cooled, and then two things happened. I actually enjoyed visiting for a few moments with the clerk, *and* he sped up. Could just putting a new label on my sensations be enough to break my pattern and truly change my experience? Could it really be that easy? What a concept!

Over the next week, I tried my new word over and over again. In each case, I found that saying it had the impact of immediately lowering my emotional intensity. Sometimes it made me laugh, but at the very minimum it stopped the momentum of being upset from rushing me into a state of anger. Within two weeks, I didn't even have to work on using the word: it became habitual. It became my *first choice* in describing my emotions, and I found myself no longer getting in these extremely angry states at all. I became more and more fascinated with this tool that I'd stumbled across. I realized that by changing my habitual vocabulary, I was transforming my experience; I was using what I would later call **"Transformational Vocabulary."** Gradually, I began to experiment with other words, and I found that if I came up with words that were potent enough, I could instantly lower or increase my intensity about virtually anything.

How does this process really work? Think of it this way: imagine that your five senses funnel a series of sensations to your brain. You're getting visual, auditory, kinesthetic, olfactory, and gustatory stimuli, and they are all translated by your sense organs into internal sensations. Then they must be organized into categories. But how do we know what these images, sounds, and other sensations mean? One of the most powerful ways that man has learned to quickly decide what sensations mean (is it pain or pleasure?) is to create labels for them, and these labels are what you and I know as "words."

Here's the challenge: all of your sensations are coming to you through this funnel, like *liquid sensation* poured through a thin spout into various molds called words. In our desire to make decisions quickly, rather than using all of the words available to us and finding the most appropriate and accurate description, we often force the experience into a disempowering mold. We form habitual favorites: molds that shape and transform our life experience. Unfortunately, most of us have not consciously evaluated the impact of the words we've grown accustomed to using. The problem occurs when we start consistently pouring any form of negative sensation into the word-mold of "furious" or "depressed" or "humiliated" or "insecure." And this word may not accurately reflect the actual experience. The moment we place this mold around our experience, the label we put on it *becomes* our experience. What was "a bit challenging" becomes "devastating."

For example, my CEO used "furious," "livid," and "enraged"; I called it "angry" or "upset"; and when it came to my friend, he poured his experience into the mold of "peeved" or "annoyed." What's interesting is that all of us, I discovered, use these same patterns of words to describe multitudes of frustrating experiences. You and I need to know that we can all have the same sensations, but the way in which we organize them—the mold or word we use for them—*becomes our experience*. I later found that by using my friend's mold (the words "peeved" or "annoyed") I instantly was able to change the intensity of my experience. It became something else. **This is the essence of Transformational Vocabulary: the words that we attach to our experience *become* our experience.** Thus, we must *consciously* choose the words we use to describe our emotional states, or suffer the penalty of creating greater pain than is truly warranted or appropriate.

Literally, words are used to re-present to us what our experience of life is. In that representation, they alter our perceptions and feelings. Remember, if three people can have the same experience, yet one person feels rage, another feels anger, and the third feels annoyance, then obviously the sensations are being changed *by each person's translation*. Since words are our primary tool for interpretation or translation, the way we label our experience immediately changes the sensations produced in our nervous systems. You and I must realize that words do indeed create a biochemical effect.

If you doubt this, I'd like you to honestly consider whether or not there are words that, if someone were to use them, would immediately create an emotional reaction. If someone hurls a racial slur at you, how does that make you feel? Or if someone were to call you a four-letter word, for example, wouldn't that change your state? There's probably a big difference between someone calling you by the initials "S.O.B." and having them articulate in graphic detail the phrase these letters stand for.

Wouldn't it produce a different level of tension in your body than if they were to call you an "angel"? Or a "genius"? Or a "dude"? We all link tremendous levels of pain to certain words. When I interviewed Dr. Leo Buscaglia, he shared with me the findings of a research study done at an eastern university in the late fifties. People were asked, "How would you define communism?" An astonishing number of the respondents were terrorized even by the question, but not many could actually define it—all they knew was that it was horrifying! One woman even went so far as to say, "Well, I don't really know what that means, but there hadn't better be any in Washington." One man said that he knew everything he needed to know about Communists and that what you needed to do was *kill* them! But he couldn't even explain what they were. There is no denying the power of labels to create sensations and emotions.

> *"Words form the thread on which we string*
> *our experiences."*
> —ALDOUS HUXLEY

As I began to explore the power of vocabulary, I still found myself fighting the idea that something as simplistic as changing the words that we use could ever make such a radical difference in our life experience. But when my study of language intensified, I came across some surprising facts that began to convince me that words absolutely do *filter* and *transform* experience. For instance, I found that, according to *Compton's*

Encyclopedia, English contains at least 500,000 words, and I've since read from other sources that the total may be closer to 750,000 words! English definitely has the largest number of words of any language on earth today, with German running a distant second, tallying roughly half the number.

What I found so fascinating was that, with the immense number of words we could possibly use, **our habitual vocabulary is extremely limited.** Various linguists have shared with me that the average person's working vocabulary consists of only between 2,000 and 10,000 words. Conservatively estimating English to contain half a million words, that means we regularly use *only ½ of 1 percent to 2 percent of the language!* What's an even greater tragedy? Of these words, how many do you think describe emotions? I was able to find over 3,000 words related to human emotion by going through a group of thesauruses. What struck me was the proportion of words that describe negative versus positive emotions. By my count, 1,051 words describe positive emotions, while 2,086 (almost twice as many!) describe negative emotions. Just as one example, I found 264 words to describe the emotion of sadness—words like "despondent," "sullen," "heavy-hearted," "moody," "woeful," "grievous," "tearful," "melancholy"—yet only 105 to describe cheerfulness, as in "blithe," "jaunty," "perky," "zestful," and "buoyant." No wonder people feel bad more than they feel good!

As I described to you in Chapter 7, when participants at my Date With Destiny seminar make out their list of emotions that they feel in a week, the majority of them come up with only about a dozen. Why? It's because we all tend to experience the same emotions again and again: certain people tend to be frustrated all of the time, or angry, or insecure, or frightened, or depressed. One of the reasons is that they constantly use these *same* words to describe their experience. If we were to analyze more critically the sensations we have in our bodies, and be more creative in our way of evaluating things, we might attach a new label to our experience and thereby change our emotional reality.

I remember reading years ago about a study conducted in a prison. Typically, it was found that when inmates experienced pain, one of the few ways they could communicate it was through physical action—their limited vocabulary limited their emotional range, channeling even the slightest feelings of discomfort into heightened levels of violent anger. What a contrast to someone like William F. Buckley, whose erudition and command of the language allow him to paint such a broad picture of emotions and thus represent within himself a variety of sensations! **If we want to change our lives and shape our destiny, we need to consciously** *select* **the words we're going to use, and we need to constantly strive to expand our level of choice.**

To give you further perspective, the Bible uses 7,200 different words; the poet and essayist John Milton's writing included 17,000; and it's said that William Shakespeare used over 24,000 words in his varied works, 5,000 of them only once. In fact, he's responsible for creating or coining many of the English words we commonly use today. Here's a list of just a few you might find interesting:

TRIPPINGLY ON THE TONGUE . . .

Here, from the book *Brush Up Your Shakespeare!* by Michael Macrone, is a smattering of powerful, state-inducing words coined by the master of the English language, Shakespeare.

amazement	money's worth	savagery
arch-villain	moonbeam	shipwrecked
assassination	mortifying	shooting star
bloodstained	to negotiate	to sire
bluster	nimble-footed	to sneak
to champion	obscene	to squabble
cold-hearted	Olympian	stealthy
disgraceful	pageantry	to swagger
eventful	to perplex	tardiness
fathomless	to puke	time-honored
gallantry	puppy dog	to torture
hostile	on purpose	tranquil
invulnerable	quarrelsome	transcendence
jaded	radiance	trippingly
lackluster	reliance	unearthly
laughable	remorseless	watchdog
lustrous	rose-cheeked	yelping
madcap	sacrificial	zany
majestic		

Linguists have proven beyond a shadow of a doubt that culturally we're shaped by our language. Doesn't it make sense that the English language is so verb-oriented? After all, as a culture we're very active and pride ourselves on our focus of *taking action*. The words we use consistently affect the way we evaluate, and therefore the way we think. By contrast, the Chinese culture places a high value on that which does not change, a fact reflected in the many dialects featuring a predominance of nouns rather than verbs. From their perspective, nouns represent things that will last, while verbs (as actions) will be here today and gone tomorrow.

Thus, it's important to realize that words shape our beliefs and impact our actions. Words are the fabric from which all questions are cut. As we noted in the last chapter, by changing one word in a question, we can instantly change the answer we'll get for the quality of our lives. The more I pursued an understanding of the impact of words, the more impressed I became with their power to sway human emotion, not only within myself, but within others as well.

> *"Without knowing the force of words, it is impossible to know men."*
> —CONFUCIUS

One day I began to realize that this idea, as simple as it was, was no fluke, that Transformational Vocabulary was a reality, and that by changing our habitual words, we could literally change the emotional patterns of our lives. Further, we could therefore mold the actions, directions, and ultimate destinies of our lives. One day I was sharing these distinctions with a longtime friend of mine, Bob Bays. As I did so, I could see him light up like a Christmas tree. He said, "Wow! I have another distinction to give you." He began to relate an experience to me that he'd had recently. He, too, had been on the road keeping an intense schedule and meeting everyone else's demands. When he finally came home, all he wanted to do was have some "space." He has a home on the ocean in Malibu, but it's a very small place, not designed to have house guests, much less three or four.

When he arrived on his doorstep, he found that his wife had invited her brother to stay with them, and that his daughter, Kelly, who was supposed to visit for two weeks, had decided to stay for two months. To add insult to injury, someone had turned off the VCR that he'd preset for a football game he'd been looking forward to viewing for days! As you can imagine, he hit his own "emotional threshold," and when he found out who had turned off his VCR—his daughter—he immediately unloaded on her, screaming all the four-letter words he could think of. This was the very first time in her life that he had even raised his voice to her, much less used language of that color. She immediately burst into tears.

Witnessing this scene, Bob's wife, Brandon, broke into peals of laughter. Since this was so unlike Bob's normal behavior, she assumed this was an outrageous and massive pattern interrupt. In reality, he *wished* he had been doing a pattern interrupt. After the smoke began to clear, and she realized he was actually furious, she became concerned, so she gave him some very valuable feedback. She said, "Bob, you're acting so strangely. You never act this way. You know, I noticed something else: you keep using a certain word that I've never heard you use before. Usually when you're stressed, you say you're *overloaded,* but lately I hear you talking all the time about how you're *overwhelmed.* You never say that; *Kelly* uses that word, and when she does, she feels this same kind of rage and behaves very much like you just did."

"Wow," I began to think as Bob told me the story, **"Is it possible that, by adopting someone else's habitual vocabulary, you began to adopt their emotional patterns as well?"** And isn't this especially true if you've adopted not only their words, but also their volume, intensity, and tonality, too?

"In the beginning was the Word . . ."
—JOHN 1:1

I'm sure that one of the reasons we often become like the people we spend time with is that we do adopt some of their emotional patterns by adopting some of their habitual vocabulary. People who spend any amount of time with me soon find themselves using words like "passionate," "outrageous," and "spectacular" to describe their experiences. Can you imagine the difference that produces in their positive states as compared to someone who says they're merely feeling "okay"? Can you imagine how using the word "passion" could cause you to peg your emotional scale? It's a word that transforms, and because I consistently use it, my life has more emotional juice.

Transformational Vocabulary can allow us to intensify or diminish any emotional state, positive or negative. This means it gives us the power to take the most negative feelings in our lives and lower their intensity to the point where they no longer bother us, and take the most positive experiences and move them to even greater heights of pleasure and empowerment.

Later that day, as Bob and I were having lunch, we became immersed in a series of projects we were working on together. At one point, he turned to me and said, "Tony, I can't believe that anyone in the world could ever be bored." I agreed. "I know what you mean. Seems crazy, doesn't it?" He said, "Yeah, boredom's not even in my vocabulary." Just as he said that, I asked, "What did you just say? Boredom is a word that's not in your vocabulary . . . Do you remember what we were talking about earlier? It's not in your vocabulary, and you don't experience the feeling. Hmmm. Is it possible that we don't experience certain emotions because we don't have a word to represent them?"

THE WORDS YOU CONSISTENTLY SELECT WILL SHAPE YOUR DESTINY

Earlier I said that the way we represent things in our minds determines how we feel about life. A related distinction is that **if you don't have a way of representing something, you can't experience it.** While it may be true that you can picture something without having a word for it, or you can represent it through sound or sensation, there's no denying that being able to articulate something gives it added dimension and substance, and thus a sense of *reality*. Words are a basic tool for representing things to ourselves, and often if there's no word, there's no way to think about the experience. For example, some Native American languages have no word for "lie"—that concept is simply not a part of their language. Nor is it a part of their thinking or behavior. Without a word for it, the concept doesn't seem to exist. In fact, the Tasaday tribe in the Philippines reportedly has no words for "dislike," "hate" or "war"—what a thought!

Returning to my initial question, if Bob never feels bored, and he doesn't have that word in his vocabulary, I had to ask further, "What's a word that I never used to describe how I'm feeling?" The answer I came up with was "depression." I may get frustrated, angry, curious, peeved, or overloaded, but I never get depressed. Why? Had it always been that way? No. Eight years ago, I'd been in a position where I felt depressed all the time. That depression drained every ounce of my will to change my life, and at the time it made me see my problems as permanent, pervasive, and personal. Fortunately I got enough pain that I pulled myself out of that pit, and as a result I linked massive pain to depression. I began to believe that being depressed was the closest thing to being dead. Because my brain associated such massive pain to the very concept of depression, without my even realizing it, I had automatically banned it from my vocabulary so that there was no way to represent or even feel it. In one stroke I had purged my vocabulary of disempowering language and thus a feeling that can devastate even the stoutest of hearts. **If an assemblage of words you're using is creating states that disempower you, get rid of those words and replace them with those that empower you!**

At this point you may be saying, "This is just semantics, isn't it? What difference does it make to play with words?" The answer is that, if *all you do is change the word*, then the experience does not change. But if using the word causes you to *break your own habitual emotional patterns*, then **everything changes.** Effectively using Transformational Vocabulary—

vocabulary that transforms our emotional experience—**breaks unresourceful patterns, makes us smile, produces totally different
feelings, changes our states, and allows us to ask more intelligent
questions.**

For instance, my wife and I are both passionate people who feel
deeply about things. Early in our relationship, we would often get into
what we used to call "pretty intense arguments." But after discovering
the power of the labels we put on our experience to alter that experience, we agreed to refer to these "conversations" as "spirited debates."
That changed our whole perception of it. A "spirited debate" has different rules than an argument, and it definitely has a different emotional intensity to it. In seven years, we've never returned to that
habitual level of emotional intensity that we had previously associated
with our "arguments."

I also began to realize that I could soften emotional intensity even
further by using **modifiers**; for example, by saying, "I'm *just a bit* peeved,"
or "I'm feeing *a tad* out of sorts." One of the things Becky will do now,
if she starts to get a little frustrated, is to say, "I'm beginning to get a
smidge cranky." We both laugh because it breaks our pattern. Our new
pattern is to make a joke of our disempowering feelings before they ever
reach the point of our being upset—we've "killed the monster while it's
little."

When I shared this Transformational Vocabulary technology with my
good friend Ken Blanchard, he related to me examples of several words
he uses to change his state. One is a word he adopted in Africa when he
was on safari and the truck he was in broke down. He turned to his wife,
Marge, and said, "Well, that's rather *inconvenient*." It worked so well in
changing their states, now they use the word on a regular basis. On the
golf course, if a shot doesn't go the way he wants, he'll say, "That shot just
underwhelms me." Tiny shifts like these change the emotional direction
and therefore the quality of our lives.

YOU CAN USE TRANSFORMATIONAL
VOCABULARY TO HELP OTHERS

Once you understand the power of words, you become highly sensitized
not only to those you use, but to those that people around you use as
well. As a result of my new understanding of Transformational Vocabulary, I found myself helping others around me. I'll never forget the first

time I began to consciously use this technology. It was in helping a friend of mine named Jim, a very successful businessman who was going through some tough times. I remember that I'd never seen him so down before.

As he talked, I noticed that he described how depressed he was, or how depressing things were, at least a dozen times in a twenty-minute period. I decided to see how quickly Transformational Vocabulary could help him to change his state, so I asked him, "Are you really depressed, or are you feeling a little frustrated?" He said, "I *am* feeling very frustrated." I said, "It looks to me like you're actually making some very positive changes that will lead to progress." Since he agreed, I described to him the impact his words might be having on his emotional state, and asked, "Do me a favor, okay? For the next ten days, promise me you won't use the word 'depressed' even once. If you begin to use it, immediately replace it with a more empowering word. Instead of 'depressed,' say, 'I'm feeling a little bit down.' Say, 'I'm getting better,' or 'I'm turning things around.' "

He agreed to commit to this as an experiment, and you can guess what happened: one simple shift in his words shifted his pattern completely. He no longer worked himself up to the same level of pain, and as a result, he stayed in more resourceful states. Two years later when I told Jim that I was writing about his experience in this book, he shared with me that he has not felt depressed one day since that time *because he never uses that word to describe his experience.*

Remember, the beauty of Transformational Vocabulary is its utter simplicity. It's truly profound knowledge—something so simple and universally applicable that the minute you use it, it can immediately increase the quality of your life.

A great example of the transformation that's possible when you change just one word is what occurred several years ago at PIE, the nationwide trucking service. Their executives found that 60 percent of all their shipping contracts were erroneous, and it was costing them more than a quarter of a million dollars a year. Dr. W. Edwards Deming was hired to find the cause. He did an intensive study and discovered that 56 percent of these errors were based on misidentification of containers by their own workers. Based on Dr. Deming's recommendations, the PIE executives decided that they must find a way to change the company-wide level of commitment to quality and that the best way would be to change how their workers viewed themselves. Instead of workers or truckers, they started referring to themselves as *craftsmen.*

At first people thought it was strange; after all, what difference could changing a job title make? They hadn't really changed anything, had they? But pretty soon, as a result of regularly using the word, the workers began to see themselves as "craftsmen," and in less than thirty days PIE cut their 56 percent erroneous shippings down to less than 10 percent, ultimately saving close to a quarter of a million dollars a year.

This illustrates a fundamental truth: **the words we use as a corporate culture and as individuals have a profound effect on our experience of reality**. One of the reasons I created the word **CANI!**, rather than borrow the Japanese term *kaizen* ("improvement"), was to build into one word the philosophy and thought patterns of constant, never-ending improvement. Once you begin to consistently use a word, it affects what you consider and how you think. The words that we use carry meaning and emotion. People invent words all the time; that's one of the marvels of the English language, which is so quick to embrace new words and concepts. If you look through a current dictionary you'll discover the contributions of many foreign languages, and especially from all kinds of special-interest groups.

For example, people in the surfing culture have created words like "tubular" and "rad" to translate their "totally awesome" experience of the waves to their day-to-day lives. Their private lingo gained such widespread acceptance that it became part of our common argot and thus the way in which we think. This also brings up the point again that we need to be conscious of the words we adopt from those around us or those we select ourselves. If you use phrases like "I'm suicidal," you have instantly raised your emotional pain to a level that could actually threaten the quality of your life. Or, if you're in a romantic relationship and tell your partner, "I'm leaving," you create the very real possibility that the relationship's about to end. If, however, you were to say, "I'm incredibly frustrated" or "I'm angry," you have a much better chance at resolution.

Most professions have a certain set of words they use to describe their work and the things particular to their type of work. Many entertainers, for example, right before they go onstage, get a feeling of tension in their stomachs. Their breathing changes, their pulse races, and they begin to perspire. Some consider this to be a natural part of the preparation to perform, while others see it as evidence that they will fail. These sensations, which Carly Simon called "stage fright," kept her from performing live for years. Bruce Springsteen, on the other hand, gets the same kind of tension in his stomach, only he labels these feelings "excitement"! He knows that he's about to have the incredibly powerful experience of entertaining thousands of people, and having them love it. He can't wait to get onstage. For Bruce Springsteen, tension in his stomach is an ally; for Carly Simon, it's an enemy.

TAKE THESE YARD APES AND GET RID OF THE GREY POUPON!

Following are some fun examples from *Newsweek*'s "Buzzwords" of Transformational Vocabulary used in the workplace ...

Daycare
Yard ape: A fully mobile preschooler. Usage: "At least yours is in school. I've got a yard ape to contend with."
Klingons: Hysterical yard apes who latch on ferociously to parents.
Chernobyl Huggies: A particularly nasty diaper, as in, "Honey, you better warn Scandinavia."
Green Elevens: The green, dripping nostrils of a yard ape.
Grey Poupon: The mess in the diapers.

Funeral Directors
This term itself is a major piece of Transformational Vocabulary. What did they used to be called? *Undertakers.* Then they became morticians, and now they're funeral directors, a term most people find a little easier to take ...
Shake 'n' Bake: Cremation without a funeral home service. Usage: "Oh, this guy's just a Shake 'n' Bake."
Peekaboo: A brief viewing of the body and short service, usually involving only family members.

SWAT Teams
Avon Calling: Blowing open a door with a shotgun.

Lawyers
Shopper: A financially dependent spouse with no personal income, as in "She'll need a ton of alimony. She's a shopper."
Bombers: Divorce lawyers who seek to destroy the opposing spouse by getting all of the assets for their own client.

Tanning Salons
Caspers: Pale-skinned customers. (Derived from Casper the Friendly Ghost.)
Iguanas: Overly tanned, leathery customers.

FROM TINKLED TO TURBO-CHARGED

What would your life be like if you could take all the negative emotions you ever felt and lower their intensity so they didn't impact you as powerfully, so you were always in charge? What would your life be like if you could take the most positive emotions and intensify them, thereby taking your life to a higher level? You can do both of these in a heartbeat. Here's your first assignment.

Take a moment right now, and write down three words that you currently use on a regular basis to make yourself feel lousy (bored, frustrated, disappointed, angry, humiliated, hurt, sad, and so forth). Whatever words you choose, be sure they are ones that you use regularly to disempower yourself. To discover some of the words you need to transform, ask yourself, "What are some negative feelings I have on a consistent basis?"

Next, having identified these three words, have some fun. **Put yourself in a crazy and outrageous state and brainstorm some new words that you think you could use to either break your pattern or at least lower your emotional intensity in some way.** Let me give you a clue on how to select some words that will really work for you over the long term. Remember that your brain loves anything that gets you out of pain and into pleasure, so pick a word that you'll *want* to use in place of the old, limiting one. One of the reasons I used "peeved" or "a bit annoyed" instead of "angry" is that they sound so ridiculous. It's a total pattern interrupt for me and anyone who's listening to me, and since I love to break patterns, I get a lot of fun and pleasure out of using these words. Once you get results like that, I guarantee you'll also get addicted to the process. To help you get started, here are some examples of simple and ridiculous words you can use to immediately lower your intensity:

Negative Emotion/Expression		Transforms Into
I'm feeling . . .	to	*I'm feeling . . .*
angry	to	**disenchanted**
afraid	to	uncomfortable
anxious	to	a little concerned
anxious	to	expectant
confused	to	curious
depressed	**to**	**calm before action**
depressed	to	not on top of it
depressed	to	on the road to a turn-around

destroyed	to	set back
that stinks	**to**	**that's a little aromatic**
pissed off	**to**	**tinkled**
disappointed	to	underwhelmed
disappointed	to	delayed
disgusted	to	surprised
dread	to	challenge
embarrassed	to	aware
embarrassed	to	stimulated
exhausted	to	recharging
exhausted	to	a little droopy
failure	to	stumble
failure	**to**	**learning**
failure	to	getting educated
fear	to	wonderment
fearful	to	curious
frightened	to	inquiring
frustrated	to	challenged
frustrated	to	fascinated
furious	to	passionate
humiliated	to	uncomfortable
humiliated	to	surprised
hurt	to	bothered
hurt	to	dinged
I hate	**to**	**I prefer**
impatient	to	anticipating
insecure	to	questioning
insulted	to	misunderstood
insulted	to	misinterpreted
irritated	**to**	**stimulated**
irritated	to	ruffled
jealous	to	overloving
lazy	to	storing energy
lonely	to	available
lonely	to	temporarily on my own
lost	to	searching
nervous	to	energized
overloaded	to	stretching
overwhelmed	to	some imbalance
overwhelmed	to	busy
overwhelmed	to	challenged
overwhelmed	to	in demand

overwhelmed	to	many opportunities
overwhelmed	**to**	**maximized**
overwhelmed	to	moving and shaking
painful	to	uncomfortable
petrified	to	challenged
rejected	to	deflected
rejected	to	learning
rejected	to	overlooked
rejected	to	underappreciated
rejected	to	**misunderstood**
sad	to	sorting my thoughts
scared	to	excited
oh, shit	to	oh, poo
sick	to	cleansing
stressed	to	busy
stressed	to	blessed
stressed	to	energized
stupid	to	discovering
stupid	to	unresourceful
stupid	to	learning
terrible	**to**	**different**

Now, you can do better than this list, I'm sure, so **come up with three words that you habitually use that create negative feelings in your life, and then write a list of alternatives** that would either break your pattern by making you laugh because they're so ridiculous, or at least lower the intensity.

Old, Disempowering Word	New, Empowering Word
1. _____	1. _____
2. _____	2. _____
3. _____	3. _____

How do you make sure that you really use these words? The answer is simple: **NAC** yourself. Remember Neuro-Associative Conditioning? Remember the first two steps?

Step One: Decide that you're committed to having much more plea-sure in your life and a lot less pain. Realize that one of the things that's kept you from having that is using language that intensifies negative emotion.

Step Two: Get leverage on yourself so that you'll use these three new words. One way to do this is to think of how ridiculous it is to work yourself into a frenzy when you have the choice of feeling good! Maybe an even more powerful way to get leverage is to do what I did: approach three friends and share with them the words that you want to change. For example, I found myself being frustrated a lot in my life, so I decided to become "fascinated" instead. I also was often saying, "I *have* to do this," and it made me feel stressed. Since I wanted a reminder about how fortunate I am, and because it really transformed my experience, I began to say, "I *get* to do this." I don't *have* to do anything! And instead of being "angry," I wanted to either be "annoyed," "peeved," or "a little bit concerned."

For the next ten days, if I caught myself using the old word, I would immediately break my pattern and replace it with the new word. **By giving myself pleasure for committing and following through, I established a new pattern**. My friends, though, were there to help me if I got off track. They were to immediately ask me, "Tony, are you angry, or are you just *peeved?*" "Are you frustrated or *fascinated?*" I made it clear to them not to use this as a weapon, but as a tool of support. Within a short period of time, these new language patterns became my consistent approach.

Does this mean that I can never feel "angry"? Of course not. Anger can be a very useful emotion at times. We just don't want our most negative emotions to be our tools of first resort. We want to add to our level of choice. We want to have more of those molds in which to pour our liquid sensations of life so that we have a greater number and quality of emotions in our lives.

If you really want to make these changes, go to three of your friends, explain to them what you're doing, what words you want, and have them ask you respectfully, "Are you (*old word*) or (*new word*)?" Make the commitment to break your own patterns as well, whenever possible. Give yourself immediate pleasure whenever you use the new alternative, and you'll develop a new level of choice for your life.

Of course, using Transformational Vocabulary is not limited to lowering negative intensity; it also offers us the opportunity to powerfully intensify our experience of positive emotions. When someone asks how you're doing, instead of saying, "Okay" or "So-so," knock their socks off by exclaiming, *"I feel spectacular!"* **As simplistic as this sounds, it creates a new pattern in your neurology—a new neural highway to pleasure**. So right now, write down three words you use to describe how you're feeling or how you're doing on a regular basis that are "just okay"

in their orientation—"I'm feeling good," "I'm fine," "Things are all right."
Then come up with new ones that will absolutely inspire you. If you want
some suggestions, look at the following list and circle the ones that you
think would be fun to add to your vocabulary to spice up your current
experience of life:

Good Word		Great Word
I'm feeling	*to*	*I'm feeling . . .*
alert	to	energized
all right	to	superb
attractive	to	gorgeous
awake	to	raring to go
comfortable	**to**	**smashing**
confident	to	unstoppable
content	to	serene
cool	to	outrageous
curious	to	fascinated
determined	**to**	**unstoppable**
energized	to	turbo-charged
enthusiastic	to	excited
excited	to	ecstatic
excited	to	impassioned
excited	to	outrageous
fantastic	to	fabulous
fast	**to**	**ballistic**
feeling good	to	cosmically charged
feeling good	to	just tremendous
fine	to	awesome
focused	to	energized
fortunate	**to**	**unbelievably blessed**
full	to	replete
fun	to	vivacious
glad	to	over the moon
good	to	better than excellent
good	to	dynamite
good	to	just doesn't get any better
good	to	magic
good	to	vibrant
great	to	exuberant

great	to	exhilarated
great	to	killer
great	to	incredible
great	**to**	**phenomenal**
happy	to	ecstatic
happy	to	jazzed
happy	to	stoked, exuberant and hyped
happy	to	totally blissed
intense	to	laser-like
interested	**to**	**enthralled**
interesting	to	captivating
like	to	enraptured
like	to	idolize
like	**to**	**relish**
loved	to	adored
loving	to	exuding love
loving	to	passionate
motivated	to	compelled
motivated	to	driven to
motivated	to	juiced
moving forward	to	moving at warp speed
nice	to	fantastic
nice	to	spectacular
no problem	to	happy to
not bad	to	couldn't be better
okay	to	energized
okay	to	fantastic
okay	**to**	**perfect!**
paying attention	to	focused
peaceful	to	serene
perfect	to	extraordinary
pleasant	to	monumental
powerful	to	invincible
pretty good	to	coolamundo
pretty good	to	great
pumped up	to	soaring
quick	**to**	**explosive**
resourceful	to	brilliant

satisfied	to	satiated
secure	to	centered
secure	to	confident
secure	to	emboldened
secure	to	empowered
smart	**to**	**gifted**
stimulated	to	charged up
strong	to	invincible
super	to	booming
tasty	to	sumptuous
terrific	**to**	**ecstatic**

Old, Mediocre Word	**New, Intensified Word**
1. _____	1. _____
2. _____	2. _____
3. _____	3. _____

Use the same system of contacting your three friends to make sure you use these new, powerful, positive words, and have fun doing it!

SOFTEN YOUR APPROACH TO PAIN WITH OTHERS

It's difficult to overestimate the impact our Transformational Vocabulary has on ourselves and on others. We need to remember the value of using what I call **softeners** and **intensifiers**; they give us a greater degree of precision in our dealings with others, whether it's a romantic relationship, a business negotiation, or all the possible scenarios in between.

Years ago, when I thought something was "screwed up" in my business, I would call the appropriate person and say, "I'm really upset" or "I'm really worried about this." Do you know what that did? My language pattern automatically put the other person into reaction, even if it wasn't my intention; often, they tended to become defensive, something that prevented both of us from finding a solution to the challenge before us.

So what I learned to do instead was to say (even if I felt more intensity), "I'm a little bit concerned about something. Can you help me?" First of all, doing this lowered my own emotional intensity. This benefited both me and the person with whom I was communicating. Why? Because "concerned" is a much different word than "worried." If you say that you're worried about something, you may be conveying the impression that you don't have faith in this person's abilities. And second, adding "a little bit" softens the message significantly. So by lowering my intensity, I enabled the person to respond from a position of strength and also enhanced my level of communication with them.

Can you see how this would improve your interactions at home as well? How do you habitually communicate with your kids? Often we don't realize the power our words have on them. Children, as well as adults, tend to take things personally, and we need to be sensitized to the possible ramifications of thoughtless remarks. Instead of continually blurting out impatiently, "You're so stupid!" or "You're so clumsy!"—a pattern that can in some cases powerfully undermine a child's sense of self-worth—break your own pattern by saying something like "I'm getting a little bit peeved with your behavior; come over here and let's talk about this." Not only does this break the pattern, allowing both of you to access a better state to intelligently communicate your feelings and desires, but it also sends the child the message that the challenge is not with them as a person but *with their behavior*—something that can be changed. This can build what I call the Reality Bridge,* the foundation for more powerful and positive communication between two people—and have a more powerful, positive impact on your kids.

The key in any of these situations is to be able to break your pattern; otherwise, in your unresourceful state, you may say things you'll regret later. This is exactly how many relationships are destroyed. In a state of anger, we may say things that hurt somebody's feelings and make them want to retaliate, or cause them to feel so hurt that they don't want to open up to us ever again. So we've got to realize the power of our words, both to create and to destroy.

> *"The German people is no warlike nation. It is a soldierly one, which means it does not want a war but does not fear it. It loves peace but it also loves its honor and freedom."*
> —ADOLF HITLER

Words have been used by demagogues throughout the ages to murder and subjugate, as when Hitler perverted a nation's frustrations into ha-

---

* The Reality Bridge is a communications strategy that our company, Robbins Success Systems, uses in corporate training programs to enhance interaction between management and employees as well as between members of the executive team.

tred for a small group of people, and in his lust for territory persuaded the German populace to gird for war. Saddam Hussein labeled his invasion of Kuwait, and the subsequent hostilities, a *jihad*, or "Holy War," which powerfully transformed the Iraqi citizens' perceptions of the justness of their cause.

To a lesser extent, we can see in our recent history plenty of examples of the careful use of words to redefine experience. During the recent Persian Gulf War, the military's jargon was unbelievably complex, but it served to soften the impact of the destruction that was occurring. During the Reagan administration, the MX missile was renamed the "Peacekeeper." The Eisenhower administration consistently referred to the Korean War as a "police action."

We've got to be precise in the words we use because they carry meaning not only to ourselves about our own experience, but also to others. If you don't like the results you're getting in your communication with others, take a closer look at the words you're using and become more selective. *I'm not suggesting that you become so sensitized that you can't use a word.* But selecting words that *empower* you is critical.

By the same token, is it always to our advantage to lower the intensity of our negative emotions? The answer is no. Sometimes we need to get ourselves into an angry state in order to create enough leverage to make a change. All human emotions have their place, as we'll talk about in Chapter 11. However, we want to make certain that we do not access our most negative and intense states to start with. So please don't misinterpret me; I'm not asking you to live a life where you don't have any negative sensations or emotions. There are places where they can be very important. We'll talk about one of them in the next chapter. Realize that our goal is to consistently feel less pain in our lives, and more pleasure. Mastering Transformational Vocabulary is one of the single most simple and powerful steps toward that goal.

Beware of labels that can limit your experience. As I mentioned in the first chapter, I worked with a young boy who was at one time labeled "learning disabled" and is now evaluated as a genius. You can imagine how that one change in words has radically transformed his perception of himself and how much of his ability he now taps. What are the words *you* want to be known by? What characteristic word or phrase do you want others to identify with you?

We've got to be very careful of accepting other people's labels, because once we put a label on something, we create a corresponding emotion. Nowhere is this truer than with diseases. Everything that I've studied in the field of psychoneuroimmunology reinforces the idea that the words we use produce powerful biochemical effects. In an interview with Norman Cousins, he told me of the work he'd done in the last

---

AND NOW, A PAUSE FOR OUR SPONSOR . . .

Sometimes vocabulary is even more transformational than bargained for—a fact to which several major advertisers can attest. After translating their slogan "Come Alive! You're in the Pepsi Generation" into Chinese, corporate officials were stunned to discover that they'd just spent millions of dollars announcing, "Pepsi Brings Your Ancestors Back from the Grave." Chevrolet, mystified by sluggish sales of its new Nova compact in Latin America, eventually discovered the Spanish translation of *no va:* "It Doesn't Go."

---

twelve years with over 2,000 patients. Time and again, he noticed that the moment a patient was diagnosed—i.e., had a *label* to attach to his symptoms—he became worse. Labels like "cancer," "multiple sclerosis," and "heart disease" tended to produce panic in the patients, leading to helplessness and depression that actually impaired the effectiveness of the body's immune system.

Conversely, studies proved that if patients could be freed of the depression produced by certain labels, a corresponding boost was automatically produced in their immune systems. **"Words can produce illness; words can kill,"** Cousins told me. "Therefore, wise physicians are very careful about the way they communicate." That's one of the reasons why, in Fortune Management,™ our practice-management company, we work with doctors not only in helping them to build their businesses, but in teaching them how to enhance their emotional sensitivity to enable them to contribute more. **If you're in a profession where you work with people, it's imperative that you understand the power of words to impact those around you.**

If you're still skeptical, I suggest that you simply test Transformational Vocabulary on yourself, and see what happens. Often in seminars, people say things like, "I'm so angry about what this person did to me!" I'll ask them, "Are you angry, or are you hurt?" Just asking them that question often makes them reevaluate the situation. When they select a new word and say, "I guess I'm hurt," you can instantly see their physiology reflect a drop in intensity. It's a lot easier for them to deal with hurt than it is with anger.

Similarly, you can try lowering your emotional intensity in areas you may not have thought of. For instance, instead of using the phrase, "I'm *starving* to death," what if instead you said, "I feel a little hungry"? By using that, you'll discover as I have that you can literally lower the intensity of your appetite in a matter of moments. Sometimes people overeat simply out of a habitual pattern of whipping themselves into an emotional frenzy. Part of it starts with the language they use consistently.

At a recent Date With Destiny seminar, we witnessed a great example of the power of using words to change someone's state instantly. One of the participants came back from dinner, absolutely radiant. She told us that right before dinner she'd had an incredible urge to cry, and ran out of the room, bawling. "Everything was all jumbled up," she said. "I felt like I was going to burst. I thought I was going to have a breakdown. But then I said to myself 'No, no, no, you're having a break-*up!*' That made me laugh. And then I thought, 'No—you're having a break-*through!*' " The only thing she had changed was one word, but by taking control of her labeling process (her vocabulary) she completely changed her state and her perception of her experience—and thus transformed her reality.

Now is your chance. **Take control.** Notice the words you habitually use, and replace them with ones that empower you, raising or lowering the emotional intensity as appropriate. Start today. Set this processional effect in motion. Write down your words, make your commitment, follow through, and know what the power of this simple tool in and of itself will accomplish without using anything else.

Next, let's take a look at something that's equally fun and equally simple in empowering you to manage your emotions consistently. Together, let's blaze a trail of possibility as you . . .

10
DESTROY THE BLOCKS, BREAK DOWN THE WALL, LET GO OF THE ROPE, AND DANCE YOUR WAY TO SUCCESS: THE POWER OF LIFE METAPHORS

"The metaphor is perhaps one of man's most fruitful potentialities. Its efficacy verges on magic, and it seems a tool for creation which God forgot inside one of His creatures when He made him."
—JOSÉ ORTEGA Y GASSET

"I'm at the end of my rope."
"I can't break through the wall."
"My head is about to burst."
"I'm at a crossroads."
"I struck out."
"I'm floating on air."
"I'm drowning."
"I'm happy as a lark."
"I've reached a dead end."
"I'm carrying the world on my shoulders."
"Life is a bowl of cherries."
"Life is the pits."

In the last chapter we talked about the power of words to shape our lives and direct our destinies. Now, let's look at certain words that carry even *more* meaning and emotional intensity: **metaphors**. In order to understand metaphors, we must first understand symbols. What creates more immediate impact: the word "Christian" or the image of a cross? If you're like many people, the cross has more power to produce immediate positive emotions. It's literally nothing but two intersecting lines, but it has the power to communicate a standard and a way of life to millions of people. Now take that cross, twist it into a swastika, and contrast it with the word "Nazi." Which has more power to influence you negatively? Again, if you're like most, the swastika will tend to produce stronger sensations more quickly than the word itself. Throughout human history, symbols have been employed to trigger emotional response and shape men's behavior. Many things serve as symbols: images, sounds, objects, actions, and, of course, words. If words are symbolic, then metaphors are heightened symbols.

What is a metaphor? **Whenever we explain or communicate a concept by likening it to something else, we are using a metaphor.** The two things may bear little actual resemblance to each other, but our familiarity with one allows us to gain an understanding of the other. Metaphors are symbols and, as such, they can create emotional intensity even more quickly and completely than the traditional words we use. Metaphors can transform us *instantly*.

As human beings, we constantly think and speak in metaphors. Often people speak of "being caught between a rock and a hard place." They feel like they're "in the dark," or that they're "struggling to keep their head above water." Do you think you might be a little bit more stressed if you thought about dealing with your challenge in terms of "struggling to keep your head above water" rather than "climbing the ladder of success"? Would you feel differently about taking a test if you talked about "sailing" through it rather than "flailing"? Would your perception and experience of time change if you talked about time "crawling" rather than "flying"? You bet it would!

One of the primary ways we learn is through metaphors. Learning is the process of making new associations in our minds, creating new meanings, and metaphors are ideally suited for this. When we don't understand something, a metaphor provides a way of seeing how what we *don't* understand is like something we *do* understand. The metaphor helps us to link up a relationship. If X is like Y, and we understand X, suddenly we understand Y. If, for example, someone tries to explain electricity to you by throwing around the terms "ohms," "amperes," "wattage," and "resistors," chances are they'll totally confuse you because it's likely you have no understanding of these words, no **references** for them, and therefore it's difficult to understand a relationship between them.

But what if I explained electricity to you by comparing it to something you were already familiar with? What if I drew you a picture of a pipe and said, "Have you ever seen water running through a pipe?" You'd say yes. Then I'd say, "What if there were a little flap that could slow down the amount of water going through the pipe? That little flap is what a resistor does in an electrical unit." Would you now know what a resistor is? You bet—and you'd know it instantly. Why? Because I told you how this was *like* something you already understood.

All great teachers—Buddha, Mohammed, Confucius, Lao-Tzu—have used metaphors to convey their meaning to the common man. Regardless of religious beliefs, most would agree that Jesus Christ was a remarkable teacher whose message of love has endured not only because of what he said, but also the way in which he said it. He didn't go to the fishermen and tell them he wanted them to recruit Christians; they would have no reference for recruiting. So he told them he wanted them to become "fishers of men."

The minute he used that metaphor, they immediately understood what they needed to do. This metaphor instantly gave them an analogous step-by-step process for how to bring others into the faith. When he told his parables, he distilled complex ideas into simple images that transformed anyone who took their message to heart. In fact, not only was Jesus a master storyteller, but he used his whole life as a metaphor to illustrate the strength of God's love and the promise of redemption.

Metaphors can empower us by expanding and enriching our experience of life. Unfortunately, though, if we're not careful, when we adopt a metaphor we instantaneously also adopt many limiting beliefs that come with it. For years physicists used the metaphor of the solar system to describe the relationship of the electrons to the protons and neutrons within the nucleus of an atom. What was great about this metaphor? It immediately helped students understand the relationship between the atom and something they already understood. They could immediately picture the nucleus as the sun and the electrons as planets revolving around it. The challenge was that by adopting this metaphor, physicists— without realizing it—adopted a belief system that electrons remained in equidistant orbits from the nucleus, very much in the same way that planets remained in basically equidistant orbits from the sun. It was an inaccurate and limiting presupposition. In fact, it locked physicists for years into a pattern of irresolution of many atomic questions, all because of a false set of presuppositions adopted due to this metaphor. Today we know that electrons don't maintain equidistant orbits; their orbits *vary* in distance from the nucleus. This new understanding wasn't adopted until the solar system metaphor had been abandoned. The result was a quantum leap in the understanding of atomic energy.

GLOBAL METAPHORS

Remember my raging CEO? The same day I made the distinctions that led to the creation of the technology of Transformational Vocabulary, I discovered the value of what I call **global metaphors.** I knew that my CEO used words that intensified his emotion, and I wondered what made him feel those negative feelings in the first place. As you and I already know, everything we do is based on the state we're in, and our state is determined by our physiology and the way we represent things in our minds.

So I asked him why he was so upset, and he said, "Well, it's like *they have us in a box with a gun to our heads.*" Do you think you'd react rather intensely if you believed or represented in your mind that you were trapped in a situation like this? It's not hard to figure out why he was in a rage. Now, for many years without realizing it, I'd helped people change how they were feeling by interrupting their patterns and **changing their metaphors.** I just wasn't aware of what I was doing. (That's part of the power of creating a label: once you have a label for what you do, you can produce a behavior consistently.)

I turned to the CEO and asked, "What color is the squirt gun?" He looked at me in a puzzled state and said, "What?" I repeated the question, "What color is the squirt gun?" This immediately broke his pattern. In order to answer my question, his mind had to focus on my weird question, which immediately changed his internal focus. When he began to picture a squirt gun, do you think his emotion changed as a result? You bet! He started to laugh. You see, virtually any question we ask repeatedly, a person will eventually entertain an answer to, and when they do answer your question, it changes their focus. For example, if I tell you over and over, "Don't think of the color blue," what color are you going to think of? The answer, obviously, is "blue." And whatever you think about, you'll feel.

Getting him to think about the situation in terms of a squirt gun, I immediately shattered his disempowering imagery, and thereby changed his emotional state in the moment. What about his box? I handled that in a different way because I knew he was competitive; I simply said, "As far as this box idea is concerned, I don't know about you, but I know no one could ever build a box big enough to hold *me*." You can imagine how quickly that destroyed his box!

This man regularly feels intense because he's operating with aggressive metaphors. If you are feeling really bad about something, take a quick look at the metaphors you're using to describe how you are feeling, or why you are not progressing, or what is getting in the way. Often you're using a metaphor that intensifies your negative feelings. When people are experiencing difficulties they frequently say things like "I feel like the weight of the world is on my back" or "There's this wall in front of me, and I just can't break through." But disempowering metaphors can be changed just as quickly as they were created. You choose to represent the metaphor as being real; you can *change* the metaphor just as quickly. So if someone tells me they feel like they have the weight of the world on their back, I'll say, "Set the world down and move on." They'll give me a funny look, but sure enough, in order to understand what I just said, they'll make a change in their focus and therefore how they feel immediately. Or if someone tells me that they just can't make progress, that they keep hitting a wall, I tell them to stop hitting it and just drill a hole through it. Or climb over it, or tunnel under it, or walk over, open the door, and go through it.

You'd be surprised, as simplistic as this sounds, how quickly people will respond. Again, the moment you represent things differently in your mind, in that moment you'll instantly change the way you feel. If someone tells me, "I'm at the end of my rope," I'll say, "Set it aside and come over here!" Often people talk about how they feel "stuck" in a situation. You're never stuck! You may be a little frustrated, you may not have clear answers, but you're not stuck. The minute you represent the situation to yourself as being stuck, though, that's exactly how you'll feel. We must be very careful about the metaphors we allow ourselves to use.

Be careful of the metaphors that other people offer you as well. Recently I read an article about the fact that Sally Field is now turning 44. The article said she's beginning to start "down the slippery slope of middle age." What a horrible and disempowering way to represent your expanding wisdom! If you feel like you're in the dark, then simply turn the lights on. If you feel like you're drowning in a sea of confusion, walk up the beach and relax on the island of understanding. I know this can sound juvenile, but what's truly juvenile is allowing ourselves to unconsciously select metaphors that disempower us on a consistent basis. **We must *take charge* of our metaphors**, not just to avoid the problem metaphors, but so that we can *adopt the empowering metaphors as well*.

Once you become sensitized to the metaphors you and other people use, making a change is very easy. All you need to do is ask yourself, *"Is this what I really mean? Is this really the way it is, or is this metaphor inaccurate?"* Remember, anytime you use the words "I feel like" or "This is like," the word "like" is often a trigger for the use of a metaphor. So ask yourself a more empowering question. Ask, "What would be a *better* metaphor? What would be a more *empowering* way of thinking of this? What else is this like?" For example, if I were to ask you what life means to you, or what your metaphor for life is, you might say, "Life is like a constant battle" or "Life is a war." If you were to adopt this metaphor, you'd begin to adopt a series of beliefs that come with it. Like the example of the atom and the solar system, you'd begin to conduct your behavior based on a set of unconscious beliefs that are carried within this metaphor.

A whole set of rules, ideas, and preconceived notions accompany any metaphor you adopt. So if you believe life is a war, how does that color your perceptions of life? You might say, "It's tough, and it ends with death." Or, "It's going to be me against everybody else." Or, "It's dog eat dog." Or, "If life is really a battle, then maybe I'm going to get hurt." All these filters impact your unconscious beliefs about people, possibility, work, effort, and life itself. This metaphor will affect your decisions about how to think, how to feel, and what to do. It will shape your actions and therefore your destiny.

LIFE IS A GAME

Different people have different global metaphors. For example, in reading interviews with Donald Trump, I've noticed that he often refers to life as a "test." You either win first place, or you lose—there's no in between. Can you imagine the stress that must create in his life, interpreting it this way? If life is a test, maybe it's going to be tough; maybe you'd better be prepared; maybe you could flunk out (or cheat, I suppose). For some people, life is a competition. That might be fun, but it could also mean that there are other people you have to beat, that there could be only one winner.

For some people, life is a game. How might that color your perceptions? Life might be fun—what a concept! It might be somewhat competitive. It might be a chance for you to play and enjoy yourself a lot more. Some people say, "If it's a game, then there are going to be losers." Other people ask, "Will it take a lot of skill?" It all depends on what *beliefs* you attach to the word "game"; but with that one metaphor, again, you have a set of filters that is going to affect the way you think and the way you feel.

Surely, Mother Teresa's metaphor for life is that it's sacred. What if you believed life is sacred? If that were your primary metaphor, you might have more reverence for it—or you might think that you weren't allowed to have so much fun. What if you believe life is a gift? All of a sudden it becomes a surprise, something fun, something special. What if you think life is a dance? Wouldn't that be a kick? It would be something beautiful, something you do with other people, something with grace, rhythm, and joy. Which of these metaphors properly represents life? They're probably *all* useful at different times to help you interpret what you need to do to make changes. But remember, all metaphors carry benefits in some context, and limitations in others.

As I've become more sensitized to metaphors, what I've begun to believe is that *having only one metaphor is a great way to limit your life.* There would be nothing wrong with the solar system metaphor if a physicist had many other ways of describing atoms as well. So if we want to expand our lives, we should expand the metaphors we use to describe what our life is or what our relationships are, or even who we are as human beings.

Are we limited to metaphors about life or about atoms? Of course not. We have metaphors for almost every area of our experience. Take work, for example. Some people will say, "Well, back to the salt mines" or "I have to put my nose to the grindstone." How do you think those people feel about their jobs? Some business people I know use global metaphors like "my assets" for the businesses they own and "my liabilities" for the people they employ. How do you think that affects the way they treat people? Others look at business as a garden where every day you have to maintain and improve it so that eventually you will reap a reward. Still others see work as a chance to be with friends, to join a winning team. As for me, I think of my businesses as families. This allows us to transform the quality of the connections we share with each other.

"Life is painting a picture, not doing a sum."
—OLIVER WENDELL HOLMES, JR.

Can you see how changing just one global metaphor from "Life is a competition" to "Life is a game" could instantly change your experience of life in many areas simultaneously? Would it change your relationships if you saw life as a dance? Could it change the way you operate in your business? You bet it could! This is an example of a **pivot point**, a global change, where just making this one change would transform the way you think and feel in multiple areas of your life. I am not saying that there is a right or wrong way of looking at things. Just realize that **changing one global metaphor can instantly transform the way you look at your entire life**. Just as with Transformational Vocabulary, the power of metaphors is in their simplicity.

Years ago I was conducting a two-week Certification program in Scottsdale, Arizona. In the middle of the seminar, a man jumped up and started stabbing out at people with his bare hands as if he were holding a knife, while screaming at the top of his lungs, *"I'm blacking out, I'm blacking out!"* A psychiatrist who was sitting two rows in front of him shouted, "Oh, my God! He's having a psychotic breakdown!" Fortunately, I didn't accept the psychiatrist's label of Transformational Vocabulary. Instead, all I knew was that I needed to change the excited man's state *instantly*. I had not developed the concept of global metaphors yet; I just did what I knew how to do best. I interrupted his pattern. I went up to him and yelled, "Then just *white it out!* Use that stuff you use when you're typing! *White it out!"* The man was stunned for a moment. He stopped what he was doing, and everybody paused to see what would happen next.

Within a matter of seconds his face and body changed, and he started to breathe differently. I said, "White out the whole thing." Then I asked him how he felt and he said, "That feels a lot better." So I said, "Well, then, sit down," and continued with the seminar. Everyone looked dumbfounded, and to tell the truth, I, too, was a bit surprised that it worked this easily! Two days later this man approached me and said, "I don't know what that whole thing was about, but I turned forty that day and just lost it. I felt like stabbing out because I was in this blackness and it was swallowing me up. But when I put that White-Out on, everything just brightened up. I felt totally different. I started thinking new thoughts, and I feel fine today." And he continued to feel fine for the duration—just by changing one simple metaphor.

So far we've spoken only of how to *lower* our negative emotional intensity through the use of Transformational Vocabulary and global metaphors. However, **sometimes it's useful and important to get our-**

selves to feel negative emotions with strong intensity. For example, I know a couple who have a son who was caught up in drugs and alcohol. They knew they should do something to get him to change his destructive patterns, but at the same time they had mixed associations with interfering in his life. What finally pushed them over the edge and gave them enough leverage to get themselves to take action and *do* something was a conversation they had with someone who'd once been addicted himself. *"There are two bullets pointed at your son's head right now,"* he told them. *"One is drugs, the other is alcohol, and one or the other is going to kill him—it's only a matter of time—if you don't stop him now."*

By representing things in this way, they were driven to action. Suddenly, not taking action would mean allowing their son to die, whereas previously they had represented his problem as merely being a challenge. Until they adopted this new metaphor, they were missing the emotional potency to do whatever it would take. I am happy to tell you that they did succeed in helping this young man turn things around. Remember, the metaphors we use will determine our actions.

SELECT YOUR GLOBAL METAPHORS

As I developed "antennae" to sensitize myself to people's global metaphors, I read an interview with anthropologist Mary Catherine Bateson in which she said, "Few things are more debilitating than a toxic metaphor."* That's quite an insight, and one with which I was soon to gain firsthand experience.

At one of my Date With Destiny seminars, most everybody was complaining about a certain woman even before the program had begun. She had created a commotion at the registration area, and when she got into the room she started complaining about everything imaginable: first the room was too hot, then too cold; she was upset with the person in front of her because he was too tall; and so on. By the time I got up to speak I couldn't go for more than five minutes without her interrupting and trying to find how what I said really didn't work, or wasn't really true, or for which there was some kind of exception.

I kept trying to break her pattern, but I was focusing on the effect rather than the cause. Suddenly I realized that she must have some global belief or global metaphor about life that made her such a fanatic for detail and almost spiteful in her approach. I asked her, "What are you trying to gain by doing this? I know you must have a positive intent. What is your belief about life, or about details, or about whether things are right or

* Moyers, Bill, *A World of Ideas,* New York: Doubleday, 1989.

wrong?" She said, *"I guess I just believe that small leaks sink the ship."* If you thought you were going to drown, wouldn't you be a little fanatical about finding any possibility of a leak? That's how this woman viewed life!

Where did this metaphor come from? It turned out that this woman had experienced several situations in her life where little things cost her a lot. She attributed her divorce to some small problems that didn't get handled—problems she wasn't even aware of. Similarly, she felt that her financial woes were the result of equally small causes. She adopted this metaphor to keep her from re-experiencing pain like this in the future. Obviously, she wasn't very excited about changing metaphors without my providing a little leverage. Once I got her to feel the pain that this metaphor was constantly creating in her life, and the immediate pleasure she could have by changing it, I was able to assist her in breaking her pattern and changing her metaphor by creating a series of new ways of looking at herself and life.

She combined a variety of global metaphors—life as a game, life as a dance—and you should have seen the transformation, not just in the way she treated other people, but also in the way she treated herself, because she had always been finding small leaks in herself as well. This one change affected the way she approached everything and is a great example of how changing one global metaphor can transform every area of your life, from your self-esteem to your relationships to the way you deal with the world at large.

With all the power that metaphors wield over our lives, the scary part is that *most of us have never consciously selected the metaphors with which we represent things to ourselves.* Where did you get your metaphors? You probably picked them up from people around you, from your parents, teachers, co-workers, and friends. I'll bet you didn't think about their impact, or maybe you didn't even think about them at all, and then they just became a habit.

> ### *"All perception of truth is the detection of an analogy."*
> —HENRY DAVID THOREAU

For years, people asked me what it was I did exactly. At various times I tried different metaphors—"I'm a teacher," "I'm a student," "I'm a hunter of human excellence," "I'm a speaker," "I'm a national best-selling author," "I'm a peak performance consultant," "I'm a therapist," "I'm a counselor"—but none of them conveyed the right feeling. People gave me plenty of metaphors. I was known by many in the media as a "guru." This is a metaphor I avoided because I felt that the presupposition that went with it was that people were dependent upon me to create their change—which would never empower them. Since I believe that we all must be responsible for our own change, I avoided this metaphor.

One day, though, I finally got it. "*I'm a coach,*" I thought. What is a coach? To me, a coach is a person who is your friend, someone who really cares about you. A coach is committed to helping you be the best that you can be. A coach will challenge you, not let you off the hook. Coaches have knowledge and experience because they've been there before. They aren't any better than the people they are coaching (this took away my need to have to be perfect for the people I was "teaching"). In fact, the people they coach may have natural abilities superior to their own. But because coaches have concentrated their power in a particular area for years, they can teach you one or two distinctions that can immediately transform your performance in a matter of moments.

Sometimes coaches can teach you new information, new strategies and skills; they show you how to get measurable results. Sometimes a coach doesn't even teach you something new, but they remind you of what you need to do at just the right moment, and they push you to do it. I thought, "What I truly am is a success coach. I help to coach people on how to achieve what they really want more quickly and more easily." And everyone needs a coach, whether it's a top-level executive, a graduate student, a homemaker, a homeless person, or the president of the United States! As soon as I started using this metaphor, it immediately changed the way I felt about myself. I felt less stressed, more relaxed; I felt closer to people. I didn't have to be "perfect" or "better." I began to have more fun, and my impact on people multiplied manyfold.

A METAPHOR COULD SAVE YOUR LIFE

Two people Becky and I have the privilege to count as friends are Martin and Janet Sheen. They have been married for close to thirty years, and one of the things that I respect most about them is their absolute support for each other, for their family, and for anyone in need. As much as the public knows Martin is a committed giver, they have no idea how much he and Janet do together for others on a daily basis. These two people are the epitome of integrity. Their metaphor for humanity is that of "one giant family," and as a result they feel the deepest caring and compassion even for complete strangers.

I remember when Martin shared with me the moving story of how his life changed years ago while he was making *Apocalypse Now*. Before that time, he had seen life as something to fear. Now he sees it as an intriguing challenge. Why? *His new metaphor is that life is a mystery*. He loves the mystery of being a human being, the wonder and sense of possibility that unfolds with his experience of each new day.

What changed his metaphor? Intense pain. *Apocalypse* was shot deep in the jungles of the Philippines. The shooting schedule was normally Monday through Friday, and usually on Friday night, Martin and Janet would make the two-and-a-half-hour drive for a weekend "retreat" in Manila. On one weekend, though, Martin had to stay for an additional Saturday morning shoot. (Janet had already committed to going into town to purchase a glass eye for a crewman who was so poor he was unable to buy his own, so she went ahead.) That night, Martin found himself alone, tossing and turning, perspiring profusely, and beginning to experience intense pain. By morning he began to have a massive heart attack. Portions of his body became numb and paralyzed. He fell to the ground, and through nothing but the sheer power of his will, crawled out the door and yelled for help. Lying there on the ground, he said he actually had the experience of dying. All of a sudden, everything felt calm and smooth. He could see himself moving across the lake and the water in the distance. He thought to himself, "Oh, this is what dying is," and it was then that he realized that *he wasn't afraid of dying, that he had really been afraid of life!* In that moment, he realized that life itself was the real challenge. Instantly, he made the decision to live. He mustered every ounce of energy he had left, pushing his arm out to grab some grass. With total focus, he slowly pulled it up to his nose. He could barely feel a thing. The moment he smelled the grass, the pain came back, and he knew he was alive. He kept fighting.

When the crewmen discovered him, they were sure he would die. Both the looks on their faces and their comments made Martin question his own ability to make it. He began to lose his strength. Realizing there was no time, the top pilot on the *Apocalypse* crew risked his own life and flew the helicopter sideways through thirty- to forty-knot winds in order to get him to the hospital in town. Upon arriving, he was put on a stretcher and wheeled into the emergency room, where he continued to receive both subliminal and overt messages that he was going to die. He was becoming weaker with each moment. Then Janet came in. All she'd heard was that he'd had a heat stroke, but then the doctors informed her of the graveness of his condition. She refused to accept it—she knew that Martin needed strength; she also knew she had to break his pattern of fear as well as her own. She took immediate action, and accomplished it all with one statement. When he opened his eyes, she smiled brightly and said, *"It's just a movie, babe! It's only a movie!"* Martin said that in that moment he knew he was going to make it and began to heal. What a great metaphor! Instantly, the problem didn't seem so grave—it was something he could handle. "A movie certainly isn't worth having a heart attack over" was the implied message, but also, subliminally, I believe the metaphor cut even deeper. After all, the pain you're experiencing when you make a movie never lasts. It's not real, and at some point the director will say "Cut!" Janet's use of this brilliant pattern interrupt, this single metaphor, helped Martin to marshal his resources, and to this day he believes it saved his life.

Metaphors don't just affect us as individuals; they affect our community and our world as well. The metaphors we adopt culturally can shape our perceptions and our actions—or lack of action. In the last few decades, with the advent of moon missions, we began to adopt the metaphor of "Spaceship Earth." While this metaphor sounded great, it didn't always work well for creating an emotional response to dealing with our ecological challenges. Why? It's hard to get emotional about a spaceship; it's disassociated. Contrast that with the feelings created by the metaphor "Mother Earth." How differently would you feel about protecting your "mother" than you would about keeping a "spaceship" clean? Pilots and sailors often describe their planes or ships as beautiful women. They say, "She's a beauty." Why don't they say, "He's a beauty?" Because they'd probably be a lot rougher with that plane or ship if they thought it was some big, fat guy named Joe rather than some shapely and sleek princess gliding through the shimmering air or sea.

We use metaphors constantly during war. What was the name for the first part of the operation in the Persian Gulf War? Before war was declared, it was called "Operation Desert Shield." But as soon as the command to fight was given, Operation Desert Shield became "Desert Storm." Think how that one change of metaphor instantly changed the meaning of the experience for everyone. Instead of shielding the rest of the Arabs from Saddam Hussein, in General Norman Schwarzkopf's words, the troops became "the storm of freedom," sweeping the occupying Iraqi forces out of Kuwait.

> ### *"An iron curtain has descended across the Continent."*
> —WINSTON CHURCHILL

Think how radically the face of eastern Europe has changed just in the last couple of years. The "Iron Curtain" was a metaphor that shaped the post–World War II experience for decades, and the Berlin Wall served as a physical symbol for the imposing barrier that divided all of Europe. When the Berlin Wall came down in November 1989, more than just a stone wall was demolished. The destruction of that one symbol instantly provided a new metaphor that changed the beliefs of multitudes of people about what was possible in their lifetimes. Why did people have so much fun digging away at an old, crumbling wall when there were plenty of gates they could go through? It was because knocking down the wall was a universal metaphor for possibility, freedom, and breaking through barriers.

FIT THE WORD TO THE DEED

Being aware of the vast power contained in metaphors includes knowing how to use them in an appropriate context. The challenge is that a lot of people have metaphors that help them in their professions, but create challenges at home. I know an attorney who found herself trying to apply the same adversarial metaphors at home that served her so well at work. Her husband would start a perfectly innocent conversation with her, and the next thing he knew, he felt like he was up on the witness stand being cross-examined! That doesn't work too well in a personal relationship, does it? Or suppose someone is a totally dedicated police officer. If they can't let go of their work when they get home, do you think they might always be on the lookout for other people violating their standards?

One of the best examples of an inappropriate metaphor is a man who was so dissociated that his wife and children didn't feel any connection with him at all. They resented the way he never expressed his true feelings and the fact that he always seemed to be directing them. Do you know what his profession was? He was an air traffic controller! On the job he had to remain detached. Even if there was an emergency, he had to keep his voice absolutely calm so as not to alarm the pilots he was directing. That disassociated attitude worked well in the control tower, but it didn't work at home. Be careful not to carry the metaphors that are appropriate in one context, like the environment in which you work, into an incompatible context, like how you relate to your family or friends.

What are some of the metaphors people have for their personal relationships? Some people call the person they're in a relationship with "the old man" or "the old hag." Some call them "the dictator," "the ball and chain," "the warden." One woman actually called her husband "the Prince of Darkness"! What are some more empowering alternatives? Many people call their mate their "lover," their "better half," their "partner in life," their "teammate," their "soul mate." By the way, even changing one slight nuance of a metaphor will change the way you perceive the relationship. You may not feel passionate for a "partner," but you certainly would for your "lover."

Do you think that the metaphors you use in representing your relationship to yourself as well as to others would affect the way you feel about it and how you relate to one another? You bet! One lady who came to a Date With Destiny seminar kept referring to her husband as "this jerk I'm with," and I had noticed that whenever he talked about her, he called her "the love" of his life or his "better half" or his "gift from God." When I pointed this out to her, she was shocked, because she's a very loving woman who hadn't realized how toxic one casually adopted metaphor could be. Together we selected more appropriate metaphors for her relationship with her husband.

ALL I WANT FOR CHRISTMAS . . .

One of my friends who obviously doesn't have kids used to call them "barfers." As long as he held that metaphor, can you imagine how kids responded to him? Recently, though, he filled in for Santa Claus at a department store—several of us set him up so he had to do it—and he got to have hundreds of "barfers" come and sit on his lap. Well, that one experience gave him a totally new view of children and changed his metaphor forever. Now he calls them "cuddlies"! Do you think that changed the way he feels? You'd better believe it. Calling your kids "brats" doesn't usually make you want to take good care of them or nurture them. Make sure that you have the appropriate metaphor that supports you in dealing with your children—remember, they listen and learn from you.

One of the most empowering global metaphors that has helped me through tough times is a story shared by many speakers in personal development. It's the simple story of a stonecutter. How does a stonecutter break open a giant boulder? He starts out with a big hammer and whacks the boulder as hard as he can. The first time he hits it, there's not a scratch, not a chip—nothing. He pulls back the hammer and hits it again and again—100, 200, 300 times without even a scratch.

After all this effort, the boulder may not show even the slightest crack, but he keeps on hitting it. People sometimes pass by and laugh at him for persisting when obviously his actions are having no effect. But a stonecutter is very intelligent. He knows that just because you don't see immediate results from your current actions, it doesn't mean you're not making progress. He keeps hitting at different points in the stone, over and over again, and at some point—maybe on the 500th or 700th hit, maybe on the 1,0004th hit—the stone doesn't just chip, but literally splits in half. Was it this one single hit that broke the stone open? Of course not. It was the constant and continual pressure being applied to the challenge at hand. To me, the consistent application of the discipline of **CANI!** is the hammer that can break open any boulder that's blocking the path of your progress.

Years ago, one of my early mentors, Jim Rohn, assisted me in looking at my life in a new way by thinking in terms of the metaphor of the seasons. Often when things look bleak people think, "This is going to go on forever." Instead I say, "**Life has its seasons**, and I'm in winter right now." The great thing is, if you adopt this metaphor, what always follows winter? Spring! The sun comes out, you're no longer freezing to death, and all of a sudden you can plant new seeds. You start to notice all the beauty of nature, the new life and growth. Then comes summer. It's hot, you tend to your little plants, and you nurture them so they don't get scorched. Then there's fall, when you get to reap your rewards. Sometimes it doesn't work out—maybe a hailstorm destroys your crop. But if you trust in the cycle of the seasons, you know you'll get another chance.

A great example of the power of metaphor to transform one's life was provided by a man in one of my Date With Destiny seminars. His nickname was "Maestro." (I always have people choose a name for themselves that's a metaphor for the way they want to be treated during the weekend. Even that simple exercise can create some interesting changes in people as they begin to live up to their new "label." How differently do you think you'd act if your name was "Lightning" or "Love" or "Dancer" or "The Wizard"?) Maestro was a wonderful man who was almost 170 pounds overweight. As I worked with him, it became clear that he associated being fat with being spiritual. His belief was that if you're really overweight, then only spiritual people will get through to you because they'd be the only people not turned off by your fat. Sincere people would try to get through; shallow, nonspiritual types would be so turned off that he would never have to deal with them. He said, "I know it doesn't make any sense, but it just feels real to me that if you're fat, you really are spiritual. After all, think of all the fat gurus around the world. I think God loves fat people."

I said, "Well, I think God loves everybody . . . but I think what he does with fat people is stick them on a skewer and roast them over hell!" You should have seen his face! Now, of course I don't believe that, but it was a major pattern interrupt that created a pretty intense picture in his head. Then I asked him, "What is your body like?" He said, "It's nothing; it's just a vehicle." I said, "Is it a quality vehicle?" He said, "It doesn't matter if it's a quality vehicle, as long as it gets you there."

A change in metaphor was obviously in order. He was already a beautiful spiritual being, so I assisted him in adopting a new metaphor that was in alignment with his own beliefs. I asked him how he would treat his body if he realized it wasn't just a vehicle that got him by, *but was truly the temple of his soul.* In that moment, he nodded his head, and you could see he believed that was truly what his body was. With this one simple, perceptual shift, he made all the changes necessary in his unconscious rules about what to eat, when to eat, how to eat, and how to treat his body, in that moment. One global metaphor changed just about everything he'd ever thought about his body.

How would *you* treat a temple? Would you slam huge amounts of fatty, greasy foods into it? Maestro's newfound sense of reverence for his body transformed him. As of this writing, it's been six months since he attended the seminar, and *he's already lost 130 pounds simply by adopting this one metaphor* and living by it every single day. It has become the *habitual* metaphor that shapes his thinking and his actions. Now when he goes grocery shopping, he asks himself, "Would I put this in a temple?" Once in a rare while if he finds himself going down an aisle in the supermarket that holds all the junk food he used to eat, he just pictures his body on a skewer above hell, and that is all it takes to knock him right out of that aisle! Maestro also used to listen to music so loud that everyone around him was concerned that he would damage his ear-drums. Now he doesn't even listen to the same music because he says, "I want to take care of my temple." Are you clear now on the incredible power of global metaphors to change almost every area of your life simultaneously?

THE METAMORPHOSIS FROM CATERPILLAR TO BUTTERFLY

One day, when my son Joshua was about six or seven years old, he came home crying hysterically because one of his friends fell off some play-ground equipment at school and died. I sat down with Josh and said, "Honey, I know how you feel. You miss him, and you should feel those feelings. But you should also realize that you feel this way because you're a caterpillar." He said, "What?" I had broken his pattern a little bit. I said, "You're thinking like a caterpillar." He asked me what I meant.

"There's a point," I said, "where most caterpillars think that they have died. They think life has ended. When is that?" He said, "Oh yeah, when that thing starts wrapping around them." I said, "Yeah, pretty soon the caterpillar gets wrapped in its cocoon, buried by all this stuff. And you know what? If you were to open up that cocoon, the caterpillar is no longer there. There's just all this mush and goo and stuff. And most people, including the caterpillar, thinks it's dying. But really it's begin-ning to transform. Do you understand? It is going from one thing to something else. And pretty soon, what does it become?" And he said, "A butterfly."

I asked, "Can the other little caterpillars on the ground see that this caterpillar became a butterfly?" He said, "No." I said, "And when a caterpillar breaks out of the cocoon, what does he do?" Joshua said, "He flies." I said, "Yeah, he gets out and the sunlight dries off his wings and he flies. He's even more beautiful than when he was a caterpillar. Is he more free or less free?" Josh said, "He's much more free." And I said, "Do you think he'll have more fun?" And he said, "Yeah—he's got less legs to get tired!" And I said, "That's right, he does. He doesn't need legs anymore; he's got wings. I think your friend has wings now.

"You see, it's not for us to decide when somebody becomes a butterfly. We think it's wrong, but I think God has a better idea when the right time is. Right now it's winter and you want it to be summer, but God has a different plan. Sometimes we just have to trust that God knows how to make butterflies better than we do. And when we're caterpillars, sometimes we don't even realize that butterflies exist, because they're up above us—but maybe we should just remember that they're there." And Joshua smiled, gave me a big hug and said, "I bet he's a beautiful butterfly."

Metaphors can change the meaning you associate to anything, change what you link pain and pleasure to, and transform your life as effectively as they transform your language. Select them carefully, select them intelligently, select them so they will deepen and enrich your experience of life and that of the people you care about. Become a "metaphor detective." Whenever you hear someone using a metaphor that places limits, just step in, break their pattern, and offer a new one. Do this with others, and do it for yourself.

So try the following exercise:

1. **What is life? Write down the metaphors you've already chosen:** "Life is like . . ." what? Brainstorm everything you can think of, because you probably have more than one metaphor for life. When you're in an unresourceful state, you probably call it a battle or a war, and when you're in a good state, maybe you think of it as a gift. Write them all down. Then review your list and ask yourself, "If life is such and such, what does it mean to me?" If life is sacred, what does that mean? If life is a dream, what does that mean? If all the world is a stage, what does that mean? Each of your metaphors empower *and* limit. "All the world's a stage" may be great because it means you can go out there and make a difference and be heard. But it also may mean you're someone who's always performing, instead of sharing your true feelings. So take a good look at the metaphors that you've made available to yourself. What are their advantages and disadvantages? What new metaphors might you like

to apply to your life in order to feel more happy, free, and empowered?

2. Make a list of all the metaphors that you link to relationships or marriage. Are they empowering or disempowering? Remember, conscious awareness alone can transform your metaphors, because your brain starts to say, "That doesn't work—that's *ridiculous!*" And you can adopt a new metaphor easily. The beauty of this technology is that it's so simple.

3. Pick another area of your life that impacts you most—whether it's your business, your parents, your children, your ability to learn—**and discover your metaphors** for this area. Write these metaphors down and study their impact. Write down, "Learning is like playing." If studying is like "pulling teeth," you can imagine the pain you're giving yourself! This might be a good metaphor to change, and change *now!* Once again, notice the positive and negative consequences of each of your metaphors. Exploring them can create new choices for your life.

4. Create new, more empowering metaphors for each of these areas. Decide that from now on you're going to think of life as four or five new things to start with, at least. Life is not a war. Life is not a test. Life is a game, life is a dance, life is sacred, life is a gift, life is a picnic— whatever creates the most positive emotional intensity for you.

5. Finally, decide that you are going to live with these new, empowering metaphors for the next thirty days.

I invite you to allow the radiance of your new metaphors to "sweep you off your feet" and make you feel like you're "floating on air" until you arrive at "Cloud Nine." While you're "on top of the world," you can look down on "Easy Street" and be "tickled pink," knowing that the amount of joy you're feeling in this moment is only the "tip of the iceberg." **Take control of your metaphors now and create a new world for yourself: a world of possibility, of richness, of wonder, and of joy.**

Once you've mastered the creative art of crafting metaphors, transforming vocabulary, and asking empowering questions, you are ready to harness . . .

11
THE TEN
EMOTIONS
OF POWER

*"There can be no transforming of darkness into light
and of apathy into movement without emotion."*
—CARL JUNG

I'd like to introduce you to a fellow named Walt. Walt is a good, decent human being who always tries to do the right thing. He has his life down to a science: everything in its proper place and in the correct order. Weekdays he arises at exactly 6:30, showers and shaves, gulps down some coffee, grabs his lunch pail filled with the requisite bologna sandwich and Twinkies, and runs out the door by 7:10 to spend forty-five minutes in traffic. He arrives at his desk by 8:00, where he sits down to do the same job he's been doing for the past twenty years.

At 5:00 he goes home, pops the top on a "cold one," and grabs the TV remote-control. An hour later his wife comes home and they decide whether to eat leftovers or throw a pizza in the microwave. After dinner he watches the news while his wife bathes their kid and puts him to bed. By no later than 9:30 he's in the sack. He devotes his weekends to yard work, car maintenance, and sleeping in. Walt and his new wife have been married for three years, and while he wouldn't exactly describe their relationship as "inflamed with passion," it's comfortable—even though lately it seems to be repeating a lot of the same patterns of his first marriage.

Do you know someone just like Walt? Maybe he's someone you know *intimately*—someone who never suffers the depths of utter devastation or despondency, but also someone who never revels in the heights of passion and joy. I've heard it said that the only difference between a rut and a grave is a few feet, and over a century ago, Thoreau observed that "the mass of men lead lives of quiet desperation." As we move into the next century, this phrase is unfortunately more applicable than ever. If there's one thing I've noticed in the countless letters I've received since I wrote

Unlimited Power, it's the overwhelming prevalence of this kind of *disassociation* in people's lives—something that just "happened" out of their desire to avoid pain—and the hunger with which they seize upon an opportunity to feel more alive, more passionate, more electric. From my perspective, as I travel around the world, meeting people from all walks of life and "feeling the pulse" of literally hundreds of thousands of individuals, we all seem to instinctively realize the risk of emotional "flat line," and desperately seek ways to get our hearts pumping again.

So many suffer from the delusion that emotions are entirely out of their control, that they're just something that spontaneously occurs in reaction to the events of our lives. Often we dread emotions as if they were viruses that zero in on us and attack when we're most vulnerable. Sometimes we think of them as "inferior cousins" to our intellect and discount their validity. Or we assume that emotions arise in response to what others do or say to us. What's the common element in all these global beliefs? It's the misconception that we have no control over these mysterious things called emotions.

Out of their need to avoid feeling certain emotions, people will often go to great, even ridiculous, lengths. They'll turn to drugs, alcohol, overeating, gambling; they'll lapse into debilitating depression. In order to avoid "hurting" a loved one (or being hurt by one), they'll suppress *all* emotions, end up as emotional androids, and ultimately destroy all the feelings of connection that got them together in the first place, thus *devastating* the ones they love most.

I believe there are four basic ways in which people deal with emotion. Which of these have you used today?

1. Avoidance. We all want to avoid painful emotions. As a result, most people try to avoid any situation that could lead to the emotions that they fear—or worse, some people try not to feel any emotions at all! If, for example, they fear rejection, they try to avoid any situation that could lead to rejection. They shy away from relationships. They don't apply for challenging jobs. Dealing with emotions in this way is the ultimate trap, because while avoiding negative situations may protect you in the short term, it keeps you from feeling the very love, intimacy, and connection that you desire most. **And ultimately, you can't avoid feeling.** A much more powerful approach is to learn to find the hidden, positive meaning in those things you once thought were negative emotions.

2. Denial. A second approach to dealing with emotion is the *denial* strategy. People often try to *disassociate* from their feelings by saying, "It doesn't feel *that* bad." Meanwhile, they keep stoking the fire within themselves by thinking about how horrible things are, or how someone has taken advantage of them, or how they do everything right but things still turn out wrong, and why does this always happen to *them*? In other words, they never change their focus or physiology, and they keep asking the same disempowering questions. Experiencing an emotion and trying to pretend it's not there only creates more pain. Once again, ignoring the messages that your emotions are trying to give you will not make things better. **If the message your emotions are trying to deliver is ignored, the emotions simply increase their amperage; they *intensify* until you finally pay attention.** Trying to deny your emotions is not the solution. Understanding them and using them is the strategy you'll learn in this chapter.

   3. Competition. Many people stop fighting their painful emotions and decide to fully indulge in them. Rather than learn the positive message their emotion is trying to give them, they intensify it and make it even worse than it is. It becomes a "badge of courage," and they begin to compete with others, saying, "You think *you've* got it bad? Let me tell you how bad *I've* got it!" It literally becomes part of their identity, a way of being unique; they begin to pride themselves on being worse off than anyone else. As you can imagine, this is one of the deadliest traps of all. This approach must be avoided at all costs, because it becomes a self-fulfilling prophecy where the person ends up having an investment in feeling bad on a regular basis—and then they are truly trapped. A much more powerful and healthy approach to dealing with the emotions that we think are painful is to realize that they serve a positive purpose, and that is . . .

   4. Learning and Using. If you want to make your life really work, you *must* make your emotions work for you. You can't run from them; you can't tune them out; you can't trivialize them or delude yourself about what they mean. Nor can you just allow them to run your life. Emotions, even those that seem painful in the short term, are truly like an internal compass that points you toward the actions you must take to arrive at your goals. Without knowing how to use this compass, you'll be forever at the mercy of any psychic tempest that blows your way.

   Many therapeutic disciplines begin with the mistaken presupposition that emotions are our enemies or that our emotional well-being is rooted in our past. The truth is that you and I can go from crying to laughing in a heartbeat if the pattern of our mental focus and physiology is merely interrupted strongly enough. Freudian psychoanalysis, for example, searches for those "deep, dark secrets" in our past to explain our present difficulties. Yet we all know that whatever you continually look for, you will surely find. If you're constantly looking for the reasons why your past has hamstrung your present, or why you're so "screwed up," then your brain will comply by providing references to back up your request and generate the appropriate negative emotions. How much better it would be to adopt the global belief that "your past does not equal your future"!

The only way to effectively use your emotions is to understand that they all serve you. You must learn from your emotions and use them to create the results you want for a greater quality of life. **The emotions you once thought of as negative are merely a *call to action*.** In fact, instead of calling them negative emotions, from now on in this chapter, let's call them **Action Signals**. Once you're familiar with each signal and its message, your emotions become not your enemy but your ally. They become your friend, your mentor, your coach; they *guide* you through life's most soaring highs and its most demoralizing lows. Learning to use these signals frees you from your fears and allows you to experience all the richness of which we humans are capable. To get to this point, then, you *must* change your global beliefs about what emotions are. They are not predators, substitutes for logic, or products of other people's whims. They are Action Signals trying to *guide* you to the promise of a greater quality of life.

If you merely react to your emotions through an avoidance pattern, then you'll miss out on the invaluable message they have to offer you. If you continue to miss the message and fail to handle the emotions when they first turn up, they'll grow into full-blown crises. All our emotions are important and valuable in the proper amounts, timing, and context.

Realize that the emotions you are feeling *at this very moment* are a gift, a guideline, a support system, a *call to action*. If you suppress your emotions and try to drive them out of your life, or if you magnify them and allow them to take over everything, then you're squandering one of life's most precious resources.

So what *is* the source of emotions? **You are the source of all your emotions; *you* are the one who creates them.** So many people feel that they have to wait for certain experiences in order to feel the emotions they desire. For instance, they don't give themselves permission to feel loved or happy or confident unless a particular set of expectations is met. I'm here to tell you that **you can feel any way you choose at any moment in time.**

At the seminars I conduct near my home in Del Mar, California, we've created a fun anchor to remind us who is really responsible for our emotions. These seminars are held in an exquisite, four-star resort, the Inn L'Auberge, which sits right on the ocean, and is also near the train station. About four times a day, you can hear the train whistle loudly as it passes through. Some seminar participants would become irritated at the interruption (remember, they didn't know about Transformational Vocabulary yet!), so I decided that this was the perfect opportunity to turn frustration into fun. "From now on," I said, "whenever we hear that train howl, we'll celebrate. I want to see how good you can make yourselves feel whenever you hear that train. We're always waiting for the right person or right situation to come along before we feel good. But who determines whether this is the right person or situation? When you do feel good, who's making you feel good? *You are!* But you simply have a rule that says you have to wait until A, B, and C occur before you allow yourself to feel good. Why wait? Why not set up a rule that says that whenever you hear a train whistle, you'll automatically feel great? The good news is that the train whistle is probably more consistent and predictable than the people you're hoping will show up to make you feel good!"

Now, whenever we hear the train pass, jubilation ensues. People immediately jump out of their chairs, cheer and holler, and act like silly maniacs—including doctors, lawyers, CEOs—people who were supposedly intelligent before they arrived! As everyone sits back down, uproarious laughter ensues. What's the lesson? You don't have to wait for anything or anyone! **You don't need any special reason to feel good— you can just decide to feel good** *right now*, **simply because you're alive, simply because you want to.**

So if you're the source of all your emotions, why don't you feel good all the time? Again, it's because your so-called negative emotions are giving you a message. **What is the message of these Action Signals? They're telling you that what you're currently doing is not working, that the reason you have pain is either the way you're** *perceiving* **things or the** *procedures* **you're using: specifically, the way you're** *communicating* **your needs and desires to people, or the** *actions you're taking*.

What you're doing is not producing the result you want, and you have to *change your approach*. Remember that your perceptions are controlled by what you focus on and the meanings you interpret from things. And you can change your perception in a moment, just by changing the way you're using your physiology or by asking yourself a better question.

Your procedures include your style of communication. Maybe you're being too harsh in the way you communicate, or maybe your procedure is not even communicating your needs, and you're expecting other people to *know* what you need. This could create a lot of frustration, anger, and hurt in your life. **Maybe this Action Signal of feeling hurt is trying to tell you that you need to change your way of communicating so** you don't feel hurt again in the future. **Feeling depressed is another call to action, telling you that you need to change your perception** that the problems you're dealing with are permanent or out of control. Or, you need to take some kind of physical action to handle one area of your life so that once again you remember that you are in control.

This is the true message of all your Action Signals. They're merely trying to support you in taking action to change the way you think, change the way you're perceiving things, or change your procedures for communicating or behaving. These calls to action are there to remind you that you don't want to be like the fly who keeps banging himself against the window, trying to get through the glass—if you don't change your approach, all the persistence in the world will never pay off. Your Action Signals are whispering to you (perhaps screaming!), through the experience of pain, that you need to change what you're doing.

SIX STEPS TO EMOTIONAL MASTERY

I've found that whenever I feel a painful emotion, there are six steps I can take very quickly to break my limiting patterns, find the benefit of that emotion, and set myself up so that in the future I can get the lesson from the emotion and eliminate the pain more quickly. Let's examine them briefly.

STEP ONE

Identify What You're Really Feeling

So often people feel so overloaded they don't even *know* what they're feeling. All they know is that they're being "attacked" by all these negative emotions and feelings.

Instead of feeling overloaded, step back for a moment and ask yourself, "What am I really feeling right now?" If you think at first, "I'm feeling angry," begin to ask yourself, "Am I really feeling angry? Or is it something else? Maybe what I'm really feeling is *hurt*. Or I feel like I've *lost out* on something." Realize that a feeling of hurt or a feeling of loss is not as intense as the feeling of anger. Just in taking a moment to identify what you're really feeling, and beginning to question your emotions, you may be able to lower the emotional intensity you're experiencing, and therefore deal with the situation much more quickly and easily.

If, for example, you say, "Right now I feel rejected," you might ask yourself, "Am I feeling rejected, or am I feeling a sense of *separation* from a person I love? Am I feeling rejected, or am I feeling *disappointed*? Am I feeling rejected, or am I feeling a little *uncomfortable*?" Remember the power of Transformational Vocabulary to immediately lower your intensity. Again, as you identify what you're really feeling, you can lower the intensity even more, which makes it much easier to learn from the emotion.

STEP TWO
_____

Acknowledge and Appreciate Your Emotions, Knowing They Support You

You never want to make your emotions wrong. The idea that anything you feel is "wrong" is a great way to destroy honest communication with yourself as well as with others. Be thankful that there's a part of your brain that is sending you a signal of support, a call to action to make a change in either your perception of some aspect of your life or in your actions. If you're willing to trust your emotions, knowing that even though you don't understand them at the moment, each and every one you experience is there to support you in making a positive change, you will immediately stop the war you once had with yourself. Instead, you'll feel yourself moving toward simple solutions. Making an emotion "wrong" will rarely cause it to become less intense. Whatever you resist tends to persist. **Cultivate the feeling of appreciation for all emotions,** and like a child that needs attention, you'll find your emotions "calming down" almost immediately.

STEP THREE
_____

Get Curious about the Message This Emotion Is Offering You

Remember the power of changing emotional states? If you put yourself in a state of mind where you truly are feeling curious about learning something, this is an immediate pattern interrupt to any emotion and enables you to learn a great deal about yourself. **Getting curious helps you master your emotion, solve the challenge, and prevent the same problem from occurring in the future.**

As you begin to feel the emotion, get curious about what it really has to offer you. What do you need to do right now to make things better? If you're feeling lonely, for example, get curious and ask, "Is it possible that I'm just misinterpreting the situation to mean that I'm alone, when in reality I have all kinds of friends? If I just let them know I want to visit with them, wouldn't they love to visit with me as well? Is my loneliness giving me a message that I need to take action, reach out more and connect with people?"

Here are four questions to ask yourself to become curious about your emotions:

What do I really want to feel?

What would I have to believe in order to feel the way I've been feeling?

What am I willing to do to create a solution and handle this right now?

What can I learn from this?

As you get curious about your emotions, you'll learn important distinctions about them, not only today, but in the future as well.

STEP FOUR

Get Confident

Get confident that you can handle this emotion immediately. **The quickest, simplest, and most powerful way I know to handle any emotion is to remember a time when you felt a similar emotion and realize that *you've successfully handled this emotion before.*** Since you handled it in the past, surely you can handle it again today. The truth is, if you've ever had this Action Signal before and gotten through it, you already have a *strategy* of how to change your emotional states.

So stop right now and think about that time when you felt the same emotions and how you dealt with them in a positive way. Use this as the role model or checklist for what you can do right now to change how you feel. What did you do back then? Did you change what you were focusing on, the questions you asked yourself, your perceptions? Or did you take some kind of new action? Decide to do the same right now, with the confidence that it will work just as it did before.

If you're feeling depressed, for example, and you've been able to turn it around before, ask yourself, "What did I do then?" Did you take some new action like going for a run or making some phone calls? Once you've made some distinctions about what you've done in the past, do the same things now, and you'll find that you'll get similar results.

Get Certain You Can Handle This Not Only Today, But in the Future as Well

You want to feel *certain* that you can handle this emotion easily in the future by having a great plan to do so. One way to do this is to simply remember the ways you've handled it in the past, and *rehearse* handling situations where this Action Signal would come up in the future. See, hear, and feel yourself handling the situation easily. Repetitions of this with emotional intensity will create within you a neural pathway of certainty that you can easily deal with such challenges.

In addition, jot down on a piece of paper three or four other ways that you could change your perception when an Action Signal comes up, or ways that you could change how you were communicating your feelings or needs, or ways that you could change the actions you were taking in this particular situation.

Get Excited, and Take Action

Now that you've finished the first five steps—identified what you were really feeling, appreciated the emotion instead of fighting it, gotten curious about what it really meant and the lesson it was offering you, learned from it, figured out how to turn things around by modeling your successful past strategies for handling the emotion, and rehearsed dealing with it in future situations and installed a sense of certainty—the final step is obvious: *Get excited, and take action!* Get excited about the fact that you can easily handle this emotion, and take some action right away to prove that you've handled it. Don't stay stuck in the limiting emotions you're having. Express yourself by using what you rehearsed internally to create a change in your perceptions or your actions. Remember that the new distinctions you've just made will change the way you feel not only today, but how you deal with this emotion in the future.

With these six simple steps, you can master virtually any emotion that comes up in your life. If you find yourself dealing with the same emotion again and again, this six-step method will help you identify the pattern and change it in a very short period of time.

So practice using this system. Like anything else that's brand-new, at first this may seem cumbersome. But the more you do it, the easier it will become to use, and pretty soon you'll find yourself being able to navigate your way through what you used to think were emotional minefields. What you'll see instead will be a field of personal coaches guiding you each step of the way, showing you where you need to go to achieve your goals.

Remember, the best time to handle an emotion is when you first begin to feel it. It's much more difficult to interrupt an emotional pattern once it's full-blown. My philosophy is, "Kill the monster while it's little." Use this system quickly, as soon as the Action Signal makes itself known, and you'll find yourself being able to quickly handle virtually any emotion.

THE TEN ACTION SIGNALS

With the six steps alone, you can change most emotions. But in order to keep yourself from even having to use the six steps, you may find it useful to have a conscious understanding of what positive message each of your major emotions or Action Signals is trying to give you. In the next couple of pages, I'll share with you the ten primary emotions most people try to avoid but which you will instead use to drive yourself to action.

Reading this list of Action Signals won't give you instant mastery of your emotions. You've got to *use these distinctions consistently* in order to reap their benefits. I suggest that you reread this section several times, underlining the areas that are especially significant for you, and then write down the Action Signals on a 3 × 5 card you can carry with you everywhere, reminding yourself of the meaning the emotion really has for you and what action you can take to utilize it. Attach one of these little cards to the sun visor in your car, not only so you can review it throughout the day, but so if you get stuck in traffic and begin to "boil over in rage," you'll be able to pull out the card and remind yourself of the positive nature of the messages you're receiving.

Let's begin with the most basic call to action, the emotion of . . .

1. **DISCOMFORT.** Uncomfortable emotions don't have a tremendous amount of intensity, but they do bother us and create the nagging sensation that things are not quite right.
The Message:
Boredom, impatience, unease, distress, or mild embarrassment are all sending you a message that something is not quite right. Maybe the way you're perceiving things is off, or the actions you're taking are not producing the results you want.

The Solution:

Dealing with emotions of discomfort is simple:

1) Use the skills you've already learned in this book to change your state;

2) Clarify what you do want; and

3) Refine your actions. Try a slightly different approach and see if you can't immediately change the way you're feeling about the situation and/or change the quality of results you're producing.

Like all emotions, if not dealt with, uncomfortable feelings will intensify. Discomfort is somewhat painful, but the anticipation of possible emotional pain is much more intense than the discomfort you might be feeling in the moment. You and I need to remember that our imagination can make things ten times more intense than anything we could ever experience in real life. In fact, there's a saying in chess and in martial arts: "The threat of attack is greater than the attack itself." When we begin to anticipate pain, especially intense levels of it, often we begin to develop the Action Signal of . . .

2. FEAR. Fearful emotions include everything from low levels of concern and apprehension to intense worry, anxiety, fright, and even terror. Fear serves a purpose, and its message is simple.

The Message:

Fear is simply the anticipation that something that's going to happen soon needs to be prepared for. In the words of the Boy Scout motto, **"Be prepared."** We need either to prepare to cope with the situation, or to do something to change it. The tragedy is that most people either try to deny their fear, or they wallow in it. Neither of these approaches is respecting the message that fear is trying to deliver, so it will continue to pursue you as it tries to get its message across. You don't want to surrender to fear and amplify it by starting to think of the worst that could happen, nor do you want to pretend it's not there.

The Solution:

Review what you were feeling fearful about and evaluate what you must do to prepare yourself mentally. Figure out what actions you need to take to deal with the situation in the best possible way. Sometimes we've done all the preparation we could for something; there's nothing else we can do—but we still sit around in fear. This is the point when you must use the **antidote to fear: you must make a decision to have faith**, knowing you've done all you can to prepare for whatever you're fearing, and that most fears in life rarely come to fruition. If they do, you may experience . . .

3. HURT. If there's any one emotion that seems to dominate human relationships, both personal and professional, it's the emotion of hurt. **Feelings of hurt are usually generated by a sense of loss.** When people are hurt, they often lash out at others. We need to hear the real message hurt gives us.

The Message:

The message the hurt signal gives us is that we have an expectation that has not been met. Many times this feeling arises when we've expected somebody to keep their word and they didn't (even if you didn't tell them your expectation that, for example, they not share with someone else what you talked with them about). In this case, you feel a loss of intimacy with this person, maybe a loss of trust. That sense of loss is what creates the feeling of hurt.

The Solution:

1) Realize that in reality you may not have lost anything. Maybe what you need to lose is the false perception that this person is trying to wound or hurt you. Maybe they really don't realize the impact of their actions on your life.

2) Secondly, take a moment and reevaluate the situation. **Ask yourself, "Is there really loss here? Or am I judging this situation too soon, or too harshly?"**

3) A third solution that can help you get out of a sense of hurt is to elegantly and appropriately communicate your feeling of loss to the person involved. Tell them, "The other day when X-Y-Z happened, I misinterpreted that to mean that you didn't care, and I have a sense of loss. Can you clarify for me what really happened?" Simply by changing your communication style and clarifying what's really going on, you will often find that hurt disappears in a matter of moments.

However, if hurt is not dealt with, it often becomes amplified and turns into . . .

4. ANGER. Angry emotions include everything from being mildly irritated to being angry, resentful, furious, or even enraged.

The Message:

The message of anger is that an important *rule* or standard that you hold for your life has been violated by someone else, or maybe even by you. (We'll talk more about this in Chapter 16 on rules.) When you get the message of anger, you need to understand that you can literally change this emotion in a moment.

The Solution:

1) Realize that you may have misinterpreted the situation completely, that your anger about this person breaking your rules may be based on the fact that they don't know what's most important to you (even though you *believe* they should).

2) Realize that even if a person did violate one of your standards, your rules are not necessarily the "right" rules, even though you feel as strongly as you do about them.

3) Ask yourself a more empowering question like "In the long run, is it true that this person really cares about me?" Interrupt the anger by asking yourself, "What can I learn from this? How can I communicate the importance of these standards I hold for myself to this person in a way that causes them to want to help me, and not violate my standards again in the future?"

For example, **if you're angry, change your perception**—maybe this person really didn't know your rules. Or **change your procedure**— maybe you didn't effectively communicate your real needs. Or **change your behavior**—tell people up front, for example, "Hey, this is private. Please promise me you won't share this with anybody; it's really important to me."

For many people, consistent anger, or the failure to be able to meet their own standards and rules, leads to . . . .

5. FRUSTRATION. Frustration can come from many avenues. Any time we feel like we're surrounded by roadblocks in our lives, where we are continuously putting out effort but not receiving rewards, we tend to feel the emotion of frustration.

The Message:

The message of frustration is an exciting signal. It means that your brain believes you could be doing better than you currently are. Frustration is very different from disappointment, which is the feeling that there's something you want in your life but you'll never get it. **By contrast, frustration is a very positive sign.** It means that the solution to your problem is within range, but what you're currently doing isn't working, and you need to change your approach in order to achieve your goal. It's a signal for you to become more flexible! How do you deal with frustration?

The Solution:

1) Realize that frustration is your friend, and brainstorm new ways to get a result. How can you flex your approach?

2) Get some input on how to deal with the situation. Find a role model, someone who has found a way to get what you want. Ask them for input on how you might more effectively produce your desired result.

3) Get fascinated by what you can learn that could help you handle this challenge not only today, but in the future, in a way that consumes very little time or energy and actually creates joy.

Much more devastating than frustration, however, is the emotion of . . .

6. **DISAPPOINTMENT.** Disappointment can be a very destructive emotion if you don't deal with it quickly. Disappointment is the devastating feeling of being "let down" or that you're going to miss out on something forever. Anything that makes you feel sad or defeated as a result of expecting more than you get is disappointing.

The Message:

The message disappointment offers you is that **an expectation you have had—a goal you were really going for—is probably not going to happen, so it's time to change your expectations to make them more appropriate for this situation and take action to set and achieve a new goal immediately.** And *that is* the solution.

The Solution:

1) Immediately figure out something you can learn from this situation that could help you in the future to achieve the very thing you were after in the first place.

2) Set a new goal, something that will be even more inspiring, and something you can make immediate progress toward.

3) Realize that you may be judging too soon. Often the things you're disappointed about are only temporary challenges, very much like in the story of Billy Joel in Chapter 2. As I've said, you and I need to remember that **God's delays are not God's denials.** You may just be in what I call "lag time." People often set themselves up for disappointment by having completely unrealistic expectations. If you go out today and plant a seed, you can't go back tomorrow and expect to see a tree.

4) A fourth major solution to dealing with disappointment is to **realize that a situation isn't over yet, and develop more patience. Completely reevaluate what you truly want, and begin to develop an even more effective plan for achieving it.**

5) The most powerful antidote to the emotion of disappointment is **cultivating an attitude of positive expectancy about what will happen in the future, regardless of what has occurred in the past.**

The ultimate disappointment that we can experience is usually expressed as the emotion of . . .

7. GUILT. The emotions of guilt, regret, and remorse are among the emotions human beings do most to avoid in life, and this is valuable. They are painful emotions for us to experience, but they, too, serve a valuable function, one which becomes apparent once we hear the message.

The Message:
Guilt tells you that you have violated one of your own highest standards, and that you must do something *immediately* to ensure that you're not going to violate that standard again in the future. If you recall, in Chapter 6 I said that leverage is accessed when someone begins to link pain to something. With enough pain linked to a behavior, that person will eventually change it, and the strongest leverage is the pain we can give ourselves. Guilt is the ultimate leverage for many people in changing a behavior. However, some people try to deal with their guilt by denying and suppressing it. Unfortunately, this rarely works. Guilt does not go away; it only comes back stronger.

The other extreme is to surrender to and wallow in guilt, where we begin to just accept the pain and experience learned helplessness. This is not the purpose of guilt. It's designed, again, to drive us to action to create a change. People fail to understand this and often feel so remorseful about something they once did that they allow themselves to feel inferior for the rest of their lives! That is not the message of guilt. It's there to make sure you either avoid behaviors out of your certainty that they'll lead to guilt, or, if you've already violated your standard, it's there to induce enough pain within you to get yourself to recommit to a higher standard once again. Once you address your old behavior that you feel guilty about, though, and you're sincere and consistent, then move on.

The Solution:
1) **Acknowledge that you have, in fact, violated a critical standard you hold for yourself.**
2) **Absolutely commit yourself to making sure this behavior will never happen again in the future. Rehearse in your mind how, if you could live it again, you could deal with the same situation you feel guilty about in a way that is consistent with your own highest personal standards.** As you commit beyond a shadow of a doubt that you'll never allow the behavior to occur again, you have the right to let go of

the guilt. Guilt has then served its purpose to drive you to hold a higher standard in the future. Utilize it; don't wallow in it!

Some people manage to beat themselves up mentally and emotionally because they are constantly failing to meet standards that they hold for themselves in virtually every area of life. As a result, most of these people experience a feeling of . . .

8. INADEQUACY. This feeling of unworthiness occurs anytime we feel we can't do something we should be able to do. The challenge, of course, is that **often we have a completely unfair rule for determining whether we're inadequate or not.** First, understand the message inadequacy is giving you.
The Message:
The message is that you don't presently have a level of skill necessary for the task at hand. It's telling you that you need more information, understanding, strategies, tools or confidence.
The Solution:
1) Simply ask yourself, "Is this really an appropriate emotion for me to feel in this situation? Am I really inadequate, or do I have to change the way I'm perceiving things?" Maybe you've convinced yourself that in order to feel adequate, you have to go out on the dance floor and outdo Michael Jackson. This is probably an inappropriate perception.

If your feeling is justified, the message of inadequacy is that you need to find a way to do something better than you've done it before. The solution in this case is also obvious:
2) Whenever you feel inadequate, appreciate the encouragement to improve. Remind yourself that you're not "perfect," and that you don't need to be. With this realization, you can begin to feel adequate the moment you decide to commit yourself to CANI!™—constant and never-ending improvement in this area.
3) Find a role model—someone who's effective in the area in which you feel inadequate—and get some coaching from them. Just the process of deciding to master this area of your life and making even the smallest amount of progress will turn a person who's inadequate into a person who's learning. This emotion is critical, because when someone feels inadequate, they tend to fall into the trap of learned helplessness, and they begin to see the problem as being a permanent one with themselves. There's no greater lie you could tell yourself. You're not inadequate. You may be untrained or unskilled in a particular area, but you're not inadequate. The capability for greatness in anything is within you even now.

When we begin to feel that problems are permanent or pervasive or we have more things to deal with than we can possibly imagine, we tend to succumb to the emotions of . . .

9. OVERLOAD OR OVERWHELM. Grief, depression, and helplessness are merely expressions of feeling overloaded or overwhelmed. Grief happens when you feel like there is no empowering meaning for something that has happened, or that your life is being negatively impacted by people, events, or forces that are outside your control. People in this state become overwhelmed and often begin to feel that nothing can change the situation, that the problem is too big—it's permanent, pervasive, and personal. People go into these emotional states whenever they perceive their world in a way that makes them feel like there's more going on than they can possibly deal with, i.e., the pace, amount, or intensity of sensations seems overwhelming.

The Message:

The message of being overwhelmed is that **you need to reevaluate what's most important to you in this situation.** The reason you're overloaded is that you're trying to deal with too many things at once, and you're trying to change everything overnight. The feeling of being overloaded or overwhelmed disrupts and destroys more people's lives than just about any other emotion.

The Solution:

1) **Decide, out of all the things you're dealing with in your life, what the absolute, most important thing is for you to focus on.**

2) **Now write down all the things that are most important for you to accomplish and put them in an order of priority. Just putting them down on paper will allow you to begin to feel a sense of control over what's going on.**

3) **Tackle the first thing on your list, and continue to take action until you've mastered it.** As soon as you've mastered one particular area, you'll begin to develop momentum. Your brain will begin to realize that you are in control and you are not overloaded, overwhelmed, or depressed, that the problem is not permanent, and that you can always come up with a solution.

4) **When you feel that it's appropriate to start letting go of an overwhelming emotion like grief, start focusing on what you *can* control and realize that there must be some empowering meaning to it all, even though you can't comprehend it yet.**

Our self-esteem is often tied to our ability to control our environments. **When we create an environment inside our minds that has too many intense and simultaneous demands upon us, of course we'll** feel overloaded. But we also have the power to change this by focusing on what we can control and dealing with it a step at a time.

Probably the emotion that most people fear the most, however, is that feeling of disconnection, also known as . . .

10. LONELINESS. Anything that makes us feel alone, apart, or separate from others belongs in this category. Have you ever felt really lonely? I don't think there's anybody alive who hasn't.

The Message:

The message of loneliness is that you need a connection with people. But what does the message mean? People often assume it means a sexual connection, or instant intimacy. Then they feel frustrated, because even when they do have intimacy, they still feel lonely.

The Solution:

1) The solution to loneliness is to realize that you can reach out and make a connection immediately and end the loneliness. There are caring people *everywhere.*

2) Identify what kind of connection you do need. Do you need an intimate connection? Maybe you just need some basic friendship, or someone to listen to you or to laugh or talk with. You simply have to identify what your true needs are.

3) Remind yourself that what's great about being lonely is that it means, "I really care about people, and I love to be with them. I need to find out what kind of connection I need with somebody right now, and then take an action immediately to make that happen."

4) Then, take immediate action to reach out and connect with someone.

So there's your list of the ten Action Signals. As you can see, every one of these emotions is offering you empowering messages and a call to change either your false and disempowering perceptions or your inappropriate procedures, that is, your communication style or actions. To fully utilize this list, remember to review it several times, and with each repetition, look for and underline the positive messages that each signal is giving you, as well as the solutions you can use in the future. Almost all "negative" emotions have their basis in these ten categories or are some hybrid of them. But you can deal with any emotion in the way we discussed earlier: by going through the six steps, getting curious, and discovering the empowering meaning it's offering you.

"We must cultivate our garden."
—VOLTAIRE

Think of your mind, your emotions, and your spirit as the ultimate garden. The way to ensure a bountiful, nourishing harvest is to plant seeds like love, warmth, and appreciation, instead of seeds like disappointment, anger, and fear. Begin to think of those Action Signals as weeds in your garden. A weed is a call to action, isn't it? It says, "You've got to do something; you've got to pull this out to make room for better, healthier plants to grow." Keep cultivating the kinds of plants you want, and pull the weeds as soon as you notice them.

Let me offer you ten emotional seeds you can plant in your garden. If you nurture these seeds by focusing on feeling what you want to feel every day, you will hold yourself to a standard of greatness. These seeds create a life that flourishes and fulfills its highest potential. Let's explore them briefly now, and realize that each of these emotions represents an antidote to any of the "negative" emotions you may have been feeling previously.

THE TEN EMOTIONS OF POWER

1. LOVE AND WARMTH. The consistent expression of love seems to be able to melt almost any negative emotions it comes in contact with. If someone is angry with you, you can easily remain loving with them by adopting a core belief such as this marvelous one from the book *A Course in Miracles*: **all communication is either a loving response or a cry for help.** If someone comes to you in a state of hurt or anger, and you consistently respond to them with love and warmth, eventually their state will change and their intensity will melt away.

> *"If you could only love enough, you could be the most powerful person in the world."*
> —EMMET FOX

2. APPRECIATION AND GRATITUDE. I believe that all of the most powerful emotions are some expression of love, each directed in different ways. For me, appreciation and gratitude are two of the most spiritual emotions, actively expressing through thought and action my appreciation and love for all the gifts that life has given me, that people have given me, that experience has given me. Living in this emotional state will enhance your life more than almost anything I know of. Cultivating this is cultivating life. Live with an attitude of gratitude.

3. CURIOSITY. If you really want to grow in your life, learn to be as curious as a child. Children know how to *wonder*—that's why they're so endearing. **If you want to cure boredom,** *be curious.* **If you're** *curious,* **nothing is a chore**; it's automatic—you *want* to study. Cultivate curiosity, and life becomes an unending study of joy.

4. EXCITEMENT AND PASSION. Excitement and passion can add juice to anything. Passion can turn any challenge into a tremendous opportunity. **Passion is unbridled power to move our lives forward at a faster tempo than ever before.** To paraphrase Benjamin Disraeli, man is only truly great when he acts from the passions. How do we "get" passion? The same way we "get" love, warmth, appreciation, gratefulness, and curiosity—**we** *decide* **to feel it!** Use your physiology: speak more rapidly, visualize images more rapidly, move your body in the direction you want to go. Don't just casually sit and think. You can't be filled with passion if you're slumping over your desk, breathing shallowly, and slurring your speech.

5. DETERMINATION. All of the above emotions are invaluable, but there is one that you must have if you're going to create lasting value in this world. It will dictate how you deal with upsets and challenges, with disappointment and disillusionments. **Determination means the difference between being stuck and being struck with the lightning power of commitment.** If you want to get yourself to lose weight, make those business calls, or follow through on anything, "pushing" yourself won't do it. Putting yourself in a state of determination will. All your actions will spring from that source, and you'll just automatically do whatever it takes to accomplish your aim. Acting with determination means making a congruent, committed decision where you've cut off any other possibility.

> *"Determination is the wake-up call*
> *to the human will."*
> —ANTHONY ROBBINS

With determination, you can accomplish anything. Without it, you're doomed to frustration and disappointment. Our willingness to do whatever it takes, to act in spite of fear, is the basis of courage. And courage is the foundation from which determination is born. The difference between feeling accomplishment or feeling despondency is the cultivation of the emotional muscle of determination. With all that determination at your command, though, be sure you can also break your own pattern and change your approach. Why smash through a wall if you can just look a little to your left and find a door? Sometimes determination can be a limitation; you need to cultivate . . .

6. FLEXIBILITY. If there's one seed to plant that will guarantee success, it's the ability to *change* your approach. In fact, all those Action Signals—those things you used to call negative emotions—are just messages to be more flexible! Choosing to be flexible is choosing to be happy. Throughout your life there will be times when there are things you will not be able to control, and your ability to be flexible in your rules, the meaning you attach to things, and your actions will determine your long-term success or failure, not to mention your level of personal joy. The reed that bends will survive the windstorm, while the mighty oak tree will crack. If you cultivate all of the above emotions, then you'll surely develop . . .

7. CONFIDENCE. Unshakable confidence is the sense of certainty we all want. The only way you can consistently experience confidence, even in environments and situations you've never previously encountered, is through the power of faith. Imagine and feel certain about the emotions you deserve to have now, rather than wait for them to spontaneously appear someday in the far distant future. When you're confident, you're willing to experiment, to put yourself on the line. One way to develop faith and confidence is simply to practice using it. If I were to ask whether you're confident that you can tie your own shoes, I'm sure you could tell me with perfect confidence that you can. Why? Only because you've done it thousands of times! So practice confidence by using it consistently, and you'll be amazed at the dividends it reaps in every area of your life.

In order to get yourself to do anything, it's imperative to exercise confidence rather than fear. The tragedy of many people's lives is that they avoid doing things because they're afraid; they even feel bad about things *in advance.* But remember: the source of success for outstanding achievers often finds its origin in a set of nurtured beliefs for which that individual had no references! The ability to act on faith is what moves the human race forward.

Another emotion you'll automatically experience once you've succeeded in cultivating all the above is . . .

8. CHEERFULNESS. When I added cheerfulness to my list of most important values, people commented, "There's something different about you. You seem so happy." I realized that I had been happy, but I hadn't told my face about it! There's a big difference between being happy on the inside, and being outwardly cheerful. Cheerfulness enhances your self-esteem, makes life more fun, and makes the people around you feel happier as well. Cheerfulness has the power to eliminate the feelings of fear, hurt, anger, frustration, disappointment, depression, guilt, and inadequacy from your life. You've achieved cheerfulness the day you realize that no matter what's happening around you, being anything other than cheerful will not make it better.

Being cheerful does not mean that you're Pollyanna or that you look at the world through rose-colored glasses and refuse to acknowledge challenges. **Being cheerful means you're incredibly intelligent because you know that if you live life in a state of pleasure—one that's so intense that you transmit a sense of joy to those around you—you can have the impact to meet virtually any challenge that comes your way.** Cultivate cheerfulness, and you won't need so many of those "painful" Action Signals to get your attention!

Make it easy for yourself to feel cheerful by planting the seed of . . .

9. VITALITY. Handling this area is critical. If you don't take care of your physical body, it's more difficult to be able to enjoy these emotions. Make sure that physical vitality is available; remember that all emotions are directed through your body. If you're feeling out of sorts emotionally, you need to look at the basics. How are you breathing? When people are stressed, they stop breathing, sapping their vitality. Learning to breathe properly is the most important avenue toward good health. Another critical element to physical vitality is ensuring that you have an abundant level of nerve energy.

How do you do this? Realize that day to day you're expending nerve energy through your actions, and as obvious as it sounds, you do need to make sure that you rest and recharge. By the way, how much sleep are you getting? If you're regularly logging eight to ten hours of sack time, you're probably getting *too much* sleep! Six to seven hours has been found to be optimum for most people. Contrary to popular belief, sitting still doesn't preserve energy. The truth is, that's usually when you feel most tired. The human nervous system needs to *move* to have energy. To a certain extent, expending energy *gives* you a greater sense of energy. As you move, oxygen flows through your system, and that physical level of health creates the emotional sense of vitality that can help you to deal with virtually any negative challenge you could have in your life.* **So realize that a sense of vitality is a critical emotion to cultivate in order to handle virtually any emotions that come up in your life,** not to mention the critical resource in experiencing consistent passion.

Once your garden is filled with these powerful emotions, then you can share your bounty through . . .

* For more information on how to enhance your physical vitality, see *Unlimited Power,* Chapter 10, "Energy: The Fuel of Excellence."

10. CONTRIBUTION. Years ago, I remember being in one of the toughest times in my life, driving down the freeway in the middle of the night. I kept asking, "What do I need to do to turn my life around?" Suddenly an insight came to me, accompanied by such intense emotion that I was compelled to pull my car off the road immediately and write down one key phrase in my journal: **"The secret to living is giving."**

There's no richer emotion I know of in life than the sense that who you are as a person, something you've said or done, has added to more than just your own life, that somehow it has enhanced life's experience for someone you care about, or maybe someone you don't even know. The stories that move me most profoundly are about people who follow the highest spiritual emotion of caring unconditionally and acting for others' benefit. When I saw the musical *Les Miserables,* I was deeply moved by the character of Jean Valjean, because he was such a good man who wanted to give so much to others. Each day we should cultivate that sense of contribution by focusing not only on ourselves, but on others as well.

Don't fall into the trap, though, of trying to contribute to others at your own expense—**playing the martyr won't give you a true sense of contribution**. But if you can consistently give to yourself and others on a measurable scale that allows you to know that your life has mattered, you'll have a sense of connection with people and a sense of pride and self-esteem that no amount of money, accomplishments, fame, or acknowledgment could ever give. A sense of contribution makes all of life worthwhile. Imagine what a better world it would be if all of us cultivated a sense of contribution!

THE TEN ACTION SIGNALS	THE TEN EMOTIONS OF POWER
1. DISCOMFORT	1. LOVE AND WARMTH
2. FEAR	2. APPRECIATION AND GRATITUDE
3. HURT	3. CURIOSITY
4. ANGER	4. EXCITEMENT AND PASSION
5. FRUSTRATION	5. DETERMINATION
6. DISAPPOINTMENT	6. FLEXIBILITY
7. GUILT	7. CONFIDENCE
8. INADEQUACY	8. CHEERFULNESS
9. OVERLOAD, OVERWHELM	9. VITALITY
10. LONELINESS	10. CONTRIBUTION

Plant these emotions daily, and watch your whole life grow with a vitality that you've never dreamed of before. Here, for review, are the ten Action Signals and the ten Emotions of Power. I cannot emphasize strongly enough the importance of learning to use the negative emotions for what they are—calls to action—and committing to cultivate the positive emotions. Do you remember the 3″ × 5″ card you created on which you wrote down all the messages and solutions your Action Signals are giving you? Review it frequently throughout the day. As you view it even now, you may notice that the positive emotions we've just covered are great antidotes to the Action Signals. In other words, if you're feeling uncomfortable emotion, then love and warmth will make changing that emotion much simpler. If you're feeling fearful, then a sense of gratitude wipes that emotion out. If you're feeling hurt and then get curious about what's going on, that replaces the sense of hurt. If you're feeling angry and you turn that emotional intensity into directed excitement and passion, think of what you can accomplish! Frustration can be broken through with the use of determination. Disappointment can be dissolved by being flexible in your approach. Guilt disappears the minute you become confident that you're going to stick to your new standards. Inadequacy departs when you're feeling cheerful; there's simply no room for it. A sense of overload disappears with a sense of personal power and vitality. Loneliness melts away the moment you figure out how to contribute to others.

I'd now like you to do an assignment that will fully associate you to the simple and powerful tool of emotions.

1) Over the next two days, **any time you feel a disempowering or negative emotion, follow the six steps to emotional mastery.** Identify what category it belongs in, and recognize its value in giving you the message that you need. Discover whether what needs to be changed are your perceptions or your actions. Get confident, get certain, and get excited.

2) Action Signals serve an important function, but if you didn't have to feel them as often, wouldn't that be preferable? In addition to the Emotions of Power, **cultivate global beliefs that help minimize your experience of the negative emotions.** For example, I've eliminated the feeling of abandonment (loneliness) from my life because I've adopted the belief that I can never really be abandoned. If someone I love ever tried to "abandon" me, I'd just follow them! (Other empowering beliefs include, "This, too, shall pass"; "Love is the only must in my life; everything else is a should"; and "There's always a way, if I'm committed.")

Utilize these Emotions of Power daily, and use the six steps to emotional mastery to transform your Action Signals into positive action. Remember: **Every feeling that you have—good or bad—is based on**

your interpretation of what things mean. Whenever you start to feel bad, ask yourself this question: "What *else* could this mean?" It's the first step toward taking control of your emotions.

What I hope you'll take from this chapter is an appreciation of all your emotions and a sense of excitement that they're all providing you with a chance to learn something to make your life better, literally at a moment's notice. Never again do you need to feel that painful emotions are your enemies. They're all here to serve you as a signal that some kind of change is needed. As you refine your ability to use these Action Signals, you'll start handling them up front, when they are small, rather than waiting until they turn into full-blown crises. For instance, you'll handle a situation while it's still annoying, not infuriating—like handling a weight problem when you notice the first extra pound rather than waiting until you've added another thirty.

Over the next couple of weeks, focus on enjoying the process of learning from all of your emotions. You can experience the whole kaleidoscope at any moment you choose. Don't be afraid—ride the roller coaster! Experience the joy, passion, and thrill of all the emotions, and know that you're in control! It's your life, your emotions, your destiny.

One thing I have found is that although someone may know how to do something, they might still not apply what they know. What we really need is a *reason* to use the power of our decisions, to change our beliefs, to get leverage on ourselves and interrupt our patterns, to ask better questions and sensitize ourselves to our vocabulary and metaphors. In order to be motivated on a consistent basis, we need to develop . . .

12

THE MAGNIFICENT OBSESSION— CREATING A COMPELLING FUTURE

"Nothing happens unless first a dream."
—CARL SANDBURG

Are you ready now to have some fun? Are you willing to be like a kid again and let your imagination run wild? Are you committed to grabbing hold of your life and squeezing from it all the power, passion, and "juice" you know can be yours?

I've thrown a lot at you so far. We've covered a monumental amount of material in the previous chapters, most of which you can put to use immediately. Some of it, however, will stay tucked away in a corner of your brain, locked in deep storage until just the right moment. We've worked hard together to get you in the position to make new decisions, decisions that can make the difference between a life of dreaming and a life of doing.

Many people in life know *what* they should do, but they *never do it.* The reason is that they're lacking the drive that only a **compelling future** can provide. This chapter is your opportunity to let go and dream at the highest level, to brainstorm out the wildest possibilities and, in so doing, to possibly discover something that will really push your life to the next level. *It will help you create energy and momentum.*

If you read this chapter actively instead of passively, if you do the exercises and take action, then the following pages will reward you with a vision for your future that will pull you like a magnet through your toughest times. It's a chapter I'm sure you'll love returning to again and again anytime you need renewed inspiration for your life. This is your chance to really have some fun and experience your true passion!

What I'm going to ask you to do in the next few pages is to unlock your imagination, throw all "common sense" to the wind, and act as if you're a kid again—a kid who can literally have anything he wants, a kid who has only to express his heart's desire, and it will instantly be his. Do you remember the Arabian tales known collectively as *The Thousand and One Nights*? Can you guess what my favorite story was? That's right: Aladdin's Lamp. I think all of us, at one time or another, have longed to get our hands on that magic lamp. All you have to do is rub it, and a mighty genie appears in order to carry out your wishes. I'm here to tell you that **you possess a lamp that is not limited to a mere three wishes!**

Now it's time for you to grab hold of this powerful force within you. Once you **decide** to awaken this giant, you'll be unstoppable in creating mental, emotional, physical, financial, and spiritual abundance beyond your wildest fantasies. Whether your dreams materialize instantly or take shape gradually over time, know that the only limit to what you can have in your life is the size of your imagination and the level of your commitment to making it real.

GIANT GOALS PRODUCE GIANT MOTIVATION

So often I hear people say, "Tony, where do you get your energy? With all that intensity, no wonder you're so successful. I just don't have your drive; I guess I'm not motivated. I guess I'm lazy." My usual response is, "You're not lazy! *You just have impotent goals!*"

Frequently I get a confused look to this response, at which point I explain that my level of excitement and drive comes from my goals. Every morning when I wake up, even if I feel physically exhausted from a lack of sleep, I'll still find the drive I need because my goals are so exciting to me. They get me up early, keep me up late, and inspire me to marshal my resources and use everything I can possibly find within the sphere of my influence to bring them to fruition. The same energy and sense of mission is available to you now, but it will never be awakened by puny goals. The first step is to develop bigger, more inspiring, more challenging goals.

Often people tell me, "My problem is that I really don't have *any* goals." This belief demonstrates their lack of understanding of how goals really work. The human mind is always pursuing something, if nothing more than the ability to reduce or eliminate pain, or avoid anything that could lead to it. Our brains also love to guide us in pursuing anything that can lead to the creation of pleasure. We all have goals. The problem, as I've stressed in virtually every chapter so far, is that **we are unconscious in our use of these resources.**

Most people's goals are to "pay their lousy bills," to get by, to survive, to make it through the day—in short, they are caught up in the trap of making a living rather than **designing a life**. Do you think these goals will give you the power to tap the vast reserve of power within you? Hardly! You and I must remember that our goals affect us, *whatever they are*. If we don't consciously plant the seeds we want in the gardens of our minds, we'll end up with weeds! Weeds are automatic; you don't have to work to get them. If we want to discover the unlimited possibilities within us, we must find a goal big enough and grand enough to challenge us to *push beyond our limits* and discover our true potential. Remember that your current conditions do not reflect your ultimate potential, but rather the size and quality of goals upon which you currently are focusing. **We all must discover or create a Magnificent Obsession**.

GOALS TAKE YOU BEYOND YOUR LIMITS TO A WORLD OF UNLIMITED POWER

When we first set large goals, they may seem impossible to achieve. But the most important key to goal setting is to find a goal big enough to inspire you, something that will cause you to unleash your power. The way I usually know I've set the right goal is when it seems impossible but at the same time it's giving me a sense of crazed excitement just to think about the possibility of achieving it. In order to truly find that inspiration and achieve those impossible goals, we must suspend our belief systems about what we're capable of achieving.

I'll never forget the true story of a young boy born into poverty in a run-down section of San Francisco and how his goals seemed impossible to everyone except him. This young man was a fan of football legend Jim Brown, then the running back for the Cleveland Browns. In spite of the fact that this boy was crippled by rickets he had endured as a result of malnutrition, and at the age of six his legs had become permanently bowed and his calves so atrophied that his nickname was "Pencil Legs," he set a goal to one day become a star running back like his hero. He had no money to attend football games, so whenever the Browns played the 49ers he would wait outside the stadium until the maintenance crew opened the gate late in the fourth quarter. He would then hobble into the stadium and soak up the balance of the game.

Finally, at the age of thirteen, the boy had an encounter he'd dreamed of his whole life. He walked into an ice cream parlor after a 49ers game against the Browns, and whom should he see but his long-time idol! He approached the football star and said, "Mr. Brown, I'm your biggest fan!" Graciously, Brown thanked him. The young boy persisted. "Mr. Brown, you know what?" Brown turned to him again and said, "What is it, son?" The young boy said, "I know every record you've ever set, every touchdown you've ever scored!" Jim Brown smiled and said, "That's great," and returned to his conversation. The young man persisted, "Mr. Brown! Mr. Brown!" Jim Brown turned to him yet again. This time the young man stared deep into his eyes with a passion so intense Brown could feel it and said, "Mr. Brown, one day I'm going to break every one of your records!"

The football legend smiled and said, "That's great, kid. What's your name?" The boy grinned from ear to ear and said, "Orenthal, sir. Orenthal James Simpson . . . My friends call me O.J."

> *"We are what and where we are because we have first imagined it."*
> —DONALD CURTIS

O.J. Simpson did indeed go on to break all of Jim Brown's records, and set some new ones of his own! How do goals create this incredible power to shape destiny? How can they take a young boy afflicted with rickets and allow him to become a legend? **Setting goals is the first step in turning the invisible into the visible—the foundation for all success in life.** It's as if infinite Intelligence will fill any mold you create using the impression of your intensely emotional thoughts. In other words, you can chisel your own existence by the thoughts you consistently project every moment of your life. The conception of your goals is the master plan that guides all thought.

Will you create a masterpiece or interpret life through the paintings of others? Will you put out a thimble to collect your life's experiences or a giant rain barrel? The answers to these questions have already been given by the goals you consistently seek.

TURNING THE INVISIBLE INTO THE VISIBLE

Look around yourself right now. What do you see? Are you sitting on a sofa, surrounded by fine art or watching a big-screen television employing the latest technology of laser disc? Or are you seated at a desk that holds a telephone, computer, and fax machine? All of these objects were once just ideas in someone's mind. If I had told you 100 years ago that invisible waves from around the world could be pulled from the air and fed into a box to generate sounds and pictures, wouldn't you have considered me crazy? Yet today just about every home in America has at least one television set (the average is two!). Someone had to *create* them, and in order for that to happen, someone had to **envision them with clarity**.

Is this true only of material objects? No, it also applies to all kinds of activities and processes: the reason a car works is that some enterprising individuals figured out how to harness the process of internal combustion. The answer to our current energy challenges will lie in the imagination and resourcefulness of today's physicists and engineers. And the resolution to our social crises, like the alarming spread of racial hate groups, homelessness, and hunger, can only be addressed with the inventiveness and compassion of dedicated individuals like you and me.

WHY DOESN'T EVERYONE SET GOALS?

You might be thinking right now, "Well, this all sounds so inspirational, but surely just setting a goal doesn't make it happen." I couldn't agree with you more. **All goal setting must be immediately followed by both the development of a plan, and massive and consistent action toward its fulfillment**. You already have this power to act. If you haven't been able to summon it, it's merely because you have failed to set goals that inspire you.

What's holding you back? Surely you've been exposed to the power of goal setting before reading this book. But *do you have a list of clearly defined goals for the results you will absolutely produce in your life mentally, emotionally, physically, spiritually, and financially?* What has stopped you? For many it's the unconscious fear of disappointment. Some people have set goals in the past and failed to achieve them and, as a result of their disappointment and their fear of future pain, they stop setting goals. They don't want to have any expectations that could be dashed. Other people set goals, but abuse themselves by tying their entire level of personal happiness to their ability to achieve goals that may be outside their control. Or they lack the flexibility to notice that as they move in the direction of their goals, there are better, more worthy goals all around them.

The process of setting goals works a lot like your eyesight. The closer you get to your destination, the greater clarity you gain, not only on the goal itself, but the details of everything around it. Who knows? You may decide that you like one of those other possibilities even better, that it inspires you even more, and go for that one instead! In fact, sometimes, as we'll talk about in more depth later, failing to achieve your goal actually draws you closer to your life's true purpose.

The drive to achieve and contribute comes in many forms. For some people it's spawned by disappointment or even tragedy. For others it's fueled simply by the stark realization one day that life is passing them by, that the quality of their life is lessening with each passing moment. For some, inspiration is the source of their motivation. Seeing what's possible, anticipating the best possible scenario, or realizing that they're in fact making significant progress can help them to develop tremendous momentum to accomplish even more.

Often, we don't realize how far we've come because we're so caught up in the process of achieving. A good metaphor for this is when a friend tells you how much your son or daughter has grown, and you say with honest surprise, "Really?" It's been happening right under your nose, so you've failed to notice it. It's even tougher to see your own growth, so I'd like to share with you a simple process. Please take a moment to do it right now. It will assist you in tapping one or both of the above-described forces of motivation.

YESTERDAY, TODAY, AND TOMORROW

Sometimes it's easy to lose track of just how far you've already come—or just how far you still need to go in life. Use the following pages to make an accurate assessment of where you stood in these ten critical areas five years ago. Specifically, **next to each of these categories, give yourself a score on a scale from 0 to 10, 0 meaning you had nothing in this area, and 10 meaning you were absolutely living your life's desire in that category.**

The second step, after giving yourself a score, is to **write a sentence next to each category to describe what you were like back then.** For instance, five years ago, what were you like physically? You might write down, "I was a 7," and then follow up with, "I was in fairly good shape, but definitely needed improvement. Five pounds overweight, was running twice a week, but still didn't eat healthfully. Mediocre levels of energy."

Take five to ten minutes and do this exercise now. You will find it quite enlightening!

Five Years Ago	Score	Sentence
Physically	6	WAS SLIGHTLY OVERWEIGHT BUT NOT EATING WELL + NO EXERCISE
Mentally	8	SCHOOL! MY MIND WAS SHARPER - LEARNING
~~Emotionally~~ RELATIONSHIPS	6	JUST BEGINNING THE RELATIONSHIP W/ MARI.
Attractiveness	7	I "FELT" ATTRACTIVE. WEARING PIECE
EMOTIONALLY ~~Relationships~~	7	I FELT PRETTY WELL BALANCED. I HAD MADE IT THROUGH THE DIVORCE.
Living environment	5	MOM'S HOUSE. LIMITED; LIMITED, LIMITED.
Socially	9	SCHOOL AGAIN! MAKING NEW FRIENDS, MEETING PEOPLE
Spiritually	7	NOT BAD, BETTER I THOUGHT THAN MOST. BUT IT WAS ACTUALLY BEGINNING TO DECLINE
Career	2	WHAT CAREER? I WAS IN SCHOOL MAKING ART WITHOUT MUCH DIRECTION
Financially	2	BROKE AND INCREASING MY DEBT.

Now, for contrast's sake, let's see how far you've come, or failed to come, in each of these categories. Answer the same questions based on today. In other words, first **give yourself a score of 1 to 10** of where you are today in each of these categories, and then **write a sentence or two describing what you're like in each of these categories today.**

Today	Score	Sentence
Physically	5	MORE WEIGHT, BUT START ING TO LOSE IT, SMOKING NO exercise
Mentally	7	NEED TO READ MORE, still I Feel intelligent
Emotionally	6	A little empty 4 MARY WHEN SHE DRINKS/DRUGS NO COMMITMENT LIFE.
Attractiveness	6	MOSTLY DUE TO WEIGHT
Relationships	5	STATIC, I MAYBE MANI FESTING THE BAD SIDE OF IT GREAT w/ ALEX
Living environment	5	MARZ'S HOUSE, STILL NOT MUCH PRIVACY, BUT A little more DESIGN
Socially	7	LESS ACQUAINTANCES, MORE FRIENDS BUT TIME NEEDED TO SPEND WITH THEM.
Spiritually	4	STABLE, BUT NO DAILY PRACTICE, NO GROWTH
Career	8	SON-DON, DOING well w/ PROMISE OF DOING Better
Financially	7	MAKING MORE MONEY, STILL IN DECENT DEBT BUT CRAWLING OUT

What have you learned by doing this so far? What distinctions have you made? Have you improved more than you realized in some categories? Have you come a long way? That feels great, doesn't it? If you haven't come as far as you would have liked, or if you think that you were doing better five years ago than you are now in some areas, that's a great message, too—one that may drive you to make changes before many more years pass you by. Remember, dissatisfaction can be a major key to success.

> Take a moment now and jot down a few key phrases describing what you've learned by this comparison:
>
> PHYSICALT GOING BACKWARDS, CRAWL ING OUT OF DEBT. NO PLAN, NO REAL GOALS AND THIS IS WHERE I AM FIVE YEARS LATER, STILL FAT, STILL SMOKING. PRETTY LAME ASS FOR A TALL WHITE GUY.

Now complete the exercise by projecting five years into the future. **Again, give yourself a score and a sentence describing what you'll be like in each of these key categories.**

Five Years from Now	Score	Sentence
Physically	9	WEIGHT - 200 - 210, EXERCISE PROGRAM, RUNNING - NO SMOKING.
Mentally	9	RELAXED ENERGIZED TIME TO LEARN, READ + GROW
Emotionally	9	FULFILLED, EASILY GIVING LOVE + RECEIVING IT.
Attractiveness	10	SEXY! FEEL IT, LOOK IT + AM IT.
Relationships	9	FULL, REWARDING RICH ALEX, MARY, THE GIRLS EVERYONE IN MY LIFE

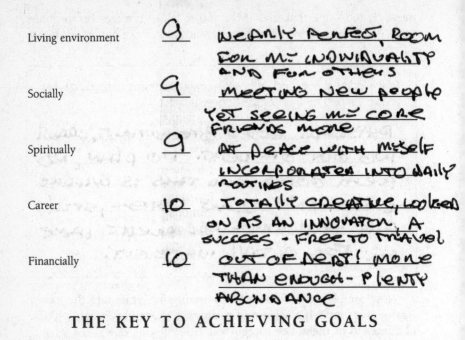

Living environment	9	NEARLY PERFECT ROOM FOR MY INDIVIDUALITY AND FOR OTHERS
Socially	9	MEETING NEW PEOPLE YET SEEING MY CORE FRIENDS MORE
Spiritually	9	AT PEACE WITH MYSELF INCORPORATED INTO DAILY ROUTINES
Career	10	TOTALLY CREATIVE, LOOKED ON AS AN INNOVATOR, A SUCCESS - FREE TO TRAVEL
Financially	10	OUT OF DEBT! MORE THAN ENOUGH - PLENTY ABUNDANCE

THE KEY TO ACHIEVING GOALS

When you set a goal, you've committed to **CANI! You've acknowledged the need that all human beings have for constant, never-ending improvement.** There is power in the pressure of dis satisfaction, in the tension of temporary discomfort. This is the kind of pain you *want* in your life, the kind of pain that you immediately transform into positive new actions.

This kind of pressure is known as **eustress** as opposed to *distress.* Eustress can be a driving, positive force that pushes you forward to constantly increase the quality of your life for yourself and all those you have the privilege to touch. Ponder it; use it to spur you forward. Many people try to avoid pressure, yet the absence of any tension or pressure usually creates a sense of boredom and the lackluster experience of life that so many people complain about. In truth, when we feel excited, we feel a sense of pressure or tension within ourselves. However, the level of stress is not overwhelming, but rather *stimulating.*

There is a difference between being stressed out and being the master of stress. *Use* stress (eustress) to drive you in the direction you desire; it can generate tremendous transformation within you. By learning to utilize pressure and make it your friend instead of your foe, you can truly hone it into a tool that assists you in livinglife to the fullest. Besides, we need to remember that our stress level is self-induced. So let's induce it intelligently.

One of the simplest ways you can use pressure as your ally is to enlist the people you respect as you commit to achieve your goals. By publicly declaring that you'll do whatever it takes to achieve your deepest and truest desires, you will find it more difficult to stray from your path when frustration or challenge set in. Often when you become tired or uncertain, and you begin to feel like things aren't working out, memories of your public announcement may keep you going, or your friends will assist you by holding you to a higher standard. You may find this a useful tool to help you continue on the road even when it gets a little bumpy.

FAILING TO ACHIEVE YOUR GOAL CAN MEAN ACHIEVING YOUR REAL GOALS

Years ago, a friend approached me and talked about a fantasy he had of living on an island paradise in Fiji. I had heard the dream many times and loved the concept in principle. But I was a practical man: getting an island paradise in Fiji was purely an opportunity for investment, and I justified to myself that if the world ever went through some cataclysm, it would be a great place for my family to escape to. So I scheduled a "business trip/vacation," and arranged to go with Becky to examine several properties in the islands to assess whether they might be a viable investment.

It took us a couple of days to start letting go of the hectic agendas we'd brought with us. But nothing was going to stop us from achieving our goal of purchasing some raw land. We were on a mission to find a sound investment, so we decided to charter a plane and explore the remote outer islands of Fiji in search of a sterling opportunity.

We spent an adventurous day, landing in several places including the "Blue Lagoon" (from the film of the same name) before finally landing on a secluded beach in the northern group of islands. We rented the only car available and drove up a coconut-strewn dirt road known as the "Hibiscus Highway" for the next three hours.

Then, in what seemed like the middle of nowhere, on the side of the road we spotted a little Fijian girl with unusual red hair that stuck straight out from her head. Becky and I were delighted and wanted to take her picture, but also wanted to be respectful to her. So we searched for her parents to ask their permission before doing so.

As we began to look for her home, we spotted a tiny village on the edge of the sea. As we approached, several villagers spotted us, and a large Fijian man came running in our direction. With a huge smile he greeted us, not in some tribal tongue, but in the Queen's English. "Hi, my name is Joe," he said in a booming voice. "Please come join us for some *kava*." As we entered the village, we were greeted by what seemed like endless smiles and laughter. I was invited into a large hut filled with thirty Fijian men to participate in a *kava* ceremony, and Becky was invited to stay outside and talk with the women as was traditional in their culture.

I was bowled over by the enthusiasm of these people. Their unbridled cheerfulness was amazing. Inside the hut, the Fijian men were all smiling so brightly, so happy to have a visitor, and they welcomed me with "Bula, bula, bula!", which roughly translated means, "Welcome, be happy, we love you!" The men had been soaking *yanggona* (a kind of peppery root) in a bowl of water for several hours, and were proudly stirring and ladling out a nonalcoholic drink they called *kava* (what looked to me like muddy water). They invited me to drink from a half-coconut shell, and as I partook of the *kava* (it tasted about as good as it looked), the men laughed and joked with me and one another. After only a few moments of being with these people, I began to feel a sense of peace that I had never experienced before.

Marveling at their sense of fun and playfulness, I asked them, "What do you think is the purpose of life?" They looked at me as if I'd cracked a cosmic joke and said, seemingly in unison, "To be happy, of course. What else is there?" I said, "It's true: you all seem so happy here in Fiji." One man replied, "Yes, I think that here in Fiji we are the happiest people on earth . . . Of course, I've never been anywhere else!" which set off another round of raucous laughter.

Then they decided to break their own rules and bring Becky into the hut. They brought over the only kerosene lamp in the village, along with ukuleles and mandolins, and pretty soon the *bure* was filled with the entire village as the men, women, and children sang to us in beautiful four-part Fijian harmony. It was one of the most powerful and deeply moving experiences of our lives. The most incredible thing about these people is that **they wanted nothing from us except to share the bountiful happiness they felt for life**.

Many hours later and after long farewell wishes, we left the village renewed, with a deep sense of peace and balance in our lives. We returned after dark that evening to a magical resort with a heightened awareness and gratitude for the beauty around us. Here we were, in this regal setting, inside our private little thatched-roof cottage perched atop a lava pinnacle, surrounded by lush greenery and moonlit coconut palms with the sounds of the gently lapping waves outside our door. We'd had an incredible day, and felt our lives deeply enriched by the people of this small village. We realized that we had not achieved our goal for the day, but by pursuing it, we'd come across an even greater gift, **a gift of value beyond compare.**

We've returned to Fiji three or four times a year for over six years now. We expected to achieve our goal of purchasing the ultimate investment on our first trip, but it took roughly twenty trips to Fiji to finally make a purchase—not just as an investment, but as an opportunity to share the joy of Fiji with our friends. Instead of buying raw land, two years ago we purchased Namale, the exquisite plantation resort at which we stayed on our first trip! We wanted to take this place of magic—121 acres and three miles of beach frontage—and enhance it even more so we could share it with our friends and other special people.

Owning Namale gives me the same joy that I get from conducting seminars where I watch people transform their capacity to enjoy life. When people arrive at Namale, the same transformation occurs, only I don't have to do anything! I get to just sit back and watch while people from all walks of life, from honeymooners to retired couples to high-powered CEOs burdened by the frenzied pace of big business, let loose and rediscover what it's like to be a child again. They happily dodge the fifteen feet of spray shooting from the remarkable blowhole on the reef, play volleyball with the locals, ride horseback down the beach, or participate in a native *kava* ceremony.

I love to see the wonder in their eyes as they discover another world under the sea, or drink in a sunset that rivals those of their greatest fantasies, or their smiles that reflect the spiritual connection they feel with the Fijian people after a Sunday morning church service in the village. I never realized when I pursued the goal of an "investment" that I would instead find an environment that would cause us all to remember what's most important in life. **It's not just getting a goal that matters, but the quality of life you experience along the way.**

LIVE THE DREAM

Many people go through life putting off their joy and happiness. To them, goal setting means that "someday," after they achieve something, only then will they be able to enjoy life to the fullest. The truth is that if we decide to be happy now, we'll automatically achieve more. While goals provide a magnificent direction and a way to focus, we must constantly strive to live each day to its fullest, squeezing all the joy we can out of each moment. Instead of measuring your success and failure in life by your ability to achieve an individualized and specific goal, remember that **the direction we're heading is more important than individual results.** If we continue to head in the right direction, we may not only achieve the goals we're pursuing but a lot more!

One man whose life I believe represents the power of a compelling future to change one's abilities, and whose life also reminds us that not achieving our intended goal may actually cause us to achieve a greater one, is the late Michael Landon. Why was this man beloved by so many? He represented many of the highest values within our culture: a strong sense of family, doing the right thing, consistency and integrity, and persistence in the face of adversity, along with a sense of deep caring and love.

This man who brightened so many lives became a cultural hero through a rather indirect route. He grew up in a physically and emotionally abusive environment where his parents fought constantly, his father being Jewish (and hating Catholics) and his mother being a Catholic (who was also anti-Semitic). His mother frequently staged melodramatic suicide attempts and often pursued Michael to the local teen hangout, where she'd jump out of a taxi to beat him with a coat hanger. A chronic bedwetter by the time he reached high school, Michael was afflicted with uncontrollable facial tics and was making involuntary gulping sounds. He was skinny and filled with fear. This doesn't sound very much like the confident, self-assured patriarch of the Ingalls family he portrayed on TV's *Little House on the Prairie,* does it? What changed his life?

One day, in his sophomore year in high school, the gym teacher took the class out onto the football field to take a shot at throwing an old, rusty javelin. Michael was about to have an experience that would reshape his view of himself forever. When his turn came, he approached the javelin with the same fear and lack of confidence with which he had approached everything else in his life up until then.

But that day a miracle happened. Michael hurled that javelin forward, and it flew out of the track area thirty feet farther than anyone else had ever thrown it. In that moment, Michael knew he had a future. As he was to say later in an interview with *Life* magazine, "On that day, I had found something I could do better than other people, something I could grab on to. And I grabbed. I begged the coach to let me take that javelin home for the summer, and he let me. And I threw it and threw it and threw it."*

Michael had found his compelling future, and he pursued it with a ferocious intensity. The results were absolutely amazing. By the time he returned from summer vacation, his body had begun to transform. In his sophomore year he began doing exercises to build his upper body. And

* Darrach, Brad. "I Want to See My Kids Grow Up," *Life* magazine, June 1991.

by his senior year, he had broken the U.S. record for high school students in the javelin throw, winning an athletic scholarship to the University of Southern California. To put it in his words, the "mouse" had "become a lion." How's that for a metaphor?

The story doesn't end here. Part of Michael's strength emanated from a belief he developed by watching a movie about Samson and Delilah. He believed that if he grew his hair long, he'd become strong. Indeed, it worked while he was in high school. Unfortunately, his belief was in for a rude awakening when he arrived at USC in the crew-cut era of the fifties. A group of short-haired athletes slammed him to the ground and cut off his long, leonine locks. Even though intellectually he knew better, his strength immediately disappeared. In fact, his javelin throw dropped by more than 30 feet. As he pushed himself to match his past performances, he injured himself so badly that he was out for the year, and the athletic department made it so difficult for him he was compelled to leave. In order to support himself, he had to unload freight in a manufacturing plant. It looked as though his dream had died. How would he ever meet his vision of being an international track star?

Fortunately, one day he was spotted by a Hollywood talent agent who asked him to try out for the part of Little Joe Cartwright in what would be the first color western on television, *Bonanza*. After that, there was no looking back. Michael's career as an actor, and eventually a director and producer, was launched. **Missing his dream had given him his future.** But the pursuit of his original goals, and the direction they took him, sculpted both his physical body and his character, two of the elements of growth that were necessary to prepare him for his ultimate future. **Sometimes we need to trust that our disappointments may truly be *opportunities in disguise*.**

THE KEY TO ACHIEVING GOALS

Does this mean that if you pursue your goals and meet with initial failure and frustration, you should move on and do something else? Of course not. No one ever achieved a goal by being *interested* in its achievement. One must be *committed*. In fact, in studying the source of people's success, I've found that persistence overshadows even talent as the most valued and effective resource in creating and shaping the quality of life. Most people give up a maddening *five feet* from their goal!

I believe that life is constantly testing us for our level of commitment, and life's greatest rewards are reserved for those who demonstrate a never-ending commitment to act until they achieve. This level of resolve can move mountains, but it must be constant and consistent. As simplistic as this may sound, it is still the common denominator separating those who live their dreams from those who live in regret.

I'm a student of those who have learned to take the invisible and make it visible. That's why I respect poets, writers, actors, and entrepreneurs—people who take an idea and bring it to life. One of the people I believe is an outstanding role model of creativity and ever-expanding personal growth and success is Peter Guber, the chairman of the board and CEO of Sony Pictures Entertainment Inc. (formerly known as Columbia Pictures). At the age of 48 Peter has become one of the most powerful and respected men in the motion picture industry. He and his partner, Jon Peters, have racked up a combined total of over 52 Academy Award nominations. His work includes films from *Midnight Express* to *Missing,* from *Rain Man* to *Batman.* In 1989 their joint company, Guber-Peters Entertainment Company, was purchased by Sony for over $200 million in order to get the duo to take charge of the Columbia Pictures empire. How does someone at such a young age achieve such impact in an incredibly competitive industry? The answer is through vision and absolute, never-ending persistence.

One day I had the privilege of receiving a phone call from him and finding out that he was a great fan of my Personal Power™ audiotape program. Each morning as he worked out, he listened to my tapes so that as he got his body in shape he could simultaneously get his mind in shape! He wanted to thank me because he'd never made a purchase like this before from television, and certainly never listened to tapes such as these. As a result of this conversation, I got a chance to meet Peter and develop a friendship with him.

I have found that one key ingredient of his incredible success is his ability never to let go once he locks on to a goal. Back in 1979, he and Jon Peters had bought the rights to produce *Batman,* but it wasn't until 1988 that they could begin production. Along the way, virtually everybody tried to kill the film. Studio executives said there was no market for it, and that the only people who would see it were kids and comic book nuts (who became inflamed when Michael Keaton was selected to play the powerhouse role of Batman). In spite of continuous disappointment, frustration, and considerable risk, the team of Guber and Peters made *Batman* one of the biggest blockbusters of all time, netting the highest opening-weekend revenues of any film ever released. Proceeds from the film and all ancillary products are estimated to have produced over $1 billion!

Another example of Guber's persistence was making the film *Rain Man.* This film should never even have survived. At various stages of its completion, the script was handled by five writers, and three directors walked off the project, including Steven Spielberg. Some of them wanted

Peter Guber to change the script by adding some action, some murders, or at least some sex. They argued that no one would ever watch a film that featured nothing but two guys sitting in a car and traveling across the country, especially when one was "retarded."

But Peter understands the power of emotion; he consistently chooses to produce movies that move the human spirit. He knows what touches people's souls, and he refused to budge, telling everyone that this was a film about a relationship, that this story of two brothers getting to know each other was all the action the film needed, and that *Rain Man* would in fact win an Oscar. The best minds tried to convince him otherwise, including Spielberg, but he would not relent. Sure enough, the 1988 film went on to garner four Academy Awards, including Best Picture, Best Actor, Best Director, and Best Screenplay. Persistence pays. Guber believes that with every new film you're starting over, that in Hollywood you're only as good as your last film. Doesn't this create a lot of fear? You bet! But he says he uses his fear and the stress of the environment not to paralyze, but rather to *propel himself forward.*

Too often people never even begin to pursue a goal out of their fear that they'll fail. Or worse, they start pursuing a goal, then give up too soon. They may have been on track to achieve what they want, but they fail to maintain the patience of the stonecutter. Because they're not getting immediate feedback, they give up far too soon. If there's any one skill that I've seen in champions—people who have really achieved their highest desires—it's an unbelievable level of persistence. They'll *change their approach* as necessary, but they won't abandon their ultimate vision.

UNLEASH THE POWER OF THE RETICULAR ACTIVATING SYSTEM TO ACHIEVE YOUR GOALS

What is the power that a Peter Guber or a Michael Landon taps into? What is this seemingly extrasensory perception they have to notice anything and everything that relates to their goal or can be used to achieve their heart's desire? I believe that in each case, these individuals have learned to use a mechanism in their brains known as the Reticular Activating System.

It sounds complex, and undoubtedly the actual process is, but the function of your RAS is simple and profound: it determines what you will notice and what you will pay attention to. It is the screening device of your mind. Remember that your conscious mind can focus only on a limited number of elements at any one time, so your brain expends a lot of effort deciding what *not* to pay attention to. There are countless stimuli bombarding you right now, but your brain deletes most of it and focuses on what you believe is important. Its mechanism for achieving this is the RAS. Thus your RAS is directly responsible for how much of reality you consciously experience.

Let me offer you an example. Have you ever bought a new outfit or car, and then suddenly noticed it everywhere you looked? Why was that? Didn't they exist before? Yes, of course they did, but you're noticing them now because your purchase of this item was a clear demonstration to your RAS that anything related to this object is now significant and needs to be noted. You have an immediate and heightened awareness of something that actually has always been around you.

This shift in mental posture aligns you more precisely with your goals. Once you decide that something is a priority, you give it tremendous emotional intensity, and by continually focusing on it, any resource that supports its attainment will eventually become clear. Therefore, it's not crucial to understand exactly *how* you'll achieve your goals when you first set them. Trust that your RAS will point out what you need to know along the way.

> *"Climb high; Climb far.*
> *Your goal the sky; Your aim the star."*
> —INSCRIPTION AT WILLIAMS COLLEGE

Eight years ago, in 1983, I did an exercise that created a future so compelling that my whole life changed as a result. As part of the overall process of raising my standards, I established a whole new set of goals, writing down all the things I would no longer settle for, as well as what I was committed to having in my life. I set aside all my limiting beliefs and sat down on the beach with my journal.

I wrote continuously for three hours, brainstorming every possibility of what I could ever imagine doing, being, having, creating, experiencing, or contributing. The time line I gave myself for achieving these goals was any time from tomorrow to the next twenty years. I never stopped to think whether I could actually achieve these goals or not. I simply captured any possibility that inspired me, and wrote it down.

From that beginning, I refined the process six months later when I was invited along with a group of parapsychologists to the USSR to study psychic phenomena directly from university experts throughout Russia. As my group traveled the country, I spent many hours on the train from Moscow to Siberia and back to Leningrad. With nothing to write on but the back of an old Russian map, I wrote down all my long-term goals for my spiritual, mental, emotional, physical, and financial destinies, and then created a series of milestones for each one, working backward.

For example, in order to achieve my top spiritual goal ten years from now, what kind of person would I have to be, and what things would I need to accomplish by nine years from now, eight years, seven years, and so on, reaching all the way back until today? **What specific action could I take *today* that would lead me on that road to the destiny of my choice?**

On that day, I set specific goals that transformed my life. I described the woman of my dreams, detailing what she would be like mentally, emotionally, physically, spiritually. I described what my kids would be like, the huge income that I would enjoy, and the home that I would live in, including the third-story circular office area that would overlook the ocean.

A year and a half later, *Life* magazine was in my home, interviewing me as to how I had made such incredible shifts in my life. When I pulled out my map to show them all the goals I had written down, it was amazing to see how many I'd achieved. I had met the woman I described, and married her. I had found and purchased the home I'd envisioned, down to the finest detail, including the third-story office in the turret of the castle, overlooking the ocean. When I wrote them down initially, I had no assurances whatsoever that these goals could be achieved. But I had been **willing to suspend judgment for a short period of time in order to make it work**.

TAKE YOUR FIRST STEP NOW!

What we are going to do now is take the first step in turning the invisible into the visible, in making your dreams a reality. By the time we are finished, you will have created for yourself an anticipation so great, a future so compelling, that you can't help but take the first steps today.

We'll be covering four areas:
1) **Personal development goals,**
2) **Career/business/economic goals,**
3) **Toys/adventure goals, and**
4) **Contribution goals.**

For each of these you'll have a set period of time in which to brainstorm. Write rapidly—keep your pen moving, don't censor yourself, just get it all down on paper. Constantly ask yourself, **what would I want for my life if I knew I could have it any way I wanted it? What would I**

go for if I knew I could not fail? Suspend the need to know precisely *how*. Just discover what it is you truly want. Do this without questioning or doubting your capability.

Remember, if you get inspired enough, the power you'll unleash from within will find a way to manifest your desire. Also, initially, don't waste time getting overly specific with things like, "I want a split-level house on Nob Hill, in San Francisco, with all-white, contemporary furniture and a splash of color here and there—oh, and don't forget the Victorian rose garden." Just write, "Dream house. Big garden. San Francisco." You'll fill in the details later.

So right now, put yourself in a state of mind of absolute faith and total expectation that you can create anything you want. I'd like you to imagine that you are a kid again on Christmas Eve. You're in a department store, about to sit on Santa's lap. Do you remember what this was like? If you talk to kids before Christmas, they have no trouble at all coming up with a fun, outrageous list; they'll say, "I'll tell you what I want. I want a swimming pool. In fact, I want *two* swimming pools: one for you, and one for me!" An adult would probably turn to them and say, "What? You'll be lucky to get a tub in the backyard!" We'll get practical later, but for now, the point is to be a kid: give yourself the freedom to explore the possibility of life without limits.

I. Personal Development Goals

Step 1: On the chart provided (or on additional sheets of paper when you need more room) **write down everything that you'd like to improve in your life that relates to your own personal growth.** How would you like to improve your physical body? What are your goals for your mental and social development? Would you like to learn, for example, to speak another language? Become a speed reader? Would there be value in reading all of Shakespeare's works? Emotionally, what would you like to experience, achieve, or master in your life? Maybe you want to be able to instantly break patterns of frustration or rejection. Maybe you want to feel compassion for those people you used to feel anger toward. What are some of your spiritual goals? Do you want to feel a greater sense of connection with your Creator? Or have an expanded feeling of compassion for your neighbor?

The key in writing these goals is to write down everything and anything you can imagine without letting your mind stop. They can be short-term goals—something you want to accomplish this week, this year—or they can be long-term goals, something you want to accomplish any time between now and the next twenty years. **Brainstorm for a minimum of five minutes. Don't stop writing at any time.** Be silly, be crazy, be a kid—sometimes a weird idea leads to a great destiny! Here are a few questions you may want to review just before beginning, but after you review them, go to work and begin your goal setting right now!

What would you like to learn?
What are some skills you want to master in your lifetime?
What are some character traits you'd like to develop?
Who do you want your friends to be?
Who do you want to be?

What could you do for your physical well-being?
Get a massage every week? Every day?
Create the body of your dreams?
Join a gym—and actually *use* it?
Hire a vegetarian chef?
Complete the Iron Man Triathlon in Honolulu?

Would you like to conquer your fear of flying?
Or of public speaking?
Or of swimming?

What would you want to learn?
To speak French?
Study the Dead Sea Scrolls?
Dance and/or sing?
Study with violin virtuoso Itzhak Perlman?
Who else would you like to study with?
Would you like to take in a foreign exchange student?

Step 2: Now that you've got a list of goals for your personal development that you can get excited about, **take a minute now to give a time line to each and every one of these.** At this stage, it's not important to know how you're going to accomplish these goals. Just give yourself a time frame from which to operate. **Remember that goals are dreams with a deadline.** The simple act of deciding when you'll achieve a goal sets in motion conscious and unconscious forces to make your goals a reality. So if you're committed to accomplishing a goal within one year or less, put a 1 next to it. If you're committed to accomplishing it within three years, put a 3 next to it, and so on for five, ten, and twenty years.

Step 3: Now **choose your single most important one-year goal in this category**—a goal that, if you were to accomplish it this year, would give you tremendous excitement and make you feel that the year was well invested. **Take *two minutes* to write a paragraph about why you are absolutely committed to achieving this goal within the year.** Why is this compelling for you? What will you gain by achieving it? What would you miss out on if you *didn't* achieve it? Are these reasons strong enough to get you to actually follow through? If not, either come up with a better goal or better reasons.

The most important distinction that I made about goals years ago was that if I had a big enough *why* to do something—a strong enough set of reasons—I could always figure out *how* to achieve it. Goals alone can inspire, but knowing the deepest reasons why you want them in the first place can provide you with the long-lasting drive and motivation necessary to persist and achieve.

PERSONAL DEVELOPMENT GOALS

II. Career/Business/Economic Goals

The next step is setting your **career/business/economic goals**.

Step 1: **Write down anything you want for your career, business, or financial life.** What levels of financial abundance do you want to achieve? To what position do you want to rise? **Take five minutes now to create a list that's worth a million!**

Do you want to earn:
$50,000 a year?
$100,000 a year?
$500,000 a year?
$1 million a year?
$10 million a year?
So much that you can't possibly count it?

What goals do you have for your company?
Would you like to take your company public?
Would you like to become the leader in your industry?

What do you want your net worth to be?
When do you want to retire?
How much investment income would you like to have so you no longer have to work?
By what age do you want to achieve financial independence?

What are your money management goals? Do you need to:
Balance your budget?
Balance your checkbook?
Get a financial coach?

What investments would you make? Would you:
Finance an exciting start-up business?
Buy a vintage coin collection?
Start a diaper delivery service?
Invest in a mutual fund?
Set up a living trust?
Contribute to a pension plan?

How much do you want to save toward giving your kids a college education?
How much do you want to be able to spend on travel and adventure?
How much do you want to be able to spend on new "toys"?

What are your career goals?
 What would you like to contribute to your company?
 What breakthroughs would you like to create?
 Would you like to become a supervisor? A manager? A CEO?
 What would you like to be known for within your profession?
 What kind of impact do you want to have?

Step 2: Now that you've written down all your most compelling career, business, and economic goals, **take a minute to give a time line to each one**, as you did with your personal development goals. If you're committed to accomplishing that goal in the next year or less, write a 1 next to it. If you're committed to achieving it within the next five years, write a 5, and so on. Remember, what matters is not whether you know how you will attain that goal, or whether the time line is reasonable, but whether you are *absolutely committed* to attaining it.

Step 3: Next, **choose your top one-year goal in the category of business and economics, and take two minutes to write a paragraph about it**, explaining why you are absolutely committed to achieving this goal within the year. Be sure to stack up as many reasons as you can for achieving this goal. Pick reasons that will really drive you, that make you passionate and excited about the process. Again, if these reasons aren't compelling enough to get you to actually follow through, then come up with either better reasons or a better goal.

CAREER/BUSINESS/ECONOMIC GOALS

III. Toys/Adventure Goals

If there were no limits economically, what are some of the things you would like to have? What are some of the things you would like to do? If the genie were before you and any wish you made would immediately be fulfilled, what would you want most in the world?

Step 1: Take five minutes to write down everything you could ever want, have, do or experience in your life. Here are some questions to get you going:

Would you like to build, create, or purchase a:
Cottage?
Castle?
Beach house?
Catamaran sailboat?
Private yacht?
Island?
Lamborghini sports car?
Chanel wardrobe?
Helicopter?
Jet plane?
Music studio?
Art collection?
Private zoo stocked with giraffes, alligators, and hippos?
Virtual Reality machine?

Would you like to attend:
An opening of a Broadway play?
A film premiere in Cannes?
A Bruce Springsteen concert?
A Kabuki theater production in Osaka, Japan?

Would you like to:
Race any of the Andrettis at the next Indy 500?
Play Monica Seles and Steffi Graf, or Boris Becker and Ivan Lendl, in a doubles match?
Pitch the World Series?
Carry the Olympic torch?
Go one-on-one with Michael Jordan?
Swim with the pink dolphins in the oceans of Peru?
Race camels between the pyramids of Egypt with your best friend? And *win*?
Trek with the Sherpas in the Himalayas?

Would you like to:
  Star in a Broadway play?
  Share an on-screen kiss with Kim Basinger?
  Dirty dance with Patrick Swayze?
  Choreograph a modern ballet with Mikhail Baryshnikov?

What exotic places would you visit? Would you:
  Sail around the world like Thor Heyerdahl in the
    Kon-Tiki?
  Visit Tanzania and study chimpanzees with Jane
    Goodall?
  Sail on the *Calypso* with Jacques Cousteau?
  Lounge on the sands of the French Riviera?
  Sail a yacht around the Greek Isles?
  Participate in the Dragon Festivals in China?
  Take part in a shadow dance in Bangkok?
  Scuba dive in Fiji?
  Meditate in a Buddhist monastery?
  Take a stroll through the Prado in Madrid?
  Book a ride on the next space shuttle flight?

Steps 2 and 3: Again, **give a time line to each one, choose your top one-year goal in this category, and take two minutes to write a paragraph explaining why you are absolutely committed to achieving it within the next year**. Back it up with strong reasons, and, of course, if these reasons aren't compelling enough to get you to actually follow through, then come up with either better reasons or a better goal.

TOYS/ADVENTURE GOALS

IV. Contribution Goals

These can be the most inspiring, compelling goals of all, because **this is your opportunity to leave your mark, creating a legacy that makes a true difference in people's lives.** It could be something as simple as tithing to your church or committing your household to a recycling program, or as broad as setting up a foundation to offer opportunities to disadvantaged people.

<u>**Step 1: Take five minutes to brainstorm out all the possibilities.**</u>

How could you contribute? Would you:
Help build a shelter for the homeless?
Adopt a child?
Volunteer at a soup kitchen?
Read to the blind?
Visit a man or woman serving a prison sentence?
Volunteer with the Peace Corps for six months?
Take balloons to an old folks' home?

How could you help to:
Protect the ozone layer?
Clean up the oceans?
Eliminate racial discrimination?
Halt the destruction of the rain forests?

What could you create? Would you:
Come up with a perpetual motion machine?
Develop a car that runs on garbage?
Design a system for distributing food to all who hunger?

<u>**Steps 2 and 3**: As before, **give each goal a time line**, select your top one-year goal in this category, and take two minutes to write a paragraph</u> explaining why you are absolutely committed to achieving it within the next year.

"There is nothing like dream to create the future. Utopia today, flesh and blood tomorrow."
—VICTOR HUGO

Now you should have four master one-year goals that absolutely excite and inspire you, with sound, compelling reasons behind them. How would you feel if in one year you had mastered and attained them all? How would you feel about yourself? How would you feel about your life? I can't stress enough the importance of developing strong enough reasons to achieve these goals. Having a powerful enough *why* will provide you with the necessary *how*.

Make sure that you look at these four goals *daily*. Put them where you'll see them *every day*, either in your journal, on your desk at the office, or over your bathroom mirror while you're shaving or putting on makeup. If you back your goals up with a solid commitment to **CANI!**, to constant and never-ending improvement of each of these areas, then you're sure to make progress daily. Make the decision now to begin to follow through on these goals, beginning *immediately*.

HOW TO MAKE YOUR GOALS REAL

Now that you have a set of compelling goals and clear-cut reasons for their achievement, the process for making the goals real has already begun. Your RAS will become sensitized as you consistently review your goals and reasons, and will attract to you any resource of value toward the achievement of your clearly defined desire. To ensure the absolute attainment of your goals, you must condition your nervous system *in advance* to feel the pleasure they will surely bring. In other words, **at least twice a day, you must rehearse and emotionally enjoy the experience of achieving each one of your most valued goals**. Each time you do this, you need to create more emotional joy as you see, feel, and hear yourself living your dream.

This continuous focus will create a neural pathway between where you are and where you want to go. Because of this intense conditioning you'll find yourself feeling a sense of *absolute certainty* that you'll achieve your desires, and this certainty will translate into a quality of action that ensures your success. Your confidence will allow you to attract the appropriate coaches and role models who will guide you in taking the most effective actions to produce results quickly rather than the traditional trial-and-error method that can take decades or more. Don't wait another day to begin this process. Start today!

THE PURPOSE OF THE GOAL

Often as we pursue our goals we fail to realize their true impact on the environment around us. We think that achieving our goal is the end. But if we had a greater understanding we'd realize that often in the pursuit of our goals, we set in motion **processional effects** that have consequences even more far reaching than we ever intended. After all, does the honeybee deliberate on how to propagate flowers? Of course not, but in the process of seeking the sweet nectar from the flowers, a bee will invariably pick up pollen on its legs, fly to the next flower, and set in motion a chain of pollination that will result in a hillside awash in color. The businessman pursues profit, and in so doing can create jobs that offer people a chance for incredible personal growth and an increase in the quality of life. The process of earning a livelihood enables people to meet such goals as putting their kids through college. Children in turn contribute by becoming doctors, lawyers, artists, businessmen, scientists, and parents. The chain is never ending.

Goals are a means to an end, not the ultimate purpose of our lives. They are simply a tool to concentrate our focus and move us in a direction. The only reason we really pursue goals is to cause ourselves to expand and grow. **Achieving goals by themselves will never make us happy in the long term; it's who you become, as you overcome the obstacles necessary to achieve your goals, that can give you the deepest and most long-lasting sense of fulfillment.** So maybe the key question you and I need to ask is, **"What kind of person will I have to become in order to achieve all that I want?"** This may be the most important question that you can ask yourself, for its answer will determine the direction you need to head personally.

Please take a moment now, and **write a paragraph describing all the character traits, skills, abilities, attitudes, and beliefs that you would need to develop in order to achieve all of the goals you've written down previously.** Certainly you'll have to take action to achieve those goals. But what qualities will you need to have as a person in order to turn this invisible set of commitments into your visible reality? Before going on, take a moment right now and write this paragraph.

**THE KIND OF PERSON I NEED TO BECOME IN ORDER
TO ACHIEVE ALL THAT I WANT:**

I will need to become very
disciplined with myself. Set
high standards and do not
accept anything less. I will
be kind, loving and energetic.
A focused individual committed
to constant + necessary imp.
everyday.

THE MOST IMPORTANT STEP

For years I had set goals and not followed through. I'd get inspired in the moment, get all pumped up, but three weeks later I noticed I wasn't following through on anything I'd written down. Writing a goal is certainly the first step, and most people don't even do that; just the action of committing your ideas to paper begins to make them more real.

But the most important thing you can do to achieve your goals is to make sure that as soon as you set them, **you immediately begin to create momentum**. The most important rules that I ever adopted to help me in achieving my goals were those I learned from a very successful man who taught me to first write down the goal, and then to **never leave the site of setting a goal without first taking some form of positive action toward its attainment**.

As I emphasized in Chapter 2, a true decision is one that you act upon, and one that you act upon *now*. Use the momentum you've built up in coming up with your top four one-year goals. The most powerful way to continue this momentum is to **take immediate action as soon as you finish this chapter**. Even the smallest step—a phone call, a commitment, sketching out an initial plan—will move you forward. Then develop a list of simple things you can do every day for the next ten days. I can promise you that ten days of small actions in the direction of your goals will begin to create a chain of habits that will ensure your long-term success.

If your number-one personal development goal for the next year is to learn jazz dancing, for instance, "let your fingers do the walking" through those yellow pages *today*. Call the dance studio for a schedule, and enroll in a class.

If your top toy/adventure goal for the next year is a Mercedes-Benz, call your local dealership for a brochure, or visit them *this afternoon* and take a test drive. I'm not saying that you need to buy it today, but at least find out what it costs or drive it so that it becomes more real. Your intensified desire will help you to start putting together a plan.

If your top economic goal for the next year is to earn $100,000, then start **evaluating now what steps you must take**. Who's already earning this kind of income who can teach you the keys to their effectiveness? Do you need to get a second job in order to earn this kind of income? What skills do you need to hone in order to achieve it? Do you need to start saving more than you spend, and invest the difference so that your income can flow from more than just your work? Do you need to start a new venture? What resources do you really need to gather?

Remember, you need to experience the feeling of achieving your top one-year goals in each of the four categories at least once a day. Ideally, you'll look at them once in the morning and once at night. Review your entire list every six months to ensure that your goals stay vital. You may want to go through the brainstorming process again in order to create some new goals, and I'm sure you'll want to add and delete goals as your life takes on exciting new shape.

An additional distinction that's critical for long-term success is that **achieving our goals can be a curse unless we have already set up a new set of higher goals before we reach the first.** As soon as you find yourself about to achieve a goal, you need to make sure that you design the next set of goals immediately. Otherwise you'll experience something we all need to avoid: outrunning our dream. How many times have we read about people who achieve their ultimate life goals only to say, "Is that all there is?" because they feel they have no place to go from the top?

A classic example of this is several Apollo astronauts who prepared their entire lives for the ultimate mission: to land on the moon. When they finally did it they were euphoric, but after returning to earth, some of them developed a level of emotional depression beyond what most people could imagine. After all, there was now nothing to look forward to. What could be a bigger goal than making it to the moon, doing the impossible, and exploring outer space? Maybe the answer is in exploring the equally uncharted frontier of *inner space* of our minds, our hearts, and our souls.

I've heard about young women who plan their weddings for months, sometimes years, pouring all of their creativity, resources, and even *identity,* into a perfect fairytale fantasy. They pin all their hopes and dreams on what they expect will be a once-in-a-lifetime event. After the glow wears off, the young bride, like the astronaut, feels let down. How do you follow up the peak moment of your life? She needs to look forward to the more important, never-ending adventure of building a relationship.

How do people achieve their heart's desire and still feel the excitement and passion that come from aiming toward a goal? **As they approach what they've pursued for so long, they immediately establish a new set of compelling goals.** This guarantees a smooth transition from completion to new inspiration and a continued commitment to growth. Without that commitment, we'll do what's necessary to feel satisfied, but never venture outside our comfort zones. That's when we lose our drive: we lose our desire to expand, and we begin to stagnate. Often people die emotional and spiritual deaths long before they ever leave their physical bodies.

The way to break out of this trap is to realize that **contribution may be the ultimate goal.** Finding a way to help others—those we care about deeply—can inspire us for a lifetime. There is always a place in the world for those who are willing to give of their time, energy, capital, creativity, and commitment.

Consider Robin Williams, for example. Here is a man who has a great advantage over his late friend John Belushi because he has discovered a way to make sure he never runs out of goals. Robin and his friends, Whoopi Goldberg and Billy Crystal, have found a mission that will continually tap their greatest resources: helping the homeless. Arnold Schwarzenegger has found a similar emotional reward in his relationship with the Special Olympics and the President's Council on Physical Fitness. All these successful people have learned that there's nothing quite so compelling as a feeling of sincere contribution.

Make sure your next level of dreams will continually pull you forward in a constant, never-ending search for improvement. A commitment to **CANI!** is truly the universal insurance policy for life-long happiness. Remember that a **compelling future is the food on which our souls thrive**—we all need a continued sense of emotional and spiritual growth.

PROGRAM YOURSELF FOR SUCCESS

Now that you have goals that truly inspire you, that will drive you forward, you've got to make them so compelling that they feel real in your nervous system. How do you develop that ironclad sense of certainty? First, clear away any roadblocks by figuring out up front what could possibly prevent you, and deal with them *now* rather than fifty miles down the road. Then, make commitments to people you know will hold you to your higher standard. Reinforce your new neural pathways by continous rehearsal, with repetition and emotional intensity. Imagine your goals vividly again and again. Incorporate the visual, auditory, and kinesthetic elements that will make your goal a reality!

THE ULTIMATE LESSON

The most important lesson in this chapter is that a compelling future creates a dynamic sense of growth. Without this, we're only half alive. A compelling future is not an accessory, but a *necessity*. It allows us not only to achieve, but to partake of the deep sense of joy, contribution, and growth that gives meaning to life itself.

> *"Where there is no vision, the people perish . . . ."*
> —PROVERBS, 29:18

I remember reading about the astounding number of people in this country who die within three years of retiring, which proves to me that if you lose the sense that you are producing or contributing in some way, you literally lose the will to live, and that if you do have a reason to hang on, you will. In fact, studies have found that elderly or ill people who are close to death often hang on until just after the holidays. As long as they had something like Christmas and the family visit to look forward to, they had a reason to live, but after it passed, they had no compelling future. This phenomenon isn't true only of our own country; it's been noted in cultures around the world. For example, in China the death rate drops off right before and during major festivals, and picks up again as soon as the festivals are over.

It doesn't matter if you're eighteen or eighty—you'll still need something to drive you forward. The inspiration you seek is found within, waiting to be called upon by an unforeseen challenge or inspired request. Colonel Harlan Sanders found it at age sixty-five, when his meager Social Security check arrived. His anger drove him to action. We don't have to wait for an event in order to have the inspiration. We can **design it.**

Venerable funnyman George Burns understands the importance and power of a compelling future. When asked to sum up his philosophy of life, he once replied, "You have to have something to get you out of bed. I can't do anything in bed, anyway. The most important thing is to have a point, a direction you're headed."* Now in his nineties, he's still sharpening his wit, still taking on movie and TV projects, and I recently heard

* George Burns interviewed by Arthur Cooper, *Playboy* magazine, June 1978.

that he booked himself at the London Palladium in the year 2000, when he'll be 104 years old—how's that for creating a compelling future?!

Use your power. You now know what to do to inspire yourself. It's time to *do it!* If you've read this chapter passively up until now, go back and do the exercises. They're fun, and they're easy. First, get your list of your top four one-year goals. Second, get clear on the "why." Third, develop the ritual of reviewing your goals and rehearsing the joy of their achievement daily for ten days. Fourth, surround yourself with role models and those who can help you develop a plan that will guide you in making it all real. Each of these steps will help you to program your RAS and sensitize you to all the possible resources you can incorporate to bring your goals to fruition. This consistent review will also provide for you the sense of certainty that you need to get yourself to take action.

So let's turn to the next chapter, and let me share with you a way to break up any obstacles that would stop you by taking on . . .

13
THE TEN-DAY MENTAL CHALLENGE

"Habit is either the best of servants or the worst of masters."
—NATHANIEL EMMONS

Consistency . . . Isn't this what we're all after? We don't want to create results *once in a while*. We don't want to feel joyous just *for the moment*. We don't want to be at our best *sporadically*. The mark of a champion is **consistency**—and true consistency is established by our habits.

I'm sure you realize by now that I didn't write this book just to help you make a few distinctions. Nor is it designed to inspire you with a few stories or share with you a bit of interesting information that you might use every now and then to create a little "personal development." This book—and my entire life—is dedicated to producing a measurable increase in the quality of our lives.

This can be accomplished only through a new pattern of taking massive action. The true value to an individual of any new strategy or skill is in direct proportion to the frequency of its use. As I've said so many times, knowing what to do is not enough: you must *do what you know*. This chapter is designed to assist you in establishing habits of excellence—the patterns of focus that will help you maximize the impact you have on yourself and others.

In order to take our lives to the next level, however, we must realize that **the same pattern of thinking that has gotten us to where we are will not get us to where we want to go.** One of the biggest challenges I see in both individuals and corporations is that they resist change (their greatest ally), justifying their actions by pointing out that their current behavior is what got them to the level of success that they now enjoy. This is absolutely true and, in reality, **a new level of thinking is now required in order to experience a new level of personal and professional success.**

To do this, we must once and for all break through the barriers of our fear and take control of the focus of our minds. Our old patterns of allowing our minds to be enslaved by the problems of the moment must be broken once and for all. In their place, we must establish the lifelong commitment to focus on the solutions and to enjoy the process. Throughout this book you've learned a wealth of powerful tools and strategies to make your life richer, fuller, more joyous and exciting. But if you just read this book and fail to use it, it's like buying a powerful new computer and never taking it out of the box, or buying a Ferrari and then letting it sit out in your driveway, collecting dust and grime.

So let me offer you a simple plan for interrupting your old patterns of thinking, feeling, and behaving, a way that can help you condition these new, empowering alternatives and make them absolutely consistent.

Years ago, I found myself caught up in a pattern of frustration and anger. I seemed to have problems everywhere I turned. At that point, thinking positively was not high on my list of solutions. After all, I was being "intelligent," and intelligent people don't make things look positive when they aren't! I had plenty of people around me who supported this idea (and they were equally frustrated with their lives, as well!).

In reality, at the time I was being incredibly negative and seeing things worse than they were. I was using my pessimism as a shield. It was my feeble attempt at protecting myself from the pain of failed expectations: I'd do anything to keep from being disappointed once again. But in adopting this pattern, this same barrier that kept me out of pain also kept me out of pleasure. It barred me from solutions and sealed me in a tomb of emotional death where one never experiences too much pain or too much pleasure, and where one continuously justifies one's limited actions by stating they're "just being realistic."

In truth, life is a balance. If we allow ourselves to become the kind of people who refuse to see the weeds that are taking root in our gardens, our delusions will destroy us. Equally destructive, however, is what happens to those people who, out of fear, constantly imagine the garden overgrown and choked with intractable weeds. The leader's path is one of balance. He notes the weeds with a smile upon his face, knowing that the weeds' visit to the garden is all but over—because he's spotted them, he can and will immediately act to remove them.

We don't have to feel negative about weeds. They're part of life. We need to see them, acknowledge them, focus on the solution, and immediately do whatever it takes to eliminate their influence from our lives. Pretending they're not there won't make things better; neither will becoming inflamed with anger by their presence nor devastated by fear. Their continual attempt to be part of your garden is a fact of life. Simply *remove them.* And do it in an emotional state of playfulness or joy while you're getting the job done; otherwise you'll spend the rest of your life being upset, because I can promise you one thing: there *will* be more "weeds" that continue to come up. And unless you want to live in reaction to the world every time problems occur, you need to remember that they're actually an important part of life. They keep you vigorous, they keep you strong, they keep you vigilant in noticing what needs to be done to keep the garden of your life healthy and rich.

We need to practice this same approach in weeding the gardens of our minds. We have to be able to notice when we start to have a negative pattern—not beat ourselves up about it, and not dwell on it—but simply break the patterns as quickly as we discover them, and replace them with the new seeds of mental, emotional, physical, financial, spiritual, and professional success. How do we break these patterns when they show up? Simply remember the steps of NAC you learned in Chapter 6.

1) You need to decide what you do want. If you really want to feel a sense of passion, joy, and control over your life—which obviously you must, or you wouldn't be reading this now—then you know what you want.

2) You've got to get leverage on yourself. If you read this whole book and don't establish any new patterns, wouldn't that be an unbelievable waste of time? In contrast, how will you feel as you truly use what you've learned to take immediate control of your mind, body, emotions, finances, and relationships? Let your desire to avoid pain and induce massive pleasure drive you to make the changes necessary to take your life to the next level now. In order to accomplish this, you must . . .

3) Interrupt the limiting pattern. The best way I know to do this is to simply go on a **"Mental Diet"**—that is, take a set period of time and take conscious control of all your thoughts. A Mental Diet is an opportunity to eliminate the negative and destructive patterns of thinking and feeling that inevitably come from living life in an emotionally reactionary and mentally undisciplined fashion. I committed myself to such a mental cleansing almost eight years ago, and found it to be a very profound and invaluable process.

I came across the idea in a small pamphlet by Emmet Fox.* In it, he expounded upon the value of spending seven days without ever holding a negative thought. The idea seemed so Pollyanna, so ridiculously simple, that at first I thought the whole concept was a total waste of time. But as he began to lay out the rules of this diet he was prescribing to cleanse the mental system, I began to realize it might be more difficult than I thought. The challenge intrigued me, and the final results astounded me. I'd like

* Fox, Emmet, *The Seven-Day Mental Diet*, Marina del Rey: DeVorss & Co. Publishers, © 1935.

to broaden the challenge Mr. Fox created in 1935 and expand it as a tool that can help you integrate the master tools of change that you've been learning thus far in this book, beginning *today*.

Here's your opportunity now to really apply all the new disciplines you've learned in the previous chapters. My challenge to you is simply this:

For the next ten days, beginning immediately, commit to taking full control of all your mental and emotional faculties by deciding right now that <u>you will not indulge in or dwell on any unresourceful thoughts or emotions for ten consecutive days</u>.

It sounds easy, doesn't it? And I'm sure it could be. But those who begin it are frequently surprised to discover how often their brains are engaged in nonproductive, fearful, worrisome, or destructive thinking.

Why would we continually indulge in mental and emotional patterns that create unnecessary stress in our lives? The answer is simple: we actually think it helps! Many people live in a state of worry. In order to accomplish this state, they continually focus and dwell on the worst possible scenario. Why would they do this? Because they believe it will get them to do something—to take action. But the truth of the matter is that worry usually puts a person in an extremely unresourceful emotional state. It doesn't usually empower us to take action, but rather, it tends to cause us to become overwhelmed with frustration or fear.

Yet, using some of the simplest tools in this book, you could change your worried state immediately by **focusing on a solution.** You could ask yourself a better question like, "What do I need to do right now to make this better?" Or you could change your state by changing the vocabulary you use to describe the sensations you're feeling: from "worried" to "a little bit concerned."

In essence, if you decide to accept my Ten-Day Challenge, it means that you've committed to putting yourself and keeping yourself in a passionately positive state, no matter what happens. It means that if you find yourself in any unresourceful emotional states, you'll instantaneously change your physiology or focus into a resourceful state regardless of your desires of the moment. For example, if someone does something that you believe is destructive or even hateful toward you, and you begin to find yourself becoming angry, you must immediately change your emotional state, regardless of the situation, during these ten consecutive days.

Again, remember that you have a multitude of strategies for changing your state. You could ask yourself a more empowering question like, "What could I learn from this?" or "What's great about this situation, and what's not yet perfect?" These questions will lead you into resourceful states where you'll find solutions instead of dwelling on and habitually running the cycle of increased anger and frustration. How many other ways could you change your state if you were really committed?

Remember, our goal is not to ignore the problems of life, but to put ourselves in better mental and emotional states where we can not only come up with solutions, but act upon them. Those people who focus on what they can't control are continually disempowered.

Yes, it's true, we can't control the wind or the rain or the other vagaries of weather, but we can tack our sails in a way that allows us to shape the direction of our lives.

When I first considered going on Fox's mental diet, I believed that staying positive would get me hurt. After all, I had been positive in the past, and my expectations weren't met. I had felt devastated. Eventually, though, I found that by changing my focus I was able to take more control of my life by avoiding the problem state and immediately focusing on solutions. My requests for inner answers were quickly met when I was in a resourceful state.

Every great, successful person I know shares the capacity to remain centered, clear and powerful in the midst of emotional "storms." How do they accomplish this? Most of them have a fundamental rule: **In life, never spend more than 10 percent of your time on the problem, and spend at least 90 percent of your time on the solution.** Most important, **don't sweat the small stuff . . . and remember, it's all small stuff!**

If you decide that you're going to take on my Ten-Day Challenge— and I sense you will, since you've made it this far in the book—then realize that for the next ten days, you're going to spend 100 percent of your time on solutions, and *no* time on problems!

But won't this make the problems worse? "If I don't worry about my problems, won't they get out of control?" I seriously doubt it. Ten days of focusing entirely upon solutions, on what's great in your life, on what works and how lucky you are will not make your problems worse. But these new patterns may make you so strong that what you once thought was a problem may disappear as you assume a new identity of an unstoppable and joyous human being.

There are four simple yet important rules to this Ten-Day Challenge. So if you're going to take it on, remember the following:

THE TEN-DAY MENTAL CHALLENGE—RULES OF THE GAME

Rule 1. In the next *ten consecutive days, refuse* to dwell on any unresourceful thoughts or feelings. Refuse to indulge in any disempowering questions or devitalizing vocabulary or metaphors.

Rule 2. When you catch yourself beginning to focus on the negative—and you certainly will—you are to immediately use the techniques you've learned to redirect your focus toward a better emotional state. Specifically, use the Problem-Solving Questions* as your first line of attack; for example: "What's great about this? What's not perfect yet?" Remember, by asking a question like, "What's not perfect yet?," you're presupposing that things will be perfect. This will change your state. It doesn't ignore the problem, but it keeps you in the right state while you identify what needs to be changed.

In addition, set yourself up for success each morning for the next ten days by asking yourself the Morning Power Questions. You can do them before you get out of bed or while you're in the shower, but make sure you do them right away. This will focus you in the direction of establishing empowering mental and emotional patterns each day as you awake. In the evening, use the Evening Power Questions, or any questions you believe will put you in a great state before you drop off to sleep.

Rule 3. For the next *ten consecutive days,* make certain that your whole focus in life is on **solutions** and not on problems. The minute you see a possible challenge, immediately focus on what the solution could be.

Rule 4. If you backslide—that is, if you catch yourself indulging in or dwelling on an unresourceful thought or feeling—don't beat yourself up. There's no problem with this as long as you change immediately. However, if you *continue to dwell on unresourceful thoughts or feelings for any measurable length of time*, you must wait until the following morning and start the ten days over. The goal of this program is *ten consecutive days* without holding or dwelling on a negative thought. This starting-over process must happen no matter how many days in a row you've already accomplished the task.

* The Problem-Solving Questions, Morning Power Questions, and Evening Power Questions are all listed in Chapter 8.

You may ask, "How long can I focus on the negative before it's considered 'dwelling'?" To me, one minute of continual focus on, and emotional attachment to, what's wrong is dwelling. One minute is more than enough time for us to be able to catch ourselves and create a change. Our whole goal is to catch the monster while it's little. Certainly, within twenty to forty seconds you know if you're being negative about something.

If I were you, though, I'd give myself up to a maximum of two minutes to notice the challenge and begin to change your state. Two minutes is certainly enough time to identify that you're in a negative state. Break the pattern. If you allow yourself to go as long as five minutes or more, you'll find the Mental Challenge won't accomplish its task; instead, you'll just learn to vent your emotions more quickly. The goal is to knock things out before you ever get in a negative emotional state in the first place.

When I first tried this exercise, after doing it for three days I got caught up and angry about something and indulged for about five minutes in negative emotions before I realized what I was doing. I had to start all over. On my second trip through, on the sixth day, I ran into some major challenges, but at this point I was committed. I wasn't about to start over again! So I immediately found myself focusing on the solution. The benefit, as you can guess, was not just staying with my mental diet, but I began conditioning myself for a tremendous, lifelong pattern of staying in a positive emotional state, even when there were challenges around me, and focusing the majority of my energy on solutions.

To this day, even when I hear about problems, as you've probably noticed, I tend to call them challenges. I don't dwell on them, and I immediately focus on how I can convert the challenge into an opportunity.

> *"We first make our habits, and then our habits make us."*
> —JOHN DRYDEN

You may decide that while you're taking this Mental Challenge you may want to cleanse your body as well. In *Unlimited Power* I issued a ten-day physical challenge. Combining both the ten-day Living Health Vitality Challenge* with the ten-day Mental Challenge can produce powerful results that can take your life to another level in the next ten days.

By committing and following through on this Mental Challenge, you'll

---

* See *Unlimited Power*, "Energy: The Fuel of Excellence."

be giving yourself a break from limiting habits and flexing the muscles of empowerment. You'll be sending your brain a new message and *commanding* new results. **You will be demanding empowering emotions, enriching thoughts, inspiring questions.**

With a clear-cut moving-away idea (the pain of starting over) you are giving your brain strong signals to search for empowering patterns. By setting a higher standard for what thoughts you'll allow your mind to dwell on, you'll begin to notice the garbage and destructive patterns you used to blindly or lazily accept from yourself. And as a result, you'll find it difficult to ever go back to the old ways again. The starkness of this approach will cause you to remember these patterns in the future and make it difficult to go back to the old patterns again.

A word of caution: **Don't begin this ten-day commitment unless and until you are certain that you are going to live by it for the full length of time.** If you don't start out with a sense of commitment, you certainly won't make it through the ten days. This is not a challenge for the weak at heart. This is only for those who are really committed to conditioning their nervous systems for new, empowering emotional patterns that can take their lives to the next level.

Have you decided yet whether you're going to do this? Think about it carefully before committing yourself, because once you do, you need to hold yourself to your word and experience the joy that comes with a disciplined effort. If your answer is yes, for the next ten days you'll be taking the things you've learned intellectually up until now and making them part of your daily experience of life. These ten days will help you use the NAC technology to condition yourself for success. You'll be asking new questions, using Transformational Vocabulary and more empowering global metaphors, and instantly changing your focus and physiology.

Let's face it, we all have our indulgences in life. If you're overweight, your indulgences may be chocolate fudge sundaes or double-cheese pizza. When you diet, you say to yourself, "*Enough is enough. This is where I draw the line.*" You hold yourself to a higher standard and enjoy the self-esteem that comes with that single, small, disciplined act. But we all have our mental indulgences, too. Some people feel sorry for themselves. Some get angry in a way that subverts their own best interests. Some of us fail to focus on the things that need attention. My challenge to you is to decide that for ten days, you will not allow yourself a single one of these destructive mental indulgences.

What stands in the way of just deciding to banish them? Three things, really. One is *laziness*. A lot of people know what they should do, but never quite get up the energy to do it. Many know their lives could be something more, yet they're sitting in front of the tube, eating junk food, depriving their minds and bodies of the fuel they need to spark new growth.

The second obstacle is *fear*. **All too often, the security of a mediocre present is more comfortable than the adventure of trying to be more in the future.** So many people get to the end of their lives wondering what could have been—don't let this happen to you.

The third challenge is *force of habit*. We have our old emotional patterns: the deadening force of routine. Like a plane on automatic pilot, our brain dredges up the same old responses it always has. We face an obstacle and see the problem instead of the solution. We suffer a reversal and feel sorry for ourselves instead of deciding how to learn from it. We make a mistake and see it as some sort of baleful judgment on what we can't do, instead of deciding to learn from it and move forward. **This exercise is a way to get beyond all three and produce lasting changes with benefits that can multiply over time.** This is your opportunity to make a true commitment to **CANI!**

This Ten-Day Challenge is not easy. If you habitually feel sorry for yourself, it's not easy to stop. If you're focusing on financial pressure, operating out of fear won't make it any better. If you blame your spouse for everything that goes wrong in your life, the easy thing is to keep doing it. If you mask your insecurities by being angry all the time, if you wallow in guilt, if you blame your looks or your financial situation or your upbringing for all your problems, it's not easy to change. **But you already have so many tools to improve your life. This is my challenge to you to start using them.**

Believe me, the power inherent in this little exercise is amazing. If you stick with it, it will do four things for you. **First,** it will make you **acutely aware** of all the habitual mental patterns that hold you back. **Second,** it will make your brain search for **empowering alternatives** to them. **Third,** it will give you an incredible jolt of confidence as you see that **you can turn your life around. Fourth,** and most importantly, it will **create new habits, new standards, and new expectations** that will help you expand more than you could ever believe.

Success is processional. It's the result of a series of small disciplines that lead us into habitual patterns of success that no longer require consistent will or effort. Like a freight train picking up speed, this exercise in *doing things right* consciously, in erasing the patterns that hold you back and installing new ones that can propel you forward, will give you a sense of momentum like very few things you've done in your life.

The great news about this is that, unlike a diet where you starve yourself and eventually have to go back to eating, *your old pattern of finding the negative is not one you ever have to return to again.* This may not be a ten-day exercise in the end. It's really an opportunity for you to become "addicted" to a positive focus for the rest of your life. But if, after banishing your toxic mental patterns for ten days, you want to return, be my guest. The truth is that once you experience life in this mentally vital and alive way, going back would disgust you. But if you ever find yourself getting off track, you have the tools to immediately put yourself back on the high road again.

Remember, though, only you can make this ten-day Mental Challenge work. Only *you* can make the commitment to really follow through. You might consider getting extra leverage on yourself to make certain you follow through. One way of providing yourself extra incentive is to announce to the people around you what you're committing to, or find a partner who wants to take on this ten-day Mental Challenge with you. In addition, it would be ideal for you to keep a written journal while you're meeting the ten-day Mental Challenge, writing your experiences each day and recording how you successfully dealt with those various challenges. I think you'll find it invaluable to review later on.

Finally, one of the most valuable tools in creating a change is not just interrupting your old pattern, but replacing it with something new. What you may decide to commit to doing is something I do on an ongoing basis throughout my life: **become a reader.**

LEADERS ARE READERS

Years ago, one of my teachers, Jim Rohn, taught me that reading something of substance, something of value, something that was nurturing, something that taught you new distinctions every day, was more important than eating. He got me hooked on the idea of reading a minimum of thirty minutes a day. He said, "Miss a meal, but don't miss your reading." I've found this to be one of the most valuable distinctions in my life. So while you're cleansing your system of the old, you might want to be empowering it by continuing to read the new. And there are plenty of pages of valuable insight and strategy ahead of you that you can be utilizing during these ten days.

If you've learned anything from this book, it's the power of decisions. You're at a critical point in our journey together. You've learned a variety of fundamental strategies and distinctions that can now be used to powerfully and positively shape your life. **My question to you right now is: Have you made the decision to use them?** Don't you owe it to yourself to make the most out of what this book has to offer you? This is one of the most important ways to follow through. Commit now to do this only as quickly as you're committed to living the quality of life that you once only dreamed of.

So realize that this chapter is my personal challenge to you. It's an opportunity and an invitation to demand more from yourself than other people would ever expect, and to reap the rewards that come from this commitment. It's a time to put in practice what you've learned. But it's also a time to decide whether you're willing to make the commitment to make some simple yet powerful improvements in your life. I know that's what you desire. If you need evidence that you *can* do it, I sincerely believe this chapter will provide it—*if* you're willing to go for it full out.

At this point, you're ready to move on to the next section of this book. You've learned the fundamental tools for shaping your life by making decisions. But now let's study the Master System that's controlling every decision you make throughout your life. Understanding the basis of your own personal philosophy is accomplished by . . .

PART · TWO

TAKING CONTROL—THE MASTER SYSTEM

14

ULTIMATE INFLUENCE: YOUR MASTER SYSTEM

"Elementary, my dear Watson..."
—WITH APOLOGIES TO SIR ARTHUR
CONAN DOYLE

One of the things I love most about what I do is the opportunity to unravel the mystery of human behavior and thereby to offer solutions that truly make a difference in the quality of people's lives. I'm fascinated to probe below the surface to find out the "why" behind a person's behavior, to discover their core beliefs, questions, metaphors, references and values. Because my forte is being able to produce immediate and measurable results, out of necessity I've learned how to quickly locate key leverage points for facilitating change. Every day, I get to live the role of Sherlock Holmes, sleuthing minute details to piece together the jigsaw puzzle of each person's unique experience—I guess you could say that I'm a *very* private detective! There are telltale clues to human behavior just as blatant as the smoking gun.

Sometimes the clues are a little more subtle, and it takes further investigation to uncover them. However, as diverse as human behavior is, one of the things that has allowed me to do what I do so successfully is that ultimately it all comes down to certain patterns made up of specific key elements. If you and I have a grasp of these organizing principles, then we are empowered not only to influence people for positive change, but also to *understand why* they do what they do.

Understanding the Master System that directs all human behavior is as much a science as are chemistry and physics, governed by predictable laws and patterns of action and reaction. You can think of your own Master System—the five components that determine how you *evaluate* everything that happens in your life—as a kind of Periodic Table, detailing the elements of human behavior. Just as all physical matter breaks down to the same basic units, so does the process of human behavior to one who knows what to look for. It's the combination and structure— *how we use these elements*—that makes each of us unique. Some mixtures are volatile and produce explosive results. Other combinations neutralize, some catalyze, and some paralyze.

Bombarded as we are with the countless things that happen to us every day, most of us don't even realize that we have a personal philosophy, much less the power it has to direct our evaluations of what things mean to us. The second section of this book is dedicated to assisting you in taking direct control of your *Master System of evaluation*—the force that controls the way you feel and what you do every moment of your life.

Understanding the Master System of others allows you to immediately get to the essence of a person, whether it's your spouse, your child, your boss or business partner, even the people you meet every day. Wouldn't this be one of the greatest gifts you could ever receive: to be able to know what is driving all the people who are most important to you—*including yourself?* Wouldn't it be great to get beyond any upsets or challenges with someone and understand why they're behaving this way—and then, without judgment, to be able to immediately reconnect with who they *really* are?

With children, we usually remember that crankiness indicates a need for a nap, rather than a sour disposition. In a marriage, it's especially important to be able to see through the day-to-day stresses so that you can support each other and nurture the bond that brought you together in the first place. If your spouse is feeling pressure from work, and is venting his or her frustration, it doesn't mean that your marriage is over, but it's a sign to be more attentive and to put your focus on supporting this person you love. After all, you wouldn't judge the stock market based solely on one day when the Dow-Jones Average plunges twenty points. By the same token, you can't judge a person's character by one isolated incident. **People are not their behaviors.**

The key to understanding people is to understand their Master Systems so you can appreciate their individual, systematic way of reasoning. **We all have a system or procedure that we go through in order to determine what things mean to us and what we need to do about them in virtually any situation in life.** You and I need to remember that different things are important to different people, and they'll evaluate what's happening differently based upon their perspective and conditioning.

Imagine playing tennis and hitting a poor serve. From your perspective, you blew it. From your opponent's perspective, it was a great shot— for him. From the line judge's perspective, the serve was neither good nor bad; it was simply "in" or "out." What often happens after hitting a poor shot? People start *generalizing* —and more often than not, in a disempowering way. "What a terrible serve" becomes "I couldn't serve today to save my life." Their next few serves are likely to be equally <u>underwhelming</u>. Then the train of generalization picks up speed, moving from "I couldn't serve today to save my life" to "I never did have that great a serve" to "I'm really not such a hot tennis player" to "I never seem to be able to master anything" to "I'm a horrible person." It looks ludicrous here, spelled out in lurid detail, but isn't this the way it happens in so many areas of our lives? If we fail to take control of our evaluation process, it literally runs wild and sweeps us into the spiraling pattern of self-recrimination.

SUPERIOR EVALUATIONS CREATE SUPERIOR LIVES

In modeling the most successful people in our culture, one common denominator I notice without fail is that they make **superior evaluations**. Think of anyone you consider to be a master of anything, in business, politics, law, the arts, relationships, physical health, spirituality. What has brought them to their personal pinnacle? What has made prosecuting attorney Gerry Spence win almost every case he has taken on in the last fifteen years? Why does Bill Cosby seem to delight his audiences virtually every time he takes the stage? What makes Andrew Lloyd Webber's music so hauntingly perfect?

It all comes down to these people making superior evaluations in their areas of expertise. Spence has honed a superior understanding of what influences human emotion and decision. Cosby has spent years developing key references, beliefs, and rules about how to use anything in his environment as material to make people laugh. Webber's mastery of melody, orchestration, arrangement, and other elements enables him to write music that touches us at the deepest level.

Consider Wayne Gretzky of the Los Angeles Kings. He has scored more points than anyone in the history of the National Hockey League. What makes him so powerful? Is it because he's the biggest, strongest, or fastest player in the league? By his own admission, the answer to all three of these questions is no. Yet he was consistently the number-one scorer in the league. When asked what makes him so effective, his response is that while most players skate to where the puck is, he tends to skate to *where the puck is going.* At any moment in time, his ability to anticipate—to evaluate the velocity of the puck, its direction, the present strategies and physical momentum of the players around him—allows him to place himself in the optimum position for scoring.

One of the top money managers in the world is Sir John Templeton, dean of international investing, whose track record for the last fifty years is unrivaled. A sum of $10,000 invested in the Templeton Growth Fund at its inception in 1954 would be worth $2.2 million today! In order to have him personally work with you on your portfolio, you must invest a minimum of $10 million cash; his top client entrusted him with over $1 billion to invest. What has made Templeton one of the greatest investment advisors of all time? When I asked him this question, he didn't hesitate a moment. He said, "My ability to evaluate the *true value* of an investment." He's been able to do this despite the vagaries of trends and short-term market fluctuations.

WEALTH IS THE RESULT OF EFFECTIVE EVALUATIONS

Other top investment advisors whom I've studied and modeled in the past year include Peter Lynch, Robert Prechter, and Warren Buffet. To help him in his financial evaluations, Buffet employs a powerful metaphor he learned from his friend and mentor Ben Graham: "[As a metaphor for looking at market fluctuations, just imagine them] as coming from a remarkably accommodating fellow named Mr. Market who's your partner in private business. . . . Mr. Market's quotations are anything but [stable]. Why? Well, for the sad-to-say reason that the poor fellow has incurable emotional problems. At times he feels euphoric and we can see only the favorable factors affecting the business, and when he's in that mood he names a very high buy-sell price because he fears that you'll snap up his interest and rob him of imminent gains. At other times he's depressed and he can see nothing but trouble ahead for both the business and the world. On those occasions he'll name a very low price since he's terrified that you will unload your interest on him. . . . But like Cinderella at the ball, you must heed one warning or everything will turn into pumpkins and mice. **Mr. Market is there to serve you, not to guide you.** It is his pocketbook, not his wisdom, that you will find useful. If he shows up someday in a particularly foolish mood, you are free to either ignore him, or take advantage of him, but it will be disastrous if you fall under his influence. **Indeed, if you aren't certain that you understand and can value your business far better than Mr. Market, you don't belong in the game."***

Clearly, Buffet evaluates his investment decisions quite differently

---

* Buffet, Warren, Berkshire Annual Report, 1987, per James Hansberger, *A Guide to Excellence in Investing,* 1976.

from those who are extremely worried when the market crashes or eu-phoric when it soars. And because he evaluates differently, he produces a different quality of result. **If someone is doing better than we are in any area of life, it's simply because they have a better way of eval-uating what things mean and what they should do about it.** We must never forget that the impact of our evaluations goes far beyond hockey or finances. How you evaluate what you're going to eat each night may determine the length and quality of your life. Poor evaluations of how to raise your kids can create the potential for lifelong pain. Failure to un-derstand someone else's evaluation procedures can destroy a beautiful and loving relationship.

The goal, then, is to be able to evaluate everything in your life in a way that consistently guides you to make choices that produce the results you desire. The challenge is that seldom do we take control of what seems like a complex process. But I've developed ways to simplify it so that we can take the helm and begin steering our own evaluation pro-cedures, and therefore our destinies. Here is a brief overview of the five elements of evaluation, some of which you already know, and the rest of which we'll be covering in the following chapters. Below you'll find an arrow pointed toward twin targets. This diagram demonstrates how our Master System of evaluation works. Let's review the five elements one at a time and add each to the diagram as we go.

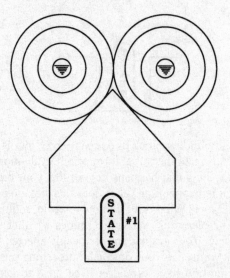

1) The first element that affects all of your evaluations is the mental and emotional **state** you're in while you're making an evaluation. There

are times in your life when somebody can say one thing to you and it will make you cry, while other times the same comment makes you laugh. What's the difference? It might simply be the state you're in. When you're in a fearful, vulnerable state, the crunching of footsteps outside your window in the night, along with the creak of a door opening, will feel and mean something totally different than if you're in a state of excitement or positive anticipation. Whether you quiver under the sheets or leap out and run to the door with open arms is the result of the *evaluations* you make about the meaning of these sounds. One major key to making superior evaluations, then, is to make certain that when we're making decisions about what things mean and what to do, we're in an extremely resourceful state of mind and emotion rather than in a survival mode.

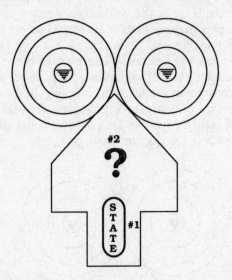

2) The second building block of our Master System is the **questions** we ask. Questions create the initial form of our evaluations. Remember, in response to anything that happens in your life, your brain evaluates it by asking, "What is happening? What does this situation mean? Does it mean pain or pleasure? What can I do now to avoid, reduce, or eliminate pain or gain some pleasure?" What determines whether you ask somebody out for a date? Your evaluations are deeply affected by the specific question you ask yourself as you consider approaching this person. If you ask yourself a question like "Wouldn't it be great to get to know this person?", you're likely to feel motivated to approach them. If, however, you habitually ask questions like "What if they reject me? What if they're offended when I approach them? What if I get hurt?" then obviously

these questions will lead you through a set of evaluations that result in your passing up the opportunity to connect with someone you're truly interested in.

What determines the kind of food you'll put on your dinner plate also depends on the questions you ask. If when you look at food, you consistently ask the question "What could I eat quickly that would give me an immediate lift?", the foods you may choose will tend to be heavily processed convenience foods—in layman's terms, *junk*. If instead you asked, "What could I have now that would nourish me?", it's more likely you'll pull from such food groups as fruits, juices, vegetables, and salads. The difference between having a Snickers bar on a regular basis or having a glass of fresh-squeezed juice will determine the quality of your physical body, and this has resulted from the way you've evaluated. Your habitual questions play a major role in this process.

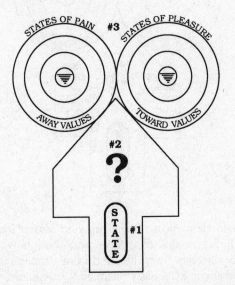

3) The third element that affects your evaluations is your hierarchy of **values**. Each of us throughout our lives has learned to value certain emotions more than others. We all want to feel good, i.e., pleasure, and avoid feeling bad, i.e., pain. But our life's experience has taught each of us a unique coding system for what equals pain and what equals pleasure. This can be found in the guidance system of our values. For example, one person may have learned to link pleasure to the idea of feeling secure, while someone else may have linked *pain* to the same idea because their family's obsession with security caused them never to experience a sense of freedom. Some people try to succeed, yet at the same

time they avoid rejection at all costs. Can you see how this values conflict
might cause a person to feel frustrated or immobilized?

The values you select will shape every decision you make in your life.
There are two types of values you'll learn about in the next chapter: the
emotional states of pleasure we're always trying to **move toward**—values
like love, joy, compassion, and excitement—and the emotional states of
pain that we're trying to **avoid or move away from**—like humiliation,
frustration, depression, and anger. The dynamic created by these two
targets will determine the direction of your life.

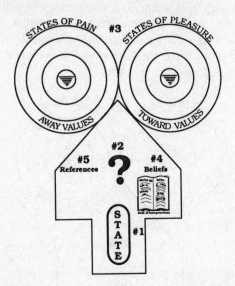

4) The fourth element that makes up your Master System is **beliefs.**
Our **global beliefs** give us a sense of certainty about how to feel and what
to expect from ourselves, from life, and from people; our **rules** are the
beliefs we have about what has to happen for us to feel that our values
have been met. For example, some people believe, "*If* you love me, *then*
you never raise your voice." This rule will cause this person to evaluate
a raised voice as evidence that there is no love in the relationship. This
may have no basis in fact, but the rule will dominate the evaluation and
therefore that person's perceptions and experience of what's true. Other
such limiting rules might be ideas like "*If* you're successful, *then* you
make millions of dollars" or "*If* you're a good parent, *then* you never have
a conflict with your children."

Our global beliefs determine our expectations and often control what
we're even willing to evaluate in the first place. Together, the force of

these beliefs determines when we give ourselves an experience of pain or pleasure, and they are a core element in every evaluation we'll ever make.

5) The fifth element of your Master System is the hodgepodge of **reference experiences** you can access from the giant filing cabinet you call your brain. In it, you've stored everything you've ever experienced in your life—and, for that matter, everything you've ever imagined. These references form the raw material that we use to construct our beliefs and guide our decisions. In order to decide what something means to us, we have to compare it to something; for example, is this situation good or bad? Think of the tennis example earlier in this chapter: is it good or bad, compared to what? Is it good compared to what your friends do or have? Is it bad compared to the worst situation you've ever heard of? You have unlimited references you can use in making any decision. Which references you choose will determine the meaning you take from any experience, how you feel about it, and to a certain extent what you'll do.

Without a doubt, references shape our beliefs and values. Can you see how it would make a difference, for example, if you grew up in an environment where you felt you were consistently being taken advantage of, as opposed to growing up feeling unconditionally loved? How might this color your beliefs or your values, the way you looked at life or people or opportunity?

If, for example, you had learned skydiving when you were sixteen years old, you might develop different values about the idea of adventure than someone who was rejected every time they attempted a new skill, concept, or idea. Masters are often people who just have more references than you do about what leads to success or frustration in any given situation. Clearly, after forty years of investing, John Templeton has more references to assist him in deciding what is an excellent investment than someone who is putting together their first deal.

Additional references offer us the potential for mastery. Yet, regardless of our experience or lack thereof, we have unlimited ways to organize our references into beliefs and rules that either empower or disempower us. Each day you and I have the opportunity to take in new references that can help us to bolster our beliefs, refine our values, ask new questions, access the states that propel us in the direction we want to go, and truly shape our destinies for the better.

> *"Men are wise in proportion, not to their experience,*
> *but to their capacity for experience."*
> —GEORGE BERNARD SHAW

Several years ago, I began to hear about the incredible success of a man named Dwayne Chapman in tracking down and capturing felons who had eluded the law for years. Known to most as "Dog," he has become known as the top bounty hunter in the country. I was fascinated and wanted to meet him and discover what makes him so effective. Dog is a deeply spiritual man whose goal is not only to catch the felon, but also to help him make changes in his life. Where did this desire come from? It came from his own pain.

As a young man, Dog made poor evaluations about whom he chose as friends. Out of his desire to belong to a group, he joined a motorcycle gang, the Devil's Disciples. One day, in the midst of a drug deal gone bad, a gang member shot and mortally wounded a man at the scene. Panic ensued; the members immediately fled. Although Dog did not commit the murder, in that state there was no line drawn between being an accessory to murder and being the man who actually pulled the trigger. He ended up serving years of hard time, working on a chain gang, in the Texas prison system. Doing time gave him so much pain that he reevaluated his entire philosophy of life. He began to realize that his core beliefs, values, and rules had created his pain. He began to ask himself new questions and to focus on his prison experiences (references) as being the effect of choices he'd made with his previous life philosophy. This got him to the point where he believed he must change his life once and for all.

In the years following his release, Dog pursued a number of colorful careers and finally settled on starting a private investigation business. When he was brought before a judge for back child-support payments (payments he'd been unable to make while in prison and in the financially unstable period following his release), the judge offered Dog a money-making opportunity in lieu of a payment he knew would never materialize. He suggested that Dog track down a rapist who had victimized many women in the Denver area. The judge suggested Dog use the distinctions he'd made in prison to assist him in figuring out what this criminal might be doing and where he might be hiding. Although law-enforcement officials had tried unsuccessfully to find this rapist for over a year, Dog delivered him within three days!

To say the least, the judge was impressed. This was the start of a brilliant career, and today, more than 3,000 arrests later, Dog has one of the best records in the country, if not *the* best. He has averaged over 360 arrests a year—*essentially one arrest a day*. What is the key to his success? Certainly a critical factor is the evaluations he makes. Dog interviews his quarry's relatives or loved ones, and in a variety of ways he elicits the information he needs. He discovers some of the beliefs, values, and habitual rules of the man or woman he's pursuing. He now understands their life references, which enables him to think the *same way* they would and *anticipate* their moves with uncanny precision. He understands their Master System and his results speak for themselves.

TWO KINDS OF CHANGE

If you and I want to change anything in our lives, it's invariably one of two things: either *how we're feeling* or *our behaviors*. Certainly we can learn how to change our emotions or feelings *within a context*. For example, if you feel fearful of being rejected as an actor, I can help you to condition yourself so that you no longer feel fearful. Or we can make the second kind of change: a **global change**. A metaphor for this might be that if we want to change the way your computer is processing data, I can change the software that you're using so that when you hit the keys what shows up on the screen is formatted differently. Or if I really want to make a change that will not only affect this type of file, but multiple environments, I can change the computer's operating system. By changing the Master System, we can change how you'll interact in a variety of circumstances.

So instead of just conditioning yourself to feel differently about rejection and eliminating the fearful behaviors, you can adopt a new global *belief* that says, "**I am the source of all my emotions. Nothing and no one can change how I feel except me. If I find myself in reaction to**

anything, I can change it in a moment." If you truly adopt this belief, not intellectually, but emotionally where you feel it with absolute certainty, can you see how that would eliminate not only your fear of rejection, but also your feelings of anger or frustration or inadequacy? Suddenly, you become the master of your fate.

Or we could change your *values*, and make your highest value one of contributing. Then, if somebody rejected you, it wouldn't matter: you'd still want to contribute to them, and through constant contribution, you'd find yourself no longer being rejected by people. You'd also find yourself permeated with a sense of joy and connection that you may never have had before in other areas of your life. Or we can change your conditioned feelings toward smoking by getting you to move health and vitality to the top of your values list. Once that becomes the highest priority of your life, the smoking behavior will disappear, and more importantly, it can be replaced by other behaviors that will support your new value of health and vitality: eating differently, breathing differently, and so on. Both types of changes are valuable.

The focus of the second section of the book is how to create these global changes, where **a single shift in one of the five elements of the Master System will powerfully affect the way you think, feel, and behave in multiple areas of your life simultaneously**. If you change just one element in your Master System, there are certain evaluations you won't even consider anymore, certain questions you won't even ask, certain beliefs the computer won't even accept. This process of creating a global change can be a powerful force for shaping destiny.

> *"Take away the cause, and the effect ceases."*
> —MIGUEL DE CERVANTES

There's a story I love to tell of a fellow standing on the banks of a river. Suddenly, he sees someone caught in the raging current, bounced about on the jagged rocks, and hears him calling for help. He leaps in, pulls the drowning man to safety, gives him mouth-to-mouth resuscitation, attends to the man's wounds, and calls for medical help. As he's still catching his breath, he hears two more screams emanating from the river. Again, he jumps in and makes another daring rescue, this time of two young women. Before he even has a chance to think, he hears four more people calling for help.

Pretty soon the man is exhausted, having rescued victim after victim, and yet the screams continue. If only he had taken the time to travel a short distance upriver, he could have discovered who was throwing all those people in the water in the first place! He could have saved all his efforts by addressing the problem at its cause rather than its effect.

Similarly, understanding the Master System allows you to eliminate the cause instead of exhausting yourself fighting the effects.

One of the finest programs I ever designed is my three-day Date With Destiny seminar. Instead of the usual 2,000 participants, I limit this program to 200 people. At Date With Destiny, we work together to assist each person to understand exactly how their Master System is set up. This understanding transforms people: suddenly they understand *why* they feel the things they feel and do the things they do. They also learn how to change virtually anything in their lives. Most importantly, we then have them design what their Master System needs to be in order for them to achieve their ultimate purpose in life. How can they organize themselves so they can be effortlessly pulled in the direction of their desires rather than be pulled apart by a sense of conflicting values, beliefs, or rules?

Some of the most important questions we ask in this program are "What are the values that are controlling me? How do I know when my values are being met—what are my rules?" Date With Destiny has been attended not only by U.S. senators and congressmen, Fortune 500 CEOs, and movie stars, but also by people from every walk of life. All of us have in common some of the same challenges. How do we deal with disappointment, frustration, failure, and certain events in our environment that we can't control no matter how successful we become?

The emotions we feel and the actions we take are based on how we evaluate things. And yet, most of us have not set up this system of evaluation for ourselves. The profound changes that people experience in this program in a mere three days are beyond words. People literally change the way they think and the way they feel about their lives in a matter of moments, because they take control of the portion of their brain that controls their experience of life. The changes end up being emotional and even physical as the brain sets new priorities for what's most important. While this book is not a replacement for Date With Destiny, I want to provide the same foundational tools that we use in that program for your immediate use. With the chapters that follow, you can produce the same kinds of changes in your life starting *now*.

TEST WHAT YOU'VE LEARNED

To stimulate your thinking about how your Master System works, let me ask you a few provocative questions that should open the floodgates of your thought and help you to identify how different portions of your system are used to make decisions.

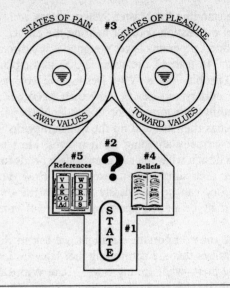

ANSWER THE FOLLOWING FOUR QUESTIONS BEFORE YOU READ ON:

1. What is your most treasured memory?
2. If you could end world hunger today by killing one innocent person, would you? Why or why not?
3. If you bumped a red Porsche and scratched it, and no one was around, would you leave a note? Why or why not?
4. If you could earn $10,000 for eating a bowlful of live cockroaches, would you? Why or why not?

Now let's review how you answered each of these questions.

As you look at the diagram of your Master System, **which of the five areas of evaluation did you use to answer the first question?** Certainly you asked a *question* of yourself in order to begin to evaluate—you probably repeated the question I asked. The answer, though, was retrieved from your *references*, wasn't it? You picked through the myriad experiences you've had in your life, and finally selected one as your most treasured memory. Or maybe you failed to select one because you have a *belief* that says, "All experiences of life are treasured" or "Selecting one over another will be denigrating to some other life experience." Those beliefs would prevent you from answering the question. You see, our Master System of evaluation not only determines what we evaluate and how we evaluate, but even *what we're willing to evaluate.*

Let's review the second question, one that is more intense and which I read in *The Book of Questions*: **If you could end world hunger today by killing one innocent person, would you?**

When I ask people this question, I usually get a rather intense set of answers. Some people say, "Absolutely," their rationale being that the lives of the many outweigh the life of an individual. The way they see it, if one person were willing to suffer, and it would end all suffering on earth, the end would justify the means. Others are aghast at this thought. They believe every human life is valuable. That's also based on a set of *beliefs*, isn't it? Others have a *global belief* that everything in life is exactly as it should be, and that all these people who are starving are getting invaluable lessons for their next incarnation. And some people say, "Yes, I would do it, but I'd take my own life." It's interesting how individuals respond with such varying reactions to the same question based on which of the five elements of evaluation they use and the content they've stored.

How about the third question: **If you bumped a red Porsche and scratched it, and no one was around, would you leave a note?** Some people would say, "Absolutely." Why? Their highest *value* is honesty. Other people say, "Absolutely," but the reason they would do it is that one of the things they avoid most in the world is guilt. Not leaving a note would make them feel guilty, and that's too painful. Others will say, "I wouldn't leave a note," and when asked why they'll say, "Well, it's happened to me several times, and nobody left *me* a note." So they're saying they have personal *references* that made them develop the belief, "Do unto others as they've done unto you."

Here's the fourth question: **If you could earn $10,000 for eating a bowlful of live cockroaches, would you?** Invariably I get very few affirmative responses. Why? Most people's *references* for cockroaches— the images and sensations that they've stored in their bodies—are intensely negative. Certainly cockroaches are not something they'd want to put in their systems. But then I raise the ante: **How many of you would do it for $100,000?** Gradually there is a shift in the room as people begin to raise their hands who previously had said no. Why will they suddenly do it for $100,000? Well, what happened to their evaluation system? Two things: I asked a different question by changing one word, and second, they have a belief that $100,000 could eliminate a lot of pain in their lives, maybe some of the long-term pain that would be more difficult to deal with than the short-term pain of live cockroaches squiggling down their throats.

How about $1 million? How about $10 million? Suddenly the majority of the people in the room are raising their hands. They believe the long-term pleasure that the $10 million would allow them to give to themselves and others would far outweigh the short-term pain. Still, some people would not eat live cockroaches for any amount of money. When asked why not, they say things like "I could never kill a living thing" or "What goes around comes around." Other people say, "I kill cockroaches all the time, just because they're in my way!" One man even said he could eat them easily, and that he would do it for fun, not the money! Why? The reason is that he grew up in a country where cockroaches and other insects are considered a delicacy. Different people have different references and different ways of evaluating things—interesting, isn't it?

THERE COMES A TIME . . .

As we study these five elements of the Master System, there's one other theme we need to bear in mind: it's certainly possible to overevaluate. Human beings love to analyze things to death. There is a point, however, when we've got to stop evaluating and *take action*. For example, some people make so many evaluations that even a minor decision turns into a major production: maybe they can't get themselves to exercise regularly as part of their lifestyle. Why? They see it as a major production. The way they "chunk" the experience, the way they look at it, there are so many steps that they're intimidated.

In order to exercise, they must 1) get up; 2) find some workout wear they don't look too fat in; 3) pick out the right athletic shoes; 4) pack everything up in their gym bag; 5) *schlepp* over to the gym; 6) find a parking spot; 7) climb the stairs; 8) sign in; 9) go into the locker room; 10) squeeze into the workout clothes; and 11) finally attend the class, hit the stationary bicycle, and sweat like crazy. And then when they're done, 12) they have to do all of this again in reverse. Of course, these same people can *easily* get themselves to go to the beach. They're ready in a heartbeat! If you ask them why, they'll tell you, "Well, to go to the beach, you just hop in the car and go!" They don't stop to evaluate each and every step along the way; they see it as one giant step, evaluating only whether to go or not, not every little detail. Sometimes evaluating too many details can cause us to feel overloaded or overwhelmed. One of the things we'll learn here, then, is to put many minor steps together into one big "chunk"—one giant step, if you will—that the minute you take it you'll get the result that you want.

In this section, we're going to analyze our evaluation system, put it together in a way that makes sense, and then start using it instead of deliberating about it. As you continue through the next few chapters,

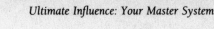

NAC™ - THE MASTER SYSTEM

The Psychology of Change

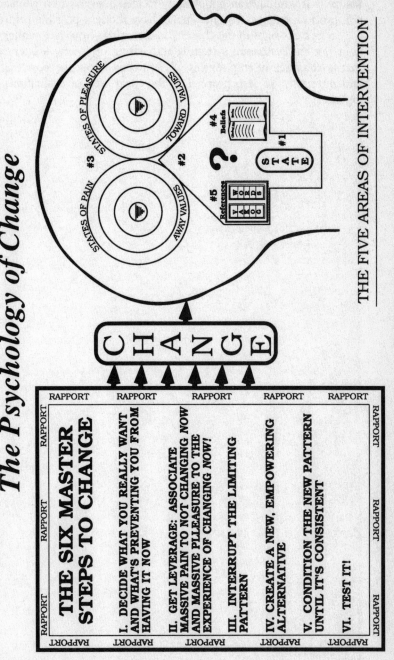

#3 STATES OF PLEASURE

#3 STATES OF PAIN

TOWARD VALUES

AWAY VALUES

#2

#4 Beliefs

#1 S T A T E

#5 References WORDS

THE FIVE AREAS OF INTERVENTION

C H A N G E

RAPPORT   RAPPORT   RAPPORT   RAPPORT   RAPPORT

THE SIX MASTER STEPS TO CHANGE

I. DECIDE WHAT YOU REALLY WANT AND WHAT'S PREVENTING YOU FROM HAVING IT NOW

II. GET LEVERAGE: ASSOCIATE MASSIVE PAIN TO NOT CHANGING *NOW* AND MASSIVE PLEASURE TO THE EXPERIENCE OF CHANGING *NOW!*

III. INTERRUPT THE LIMITING PATTERN

IV. CREATE A NEW, EMPOWERING ALTERNATIVE

V. CONDITION THE NEW PATTERN UNTIL IT'S CONSISTENT

VI. TEST IT!

realize that you have an opportunity to create leverage on yourself that will produce changes you may never have thought possible before.

So let's cut right to the chase. I'll be coaching you on revealing what your present evaluation system is and setting up a new Master System that is consistently empowering. You already know the power of state and questions, so let's proceed to the third area of evaluations. Let's look at . . .

15
LIFE VALUES: YOUR PERSONAL COMPASS

"Nothing splendid has ever been achieved except by those who dared believe that something inside of them was superior to circumstance."
—BRUCE BARTON

Courage, determination, perseverance, dedication . . . As Ross Perot conducted the tense briefing in Dallas, he saw those qualities reflected in the faces of the men he had handpicked for an extraordinary rescue mission. In the early days of 1979, civil unrest and anti-America hysteria were rising to a fever pitch in Iran, and only a few days before, two of Perot's corporate executives in Teheran had been inexplicably jailed. Bail was set at *$13 million.*

When high-powered diplomatic negotiations failed to get results, Perot decided that there was only one way to get his men out: he'd have to do it himself. Calling upon the expertise of legendary army colonel Arthur "Bull" Simons to lead this daring raid, Perot quickly assembled a crack team of his top executives to pull off the jailbreak. They were selected because they'd all been in Teheran and had military experience. He called his men "Eagles" to signify "high fliers who used their initiative, got the job done, and gave results, not excuses."*

The rewards would be high if they won, but the risks were even greater: the mission was completely unauthorized, and not only was failure a possibility, but so was death. What drove Ross Perot to muster all his resources, to take the risks and defy the odds? Clearly, he's a man who lives by his values. Courage, loyalty, love, commitment, and determination are all values that give him an exceptional capacity to care and a strength of will that is legendary. These same values were the force that drove him to build his company, EDS (Electronic Data Systems Corpo-

* Follett, Ken, *On Wings of Eagles,* New York: Penguin, 1989.

ration), from a thousand-dollar investment into an enterprise worth billions of dollars. He rose to the top because of his capacity to evaluate and select the right men. He chose them based on a strict code of values and he knew that with the right people, those who held high enough standards, all he'd have to do was give them the job to do and get out of their way.

Now he would have the ultimate test of the people he'd selected as he called upon them to summon their finest resources and rescue a few members of the corporate "family." The story of their mission and the challenges they met can be found in the book *On Wings of Eagles*. Suffice it to say that despite obstacles beyond compare, Perot's heroic rescue mission succeeded and brought home his most valued assets: his people.

> ## "A man's character is his guardian divinity."
> —HERACLITUS

Values guide our every decision and, therefore, our destiny. Those who know their values and live by them become the leaders of our society. They are exemplified by outstanding individuals throughout our nation, from the boardroom to the classroom. For example, did you see the movie *Stand and Deliver*? It told the story of the maverick math teacher Jaime Escalante.

Were you as inspired as I was by the heroic strides he made in transmitting to his students his passion for learning? He got them to associate in their nervous systems, at the deepest level, a sense of pride in their capacity to master those things others were certain they could never learn. His example of commitment translated to these young people the power of values. They learned from him discipline, confidence, the importance of the team, flexibility, and the power of absolute determination.

He didn't talk to these kids in the barrio about what they should do with their lives; he was a living demonstration, a new definition of what was possible. He not only got them to pass a calculus placement test in numbers that everyone thought were impossible, but he also got them to change their beliefs about who they were and what they were capable of if they consistently committed to holding themselves to a higher standard.

If we want the deepest level of life fulfillment, we can achieve it in only one way, and that is by doing what these two men have done: by deciding upon what we value most in life, what our highest values are, and then committing to live by them every single day. Unfortunately, this action is far too rare in today's society. Too often, people have no clear idea of what's important to them. They waffle on any issue; the world is a mass of gray to them; they never take a stand for anything or anyone.

If you and I are not clear about what's most important in our lives—what we truly stand for—then how can we ever expect to lay the foundation for a sense of self-esteem, much less have the capacity to make effective decisions? If you've ever found yourself in a situation where you had a tough time making a decision about something, the reason is that you weren't clear about what you value most within that situation. **We must remember that all decision making comes down to values clarification.**

When you know what's most important to you, making a decision is quite simple. Most people, though, are unclear about what's most important in their lives, and thus decision making becomes a form of internal torture. This is not true for those who've clearly defined the highest principles of their lives. It wasn't tough for Ross Perot to know what to do. His values *dictated* it. They acted as his personal compass to guide him through a situation fraught with peril. Recently, Escalante left the Los Angeles school system that he'd been working in to move to northern California. Why? He could no longer be a part of an organization where he believed there were no standards for a teacher's performance.

Who are the most universally admired and respected people in our culture? Aren't they those who have a solid grasp of their own values, people who not only profess their standards, but live by them? We all respect people who take a stand for what they believe, even if we don't concur with their ideas about what's right and what's wrong. There is power in individuals who congruently lead lives where their philosophies and actions are one.

Most often we recognize this unique state of the human condition as an individual with integrity. Culturally, these people have come in many forms, from the John Waynes and Ross Perots, to the Bob Hopes and Jerry Lewises, to the Martin Sheens and Ralph Naders, to the Norman Cousinses and Walter Cronkites. The fact of the matter is that those we perceive to be congruent in their values have a tremendous capacity to have an influence within our culture.

Do you remember the nightly newscasts with Walter Cronkite? Walter was with us on all the most important days of our lives: during tragedies and triumphs, when John F. Kennedy was assassinated, and when Neil Armstrong first set foot on the moon. Walter was part of our family. We trusted him implicitly.

At the beginning of the Vietnam War, he reported on it in the standard way, with an objective view of our involvement, but after visiting Vietnam his view of the war changed, and his values of integrity and honesty required that, rightly or wrongly, he communicate his disillusionment. Regardless of whether you agreed with him or not, the impact he had may have been one of the final straws that caused many in Middle America to begin to question the war for the first time. Now it wasn't just a few radical students protesting Vietnam, but "Uncle Walt."

The conflict in Vietnam was truly a values conflict within our culture. People's perception of what was right and wrong, what could make a difference, was the battle fought at home while the boys overseas put their blood and guts on the line, some not knowing why. An inconsistency of values among our leaders has been one of the greatest sources of pain in our culture. Watergate certainly wounded many Americans. Yet, through it all, our country has continued to grow and expand because there are individuals who continually come forth to demonstrate what's possible and hold us to a higher standard—whether it's Bob Geldof focusing the attention of the world on the famine in Africa or Ed Roberts mobilizing the political forces necessary to change the quality of life for the physically challenged.

> *"Every time a value is born, existence takes on a new meaning; every time one dies, some part of that meaning passes away."*
> —JOSEPH WOOD KRUTCH

We need to realize that the direction of our lives is controlled by the magnetic pull of our values. They are the force in front of us, consistently leading us to make decisions that create the direction and ultimate destination of our lives. This is true, not only for us as individuals, but also for the companies, organizations, and the nation of which we're a part. Clearly, the values that our Founding Fathers held most dear have shaped our nation's destiny: the values of freedom, choice, equality, a sense of community, hard work, individuality, challenge, competition, prosperity, and respect for those who have the strength to overcome great adversity have consistently sculpted the experience of American life and thus our joint destinies. These values have caused us to be an ever-expanding country that innovates and continually provides a vision of possibility for people the world over.

Would a different set of national and cultural values have shaped our country differently? You bet! What if the value held most important by our forefathers was stability? Or conformity? How would that have changed the face of our great land? In China, for example, one of the highest values in the culture is the value of the group versus that of the individual, the idea that an individual's needs must be subservient to the group's. How has this shaped Chinese life differently than American life? The fact is, within our own nation there are constant shifts going on within the values of the culture as a whole. While there are certain foundational values, **significant emotional events can create shifts in individuals and therefore in the companies, organizations, and countries that they make up. The changes in Eastern Europe are clearly the most profound value shifts that have occurred in the world community in our lifetimes.**

What happens with countries and individuals also happens with companies. IBM is an example of a corporation whose direction and destiny was set up by its founder, Tom Watson. How? He clearly defined what the company stood for, what would be most important for all people to experience regardless of what products, services, or financial climates they would enter in the future. He guided "Big Blue" into being one of the world's largest and most successful companies.

What can we learn from all this? In our personal and professional lives, as well as on the global front, we must **get clear about what is most important in our lives and decide that we will live by these values, no matter what happens.** This consistency must occur regardless of whether the environment rewards us for living by our standards or not. We must live by our principles even when it "rains on our parade," even if no one gives us the support we need. **The only way for us to have long-term happiness is to live by our highest ideals,** to consistently act in acccordance with what we believe our life is truly about.

But we can't do this if we don't clearly know what our values are! This is the biggest tragedy in most people's lives: *many people know what they want to have, but have no idea of who they want to be.* Getting "things" simply will not fulfill you. Only living and doing what you believe is "the right thing" will give you that sense of inner strength that we all deserve.

Remember that your values—whatever they are—are the compass that is guiding you to your ultimate destiny. They are creating your life path by guiding you to make certain decisions and take certain actions *consistently*. Not using your internal compass intelligently results in frustration, disappointment, lack of fulfillment, and a nagging sense that life could be more if only somehow, *something* were different. On the other hand, there's an unbelievable power in living your values: a sense of certainty, an inner peace, a total congruency that few people ever experience.

IF YOU DON'T KNOW YOUR TRUE
VALUES, PREPARE FOR PAIN

The only way we can ever feel happy and fulfilled in the long term is to live in accordance with our true values. If we don't, we're sure to experience intense pain. So often, people develop habitual patterns of behavior that frustrate or could potentially destroy them: smoking, drinking, overeating, abusing drugs, attempting to control or dominate others, watching hour upon hour of television, and so on.

What's the real problem here? These behaviors are really the result of frustration, anger, and emptiness that people feel because they don't have a sense of fulfillment in their lives. They're trying to distract themselves from those empty feelings by filling the gap with the behavior that produces a "quick fix" change of state. This behavior becomes a pattern, and people often focus on changing the behavior itself rather than dealing with the cause. They don't just have a drinking problem; they have a *values* problem. The only reason they're drinking is to try to change their emotional state because they don't like the way they feel, moment by moment. They don't know what's most important to them in their lives.

The consolation is that whenever we do live by our highest standards, whenever we fulfill and meet our values, we feel immense joy. We don't need the excess food or drink. We don't need to put ourselves into a stupor, because life itself becomes so incredibly rich without these excesses. Distracting ourselves from such incredible heights would be like taking sleeping pills on Christmas morning.

Guess what the challenge is! As always, we were already asleep when the essence of what would shape our lives was formed. We were children who didn't understand the importance of having a clear sense of our values, or adults dealing with the pressures of life, already distracted to the point where we couldn't direct the formation of our values. I must reiterate that **every decision is guided by these values,** *and in most cases, we didn't set them up.*

If I asked you to make a list of your top ten values in life, to write them in precise order of importance, I'd be willing to bet that only one in 10,000 could do it. (And that $\frac{1}{100}$th of a percent would have attended my Date With Destiny seminar!) But if you don't know the answer to this question, how can you make any clear decisions at all? How can you make choices that you know in the long term will meet your deepest emotional needs? It's hard to hit a target when you don't know what it is! Knowing your values is critical to being able to live them.

Anytime you have difficulty making an important decision, you can be sure that it's the result of being unclear about your values. What if you were asked to move your family across the country in connection with a new job? If you knew that there was some risk involved, but that the compensation would be better and the job would be more interesting, what would you do? How you answer this question will depend entirely on what's most important to you: personal growth or security? Adventure or comfort?

By the way, what determines whether you value adventure more than comfort? Your values came from a mixed bag of experiences, of lifelong conditioning through punishment and reward. Your parents congratulated and supported you when you did things that agreed with their values, and when you clashed with their values, you were punished either physically, verbally, or through the pain of being ignored. Your teachers, too, encouraged and applauded you when you did things they agreed with, and applied similar forms of punishment when you violated their most deeply held views. This cycle was perpetuated by your friends and employers. You modeled the values of your heroes, and maybe some of your antiheroes as well.

Today, new economic factors come into play. With most families having both parents working outside the home, there is no traditional role model for values in the home. Schools, churches, and, on the less appetizing side, TV have all stepped in to fill the gap. Indeed, TV is our most convenient babysitter, with the average person now watching television *seven hours* a day! Am I suggesting that the "traditional" family structure is the only way to raise children who have strong values? Of course not. What I suggest is that we teach our children our philosophy of life by being strong role models, by knowing our own values and living by them.

WHAT ARE VALUES?

To value something means to place importance upon it; anything that you hold dear can be called a "value." In this chapter, I'm specifically referring to life values, those things that are most important to you in life. For this kind of value, there are two types: **ends** and **means**. If I ask you, "What do you value most?," you might answer, "Love, family, money . . ." Of these, love is the end value you're pursuing; in other words, the emotional state you desire. Conversely, family and money are merely means values. In other words, they are simply a way for you to trigger the emotional states you really desire.

If I asked you, "What does family give you?," you might say, "Love,

"I put the kids to bed. I don't want them watching stuff like this."

security, happiness." What you truly value—**the ends you're after**—are love, security, and happiness. Similarly, with money, I could ask you, "What does money really mean to you? What does it give you?" You might say, "Freedom, impact, the ability to contribute, a sense of security." Again, you see, money is merely a means to achieving a much deeper set of values, a set of emotions that you desire to experience on a consistent basis in your life.

The challenge in life is that most people are not clear on the difference between means and ends values, and therefore, they experience a lot of pain. **So often people are too busy pursuing means values that they don't achieve their true desire: their ends values.** The ends values are those that will fulfill you, make your life rich and rewarding. One of the biggest challenges I see is that people keep setting goals without knowing what they truly value in life, and therefore they end up achieving their goals and saying, "Is this all there is?"

For example, let's say a woman's highest values are caring and contribution, and she chooses to become an attorney because she once met a lawyer who really impressed her as being able to make a difference and help people through his work. As time goes by, she gets caught up in the whirlwind of practicing law, and aspires to become a partner in her firm. As she pursues this position, her work takes on an entirely different focus. She begins to dominate and run the firm, and becomes one of the most successful women she knows, yet she feels unhappy because she no longer has any contact with clients. Her position has created a different relationship with her peers, and she spends all her time in meetings ironing out protocol and procedure. **She achieved her goal, but missed out on her life's desire.** Have you ever fallen into this trap of pursuing the means *as if they were the end you were after?* In order to be truly happy, we must know the difference, and be sure to pursue the end itself.

MOVING-TOWARD VALUES

While it's absolutely true that you and I are constantly motivated to move toward pleasurable emotional states, it's also true that we value some emotions more than others. For example, what are the emotional states that you value most in life? What are the emotions that you think will give you the most pleasure? Love or success? Freedom or intimacy? Adventure or security?

I call these pleasurable states that we value most **moving-toward** values because these are the emotional states we'll do the most to attain. What are some of the feelings that are most important for you to experience in your life on a consistent basis? When asked this question at seminars, my audiences invariably respond with words like:

Love ·	1.	FREEDOM
Success ·	2.	Love
Freedom ·	3.	PASSION
Intimacy ·	4.	SUCCESS
Security ·	5.	HEALTH
Adventure ·	6.	INTIMACY
Power ·	7.	POWER
Passion ·	8.	ADVENTURE
Comfort	9.	SECURITY
Health ·	10.	COMFORT

It's certainly true that you probably value all of these emotions, and that they're all important for you to feel. But wouldn't it be fair to say that you don't value them all *equally?* **Obviously there are some emotional states that you'll do more to achieve than others.** In truth, we all have a **hierarchy of values.** Each person who looks at this list will see some emotional states as being more important to them than others. The hierarchy of your values is controlling the way you make decisions in each moment. Some people value comfort over passion, or freedom over security, or intimacy over success.

Take a moment right now, and discover from this list which of these emotions you value most. Simply rewrite the list in your order of importance, with 1 being the emotional state you hold as most important, and 10 being least important. Please take a moment now and fill in the blanks in your order of importance.

> *"Be more concerned with your character than your reputation, because your character is what you really are, while your reputation is merely what others think you are."*
> —JOHN WOODEN

So what did you learn by doing this ranking? If I were sitting next to you, I could probably give you some quality feedback. For example, I'd know a lot about you if your number-one value was freedom, followed by passion, adventure, and power. I know you're going to make different decisions than someone whose top values are security, comfort, intimacy, and health. Do you think a person whose number-one value is adventure makes decisions the same way as someone whose number-one value is security? Do you think these people would drive the same kind of car? Take the same kind of vacation? Seek out the same profession? Far from it.

Remember, whatever your values are, they affect the direction of your life. We have all learned through our life's experience that certain emotions give us more pleasure than others. For example, some people have learned that the way to have the most pleasurable emotions in life is to have a sense of control, so they pursue it with incredible vigor. It becomes the dominant focus of all their actions: it shapes who they will have relationships with, what they will do within those relationships, and how they'll live. It also causes them, as you can imagine, to feel quite uncomfortable in any environment where they're not in charge.

Conversely, some people link pain to the idea of control. What they want more than anything else is a sense of freedom and adventure. Therefore, they make decisions completely differently. Others get the same level of pleasure through a different emotion: contribution. This value causes that person to constantly ask, "What can I give? How can I make a difference?" This would certainly send them in a different direction from someone whose highest value was control.

Once you know what your values are, you can clearly understand why you head in the directions that you do on a consistent basis. Also, by seeing the hierarchy of your values, you can see why sometimes you have difficulty making decisions or why there may be conflicts in your life. For example, if a person's number-one value is freedom, and number two is intimacy, these two incompatible values are so closely ranked that often this person will have challenges.

I remember a man I counseled at one time who was constantly feeling this push-pull. He consistently sought autonomy, but when he achieved it, he felt alone and craved intimacy. Then, as he pursued intimacy, he became fearful he would lose his freedom, and so he'd sabotage the relationship. One particular relationship was continually on-again, off-again while he cycled between these two values. After I helped him make a simple change in the hierarchy of his values, his relationship and his life was instantly changed. Shifting priorities produces power.

Knowing your own values helps you to get more clarity as to why you do what you do and how you can live more consistently, but knowing the values of others is equally important. Might it be valuable to know the values of someone you're in a relationship with, or somebody you're in business with? Knowing a person's values gives you a fix on their compass, and allows you to have insight into their decision making.

Knowing your own hierarchy is also absolutely critical because your top values are those that are going to bring you the most happiness. Of course, what you really want to do is **set it up so that you're meeting all of your values every day.** If you don't, you'll experience what seems like an inexplicable feeling of emptiness or unhappiness.

My daugher, Jolie, lives an incredibly rich life in which her highest values are almost always met. She is also a wonderful actress, dancer, and singer. At the age of sixteen, she auditioned to perform at Disneyland (something she knew would fulfill her value of accomplishment if she succeeded). Incredibly, she beat out 700 other girls to win a part in the fabled amusement park's Electric Light Parade.

Initially, Jolie was ecstatic. We, along with her friends, were all so delighted and proud of her, and we would frequently drive up on weekends to see her perform. Her schedule, however, was extremely taxing. Jolie had to perform every weeknight as well as weekends, and her school term wasn't over for the summer yet. So she had to drive from San Diego to Orange County every evening in rush-hour traffic, rehearse and perform for several hours, then drive back home in the wee hours of the night so she could get up again early the next morning in time for school. As you can imagine, the daily commute and long hours soon turned the experience into a grueling ordeal, not to mention the extremely heavy costume she had to wear which hurt her back.

Even worse, however, from Jolie's perspective, was the fact that her demanding schedule cut drastically into her personal life and prevented her from spending any time with our family and her friends. I began to notice her wandering about in a series of very unresourceful emotional states. She would cry at the drop of a hat, and began to complain about things on a consistent basis. This was totally unlike Jolie. The final straw was that the whole family was preparing to go to Hawaii for our three-week Certification program—everyone except Jolie, who had to stay home in order to continue to work at Disneyland.

One morning, she hit threshold and came to me in tears, undecided and confused. She felt so frustrated, so unhappy and unfulfilled, yet she had achieved what seemed like an unbelievable goal only six months earlier. Disneyland had become painful for her. Why? Because it became an obstacle to her ability to spend time with all those she loved most. Plus Jolie always had felt that the time she spent at Certification, where she participated as a trainer, helped her to grow more than virtually anything else in her life. Many of her friends from around the country attended this program each year, and Disneyland was beginning to feel frustrating to her because she really didn't feel like she was expanding or growing there at all. She was feeling pain if she decided to come with us to Certification (because she didn't want to be a quitter) and pain if she continued to work at Disneyland because it would mean she'd miss out on the things that seemed so important to her.

We sat down together so that I could help her take a close look at what her top four values are in life. They turned out to be: 1) love, 2) health and vibrancy, 3) growth, and 4) accomplishment. By turning to her values, I knew that I could help her get the clarity she needed to make the decision that would be right for her. So I asked her, "What does working at Disneyland give you? What's important about working at Disneyland?" She told me that she was originally excited about it because she saw it as an opportunity to make new friends, receive recognition for her work, have fun, and experience a tremendous sense of accomplishment.

At this point, though, she said she wasn't feeling very much accomplishment at all because she didn't feel like she was growing anymore, and she knew there were other things she could be doing that would accelerate her career more rapidly. She also said, "I'm burning myself into the ground. I'm not healthy, and I miss being with the family tremendously."

Then I asked her, "What would making a change in this area of your life mean? If you left Disneyland, spent time at home, and then went to Hawaii, what would that give you?" She immediately brightened. Smiling, she said, "Well, I'd get to be with you guys. I could have some time with my boyfriend. I'd feel free again. I could get some rest and start exercising to get my body back in shape. I'd keep my 4.0 grade point average in school. I could find other ways to grow and achieve. I'd be happy!"

Her answer as to what to do was plainly in front of her. The source of her unhappiness was also clear. Before she started working at Disneyland, she was fulfilling her top three values: she felt <u>loved</u>, she was very <u>healthy</u> and <u>fit</u>, and she felt like she was <u>growing</u>. Thus she began to pursue the next value on her list: accomplishment. But in so doing, she'd created an environment where she achieved, but missed out on her top three values.

This is such a common experience. We all need to realize that we must accomplish our highest values first—these are our utmost priority. And remember, there is always a way to accomplish all our values simultaneously, and we need to make certain we don't settle for anything less.

There still was one final obstacle to Jolie's decision: she also linked pain to leaving Disneyland. One of the things she avoided most in life was quitting. I certainly had contributed to this view, since I believe nothing is ever achieved by those who give up whenever it gets tough. So she saw leaving her work at Disneyland as giving up. I assured her that making a decision to live congruently with your values is not quitting, nor is foolish consistency a virtue. I would be the first person to ensure that she continue if I thought she was just giving up because the work was too tough. But that was not the case, and I offered her the opportunity to turn this transition into a gift for someone else.

I said, "Jolie, can you imagine how you'd feel if you were the first runner-up, and all of a sudden the winner stepped down, and now you had a chance to be in the parade? Why don't you give that gift to someone else?" Because part of Jolie's definition of love is contribution, this immediately tapped into her highest value. She stopped linking pain to quitting, and now associated pleasure to her decision.

This values lesson is one she's never forgotten, and the most exciting thing was that she found a new way to meet all of her values that began to move her more precisely in the direction of her goals. She not only began to feel more fun and happiness, but shortly thereafter she got her first job in a San Diego Starlight Theater production.

LESSONS IN PAIN

Just as there are emotions we desire to experience because they're pleasurable, and that's why we're always moving toward them, we also have a list of emotions that we'll do almost anything to move away from. Very early in my career, when I was just beginning to build my first company, I experienced tremendous frustration in being on the road and trying to run my business simultaneously. At one point, it appeared that a person representing me had not been completely honest. When you deal, as I have, with hundreds of thousands of people, and literally thousands of business arrangements, the law of averages says that a few will attempt to take advantage of you. Unfortunately, these are the ones that tend to stick out in our minds rather than the hundreds or even thousands of business relationships that have far surpassed our expectations.

As a result of one such painful situation, I sought out a new CEO, a man who I thought could really run my company. Armed with my new tool of being able to elicit someone's values, I asked each of the potential candidates, "What's most important to you in your life?" Some of them said things like "success" or "accomplishment" or "being the best." But one man used the magic word. He said, "Honesty."

I didn't just take him at his word; I checked him out with several people he'd worked with. They confirmed that he was "honest as the day was long" and that, in fact, at times he had set aside his own needs if there was any question of integrity. I thought, "This is the kind of man I want representing me." And he did a fine job. Soon, though, it became clear that we needed an additional associate in order to really run my rapidly expanding business: someone who had additional skills. My CEO recommended someone he thought could become his partner, and they could jointly run my organization. This sounded great to me.

I met this man, whom I'll call Mr. Smith (names have been changed to protect the not so innocent), and he did a fabulous presentation, demonstrating for me how he could use all the skills he'd developed throughout the years to take my company to the next level. He could free up my time, and allow me to do even larger seminars and impact even more people without having to live on the road. At the time, I was spending almost 150 days a year away from home, conducting my seminars. In addition, he didn't want to be paid until he'd produced the result! It sounded almost too good to be true. I agreed to the arrangement. Mr. Smith and my honest CEO would run my company.

A year and a half later, I woke up and discovered that it *was* too good to be true. Yes, my seminars had gotten bigger, but now I was on the road almost 270 days a year. My skill and impact had grown, I'd helped more people than ever before, but suddenly I was informed that I was $758,000 in debt after I'd given more than I ever had in my entire lifetime. How could this possibly be? Well, management is everything, both within companies and within ourselves. And I clearly did not have the right managers.

But worse, Mr. Smith had over this eighteen-month period of time misappropriated more than a quarter of a million dollars from our coffers. He had a new house, a new car—I had assumed he'd gotten them from his other businesses. Boy, was I in for a surprise! To say that I was angry or devastated by this experience would certainly be using Transformational Vocabulary to lower the intensity of my feelings. The metaphors I used at the time were things like "I feel stabbed in the back" and "He tried to murder my firstborn." How's that for emotional intensity?

However, the thing that perplexed me the most was how my honest CEO could stand by and not warn me that all this was happening. He was aware of what was going on! This was when I began to realize that **people don't just pursue pleasure, but they clearly also move away from pain.** My honest CEO *had* tried to tell me that he was concerned about his partner. He came to me after I'd been on the road for three straight months. On my first day home, he approached me to tell me that he had questions about Mr. Smith's integrity. I immediately became concerned and asked him why. He said, "When we moved to our new offices, he took the biggest office." This was so petty that I got extremely angry and said, "Listen. You brought him into this business; you deal with him yourself personally." And I stormed off.

I should have realized that day that I'd given this man pain when he was trying to give me information. In my exhausted and stressed state I failed to evaluate the deeper meaning of what was going on. As if this weren't bad enough, my honest CEO approached me again to give me similar feedback. I told him that he was not being totally honest by talking to me instead of Mr. Smith. I marched into his associate's office and said, "He's telling me all these things about you. You guys work this out!" Can you imagine the pain he got from Mr. Smith?

As I look back on the experience now, I can see clearly why he didn't tell me the truth. Telling me the truth—that he'd brought someone into my business who'd misappropriate more than a quarter of a million dollars—seemed to him, in the short term, to be much more painful than just putting it off and trying to find some other way to deal with it eventually.

In fact, as I look back on all the upsets I ever had with this CEO, invariably they all came down to times when he didn't do things he needed to do simply because *he wanted to avoid the feeling of confrontation.* This was the ultimate pain for him. So while honesty was important to him, avoiding confrontation was more important. Thus he simply did not communicate to me, and rationalized that he was being honest because, after all, I had never asked him if Mr. Smith was taking money. If I had, he would have told me.

As angry as this situation made me, and as painful as it was financially and emotionally, it provided me with one of the most valuable lessons of my life because it gave me one of the final pieces in the puzzle of understanding human behavior. Understanding these twin forces of pain and pleasure has helped me not only to positively influence myself and my family, but people around the world with greater precision.

MOVING-AWAY-FROM VALUES

We must remember, then, that any time we make a decision about what to do, our brain first evaluates whether that action can possibly lead to either pleasurable or painful states. Your brain is constantly juggling, or weighing, your alternatives to see what the impact may be, based upon your value hierarchy. If, for example, I asked you to go skydiving, and the number-one emotion you try to avoid at all costs is a sense of fear, it's pretty obvious that you're not going to take action, are you? If, however, the number-one value you want to avoid at all costs is a feeling of rejection, and you believe that I may reject you if you *don't* go, you may decide to jump out of a plane in spite of your fear. **The relative levels of pain we associate with certain emotions will affect all of our decisions.**

What are some of the emotions that are most important for you to *avoid* experiencing on a consistent basis? Often when I ask people this question at seminars, they come up with a list such as the following:

Rejection	1.	*Rejection*
Anger •	2.	*Humiliation*
Frustration	3.	*Guilt*
Loneliness	4.	*Failure*
Depression	5.	*Loneliness*
Failure	6.	*Depression*
Humiliation	7.	*Frustration*
Guilt	8.	*Anger*

Again, would it be fair to say that all these emotions are states you'd like to avoid having to feel? Of course, because they're painful. Wouldn't it also be true to say that, while you want to avoid feeling all of these emotions, some are more painful to you than others? That, in fact, you have a hierarchy of moving-away-from values as well? **Which value on** the above list would you do the most to avoid having to feel? Rejection, depression, humiliation? The answer to this question will determine your behavior in almost any environment.

Take a moment before we go any further, and write this list out in the above blanks, ranking them from the emotional states you'll do the most to avoid having to feel, to those you'll do the least to avoid having to feel.

> *"I hope we can build a university our football team can be proud of."*
> —UNIVERSITY OF OKLAHOMA

As you look at your list, what does it tell you? If, for example, you put at the top of your list that the emotion you would do the most to avoid having to feel is humiliation, then can you see how you would consistently avoid entering any situations where you might be judged harshly? If loneliness is the emotion you want to avoid most, it may drive you to be a nurturing person, reaching out to others and trying to give to them on a regular basis so that they'll want to be with you, and so that you'll be surrounded by many grateful friends.

THE SOURCE OF SELF-SABOTAGE: VALUES CONFLICTS

Now let's look at the dynamics created by your values hierarchy. If you selected **success**, for example, as your top moving-toward value, and **rejection** as your top moving-away-from value, do you see any possible challenges that this hierarchy might create in your life? I'm here to tell you that a person who's trying to achieve the pleasure of success without ever experiencing the pain of rejection will never succeed long term. In fact, this person will sabotage himself before he ever truly succeeds on a major scale.

How can I make such a claim? Remember the basic organizing principle we've talked about so often here: **People will do more to avoid pain than they will to gain pleasure.** If you're truly going to succeed at the highest level in life, don't you have to be willing to risk rejection? Don't you have to be willing to experience it? Isn't it true that even if you're an honest and sincere person and give your all to others every day, there are still people who will misinterpret your actions and judge you without even having met you? Whether you want to be a writer, a singer, a speaker, or a business person, the potential for rejection is ever-present. Since your brain inherently knows that in order to succeed you have to risk rejection, and it's already decided that the feelings of rejection are the ultimate levels of pain, it will make the decision that the pleasure of success is not worth the price, and will cause you to sabotage your behavior before you even get in this position!

So often I see people who take huge strides forward, only to mysteriously pull back at the last minute. Or they'll say or do things that sabotage the very personal, emotional, or physical success they're pursuing. Invariably the reason is that they have a major values conflict. Part of their brain is saying, "Go for it!" while the other part is saying, "If you do, you're going to get too much pain." So they take two steps forward, and one step back.

During the 1988 election year, I used to call this principle the "Gary Hart Syndrome." Here was a nice guy who truly seemed to care passionately about people and society, but whose value conflicts were played out for all to see. Was Gary Hart a horrible guy? I doubt it. He was just someone who had values in massive conflict. He grew up in a church that taught him he was committing a sin if he even danced. Simultaneously, he was exposed to role models like Warren Beatty. These conflicting desires obviously played a role in his political downfall.

Do you think that a person as intelligent as Gary Hart clearly seemed to be would tell the media, "If you've got questions about me, follow me," and then immediately afterward go visit his mistress? Clearly this was his brain's way of getting out of the pain of being in a position where he had to play by rules other than his own. You can call this pop psychology if you want, but doesn't it make sense that if you are being pulled in two different directions, you will not be able to serve both masters? Something has to give. We'll do whatever's necessary, consciously or unconsciously, to keep ourselves from having to experience our most intense levels of pain.

We've all seen people in the public eye who've experienced the pain of values conflicts, but rather than be judgmental, we need to realize that each of us has values conflicts within ourselves. Why? Again, simply because we never set the system up for ourselves. We've allowed our environment to shape us, but we can begin to change this now. How? Simply by taking two steps:

Step One is to gain awareness of what your current values are so you understand why you do what you do. What are the emotional states you are moving toward, and what are the states you are moving away from? By reviewing your lists side by side, you'll be able to have an understanding of the force that's creating your present and future.

Step Two: You can then make conscious decisions about what values you want to live by in order to shape the quality of life and destiny you truly desire and deserve.

HOW TO DISCOVER YOUR CURRENT VALUES

So let's get started. You've done some sample value lists by ranking the lists I gave you. What you really need to do is **start fresh with your own lists.** All you have to do to discover your values is answer one simple question: **"What's most important to me in life?"** Brainstorm the answer to this question. Is it peace of mind? Impact? Love?

Now put your values in order, from most important to least important. Take a moment and do this now . . .

WHAT'S MOST IMPORTANT TO ME IN LIFE:

CREATIVITY   ADVENTURE
LOVE   SUCCESS
Power/control   HEALTH
FREEDOM   INTIMACY
PASSION   IMPACT
SECURITY

When I first created my list of moving-toward values, this is what I came up with, and the order in which they occurred:

CREATIVITY,   ~~GROF~~
IMPACT
LOVE
PASSION
HEALTH
SUCCESS
FREEDOM
Power/control

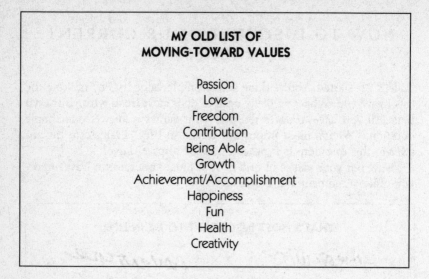

**MY OLD LIST OF
MOVING-TOWARD VALUES**

Passion
Love
Freedom
Contribution
Being Able
Growth
Achievement/Accomplishment
Happiness
Fun
Health
Creativity

As I looked at my list, I understood why I was doing what I was doing. I was such an intense individual; by anybody's description I was explosive in my approach. I saw it as my **passion**. My **love** for my family and my friends and wanting to share it in seminars was clear. My desire was to **free** people, and I figured that if I freed the individuals around me and **contributed** to them, I'd feel like I was **able** to do almost anything. I'd **grow** and **achieve** and eventually have **fun** and be **healthy** and **creative**. Knowing my values list helped me stay on track and to live consistently with what was most important to me. For years, I felt a greater sense of congruency in my life.

But I was soon to make another distinction that would transform the quality of my life forever.

CHANGE YOUR VALUES, AND YOU CHANGE YOUR LIFE

After my experience with the infamous Mr. Smith, I went to Fiji to get away from it all. I needed to balance myself emotionally, and gain some perspective and clarity on the situation. Most importantly, I had to decide what I was going to do and how I was going to turn things around. The first night I was there, before I went to sleep, I asked myself a very important question. Instead of "Why did all this happen to me?", I began to ask a better question: "What is the source of all human behavior? What makes people do what they do?"

When I woke up the following morning at 8 A.M., I felt a frenzy of ideas pouring through me. I grabbed my journal and began to write continuously, sitting in the main cabana. People walked in and out throughout the day as I wrote nonstop from 8 A.M. to 6:30 P.M. My arm was sore; my fingers were numb. I wasn't just thinking calmly and writing; the ideas were literally *exploding* through me. From this unstoppable river of ideas, I designed Destiny Technologies™ and a good portion of the science of Neuro-Associative Conditioning.™ When I went back to review my notes, however, I couldn't read a word!

But the ideas and feelings were anchored within me. I immediately realized the potency of what I had created: a program that could help a person redesign the life priorities of their nervous system, to literally redirect the process of how people make all their decisions about how to think, how to feel, and what to do in virtually every area of their lives!

I began to think about what would happen if, instead of just teaching people what their values were and clarifying them, I actually got people to consciously select or redirect the order and content of their values hierarchy system. What if I took someone whose number-one value was security, and whose number-fifteen value was adventure, and I *switched the order*, not only intellectually but so that adventure became the new highest priority in their nervous system? What kind of change do you think that might make in someone's life? A minor one, or a major one?

The answer is obvious. By doing this, you literally change the way a person thinks, feels, and behaves in virtually every area of their life. I couldn't imagine a more profound shift that a human being could make. In essence, this would be the kind of change that has been described throughout history: a conversion from Saul to Paul, if you will, with the things that a person hated most becoming the things they loved most, and vice versa.

Could this really be done? I decided that the best person to test this out on was, of course, myself. I began to look at my values list. At first I thought, "My values are great! I love my values. After all, this is who I am." But I had to keep reminding myself that **we are not our values. We are much *more* than our values.** These values were not the result of intelligent choices and a master plan. What I had merely accomplished until now was discovering what priorities were conditioned into my life, and I had consciously chosen to live within the system of pain and pleasure that had been programmed into me. But if I were to really design my own life, if I were going to create a set of values that would shape the ultimate destiny I desired, what would they need to be?

"We have made thee neither of heaven nor of earth,
Neither mortal nor immortal,

So that with freedom of choice and with honor,
As though the maker and molder of thyself,
Thou mayest fashion thyself in whatever shape thou
shalt prefer.
Thou shalt have the power out of thy soul's
judgment,
To be reborn into the higher forms, which are
divine."

—GOD'S SPEECH TO ADAM FROM PICO DELLA MIRANDOLA'S
ORATION ON THE DIGNITY OF MAN

I felt unbelievably inspired as I began to realize that in this moment I was about to make decisions that would change the direction of my life forever. I began to look at my values and ask the question, **"What do my values need to be in order to create my ultimate destiny, in order to be the best person I could possibly be, in order to have the largest impact in my lifetime?"**

I thought, "The values I have right now are helping me," but then I thought, **"What other values would I need to add?"** I began to realize that one of the things that wasn't on my list was *intelligence*. Certainly I was an intelligent person, but I hadn't made *being intelligent* as high a priority as being passionate. In fact, in my passion I'd made some pretty stupid choices—including who my CEO was going to be!

I began to realize that unless I made intelligence a conscious priority of my nervous system (i.e., unless I learned to take a moment or two in advance to consciously evaluate the consequences of my decision making), I would continuously fail to achieve my deepest desires. There was now no question that intelligence needed to be placed high on my list. I then discovered an additional series of values to add, and I decided where they needed to be placed in my hierarchy.

Then I asked a question I had never asked before: **"What values should I eliminate from my list in order to achieve my ultimate destiny?"** I began to realize that by constantly focusing on how to be **free**, I was missing out on the freedom I already had. I realized that there was no way I could be any more free than I was in this moment. Maybe my feelings would be different if I lived in a country where the choices I have here don't exist, but for me, there is no way to have any more freedom than I have today. So I decided to drop it from my list and not to make it an issue anymore. It was amazing the *freedom* I felt by getting freedom off my list!

Next, I began to evaluate each value individually as to its true merit.

I began to ask, **"What benefit do I get by having this value in this position on my hierarchy?"** I looked first at passion and asked, "What benefit do I get by having passion here?" I thought, "It gives me drive and excitement and energy and the power to impact people in positive ways. It makes my life juicy."

Then I asked a question that kind of scared me, a question I had never asked before: *"What could having passion at the top of my list cost me?"* In that moment, the answer became obvious. I had just recently returned from conducting a seminar in Denver, where for the first time in years I had felt unbelievably ill. Health was always on my values list; it was important. But it wasn't very high up on the list.

By the way, if you have anything on your values list, you think it's important, because there are hundreds of things that could have been on the list that aren't. But my idea of health was to eat right. I wasn't exercising, and I certainly wasn't getting enough rest. Finally, my body was giving out under my constant demands for unlimited energy. I began to remember that in that day, when I felt like I had no health, I pushed myself and did the seminars in spite of it all. But I didn't feel passionate, I didn't feel loving, I didn't feel like I could have impact. I began to realize that by having passion as the highest value on my list, it would cause me to burn out and therefore potentially cost me the very destiny I was pursuing.

I finally asked the last question: **"In what order do my values need to be to achieve my ultimate destiny?"** Not "What's important to me?" but "What do they need to be?" As I began to do this process, my list began to evolve until it looked like this:

MY NEW LIST OF MOVING-TOWARD VALUES

Health/Vitality
Love/Warmth
Intelligence
Cheerfulness
Honesty
Passion
Gratefulness
Fun/Happiness
Making a difference
Learning/Growing
Achieving
Being the best
Investing
Contribution
Creativity

These shifts may look subtle to you, but they were profound in their emotional impact upon me. Just creating this new list of life priorities created some intense fear and struggle at times. Probably the most difficult one was changing the order that I had between achievement and happiness. If you recall, on my previous list I had to feel **passion, love, freedom, contribution, being able, growth,** and **achievement,** and a lower priority was feeling **happy.** I began to think, "What would happen if I made happiness a priority? What would happen if I made that a higher priority than achieving?"

Quite honestly, this was another question that created fear in me. I thought, "If it's easy for me to feel happy, maybe I'll lose my drive. Maybe I won't want to achieve. Maybe I won't want to have the same impact. Maybe I won't contribute as much to people." After all, I linked my identity to my capacity to passionately make a difference. It took me almost two hours to make the decision to "go for the gusto" and decide to make myself happy. How ridiculous!

But I can tell you, having worked with tens of thousands of people in Date With Destiny, of whom the majority of attendees would be considered achievers, this is one of the biggest fears they have. *They generally fear that they'll lose their power or drive if they feel happy first.* I'm here to tell you that what happened in my life is that **instead of achieving to be happy, I began to happily achieve,** and the difference in the quality of my life is so profound that it is beyond verbal description. I didn't lose my drive—quite conversely, I felt so good, I wanted to do even more!

When my list was complete, I felt an emotion that I could not ever remember feeling previously: a sense of calm. I felt a sense of certainty I hadn't experienced before, because I now knew that every part of me was going to be pulled in the direction of my dreams. I was no longer in a tug-of-war with myself. By no longer striving constantly for freedom, I could have even more intimacy and love—I could feel even more free. I would happily achieve now. I would be healthy and vital and intelligent. With the decision to change my life's priorities, I could immediately feel the changes in my physical body.

I also then began to realize that there were certain emotional states that I must avoid indulging in if I was going to succeed. One of those clearly was worry. I found myself emotionally and physically racked by the pain of trying to figure out how I was going to keep my company going and keep the doors open. At the time, I believed that if I worried, maybe I'd be more motivated, but what I found was that *worry made me less resourceful.* So I decided I couldn't worry anymore. I could have legitimate concern, but more importantly, I could focus on taking the actions that would make things work. Once I decided worry would destroy my destiny, I began to avoid experiencing it at all costs. Clearly, this became an emotion too painful to indulge in. I began to construct a moving-away-from list.

I then flew back to the United States, having designed my own destiny. Boy, were my friends and associates in for a surprise! On my first day back at the office, people started approaching me to ask, "What's happened to you? You seem so different! You look so relaxed." I began to unload my entire new technology for hours at a time on each individual until finally I realized I needed to take it, refine it, and put it in a seminar. That's how Date With Destiny was born.

I wrote this book out of my desire to spread the Destiny-NAC technology to as many people as possible. I hope you'll use it now. **Remember, we truly can design who we become.**

> *"Give me beauty in the inward soul; may the outward and the inward man be at one."*
> —SOCRATES

So how can you now take control of this third element of your Master System known as values? Take the following two simple steps:

Step 1. Find out what your current values are, and rank them in order of importance. This will give you insight into what you want to experience most—your moving-toward values—and what you want to avoid most in your life—your moving-away-from values. It will give you an understanding of why you do what you do. It will also offer you the opportunity, if you'd like, to consistently experience more pleasure in your life by understanding the pain-pleasure system that's already built within you.

Step 2. If you're willing to take the bull by the horns, you have an opportunity to redirect your destiny. **Ask yourself a new question: "What do my values need to be in order to achieve the destiny I desire and deserve?" Brainstorm out a list. Put them in order. See which values you might get rid of and which values you might add in order to create the quality of life you truly want.**

You may be wondering, "What the heck *is* my destiny, anyway?" If you're stumbling over this, go back to Chapter 12. In it, I asked you what type of person you'd have to be in order to achieve all that you want. In order to be that person, what would your values need to be? What values would you need to add or eliminate?

For example, how would your capacity to deal with fear, frustration, and rejection be affected by deciding to place courage high upon your moving-toward value list? Or, what might be the impact of giving playfulness a higher priority? Might it enable you to have more fun in life, possibly enjoy all experiences as they come, grow closer to your children and be more to them than just a "provider"?

So what have you accomplished by creating your new list of values? Isn't it just a bunch of words on a piece of paper? The answer is yes—if you don't *condition* yourself to use them as your new compass. If you do, however, they become the solid foundation of every decision you will make. It is difficult to give you in this book the full range of conditioning tools that I use in seminars, but let me remind you of the power of leverage. Many people who have attended Date With Destiny post their values prominently at work, at home, *anywhere they will be seen by people who will hold them to this new, higher standard.*

So use the same kind of leverage to strengthen your commitment to your new values. The next time you find yourself yelling at the kids, maybe someone who loves you will walk by and remind you, "Isn't compassion number one on your list?"

> *"I touch the future; I teach."*
> —ANONYMOUS

Watching people take control of their value hierarchies in Date With Destiny is so rewarding because of the huge contrast between what they're like Friday morning and who they become by Sunday night. As transformations occur, magic happens. I remember one man who was dragged by his wife to the program and didn't want to be there. As we started talking about values and the possibility of making changes in that area, he insisted, "I don't need to change any of my values." His number-one value, by the way, was freedom! He balked at being "forced" to change anything in his life that he didn't want to; it became a control issue as he steadfastly refused to make any changes.

Finally I said to him, "I know you don't have to make any changes. I also know that you're free. So I'm sure you're *free* to add a few values. What would be some values that might be useful for you to add in order for you to increase the quality of your life and maybe even impact your ultimate destiny?" After several moments of thought he said, "Well, maybe *flexibility* might be a good one to add." The audience cracked up. "That's great," I said. "Where would you put flexibility on your list?" We started from the bottom and moved up, and it ended up being number four on his list.

The moment this man decided that was indeed the right place for his new value, another participant—a chiropractor—who was sitting behind him suddenly piped up, "Did you see that?" It was so obvious that several other people in the room had also noticed it. This man's physiology had literally begun to change before our eyes. As he had adopted flexibility in his value system, his whole posture seemed to loosen up and become more relaxed. He sat in his chair differently, and seemed to be breathing with a lot more freedom. Even his expression changed as the muscles in his face released their tension. With flexibility as a new priority, his nervous system had obviously gotten the message.

Then I asked, "Are there any other values you might want to add to your list?" The man thought a moment and said, "Maybe . . . forgiveness?" with a question in his voice. Again the group broke up laughing. This was a man who had started out bristling with hostility and tension, and here he was, making a 180-degree shift. As he figured out where to put forgiveness into his values hierarchy, it was gratifying to see the further changes that took place in his demeanor, breathing, facial muscles, and gestures. Throughout the rest of the weekend people were amazed by the dramatic changes that had been wrought with two simple additions to his values. He talked to people with more softness in his voice, his face seemed to "open up" with more expression, and he really seemed to connect with people in ways he hadn't before. Now, three years later, freedom is not even on his list, and the intimacy between his wife and him has expanded immeasurably.

> *"We are what we repeatedly do."*
> —ARISTOTLE

Life has a way of testing our commitment to our values. My test came as I was boarding an airplane . . . and lo and behold, there stood the illustrious Mr. Smith. I felt the anger and animosity well up inside me with an intensity I hadn't experienced for over two years, primarily because I hadn't seen him. He scurried onto the plane and seated himself in the rear. As I sat in my seat, knowing he was behind me, questions raced through my head: What should I do? Should I confront him? Should I just walk up next to him, stand there and stare at him, and make him squirm? I'm not proud of these questions, but since honesty is one of my highest values, I'm giving it to you straight.

In a moment, though, my actions were guided by my values. Why? I opened my notebook to write something down, and there were my values hierarchies, placed at the front of my book. At the top it said, "What's most important to me in life is to be **loving and warm.**" Hmmmm. "Be intelligent." Hmmmm. "Be cheerful. Be honest. Be passionate. Be grateful. Have fun. Make a difference . . ." Well, as you can imagine, my state changed pretty radically. Obviously my pattern had been broken. A reminder of who I really am and what I'm really about was staring me in the face. What to do became obvious.

When the plane landed, I approached him with sincerity and warmth and told him that while by no means did I appreciate or approve of his past behavior, I had decided to no longer hold a ferocious level of resentment toward him, and that I actually wished him well. The last memory I have was his stunned face as I turned and walked away. Wow! What an emotional hit! Even in a stressful environment, I'd lived by what I believed was right. Nothing in life can match the fulfillment of knowing you've done what you truly believe is the right thing.

Give yourself the gift of taking hold of this force that shapes your destiny. Make certain that you take the time to do the exercises that can clarify the priorities of your life.

Is it possible to have values and not feel that you're living them? You can have a great system of values that gives your life a magnificent direction but still feel unhappy, unless you understand the power of . . .

16
RULES:
IF YOU'RE NOT HAPPY, HERE'S WHY!

"Hold yourself responsible for a higher standard than anybody else expects of you."
—HENRY WARD BEECHER

As I write these words, I'm looking out over the deep blue Pacific from my room at the Hyatt Regency Waikoloa resort on the Big Island of Hawaii. I've just observed something that won't happen in North America again until the year 2017: a total eclipse of the sun. Becky and I got up this morning at 5:30 A.M. so that we, along with thousands of other visitors, could witness this rare astronomical event.

As crowds of people gathered at the viewing site, I began to entertain myself by watching the diversity of people who had come to share this occasion: everyone from top businessmen to vacationing families, from scientists lugging dozens of telescopes to hikers who'd pitched their tents in the lava pits overnight, and little children who knew this was an exciting event only because their parents had told them so. Here were hordes of people who had flown in from all over the world, at a cost of thousands of dollars, just for the chance to see something that would take about four minutes! What were we doing here? We wanted to stand in a shadow! We're an interesting species, aren't we?

By 6:28 A.M., the drama had begun to unfold. There was anxiety in the air, not just the anticipation of seeing the eclipse, but the fear of disappointment. For on this unique morning, the clouds had begun to gather, and the sky was becoming overcast. It was interesting to see how people were dealing with the possibility that their expectations would not be met. What they had come to see was not merely a brief flitting of the moon over the sun, but a four-minute total eclipse—when the shadow of the moon would completely block the sun's rays and envelop us in darkness. They even had a name for it: **totality**!

By 7:10 A.M., the clouds had increased and were getting larger by the minute. Suddenly, the sun broke through a hole in the clouds, and for a moment we could all see a partial eclipse. The crowd greeted it with excited applause, but soon the clouds rolled back in, thicker and thicker, completely obscuring our view. Nearing the moment of totality—utter darkness—it became obvious that we wouldn't be able to watch the moon overtake the sun.

Suddenly, thousands of people began to run over to a big-screen television set that one of the many TV crews had erected. There we sat, watching the eclipse on national television, just like everyone else in the world! In those moments I had a chance to observe an unlimited range of human emotion. Each person responded according to **their rules: their beliefs about what had to happen in order for them to feel good about this experience**.

One man behind me started cursing, saying, "I spent $4,000 and traveled all this way, just so I could watch this for four minutes on *television?*" A woman only a few feet away kept saying, "I can't believe we missed it!" while her bright little daughter enthusiastically reminded her, "But, Mom, it's happening right now!" Another woman sitting just to my right said, "Isn't this incredible? I feel so lucky to be here!"

Then a dramatic thing happened. As we observed on TV the last sliver of sunlight disappear behind the moon, in that instant we were engulfed in darkness. It was completely unlike nightfall, when the sky darkens gradually. This was immediate and total darkness! Initially there was a roar through the crowd, but then a hush fell upon us. The birds flew into the trees and became silent. It was a truly amazing moment. Then something hysterical happened. As people sat in the dark, staring at the eclipse on the television screen, some of those who had brought their cameras and were determined to get their outcome began taking pictures of the screen. In a moment, we were flooded with light again—not because of the sun—but because of all the flash bulbs!

Almost as soon as it had begun, though, totality was over. The most dramatic moment of the whole event for me was the instant that a thin sliver of the sun slipped out from behind the moon, instantly bringing full daylight with it. It occurred to me then that **it doesn't take very much light to wipe out the darkness**.

Within moments of the return of sunlight, a large number of people got up and began to leave. I was puzzled. After all, *the eclipse was still happening.* Most of them were muttering complaints about how they'd "come all this way and missed out on the experience of a lifetime." A few enraptured souls, however, lingered to watch every minute, feeling great excitement and joy. The most ironic thing of all was that within fifteen to twenty minutes, the trade winds had cleared all the clouds from the sky. It was now blue and clear, and the eclipse was revealed for everyone to see. But few people had remained; most had already returned to their rooms disgruntled. They continued to give themselves the sensations of pain because their expectations had not been met.

As I usually do, I started interviewing people. I wanted to find out what their experience of the eclipse had been. Many people talked about how it was the most incredible, spiritual experience of their lives. One pregnant woman rubbed her swollen tummy and shared with me that the eclipse somehow had created a feeling of stronger connection with her unborn child, and that this was just the right place on earth for her to be. What a contrast of beliefs and rules I noticed today!

What struck me as most humorous, though, was that people would get so excited and emotional about something like this, which was merely a four-minute shadow. If you really think about it, it's no more of a miracle than the sun coming up each morning! Can you imagine if every morning people from all over the world got up early so they could watch the sun come up? What if national and international news ardently covered every phase of the event with in-depth reports, passionately tracking the sun's rise into the sky, and everybody spent their mornings talking about what a miracle it is? Can you imagine the kind of days we'd have? What if CNN opened every broadcast with, "Good morning. Once again, the miracle has happened—the sun has risen!"? Why don't we respond this way? Could we? You bet we could. But the problem is that we've become *habituated*. We're so accustomed to the miracles happening around us every day that we don't even see them as miracles anymore.

For most of us, our rules for what's valuable dictate that we covet things that are scarce, instead of appreciating the miracles that abound. *What determined the differences in these people's responses,* from one man who got so upset he destroyed his camera on the spot, to those who not only experienced joy today, but would experience it every time they told others about the eclipse in the coming weeks, months, and years?

Our experience of this reality had nothing to do with reality, but was interpreted through the controlling force of our beliefs: specifically, the rules we had about *what had to happen in order for us to feel good.* **I call these specific beliefs that determine when we get pain and when we get pleasure *rules*.** Failure to understand their power can destroy any possibility for lifelong happiness, and a full understanding and utilization of them can transform your life as much as anything we've covered in this entire book.

Let met ask you a question before we go any further. **What has to happen in order for *you* to feel good?** Do you have to have someone hug you, kiss you, make love to you, tell you how much they respect and appreciate you? Must you make a million dollars? Do you have to hit below-par golf? Do you have to be acknowledged by your boss? Do you have to achieve all of your goals? Do you have to drive the right car, go to the right parties, be known by the right people? Do you have to be spiritually evolved or wait until you achieve total enlightenment? Do you have to run five miles a day? What really has to happen in order for you to feel good?

The truth is that nothing has to happen in order for you to feel good. You don't need an eclipse to feel good. You could feel good right now for absolutely *no reason whatsoever!* Think about it. If you make a million dollars, the million dollars doesn't give you any pleasure. It's your *rule* that says, "When I hit this mark, *then* I'll give myself permission to feel good." In that moment, when you decide to feel good, you send a message to your brain to change your responses in the muscles of your face, chest, and body, to change your breathing, and to change the biochemistry within your nervous system that causes you to feel the sensations you call pleasure.

Who do you think had the worst time the day of the eclipse? Those with the most intense rules about what had to happen before they could feel good! There's no doubt that the scientists, and the tourists who saw themselves as scientists, probably had the most pain. Many of them had huge agendas they were trying to complete in those four minutes before they could feel good about it.

Don't misunderstand; there's nothing wrong with being committed to accomplishing and doing everything you can. But years ago, I made a distinction that changed the quality of my life forever: **as long as we structure our lives in a way where our happiness is dependent upon something we cannot control, then we will experience pain.** Since I wasn't willing to live with the fear that pain could shake me anymore, and I considered myself to be intelligent, I redesigned my rules so that when I feel pain and when I feel pleasure is *whenever I feel it's appropriate based on my capacity to direct my own mind, body, and emotions.* Specifically, Becky and I enjoyed the eclipse immensely. We were in Hawaii for other reasons anyway (to conduct my three-week Certification program), so coming here a few days early to watch the eclipse was a bonus for us.

But the real reason we enjoyed ourselves was not that we had low expectations; we *were* looking forward to it. The key to our happiness could be found in one key rule we shared: **we decided** that our rule for the day was that **we were going to enjoy this event no matter what happened**. It wasn't that we didn't have expectations; it was that we decided that no matter what happened, we'd find a way to enjoy it.

Now, if you adopted and consistently applied this rule to your own life, can you see how that would change virtually everything you experience? When I tell people about this rule, some of them respond, "Yeah, but you're just lowering your standards." Nothing could be further from the truth! To adopt this rule is to **raise your standards.** It means you'll hold yourself to a higher standard of enjoying yourself despite the conditions of the moment. It means you've committed to being intelligent enough, flexible enough, and creative enough to direct your focus and evaluations in a way that allows you to experience the true richness of life—maybe *that's* the ultimate rule.

In the last chapter, you began to design for yourself a hierarchy of values to refine and define the direction of your life. You need to understand that **whether or not you feel like you're achieving your values is totally dependent upon your rules**—your beliefs about what has to happen for you to feel successful or happy or experiencing love. You can decide to make happiness a priority, but if your rule for happiness is that everything must go just as you planned, I guarantee you're *not* going to experience this value on a consistent basis. **Life is a variable event,** so our rules must be organized in ways that allow us to adapt, grow, and enjoy. It's critical for us to understand these unconscious beliefs that control when we give ourselves pain and when we give ourselves pleasure.

JUDGE AND JURY

We all have different rules and standards that govern not only the way we feel about the things that happen in our lives, but how we'll behave and respond to a given situation. Ultimately what we do and who we become is dependent upon the direction that our values have taken us. But equally, or possibly even more importantly, what will determine our emotions and behaviors is our **beliefs about what is good and what is bad, what we should do and what we *must* do. These precise standards and criteria are what I've labeled** *rules.*

Rules are the trigger for any pain or pleasure you feel in your nervous system at any moment. It's as if we have a miniature court system set up within our brains. *Our personal rules are the ultimate judge and jury.* They determine whether or not a certain value is met, whether we'll feel good or bad, whether we'll give ourselves pain or pleasure. If I were to ask you, for example, "Do you have a great body?," how would you respond? It would depend on whether you think you meet a certain set of criteria that you believe constitutes having a great body.

Here's another question: "Are you a great lover?" Your answer will be based upon your rules of what's required to be a great lover, the standards to which you hold yourself. If you told me, "Yes, I'm a great lover," I'd **discover your rules** by asking the key question, **"How do you know you're a great lover? What has to happen in order for you to feel you're a great lover?"**

You might say something like, "I know I'm a great lover because when I make love with a person, they usually say that it feels great." Others might say, "I know I'm a great lover because my lover tells me so." Or "I know I'm a great lover because of the responses I get from my partner." Others might say, "I know I'm a great lover because I feel good when I'm making love." (Doesn't their partner's response matter at all? Hmmm.) Or your answer might just be, "Ask around!"

On the other hand, some people don't feel that they're great lovers. Is this because they *aren't* great lovers? Or is it because their rules are *inappropriate*? This is an important question to answer. In many cases, people won't feel that they're a great lover because their partner doesn't *tell* them that they're a great lover. Their partner may respond passionately, but because they don't meet the specific rule of this individual, the person is certain they're not a great lover.

This predicament of not feeling the emotions we deserve is not limited to relationships or lovemaking. Most of us have rules that are just as inappropriate for defining success, making a difference, security, intelligence, or anything else. *Everything in our lives, from work to play, is presided over by this judge-and-jury system.*

The point here is simple: our rules are controlling our responses every moment we're alive. And, of course, as you've already guessed, they have been set up in a totally arbitrary fashion. Like so many other elements of the Master System that directs our lives, our rules have resulted from a dizzying collage of influences to which we've been exposed. The same punishment and reward system that shapes our values shapes our rules. In fact, as we develop new values, we also develop beliefs about what it will take to have those values met, so rules are added continuously. And, with the addition of more rules, we often tend to distort, generalize, and delete our past rules. We develop rules in conflict. For some people, rules are formed out of their desire to *rebel* against rules they grew up with.

Are the rules that guide your life today still appropriate for who you've become? Or have you clung to rules that helped you in the past, but hurt you in the present? Have you clung to any inappropriate rules from your childhood?

> *"Any fool can make a rule—And every fool will mind it."*
> —HENRY DAVID THOREAU

Rules are a shortcut for our brains. They help us to have a sense of certainty about the consequences of our actions; thus, they enable us to make lightning-quick decisions as to what things mean and what we should do about them.

When someone smiles at you, if you had to engage in a long, tedious set of calculations in order to figure out what that means, your life would be frustrating. But instead you have a rule that says **if** a person smiles at you, **then** it means they're happy, or they're friendly, or maybe they like you. **If** someone frowns at you, **then** it triggers another set of rules for what things mean and what you should do about it. For some people, **if** someone frowns at them, **then** their rule is that the person is in a bad state and should be avoided. Other people, however, might have a rule that says, "**If** someone's in a bad state, **then** I need to *change* their state."

ARE YOU MUDDLED OR PERFECT?

I remember reading an intricate story in Gregory Bateson's book *Steps to an Ecology of Mind*. It was a transcript of a conversation he'd had with his daughter years ago, and I'll paraphrase it for you here. One day she approached him and asked an interesting question: "Daddy, how come things get muddled so easily?"

He asked her, "What do you mean by 'muddled,' honey?"

She said, "You know, Daddy. When things aren't perfect. Look at my desk right now. Stuff is all over the place. It's muddled. And just last night I worked so hard to make it perfect. But things don't stay perfect. They get muddled so easily!"

Bateson asked his daughter, "Show me what it's like when things are perfect." She responded by moving everything on her shelf into individually assigned positions and said, "There, Daddy, now it's perfect. But it won't stay that way."

Bateson asked her, "What if I move your paint box over here twelve inches? Then what happens?"

She said, "No, Daddy, now it's muddled. Anyway, it would have to be straight, not all crooked the way you put it down."

Then he asked her, "What if I moved your pencil from this spot to the next one?"

"Now you're making it muddled again," she responded.

"What if this book were left partially open?" he continued.

"That's muddled, too!" she replied.

Bateson turned to his daughter and said, "Honey, it's not that things get muddled so easily. It's that you have *more ways* for things to get muddled. You have only one way for things to be perfect."

Most of us have created numerous ways to feel bad, and only a few ways to truly feel good. I never fail to be amazed at the overwhelming number of people whose rules wire them for pain. It's as if they have a vast and intricate network of neural pathways leading to the very state they're trying to avoid, and yet they have only a handful of neural pathways that they've connected to pleasure.

A classic example of this is a man who attended one of my Date With Destiny seminars. He was a well-known Fortune 500 executive, beloved by his community for his contributions, a father of five who was very close to his children and wife, and a man who was physically fit—a marathon runner. I asked him, "Are you successful?" To the astonishment of all present, he quite seriously answered, "No." I asked him, *"What has to happen* in order for you to feel successful?" (Remember, this is the key question you'll always ask to discover your rules or anyone else's.)

What followed was a litany of rigid rules and requirements that he felt he *must* meet in order to be successful in his life. He had to earn $3 million a year in salary (he was currently earning only $1.5 million in straight salary, but an additional $2 million in bonuses—this didn't count, though), he had to have 8 percent body fat (he was at 9 percent), and he had to never get frustrated with his kids (remember that he had five of them, all going in different directions in life). What do you think are this man's chances of feeling successful, when he has to meet all of these intense and arguably unreasonable criteria simultaneously? Will he *ever* feel successful?

By contrast, there was another gentleman who we had all noticed was practically bouncing off the walls because he had so much energy. He seemed to be enjoying the seminar and life to the utmost. I turned to him and asked the same question: "Are you successful?" He beamed back at me and said, "Absolutely!" So I asked him, "What has to happen in order for *you* to feel successful?" With a huge grin he explained, "It's so easy. All I have to do is get up, look down, and see that I am above ground!" The crowd roared. He continued, "Every day above ground is a great day!" This rule has become a favorite of the Date With Destiny staff, and now at every program we display it to remind each of us how successful we are the moment we pull back the covers each morning.

Like the CEO who wasn't meeting his own rules, **you could be winning and feel like you're losing because the scorecard you're using is unfair.** Not only is it unfair to you, it's also unfair to your spouse and children, the people you work with every day, and all the others whose lives you touch. If you've set up a system of rules that causes you to feel frustrated, angry, hurt, or unsuccessful—or you have no clear rules for knowing when you're happy, successful, and so on—those emotions affect the way you treat the people around you as well as how they feel when they're near you. Also, whether you are aware of it or not, often you are judging other people through a set of rules that you may never have expressed—but we all expect others to comply with our rules, don't we? If you're being hard on yourself, you're likely to be hard on others as well.

Why would anyone impose such strict regulations on themselves and the people they love most? A lot of it has to do with cultural conditioning. Many of us are afraid that if we don't have very intense rules, then we won't be driven to succeed, we won't be motivated to work hard and achieve. The truth is that you don't have to have ridiculously difficult rules to keep your drive! If a person makes their rules too intense, too painful, pretty soon they'll begin to realize that no matter what they do, they can't win, and they begin to experience learned helplessness. We certainly want to use the power of goals, *the allure of a compelling future,* to pull ourselves forward, but we must make sure that at the bottom of it all we have rules to allow us to be happy *anytime we want.*

DO YOUR RULES EMPOWER OR DISEMPOWER YOU?

We want to develop rules that move us to take action, that cause us to feel joy, that cause us to follow through—not rules that stop us short. I've found that there are an amazing number of men and women who set up rules for relationships that make it absolutely *impossible* for them to succeed in this area of their lives. For example, some people's rule for love is, "If you love me, then you'll do whatever I want you to do." Or "If you love me, then I can whine and complain and nag, and you should just accept it." Are these appropriate rules? Hardly! They'd be unfair to anyone you were sharing a relationship with.

One woman who attended Date With Destiny told me that she really wanted to have a close relationship with a man, but just hadn't seemed able to maintain a relationship with one past the initial "thrill of the chase" phase. As I began to ask her, "What has to happen for you to be attracted to a man?" her rules helped us both instantly understand what her challenge was. For her to feel attracted to a man, he had to pursue her constantly, even though she continued to reject him. If he kept working hard, trying to break down the barrier, that made her feel incredibly attracted to him; to her this meant he was a very powerful man.

But what's interesting was her second rule. If he kept on for more than a month, she lost her respect and therefore her attraction to him. So guess what normally would happen? A few men would take her rejection and keep on pursuing her, but of course most would give up after a short period of time. Thus she would never have a relationship with them. Then, the few who persisted would secretly have her favor for a while, but after an arbitrary period of about a month, she'd completely lose interest. She found herself unable to stay attracted to any man for more than a month because no man was able to anticipate her complex timetable.

What rules do you have that are equally unwinnable? For some people, in order to feel like they're in control in any context, they have to know what's going to happen in advance of its occurrence. For others, in order to feel like they're confident in some area, they have to have experience in doing it. If this were my rule for confidence, I couldn't accomplish most of what I've done in my life! Most of my success has come from my ability to get myself to feel certain I could achieve something, even though I had no references for it. My rule for confidence is, "If I decide to be confident, then I'll feel that way toward anything, and my confidence will help me succeed."

Competence is another interesting rule. Some people's rule for competence is, "If I've done something perfectly over a period of years, then I'm competent." Other people's rule is, "If I've done it effectively once, then I'm competent." And for others, competence is, "If I've done anything like it, then I know I can master this as well, and therefore I'm competent."

Do you see the impact these kinds of rules would have on your confidence, your happiness, your sense of control, the quality of your actions, and your life?

SET UP THE GAME SO YOU CAN WIN

In the last chapter, we devoted a great deal of time to setting up values. But as I've already stated, if you don't make the rules achievable, you'll never feel like those values are being met. When I first started to develop my ideas on designing destiny, I had only the concept of values and not rules, so whether or not a person felt like they were on track was completely arbitrary. The day I discovered rules, I began to understand the source of pain and pleasure in our experience. I understood that rules are the triggering device of human emotion, and began to evaluate how I could use rules more effectively.

As I've mentioned before, it quickly became clear to me that the majority of people are wired for pain. Their rules make it very, very difficult to feel good, and very easy to feel bad. Let me give you a powerful example. Here are the values of a woman we'll call Laurie who attended one of my earliest Date With Destiny seminars:

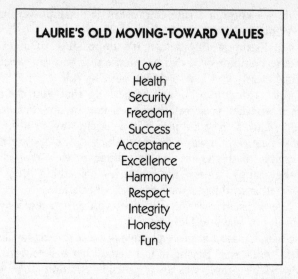

At first glance, these values look wonderful, don't they? You would think that this person is probably loving and healthy and freedom-oriented. With a closer look, though, we can already see a few challenges. Laurie's third value is security, and her fourth value is freedom. Do those two sound like they go well together?

The reality was that this woman was wired for massive pain. She was frustrated in every sense of the word, and was literally becoming a recluse, hiding out from people. No therapist she'd visited could figure out why. They were all working on her behaviors, her fears, and her emotions, instead of looking at the way her Master System of evaluating every event and experience of her life was wired.

So I began to elicit her rules for each of her values: **"What has to happen in order for you to feel _____ ?"** For her to feel love, her answer was, "I have to feel like I've earned it. *I have to feel like all my beliefs are accepted and approved of by every person I meet.* I can't feel like I'm loved unless I'm perfect. I have to be a great mother, a great wife," and so forth.

Instantly we began to see the problem. **Love** was the highest value on her list, the greatest source of pleasure she could possibly feel in her body. Yet her rules did not allow her to give herself this pleasure unless she met these complex criteria which *she couldn't control!* If any of us made our ability to feel loved dependent on everyone accepting our views, we wouldn't feel love very often, would we? There are just too many people with different ideas and beliefs, and therefore too many ways for us to feel bad.

How do we know if a rule empowers or disempowers us? There are three primary criteria:

1. It's a disempowering rule if **it's impossible to meet.** If your criteria are so complex or varied or intense that you can't ever win the game of life, clearly you have a disempowering rule.

2. A rule is disempowering if **something that you can't control determines whether your rule has been met or not.** For example, if other people have to respond to you in a certain way, or if the environment has to be a certain way, you clearly have a disempowering rule. A classic example of this is the people waiting to view the eclipse who couldn't be happy unless the weather—something they couldn't control—acted according to their specific expectations.

3. A rule is disempowering if **it gives you only a few ways to feel good and lots of ways to feel bad.**

Laurie had managed to meet all three of these criteria for disempowering rules, hadn't she? Having to feel that all her beliefs were accepted and approved by people was an impossible criterion. It required the outside environment, something she could not control—other people's opinions—to make her feel good. It provided lots of ways to feel bad, and provided no clear way to feel good.

Here are some of the rest of her rules for her values hierarchy:

LAURIE'S <u>OLD</u> MOVING-TOWARD VALUES AND RULES

Love: I have to feel like I've earned it, like all my beliefs are accepted and approved. I can't feel like I'm loved unless I'm *perfect.* I have to be a great mother and wife.

Health: I have to feel like my diet is perfect by my strict standards. I have to be completely free of physical pain. I must feel like I'm healthier than <u>everyone</u> I know and be an example.

Security: Everyone must like me. I must feel that everyone I meet is certain I'm a good person. I must be certain that **there will be no nuclear war.** I must have much more money in my savings account than I already do.

Freedom: I must be in control of my working demands, hours, fees, opinions, etc. I must be financially secure enough not to live under stress or financially related pressure.

How likely do you think it is that Laurie will meet one of her values, much less any? What about her rules for health? "I have to feel like my diet is *perfect* by my strict standards." She was not only a vegetarian, but ate only raw food, and she still didn't feel perfect! What are your chances of being healthier than everyone you know? Not much, unless you hang out in the intensive care unit!

LAURIE'S <u>OLD</u> MOVING-AWAY-FROM VALUES AND RULES

Rejection: I feel rejected if someone *doesn't* share my beliefs, if someone seemingly knows more than I do.

Failure: I feel failure if someone doesn't believe I'm a good person. I feel failure if I don't feel I support myself or my family well enough.

Anger: I feel anger when I don't feel like what I do is appreciated, when people judge me before they know me.

These moving-away-from rules are equally immobilizing. Notice how easy it is to feel bad, and how hard it is to feel good. If all it takes for her to feel rejected is someone not sharing her beliefs, then she's in for a lot of heartache. And what are the chances in your life of having people judge you before they know you? Only about one hundred percent! With these rules, can you imagine what it would be like to live in her body? She was racked with pain, and one of her biggest sources, if you look at her rules, was people. Any time she was around people, she was risking the possibility they might not share her beliefs, or might not like her, or might judge her. No wonder she was hiding out! At one point I finally said, "It's my guess that a person with values and rules like this would develop an ulcer." She said, "I already have one."

Laurie's experience, unfortunately, is not unique. Certainly some of her rules are more intense than others. But you will be absolutely surprised when you find out how unfair your *own* rules are when you begin to scrutinize them! At Date With Destiny, we attract some of the most successful people in the country—people whose level of skill and influence in the culture is unmatched. And yet, while they're successful on the outside, many are lacking the happiness and fulfillment they deserve. Invariably, it's because of values conflicts or inappropriate rules.

THE SOLUTION

The solution is very simple. All we have to do to make our lives work is set up a system of evaluating that includes rules that are *achievable,* that **make it easy to feel good and hard to feel bad**, that constantly pull us in the direction we want to go. Certainly it's useful to have some rules that give us pain. We need to have limits; we need to have some kind of pressure that drives us. I can't taste fresh orange juice unless I have a glass, something with limits to contain the juice. We all have limits, both as a society and as individuals. For starters, though, we should at least rewire ourselves so we can experience pleasure more consistently in life. When people are feeling good all the time, they tend to treat others better, and they tend to maximize their potential as human beings.

So what's our goal? Once we design our values, we must decide what evidence we need to have before we give ourselves pleasure. We need to design rules that will move us in the direction of our values, that will clearly be achievable, using criteria we can control personally so that *we're* ringing the bell instead of waiting for the outside world to do it.

Based on these requirements, Laurie changed the order of some of her values and completely changed her rules for achieving them. Here are her new values and rules:

LAURIE'S <u>NEW</u> MOVING-TOWARD VALUES AND RULES

Love: I experience love anytime I express love, give love to others, or allow myself to receive it.

Health: I am healthy when I acknowledge how wonderful I already feel!

Fun: I'm having fun when I find pleasure and joy in the process.

Gratitude: I feel grateful when I appreciate all the things I have in my life right now.

Freedom: I feel free when I live by my convictions and accept the choice to create happiness for myself.

Notice that fun is now a priority. This transformed her experience of life, not to mention her relationship with her daughter and husband. But even more powerful were the changes she made in her rules. Changing the values would have limited impact if the rules were unachievable.

What has this woman done? She has rewired her entire life so that she's in control. **You and I need to remember that our self-esteem is tied to our ability to feel like we're in control of the events in our environment.** These rules allow Laurie to always be in control without even trying.

Are her new rules for **love** achievable? You bet! Who's in control? *She* is! At any moment in time, she can decide to be loving to herself and others, and she'll now have permission to give herself the emotion called love. She'll know she's meeting her highest values. How often can she do this? *Every single day!* There are lots of ways to do it because there are lots of people she can be loving to: herself, her family, her friends, and strangers. How about her new rule for **health?** What's beautiful about it is that not only is she in charge—because she can acknowledge how wonderful she feels at any moment—and not only is it achievable, but isn't it true that if she regularly acknowledges feeling good, she'll reinforce the pattern of becoming more healthy?

In addition, Laurie adopted some new moving-away-from values. She selected emotions she knew she had to avoid indulging in order to succeed: negativity and procrastination. Remember, we want to *reverse the process of how most of us are wired. We want to make it hard to feel bad, and easy to feel good.*

LAURIE'S <u>NEW</u> MOVING-AWAY-FROM VALUES AND RULES

Negativity: I avoid <u>consistently</u> *depending on the acceptance of others* for my ultimate happiness and success.

Procrastination: I avoid <u>consistently</u> expecting perfection from myself and others.

With Laurie's new moving-away-from rules, she no longer depends upon the acceptance of others. Her rule for procrastination is based on her realization that expecting perfection created pain, and she hadn't wanted to begin projects that would create pain, so that's why she'd been procrastinating. These changes in values and rules have redirected her life to a level beyond anything she could have imagined.

Now, here's an assignment for you: based on the new values you've set up for yourself in the last chapter, **create a set of rules for your moving-toward values that makes it easy to feel good, and a set of rules for your moving-away-from values that makes it hard to feel bad. Ideally, create a *menu* of possibilities with lots of ways to feel good.** Here are a few of mine:

A SAMPLING OF MY MOVING-TOWARD VALUES AND RULES

Health and Vitality: Anytime I feel centered, powerful, or balanced; anytime I do anything that increases my strength, flexibility, or endurance; anytime I do anything that moves me toward a sense of physical well-being; anytime I eat water-rich foods or live in accordance with my own health philosophy.

Love and Warmth: Anytime I'm being warm and supportive of my friends, family, or strangers; anytime I focus on how to help; anytime I'm loving toward myself; anytime my state of being enhances how other people feel.

Learning and Growing: Anytime I make a new distinction that's useful; anytime I stretch myself beyond what was comfortable; anytime I think of a new possibility; anytime I expand or become more effective; anytime I apply anything I know in a positive way.

Achieving: Anytime I focus on the value of my life as already created; anytime I set an outcome and make it happen; anytime I learn anything or create value for myself or others.

You may say, "Isn't this just a game? Couldn't I set it up so that I meet my rule for health just by *breathing?*" Certainly you could base it on something this simple. Ideally, though, you'll design your rules so that by pursuing them you have *more* of what you want in your life. You also may say, "Won't I lose my drive to succeed if there's no pain motivation?" Trust me. Life will give you enough pain on your own if you don't follow through. You don't need to add to it by creating an intense set of rules that makes you feel lousy all the time.

In sociology there's a concept known as "ethnocentricity," which means we begin to believe that the rules, values, and beliefs of our culture are the only ones that are valid. This is an extremely limiting mindset. Every person around you has different rules and values than you do, and theirs are no better or worse than your own. The key question is not whether rules are right or wrong, but whether they **empower or disempower you**. In fact . . .

EVERY UPSET IS A RULES UPSET

Think about the last time you were upset with someone. Was it really about them, or was it about *something they did, or said, or failed to do that you thought they ought to?* Were you angry at them, or were you angry because they *violated one of your rules?* **At the base of every emotional upset you've ever had with another human being is a _rules_ upset.** Somebody did something, or failed to do something, that violated one of your beliefs about what they must or should do.

For example, some people's rule for respect is, *"If* you respect me, *then* you never raise your voice." If a person with whom you're in a relationship suddenly starts to yell, you're not going to feel respected if this is your rule. You're going to be angry because it has been violated. But your partner's rule may be, "If I'm respectful, then I'm truthful about all my feelings and all my emotions—good, bad, and indifferent—and I express them with all my intensity in the moment." Can you imagine the conflict these two people can have?

This was the scenario played out between Becky and me when we first began to develop our relationship. We had radically different rules about how to show respect for another person. Why? I grew up in an environment where you got a lot of pain if you weren't honest. If you walked out of the room in the middle of a conversation, you would never live it down. The number-one rule was that you hung in there and expressed your honest emotions, knowing you could be wrong, but you stayed there until everything was worked out.

Meanwhile, Becky grew up in a family where the rules were quite different but equally clear. She was taught, "If you don't have something good to say, don't say anything at all; if you have respect for someone, you never raise your voice to them; if someone else ever raises their voice, the only way to keep your self-respect is to get up and leave the room."

With this kind of conflict between our rules for respect, Becky and I drove each other crazy. We almost didn't get married because of this. Rules determine everything—where we go, what we wear, who we are, what's acceptable to us, what's unacceptable, who we have as friends, and whether we're happy or sad in virtually any situation.

Some people's rule for handling upset is, "If you care about me, then you leave me alone and let me deal with it my own way." Other people's rule is, "If somebody's upset, and you care about them, you immediately intervene to try to help." This creates a tremendous conflict. *Both people are trying to accomplish the same thing,* which is to respect and care about each other, but their rules dictate different behaviors, and their rules of interpretation will make their actions seem adversarial rather than supportive.

So if you ever feel angry or upset with someone, remember, it's *your* rules that are upsetting you, not their behavior. This will help you to stop blaming them. You can get past your upset quickly by first stopping and asking yourself, "Am I *reacting* to this, or am I *responding* to the situation intelligently?" Then, communicate with that person right up front and say something like, "I'm sorry I responded the way I did. It's just that you and I have different rules about what we need to do in this situation. My expectations are that if you respect me, you'll do _____ and _____ . I know those aren't your rules. So please tell me what *your* rules are. How do you express respect [love, caring, concern, etc.]?"

Once you're both clear on what the other person wants, then you can make a deal. Ask them, "Would you be willing to do _____ to make me feel respected? I'd be willing to do _____ for you." Any relationship—business or personal— can be instantly transformed just by getting clear on the rules and making an agreement to play by them. After all, how can you ever hope to win a game if you don't even know the rules?

THE CHALLENGE OF CHANGING RULES

Have you ever found yourself in a situation where you knew what the rules were, but all of a sudden exceptions started cropping up? People have the unique ability to call upon sub-rules that may be in conflict with all their other rules. A good metaphor for this might be if you and I decide to play baseball together, and I ask you, "Do you know how to play baseball?" and you say, "Of course." Then you'd review the basics: "We'd play nine innings, the person who scores the most runs wins, you've got to touch all the bases, you get three outs, and so on. If you hit a pop fly and I catch it, you're out. If I drop it, you're safe."

So we start the game. Everything's going great until the bottom of the ninth, when the score is tied, I have two men on and one man out, and I hit a high pop fly to the infield. My rules say that if you catch the ball, I'm out and the game is over, but if you drop it, I'm safe and the men on base have a chance to score, and I could win this game. I immediately run to base; you go for the ball and drop it. I'm thrilled, I'm on base, my teammate scores, and I think we've won the game.

But you come to me and say, "No, you're out!" I say, "What are you talking about? You dropped the ball! The rules are that if you drop the ball, then I'm safe." And then you say, "That's true, *except* when there are two men on and one man out. In that case, even if I drop the ball then you're still out. That's the one exception."

I protest, "You can't make up rules as we're going along!" You would answer, "I didn't make this up. It's called the *infield fly rule*. Everyone knows about it." I turn to my teammates, and they say no such rule exists. You turn to your teammates, and they all say that that's the rule—and we all end up fighting over the rules.

Have you ever had this experience in a personal relationship? You were playing by all the rules, and all of a sudden someone said, "Yes, that's true, except in this one situation," and you went ballistic. People feel very intensely about their rules. Everyone knows *their* rules are the *right* rules. People get especially angry when they think others are making up rules or changing them along the way. Yet this dynamic is a part of most interactions with other human beings.

PARADOXICAL PROVERBS

Look before you leap.	He who hesitates is lost.
Too many cooks spoil the broth.	Two heads are better than one.
Absence makes the heart grow fonder.	Out of sight, out of mind.
You can't teach an old dog new tricks.	It's never too late to learn.
The grass is always greener on the other side of the fence.	There's no place like home.
A penny saved is a penny earned.	You can't take it with you.

In fact, the paradox of conflicting beliefs and rules is one of the reasons people find so much frustration in their lives. In a relationship, one person says, "I love you, except when you leave the cap off the toothpaste," or "I love you, except when you raise your voice at me." Some of these sub-rules seem totally trivial, but they can be very damaging. The best way to deal with this is to remember that your rules are not based on reality. They're purely arbitrary. Just because you've used them and feel strongly about them doesn't mean they're the best rules or the right rules. Rules should be designed to *empower* our relationships, not destroy them. Any time a rule gets in the way, the question we need to ask ourselves is, **"What's more important? My relationship or my rules?"**

Suppose your trust was once violated in a romantic relationship, and now you're afraid to get close to anyone else again. You now have a rule that says, "If you get too close, you'll get hurt." At the same time, your highest value is love, and your rule is that in order to feel love, you must get close to someone. Now you have a major conflict: your rules and values are in absolute opposition. What can you do in this situation? The first step is to realize that you have conflicting rules. The second step is to **link enough pain to any rule that doesn't serve you, and replace it with a rule that does**. Most important, if you want to have quality relationships with other people, whether it's in your business or personal life, you must . . .

COMMUNICATE YOUR RULES

If you want to take control of your life, if you want to do well in business, if you want to be a great negotiator, if you want to be able to impact your children, if you want to be close to your spouse, then make sure you discover the rules they have for a relationship up front, and communicate yours as well. **Don't expect people to live by your rules if you don't clearly communicate what they are.** And don't expect people to live by your rules if you're not willing to compromise and live by some of theirs.

For example, in the beginning of any relationship, one of the first things I do is let the other party know my rules for the situation, and try to find out as many of their rules as possible. I ask things like "What will it take for you to know that our relationship is working? How often do we have to communicate? What is necessary?"

For example, I was once talking with a friend of mine who is a well-known celebrity, and he shared with me that he didn't feel like he had very many friends. I said, "Are you sure you don't have many friends? I see lots of people around you who truly do care about you. Is it that *you have rules* that eliminate a lot of people who could be your friends?" He said, "It just doesn't feel like they're my friends." I said, "What has to happen for you to feel like they're your friends?" He said, "Well, I guess I don't even know what my rules are, consciously."

After giving it some thought, he identified one of his top rules for friendship: if you're a friend of his, then you talk with him at least two or three times a week. "*That's* an interesting rule," I thought. "I have friends all over the world, people I truly love. But sometimes, even with my best friends, a month or more may go by before we get a chance to talk again, just because of the intensity of our schedules. Often I'll be in seminars from early morning until very late at night, and then I may have had 100 phone calls in that day. There's no physical way I could talk to all those people! Yet they all know they're my friends."

Then I asked him, "Do you think *I'm* your friend?" He said, "Well, intellectually I know you are, but sometimes it doesn't feel like it because we don't talk together often enough." I said, "Wow, I never knew that! I never would have known that was important to you if you hadn't communicated it to me. I bet you have *lots* of friends who might love meeting your rules for friendship *if they just knew what they were.*"

My definition for friendship is quite simple: if you're a friend, then you absolutely love a person unconditionally, and you'll do anything you can to support them. If they call you when they're in trouble or truly in need, you're there for them. Months go by, yet the friendship would never weaken once you decide that somebody is truly your friend. That's it! You never question it again. I think I have lots of friends because my rules for friendship are so easy to meet! All you have to do is care about me and love me, and I'll care about you and love you, and now we're friends.

It's so important to communicate your rules for any situation in life, whether it's love, friendship, or business. By the way, even if you clarify all the rules in advance, can misunderstandings still occur? You bet. Sometimes you'll forget to communicate one of your rules, or you may not even consciously know what some of your rules are. That's why ongoing communication is so important. **Never assume when it comes to rules.** *Communicate.*

THERE ARE SOME RULES YOU CANNOT BREAK!

The more I began to study people's behavior and the impact of their rules, the more interested I became in a dynamic that I noticed consistently, and that was that there are certain rules that people would *never* violate, and other rules that they would violate continuously—they'd feel bad about it each time, but they'd go ahead and do it anyway. What was the difference?

After some research, the answer became clear: we have a **hierarchy of rules**, just as we do values. There are certain rules that, to break them, would give us such intense pain that we don't even consider the possibility. We will rarely, if ever, break them. I call these rules **threshold rules**. For example, if I asked you, "What's something you would *never* do?," you'd give me a threshold rule. You'd tell me a rule that you would never violate. Why? Because you link too much pain to it.

Conversely, we have some rules that we don't want to break. I call these **personal standards**. If we do break them, we don't feel good about it, but depending upon the reasons, we're willing to break them in the short term. The difference between these two rules is often phrased with the words **must** and **should**. We have certain things that we *must* do, certain things that we *must not* do, certain things that we *must never* do, and certain things that we *must always* do. The "must" and the "must never" rules are threshold rules; the "should" and "should never" rules are personal standard rules. All of them give a structure to our lives.

Too many "must" rules can make life unlivable. I once saw a program that featured twenty families of quintuplets. Each set of parents was asked, "What is the most important thing you've learned for maintaining sanity?" The one message that was echoed repeatedly was: Don't have too many rules. With this many bodies in motion, and this many different personalities, if you've got too many rules, you'll go crazy. The law of averages says your rules are going to be violated constantly, and therefore you're going to be in continual stress, reacting to everything.

This kind of stress affects you and the people around you. Think of the rules we have today for women in our society. They even have a name for it: the "Superwoman Syndrome." Women today seem to have to do everything, and do it *perfectly*. Not only do they have to take care of their husband, children, parents, and friends, but they have to have the perfect body, they have to go out and change the world, they have to prevent nuclear war, and they have to be the consummate business person on top of it all. Do you think that could create a little stress in life, having that many musts in order to feel successful?

Of course, women aren't the only ones in society who are going through this—today's men and children are also under tremendous stress because of increased expectations. If we're burdened with too many musts to meet, we lose our enthusiasm and zest for life; we just don't want to play the game anymore. High self-esteem comes from feeling like **you have control** over events, not that events have control over you. And when you have a lot of "must" rules, the chances of them being violated are great.

What would be a "must never" rule in a relationship? Many people might say, "My husband or wife *must never* have an extramarital affair." For other people, however, that's only a should rule: "My husband or wife *should* never have an extramarital affair." Might that difference in rules have the potential to create problems down the road? It's highly possible. In fact, when people have relationship upsets, invariably it's because although they've agreed on the rules, they haven't agreed on whether it's a "*must* never" or a "*should* never." It's necessary not only to understand what kinds of rules your partner has, but also to keep in mind that both "must" and "should" rules are appropriate.

In order to achieve certain outcomes, it's important to have plenty of "must" rules to make sure that we'll follow through, that we'll take action. For example, I have a friend who's in superb physical condition. What's interesting is her set of rules for herself in the area of health: she has very few shoulds and a lot of musts. I asked her, "What must you never do if you want to be healthy?" She said, "I must never smoke. I must never violate my body with drugs. I must never pig out. I must never go more than a day without exercising."

Then I asked, "What *must* you do in order to be healthy?" Again, the list was long: "I must exercise every day for at least half an hour. I must eat the right kinds of foods. I must eat only fruit in the morning. I must combine my foods properly. I must ride at least fifty miles on my bicycle every week." And the list went on. Finally I asked for her "should" rules. She said, "I should exercise more." And that was it!

Now, this woman has an overweight friend. When I asked her what she must never do in order to be healthy, she gazed at me with a blank stare. She *had* no "must never" rules in the area of health! She *did* have a couple of must rules, however: she *must* eat, and she *must* sleep. Then I asked if she had any "should" rules. "Sure," she said, "I should eat better; I should exercise. I should take better care of my body." She also had a list of "should not" rules such as, "I should not eat meat, I should not overeat," and so on. This woman had plenty of things she knew she should do, but because she had very few "must" rules, she never got into the position of giving herself intense pain for doing unhealthy things. And it wasn't difficult to realize why she had never been able to keep the weight off.

If you've ever procrastinated on anything, were you perhaps using some "should" rules such as, "I should start this project" or "I should begin an exercise program"? What would have happened instead if you had decided, "I *must* start this project" or "I *must* start this exercise program," and then followed through by conditioning it into your nervous system?

Remember, we all need some structure. Some people have no clear rules for when they're successful. Rules can provide the contextual environment for us to create added value. Rules can motivate us to follow through; they can cause us to grow and expand. Your goal is simply to create a balance between your "must" rules and your "should" rules and to utilize both types of rules in the appropriate context.

RULES REALIGNMENT

Right now, begin to take control of your rules by writing down your answers to the following questions. Make your answers as thorough as possible.

1. **What does it take for you to feel successful?**
2. **What does it take for you to feel loved—by your kids, by your spouse, by your parents, and by whoever else is important to you?**
3. **What does it take for you to feel confident?**
4. **What does it take for you to feel you are excellent in any area of your life?**

Now look at these rules and ask yourself, **"Are they appropriate? Have I made it really hard to feel good and easy to feel bad?"** Do you have 129 things that must happen before you feel loved? Does it take only one or two things to make you feel rejected?

If that's true, change your criteria and come up with rules that empower you. What do your rules need to be in order for you to be happy and successful in this endeavor? Here's a critical distinction: **design your rules so that you're in control, so that the outside world is not what determines whether you feel good or bad. Set it up so that it's *incredibly easy* for you to feel good, and *incredibly hard* to feel bad.**

For the rules that govern your moving-toward values, use the phrase **"Anytime I . . ."** In other words, create a menu of possibilities of ways to feel good. For example, "I feel love *anytime* I give love, or *anytime* I spend time with people I love, or *anytime* I smile at someone new, or *anytime* I talk with an old friend, or *anytime* I notice someone doing something nice for me, or *anytime* I appreciate those who already love me." Do you notice what you've done? You've made the game *winnable* by stacking the deck outrageously in your favor!

Come up with *tons* of ways to satisfy your rules for feeling love; make it incredibly easy to experience that pleasure, and make sure to include plenty of criteria that are under *your* sole control, so you don't have to depend on anyone or anything else to feel good. *Any time* you do *any* of these things, you would feel love—not just by meeting some outlandish criterion that only occurred about as often as a total eclipse of the sun!

By the way, I have a rule for you: while you're doing this, *you must have fun!* Get outrageous; explore the outer edges. You've been using rules all your life to hold you back; why not get a few laughs at their expense? Maybe in order to feel love, all you have to do is wiggle your little toe. It sounds weird, but who am I to decide what gives you pleasure?

Now, be sure to discover the rules of the people around you. Go out and do some polling. Find out what your kids' rules are for being a family member, or for being successful in school, or for having fun. I bet you'll be amazed at what you discover! Find out your spouse's rules; ask your parents; ask your boss or your employees.

One thing is sure: if you don't know the rules, you're guaranteed to lose because you're bound to violate them sooner or later. But if you understand people's rules, you can predict their behavior; you can truly meet their needs and thus enrich the quality of your relationships. Remember, **the most empowering rule is to enjoy yourself no matter what happens.**

In the past few chapters we've nearly completed learning about the five elements of the Master System. We know the importance of state, the way questions direct our focus and evaluations, and the power of values and rules to shape our lives. Now let's discover the fabric from which all these elements are cut . . .

17

REFERENCES: THE FABRIC OF LIFE

"Man's mind stretched to a new idea never goes back to its original dimensions."
—OLIVER WENDELL HOLMES

As he stood on the flight deck, the young lieutenant watched a jet plane skid out of control onto the aircraft carrier, a wing slashing out and nearly cutting in half a man standing only a few feet away. The only thing that pulled him through the horror of the moment was the booming voice of his commanding officer shouting at him: "Somebody get a broom, and sweep these guts off the deck!"* There was no time to think. He had to respond immediately. He and his fellow crewmen swept their comrade's body parts off the landing strip. In that instant, nineteen-year-old George Bush had no choice but to learn to deal with the carnage of war. It would be a memory he would recite often to describe the shock of violent death and the necessity to be able to respond.

Another experience that shaped his life was a bombing mission he flew not long after the tragedy on the ship's deck. He was sent to bomb a radio tower on a small island in the South Pacific. Chichi Jima was a Prisoner of War facility run by an infamous Japanese officer, Matoba, who Bush and his crew knew had committed brutal war crimes against his prisoners: such unbelievable atrocities as cannibalizing some of the men and putting their remains into the soup for meat, feeding it to the other prisoners, and then telling them afterward that they had eaten human flesh.

As young George Bush approached the target, he was absolutely resolved to isolate this madman by destroying his only tool of communication: the radio tower. As he approached his bombing run, he was hit by enemy attack. Smoke filled the cabin, but he was determined to hit his

* "Commander in Chief," *U.S. News & World Report*, December 31, 1990.

mark. In the final seconds, he managed to release the bomb, smashing the target and destroying the antenna. Instantly he gave the orders to eject. He turned the plane back out to sea, and when his turn came, the bailout didn't take place as planned. His body was slammed against the tail of the aircraft, tearing a portion of his parachute and grazing his head. The damaged parachute functioned only partially in breaking his fall, but just before he hit the water, he cut himself loose. Struggling back to the surface with blood oozing from his head wound, he desperately groped for his life raft. He found it, but as he dragged himself into it, he saw that the water and food canisters had been destroyed upon impact with the aircraft's tail.

To make matters worse, the current was slowly pulling him directly toward the beach of the island he'd just bombed. Can you imagine what they would do to him? As his raft was drawn closer and closer to the shore, his fear grew. Then, suddenly, he began to see something in the water. At first he thought it was his imagination, then he realized it was a periscope. He was about to become a prisoner of the Japanese.

But as the huge submarine began to lift out of the water in front of him, he realized it was the *Finback,* an *American* submarine! He was rescued, but only in time for him to have to endure yet more peril. Upon picking up Bush, the *Finback* dropped quickly as the enemy boats approached and began dropping depth charges on the submarine. All the *Finback* could do was dive and remain totally still. The crew was unable to do anything but call upon their faith and pray that the explosives would not destroy them.

George Bush not only survived this experience, but also completed many other successful bombing missions, and returned a war hero. He said that his days upon that submarine were some of the most important of his life—days when he began to think about destiny, about who he was and why he was put on earth.

What role did these experiences play in shaping the character, identity, and destiny of George Bush? Clearly, they became the fabric from which many of his core beliefs and values would be cut—the fabric I call **reference experiences**—these experiences would be part of what would guide him more than forty years later to becoming President of the United States. They also helped to mold his beliefs and his sense of certainty that good must "stand up to evil." They gave him a sense of confidence that if he gave his all and didn't give up, he would produce the results he desired against all odds. How do you think these references shaped his actions almost five decades later as he sat in the Oval Office, contemplating his response to Saddam Hussein's unprovoked invasion of friendly Kuwait?

If we want to understand why people do what they do, a review of the most significant and impactful reference experiences of their lives certainly gives us clues. References—the fifth element of a person's Master System—really provide the essence, or the building blocks, for our beliefs, rules, and values. They are the clay from which our Master System is molded. There is no doubt that a person who has experienced and triumphed over tremendous adversity clearly has strong references from which to build a consistent level of confidence—a belief or faith in themselves and in others, and the capacity to overcome challenges.

The larger the number and greater the quality of our references, the greater our potential level of choices. A larger number and greater quality of references enables us to more effectively evaluate what things mean and what we can do. The reason I say "potential" choice is that, while references provide us with the foundational ingredients of our beliefs, we often fail to organize our references in ways that strengthen us. For example, a young man may have tremendous confidence and skill on the football field, but when he enters his history class, he may fail to summon that same sense of certainty that could help him to maximize his potential as well in the classroom as he does when he's facing his foe across the line on the gridiron. If he approached football with the same attitude of defeat or doubt as he did his history class, he'd be incredibly ineffective.

What determines which of our references we use? Clearly, the emotional state we're in will radically impact which files—i.e., which memories, emotions, feelings, sensations that we've stored—are available to us. When we're in a fearful state, only the references we've associated with those fearful sensations in the past seem to come to mind, and we find ourselves caught up in a loop ("fear" leading to "reference of fear" leading to "multiplied fear").

If we're feeling hurt by someone, we tend to open the file and remember every other experience when that person hurt us, rather than changing our state by remembering how this person really feels about us, remembering times when they've been loving to us. Therefore, the state we're in will determine how much of this fabric is available for the creation of a quality life. Another factor besides state is to have an **expanded reference system,** one that can clearly add to our level of understanding as to what is possible and what we're capable of, no matter what challenges may arise.

There's no doubt references are one of the most important elements of our decision-making process. They clearly will shape not only what we do, but how we feel and who we become. Contrast Saddam Hussein's reference experiences with George Bush's. We know that Saddam's father physically abused him, that his uncle taught him how to nurture a grudge and to hate the English "overlords." While Bush was rewarded for heroism, Saddam's role models were those who learned to control others with murder and propaganda.

Over a period of about fifteen to twenty years, Saddam repeatedly attempted to oust the leader of Iraq, killing anyone who got in his way. As a result, he doesn't perceive setbacks, regardless of how bloody—as failures; he's come to believe that in the long run he'll always succeed. This is a belief, by the way, that has allowed him to prevail even after his defeat in the Persian Gulf War. By the age of forty-two he had eliminated his opponents and taken control of Iraq.

To many, Saddam is a monster, and people often wonder how the Iraqis can support him. The answer is that Iraqis perceive Saddam Hussein as one who helped turn things around in their country: he helped to provide better housing, education, and so on. To the Iraqis, he is a hero. Besides, all Iraqis from the age of four or five are taught that he's a hero. His image is displayed everywhere, and they see only his best side on nationally controlled television.

Did Saddam Hussein become a murderer purely because of his references of being abused as a child? Far from it. Many people have emerged from very similar reference experiences as compassionate and sensitive people who, because of their pain, would never allow anyone else to be abused around them. Many of these people strive to help others. Could someone else have been on that same ship with George Bush and been devastated by the death of their friend, and used that as a reference for the belief that life is not worth living or that war is never justified? You bet. **Once again, it's not our references, but *our interpretations of them, the way we organize them*—that clearly determine our beliefs.**

Which references play the largest role in our life's experiences? It all depends on **what we get reinforced for.** Saddam was rewarded for cutting a wide swath of murder and destruction en route to leadership of his country. George Bush was reinforced constantly for his focus on "doing the right thing," contributing, and helping those in need. These reinforcements helped to create foundations for very different destinies for these men's lives.

WHAT ARE REFERENCES?

References are all the experiences of your life that you've recorded within your nervous system—everything you've ever seen, heard, touched, tasted, or smelled—stored away inside the giant file cabinet of your brain. Some references are picked up consciously, others unconsciously. Some result from experiences you've had yourself; others consist of information you've heard from others, and all your references, like all human experience, become somewhat distorted, deleted, and generalized as you record them within your nervous system. In fact, you also have references for things that have never happened—anything you've ever imagined in your mind is also stored in your brain as a memory.

Many of these references are organized to support beliefs and, as you learned in Chapter 4, a belief is nothing but a feeling of certainty about what something means. If you believe you are intelligent, it's because you have activated certain **references** to support that feeling of certainty. Maybe you've had the experience of successfully tackling mental challenges, such as acing a test or running a business well. All of these **reference experiences** act as "table legs" to support the idea, or "tabletop," that you are intelligent.

We have enough references within us to back up any idea we want: that we're confident or that we're weak, that we care or that we're selfish. The key is to **expand the references that are available within your life. Consciously seek out experiences that expand your sense of who you are and what you're capable of, as well as organize your references in empowering ways.**

> *"The knowledge of the world is only to be acquired in the world, and not in a closet."*
> —LORD CHESTERFIELD

Not long ago I heard about a man who found $35,000 cash in a bag on the street. He instantly sought out and returned it to the owner. Everyone who heard the story wanted to congratulate this man, but he shied away from the media and refused to be filmed. He adamantly insisted that returning the money was the right and only thing he could do. It turned out that this money was the life savings of a sixty-eight-year-old woman, and through his one act he probably saved her financial life, yet he refused to take credit. Why? Clearly the references of his past had helped him to develop a belief that taking credit for doing what obviously was the right thing would be totally inappropriate. He didn't decide to avoid the recognition on a whim; he had a sense of certainty that only his life references could create.

Think of your references, both those you consider to be good and bad, as a giant bolt of fabric woven from your experiences. With the other elements of your Master System—your state, questions, values, and beliefs—you cut a pattern from this fabric that enables you to make decisions about what to do with your life. **You have an *inexhaustible* supply of references that can be designed any way you wish.** And each day, you're adding to this supply. One important measure of a person's intelligence is the way in which they use their fabric of references. Do you craft a curtain to hide behind, or do you fashion a magic carpet that will carry you to unequalled heights? Do you consciously dig through your life experience and pull out those memories that empower you most on a consistent basis?

As you learned in Chapter 4, probably one of the most valuable things that references do for us is to provide a feeling of certainty. Without them, we would live our whole lives afraid or in doubt; we wouldn't be able to function. Would it disturb you if this book suddenly levitated, floated away, and came to rest five feet in front of you? The only reason you would feel any fear is that you have no references for this. You'd have no idea how to interpret what it means. Why will a baby reach into a dirty ashtray, pull out a cigarette butt, and chew on it? Isn't it because they don't have any references that tell them this is not good for them? (Of course, some adults still haven't figured *this* one out!)

Let me ask you again, **How do you use your references? Do you consciously interpret them in ways that empower you, in ways that support the achievement of your goals?** Or does your brain automatically latch on to individual experiences where you're not supported, and develop beliefs like "Everybody's out to get me," or "Every time I try anything, I get knocked down," or "I don't deserve to be loved"?

The way we use our references will determine how we feel, because whether something is good or bad is all based on what you're comparing it to. When a businesswoman checks into a hotel room, whether or not she thinks the room is nice is based on her past references. I guarantee that if you took someone from Eastern Europe and got them a room in the simplest budget motel here in the United States, you would find that they'd be thrilled, thinking that these were top-rate accommodations. Sometimes we lose perspective that good and bad are merely based upon our references.

Date With Destiny is one of my favorite learning environments because I'm able to consistently see how people's references are being used to shape their behavior. As part of an in-depth questionnaire participants fill out before the seminar, they list five experiences that they feel have shaped their entire lives. What they are doing is sharing with me some of their most powerful references, and it amazes me how many different meanings they take from the same references. Some people have been raped, sexually abused, abandoned. Some have come from broken or impoverished homes. Yet some people interpret these experiences in a way that helps them form the belief that their life is not worth living, and others use it to motivate themselves to study, to expand, to grow, to share, to be more sensitive.

It's true that Saddam Hussein was abused as a child, but so was Oprah Winfrey. Here is a woman who was raped and violently mistreated in her youth, yet today she touches millions of lives daily with her television show. Simply by sharing her own experiences, she has helped people to heal some of the wounds from their pasts. Millions of Americans feel close to her because they know she understands; i.e., she has references of pain, just like they do.

> *"We lift ourselves by our thought, we climb upon our vision of ourselves."*
> —ORISON SWETT MARDEN

References are not limited to your actual experience. Your imagination itself is a source of references. Remember Roger Bannister and the four-minute mile? No one believed it was physically possible for human beings to run the mile in less than four minutes, yet he created his own sense of certainty through imagined references. He visualized over and over again breaking the four-minute mile, hearing and feeling himself break the barrier until pretty soon he had so many reference legs that he felt certain he would succeed—as certain as other people were that accomplishing this task was impossible.

We need to remember that our imagination is ten times more potent than our willpower. Because Bannister was able to use his imagination as the legs supporting the tabletop of certainty, he was able to produce a result that was unheard of throughout human history. **Imagination unleashed provides us a sense of certainty and vision that goes far beyond the limitations of the past.**

Recently Mr. Akio Morita sent me his book, *Made in Japan*. Mr. Morita is the co-founder of Sony Corporation and an unbelievably brilliant man. The destiny of Sony, just like any individual's, is the result of a series of decisions. In his book, Morita discloses that one of the toughest and most important decisions he ever made was to turn down an offer from Bulova Corporation to purchase 100,000 of his breakthrough transistor radios—at a time when his company was not even moving 10,000 units a month. The amount of money they offered him was ten times what his company was worth at the time, yet after deep consideration he rejected the deal.

Why? Simply because Bulova wanted to put their own name on the radio. He realized that while in the short term saying yes would give his company a huge jump, he would be building Bulova's name instead of Sony's. The Bulova executives could not believe he would turn down their offer. He told them, "Fifty years from now, my company's name will be as big as yours, and I know that the radio I've created is going to help us develop that name."

Of course, all of Morita's partners thought he was crazy. How was he able to create this sense of certainty that enabled him to turn down such an enticing and profitable offer? He vividly imagined the future of his company, and created references where none existed. He directed his focus and envisioned his goals with clarity, and then backed it up with absolute and active faith. Today, Sony Corporation is not only a leader in the electronics industry, generating $27 billion a year, but has also diversified to industries as far-reaching as film making (acquiring Columbia and Tri-Star Pictures) and music (acquiring CBS Records and Columbia House), and is renowned for its quality around the world.

With faith, you can cling to your vision in the face of seeming failure. What if Thomas Edison had given up after his first failed attempt to make the electric light bulb? Or even after his hundredth attempt? Luckily for all of us, he persisted beyond *thousands* of attempts. He could have taken each instance as a reference to back up a belief that his invention was not feasible. Instead, he chose to use each failed attempt as a reference for the belief that he was getting *closer* to the solution. Remember, don't drive into the past using your rear-view mirror as a guide. **You want to learn from your past, not live in it—focus on the things that empower you.**

READING IS FEEDING YOUR MIND

You are not even limited to your own personal experiences as references. You can borrow the references of other people. Early in my life, I chose to focus on those who had made it, those who had succeeded and contributed and were impacting people's lives in a major way. I did so by reading biographies of successful people and learned that regardless of their background or conditions, when they held on to their sense of certainty, and consistently contributed, success eventually came. I used *their* references as my own, forming the core belief that I could truly shape my own destiny.

Do you remember my friend Captain Gerald Coffee who was a prisoner of war in Vietnam for over seven years? A good deal of that time was spent in solitary confinement. One of the things that enabled him to preserve his sanity when the outside world gave him no references for joy was to turn to his own rich internal world. As a child he had memorized various poems and stories, which he repeated to himself to create a different "environment" from the one he had to endure day after day.

You don't have to go into solitary confinement to discover the beauty and power of cultivating a bountiful treasure chest of memories and imagined references. How can you fill that chest? Explore the wealth of literature, stories, myths, poetry, and music. Read books, view movies and videotapes, listen to audiotapes, go to seminars, talk with people, and get new ideas. All references have power, and you never know which one could change your entire life.

The power of reading a great book is that you start thinking like the author. For those magical moments while you are immersed in the forests of Arden, you are William Shakespeare; while you are shipwrecked on Treasure Island, you are Robert Louis Stevenson; while you are communing with nature at Walden, you are Henry David Thoreau. You start to think like they think, feel like they feel, and use imagination as they would. Their references become your own, and you carry these with you long after you've turned the last page. That is the power of literature, of a good play, of music; that is why we constantly want to expand our references.

I used to believe that going to see a play was a waste of time. Why? Because the only plays I had ever attended were poorly acted, and their pace was painfully slow. But one day Becky and I decided to see the musical *Les Miserables*. I have never seen, read, or heard anything that moved me so deeply. Since then, I've become addicted to great theater, and each time we go to New York City, it's a priority for us to catch a show.

> ### "Imagination is more important than knowledge."
> —ALBERT EINSTEIN

One of the finest beliefs I developed years ago that helped me to enjoy all of my life experience was the idea that **there are no bad experiences**, that no matter what I go through in life—whether it's a challenging experience or a pleasurable one—*every* experience provides me something of value if I look for it. If I pull just one idea or one distinction from an experience, then it expands me.

Back when I was still in high school and scraping together money any way I could in order to attend personal development seminars, my friends were amazed that I'd go back to some of the same seminars again and again. Often they'd ask me, "Why would you go back to the same program?" Inevitably I'd tell them that I understood the power of repetition, and each time I heard something new because *I* was different. Plus I knew that hearing something again and again would eventually condition me to *use* it, that **repetition truly is the mother of skill**. Every time I reviewed a program, I made additional distinctions or heard ideas that impacted me differently and enabled me to create new references, and thus new interpretations, new actions, and new results in my life.

USE CONTRAST TO PUT YOUR LIFE IN PERSPECTIVE

While some references ennoble you and give you a higher vision, others show you a side of life you'd rather not experience. But these are the sorts of references that can be used to help you keep your life in balance. They provide a new level of contrast. No matter how bad you think things are in your life, it's good to remember that someone else has it worse.

At my nine-day Mastery™ programs, I invariably take a portion of one day to bring in people who've been through physical or emotional hell and have come out on top—the W. Mitchells of the world, or my good friend Mique Davis, who, in his drunken youth, decided to jump off a bridge but didn't realize the water was only about two feet deep. He instantly became paralyzed from the neck down. These people begin to share from their hearts how great life is, how happy they are to be alive, how much they've been able to accomplish. Or I bring in my good friend Dax, who was trapped in a fire, had his entire body burned, and was blinded. Later, in spite of all these challenges, he became a practicing attorney.

The theme for the day is to establish a simple and profound belief: "I have no problems." In contrast with the brave individuals who share their stories, everyone else in the room knows they have no challenges whatsoever. Suddenly, the problems they're having with their spouses, their children's grades, the loss of a business, or their failure to achieve goals are immediately put into perspective.

We can also use new references to motivate ourselves if we start becoming complacent. While it's true that no matter how bad things are for you, someone else is going through something worse, it's also true that no matter how well things are going for you, someone else is doing even better. Just when you think your skill has reached the highest level, you find there's someone else who's achieved even greater heights. And that's one of the beauties of life: it drives us to constantly expand and grow.

The power of having new references to raise our standards for ourselves is immense, whether it's studying the teachings of a great spiritual leader who, in spite of abuse by others, continues to give love, or seeing those who've succeeded financially and noticing what's truly possible. I'll never forget the first time I met architect and hotel magnate Chris Hemmeter. Becky and I had the privilege of being among the first people to be invited to visit Chris's new home, along with his family, in Hawaii—a $70 million residence that is beyond verbal description. The front door alone cost $1 million to create. While your rules may say, "That's an incredible waste of money," it was also an unbelievably expanding experience of what is possible in terms of business or economic growth. Suddenly, my $4 million Castle was put in perspective. It barely covered the cost of his front door and marble stairway! Certainly there was room in my life for thinking bigger, pushing limits, imagining the unimaginable. The best part of meeting Chris and his wife, Patsy, was discovering that they are incredibly warm people, that they use their wealth to create an environment that truly inspires them.

Using contrasting references is one of the most powerful ways, then, to change our perceptions and our feelings. If I ever start to lose perspective because I feel like I'm working too hard, I think about a man who attended one of my seminars years ago. He was a warm and gentle soul who unfortunately ended up in the wrong place at the wrong time. One day shy of his forty-fifth birthday he pulled into a gas station where there were two men who had just that day been released from prison. From their brief episode of freedom, these men had decided they weren't comfortable with life on the outside, and they hit upon a plan to get back into prison: they'd kill the very next person who drove into this gas station. It didn't matter who it was, what their age was, male or female; they'd just kill the next human being. When this man drove up and got out of his car to fill his tank, they attacked and brutally beat him to death.

Now, do you think *you* have problems? He left behind a wife and four small children. I was devastated by the story; I couldn't believe it. How do you come out with a positive meaning from an experience that seems to have none? I couldn't even imagine this happening to a member of my family and what it would do to me. I kept asking myself what I could do to help. I immediately called his widow and offered to help her in any way I could. My primary goal was to make sure that she was trying to find some form of empowering meaning for herself and her children from this experience. It would have been too easy to use this as a reference to back up a belief that life is not worth living, that humankind is evil and destructive, that you can do everything right and still be mowed down like a blade of grass, so why even try?

I communicated to this woman the importance for her children's sake of somehow finding in this experience a shred of meaning to empower them at some level. When I asked her what this experience could mean, she expressed how deep her pain was, but more important, the one thing about this experience that was positive was that when the story was made known in the newspapers, an unbelievable amount of love, support, and caring poured forth. She received literally hundreds of letters and offers of support from people in the community, people from all walks of life.

She said, "I realized that if I believed that people were destructive or that this meant that life was unfair, I'd destroy myself and my children.

So while it's unbelievably painful right now, I *know* that this must have happened for a reason. I don't have a way to back it up; it is just my faith." This woman found the courage to use *faith* as the ultimate reference. Her willingness to trust that there must be a reason, even if she's not aware of it, freed her from the most painful experience of her life and empowered her.

What a powerful woman! How lucky these children are! She told them, "Kids, I want you to notice all these people and how much love they are giving. People are really good. There are a few in the world who are bad, and they need to be helped, but your daddy always believed in God, and now he has gone to a better place. He had things to do while he was here, and his time was up, but *our* time is *not* up, and we have to take advantage of it while we are here. We have to use your father's death to remind us that every day we have to live life to its fullest. And we can't think about losing him, because he will always be with us."

> *"It is only with the heart that one can see rightly;*
> *what is essential is invisible to the eye."*
> —ANTOINE DE SAINT-EXUPÉRY

Could it be possible that what seem like the worst days in our lives are actually the most powerful in terms of the lessons we can choose to learn from them? Think about one of the worst experiences that has ever happened to you. As you look back upon it now, can you think of *any* ways in which it had some kind of positive impact on your life? Maybe you were fired, or mugged, or involved in a car accident, but out of that experience you gained a new resolve, or a new awareness that caused you to grow as a person and measurably increased your ability to contribute.

I realize that some situations may be more challenging than others to find something good about, but by this point in the book, you're no longer a novice. You've been stretching your imagination and flexing your muscles of empowerment. You've learned how to manage your state and direct your focus by asking better questions. If you were abused as a child, maybe it made you a more sensitive person toward children and caused you to make the decision to break that generational chain of abuse; if you grew up in a very restrictive environment, perhaps it drove you to fight for the freedom of others; if you felt that you never were loved enough, you may now be a major giver. Or maybe just that "horrible" event caused you to make new decisions, to change the direction of your life, and therefore your destiny. Perhaps your worst days have really been your best.

You may protest, "No, Tony, there are some things in my past that have no purpose. I'll never get over them; I'll always have pain." You're absolutely right: as long as you hold on to the belief that you have been taken advantage of, or that you've lost something that can never be returned, you will indeed always have that pain. Just remember, **loss is imaginary. Nothing ever disappears in the universe; it only changes form.** If there is something that still wounds you, it's because of the meaning that you have linked to it. Maybe what you need to do is to have faith and say, "Even though I don't know why this has happened, I am willing to trust. Someday, when the time is right, I will understand."

Limited references create a limited life. If you want to expand your life, you must expand your references by pursuing ideas and experiences that wouldn't be a part of your life if you didn't consciously seek them out. Remember, rarely does a good idea interrupt you; you must actively seek it. Empowering ideas and experiences must be pursued.

A UNIVERSE OF IDEAS AND EXPERIENCES

In expanding our references, we create a great contrast with which to evaluate life and possibility. If you've been magnifying your problems out of proportion, consider this: **we live in a galaxy that contains several hundred thousand million stars. Then realize that we live in a universe that has several hundred thousand million galaxies.** In other words, there are several hundred thousand million suns in our galaxy alone. And all of these suns have planets revolving around them as well! Think of the magnitude. The stars in our galaxy make one turn around the Milky Way's axis only once every several hundred million years. When you think about the immensity of this universe, and then look at the life span of an average human being (generously about eighty years), does it give you a different perspective? The human life span is but a speck in time. And yet people worry themselves to death about things like how they're going to pay the mortgage, what kind of car they drive, or how their next business meeting will go.

> *"I believe a leaf of grass is no less than the journey-work of the stars."*
> —WALT WHITMAN

I'm always trying to expand and improve my references because I believe in the old computer term GIGO: Garbage In, Garbage Out. Each day that we live, we're taking in new information, ideas, concepts, experiences, and sensations. We need to consciously stand guard at the doors of our minds to make sure that whatever we're allowing to enter will cause our lives to be enriched, that the experiences we pursue will add to our stockpile of possibility. In assisting our children to expand and grow, we need to guide them into experiences that will provide positive references for their future—references that will help them know they're capable of dealing with virtually anything.

Simultaneously, we need to teach them what to watch out for in life. Certain references denigrate our experience of life. Are you a little bit concerned when you hear music like that of the Geto Boys? One of their recent songs is a rap song about cutting a girl's throat and then having sex with her corpse. Do you think this kind of reference repeated again and again, not just in children's minds, *but in anybody's,* would be a little bit destructive? I'm not saying that someone's going to hear this and then go out and do it; I'm just saying that it's trash. Does that mean I'm promoting censorship? Absolutely not. I think one of the beauties of our country is freedom, but I think that you and I, as leaders, have the right and responsibility to know what references mean and the impact they can have on the quality of our lives.

EXPAND YOUR REFERENCES AND EXPAND YOUR LIFE

We can always use whatever life has to offer in an empowering way, but we have to do it proactively. The choices I have in my life come from a rich set of reference experiences that I have consciously pursued on an ongoing basis. Each day I look for ways to expand. Into my thirty-one years I've packed literally *hundreds* of years of experience. How can I say that? The number of challenging and enriching experiences that I have in a month relates more closely to what most people experience over a period of years.

One of the major ways I began to do this, starting at the age of seventeen, was through the rich experiences that books provide. Early in my life, I developed the belief that **leaders are readers**. Books could take me to other lands where I could meet unique people like Abraham Lincoln or Ralph Waldo Emerson whom I could utilize as my personal coaches. I also knew that within the pages of books I could find the answers to virtually any question I had. This breadth of references that hundreds of books have given me has provided countless choices for how I can assist people. I pursued these references because I realized that if I didn't feed my mind with the nourishment it craved, then I would have to settle for the intellectual junk food that could be found in the nightly "sound bites" on television news or through the opinions of the newspapers. If this is our major source of information, then we can expect to get the same results as everyone else in society does.

The most powerful way to have a great understanding of life and people, to give ourselves the greatest level of choice, is to expose ourselves to as many different types of references as possible. In my youth, I was inspired to seek spiritual understanding when I realized that I'd attended only one church and been exposed to only one religious philosophy for the majority of my life. In high school I received a scholarship in journalism to attend a two-week program held at California Polytechnic State University in San Luis Obispo. On that Sunday we were all given an assignment to write a story about a church service.

As we began to walk through the community, deciding where we would go, I found myself gravitating toward the church of my denomination. But along the way, I heard several of my friends talking about the Mormon Church we had just passed and how "horrible" those people were. It seemed to me that people just aren't that deplorable; I had to see what was going on. So I attended the service, and saw that the Mormons loved God as much as I did. The only difference was that they had a few rules that varied slightly from my own.

This started my spiritual odyssey, which developed into a personal ritual for almost a year and a half. Throughout my eighteenth and nineteenth years, two or three times a month, I would attend a totally different type of worship: Lutheran, Catholic, Baptist, Episcopalian, Methodist, Jewish, Buddhist, and so on. As a result of this, I truly began to live at a more spiritual level where I began to appreciate all people's spiritual beliefs. Even if I didn't subscribe to their particular rules or perceptions, I had a much broader base of understanding and compassion as a result.

If you want to expand your life, *go for it!* Pursue some experiences that you've never had before. Go scuba diving. Explore the undersea world, and find out what life's like and what *you're* like in a whole new environment. Go skydiving. When you're sitting on the edge of a plane 12,500 feet in the air, and you know you're going to fall for an entire minute at 120 miles an hour, to get yourself out of that plane requires absolute faith. You don't know what faith *is* until you have this reference! Go take that helicopter lesson. I assure you, it will change your life forever. Take four days and go to racing school. You'll learn more about limits and possibility than you could imagine. Go spend an evening at the symphony, if it's not something you usually do—or a rock concert, if that's what you habitually avoid. Expand your level of choice. One day, spontaneously, go by a children's hospital during visiting hours. Go meet some strangers and tell some stories. The challenge to develop rapport and find a way to touch others' lives will change you forever.

Maybe it's time to immerse yourself in another culture and see the world through others' eyes. Maybe it's time to visit Fiji and celebrate in a *kava* ceremony with the locals. Or take part in a "ride along" program at your local police department, where you sit in the back seat of a patrol car and see your community through an officer's eyes. Remember, if we want to understand and appreciate people, one of the most powerful ways is to share some of their references. Perhaps it's time to go back to school, to explore the "inner universe" in the form of biology or physiology, or understand our culture better through a study of sociology or anthropology. Remember, any limits that you have in your life are probably just the result of limited references. **Expand your references, and you'll immediately expand your life**.

While the possibilities I've touched on are exciting and inspiring, they are offered to get your juices flowing. You don't have to do all of them—or any of them—in order to gain new references. You don't have to go on safari in Africa; you can just go around the corner, and help a homeless person in your own community discover resources of their own that they never knew existed. Whole worlds open up with the addition of *just one new reference*. It could be one new thing you see or hear, a conversation or a movie or a seminar, something you read on the very next page—*you never know when it may happen*.

> *"The only way to discover the limits of the possible is to go beyond them into the impossible."*
> —ARTHUR C. CLARKE

Now let's take inventory of some of the most powerful references that have shaped your life. **Take a moment now and write down five of the most powerful experiences that have shaped who you've become as a person.** Give not only a description of the experience, but **how that experience impacted you**. If you write down anything that seems to have impacted you negatively, immediately come up with another interpretation of that event, *no matter what it takes*. This may require some faith; it may require a new perspective you never would have considered before. Remember, **everything in life happens for a reason and a purpose, and it serves us.** Sometimes it takes years or decades for us to find value. But there is value in *all* human experience.

As you review this list of all the events that have positively shaped your life, I want you to think about some new references that would be very valuable for you to pursue. What are some new experiences you need? A good question might be, **"In order to really succeed at the highest level, to achieve what I really want for my life, what are some references I need?"** Maybe what you need to do is model somebody who has really made their relationships work; find out what some of their beliefs are, what some of *their* references are about what makes a relationship work. Or maybe you just need to seek out references that make you appreciate life more or that make you feel like you are contributing.

   Now think of some *fun* references to have. Maybe you don't "need" them, but think of some that would be entertaining or would just make you feel good. I began to study martial arts because I knew what an incredible set of states the discipline would provide. I earned my black belt in *tae kwon do* in eight months by studying directly with the great Grandmaster Jhoon Rhee and modeling his incredibly intense focus. I realized that if I could have the experience of disciplining myself so fiercely in that area of my life, then that reference would spill over to many other areas—and it did. So, what else could *you* do?

   Once you've brainstormed a list of great references to acquire, put a time line and a date on each. Decide when you are going to do every one. When are you going to learn to speak Spanish or Greek or Japanese? When are you going to take that hot-air balloon ride? When are you going to go to the local old folks' home and sing carols? **When are you going to do something unusual and new?**

   What are some references you could provide for your family that would be invaluable? Maybe it is taking your kids to the Smithsonian, maybe it is something as simple as sitting down and talking about the references that the family has already shared, or getting together with some of the grandparents and talking about their lives and what they have learned. What invaluable references these sixty-, seventy-, eighty-, and ninety-plus year-olds have for those of us who are younger!

   One of the most powerful references I have shared with my family is delivering Thanksgiving dinners to those who cannot or will not visit shelters. I'll never forget my youngest son's reaction when he was four years old. It was Jairek's first time participating, and we went to a park in Oceanside, California. We found an old man who was sleeping on the floor of a bathroom with no doors, trying to cover himself with old clothes he had found in trash cans. My son marveled at his very long beard and was a little bit scared.

   I handed Jairek the basket of food and other survival goodies, and said, "Go on and give it to this man, and wish him a Happy Thanksgiving." Jairek approached cautiously. As he went into the bathroom with a basket that was as big as he was, he set it down gently. The man looked like he was either drunk or asleep. Jairek touched the man and said, "Happy Thanksgiving!" All of a sudden, the man bolted upright and grabbed my son's hand. My heart leaped into my throat, and just as I started to spring forward, the man took Jairek's hand and kissed it. He whispered hoarsely, "Thank you for caring." Boy, what a reference for a four-year-old!

Remember, it's the moments of our lives that shape us. It's up to us to pursue and create the moments that will lift us and not limit us.

So now, get off the bench and step into the game of life. Let your imagination run wild with the possibilities of all those things you could explore and experience—and begin immediately. What new experience could you pursue *today* that would expand your life? What kind of person will you become? Take action and enjoy exploring the possibilities. Let's discover the profound change that comes from . . .

18

IDENTITY:
THE KEY TO
EXPANSION

"Nothing great will ever be achieved without great men, and men are great only if they are determined to be so."
—CHARLES DE GAULLE

There were no marks on his body. The Chinese Communists had held him captive in a tiny room for more than twenty hours, but they hadn't beaten or tortured him. They had even offered him a cigarette or two . . . and as a result of their polite conversation, this GI now held a document *in his own handwriting* detailing the countless injustices and destructiveness of the American way of life—the capitalist society—and praising the superiority and ethical humanity of the Communist system. What's more, the essay this officer of the U.S. Army had written was now being broadcast to his and other POW camps in North Korea, as well as to the American forces stationed in South Korea.* He would later divulge military information, turn in his fellow prisoners, and fervently denounce his own country.

What caused this man to completely reverse his world-view and dismantle the beliefs that had been instilled in him over a lifetime? What caused him to abandon the core values he'd previously held and become a collaborator with the enemy? What single change would make such a radical shift in the thoughts, emotions, and actions of an individual?

The answer lies in understanding that he was directed down a path that caused him to literally **shift his identity**. He was now simply acting in accordance with his new image of himself.

Throughout this book you've explored with me the impact of beliefs, one of the foundational elements in the Master System that directs all of our evaluations. Beliefs guide us to conclusions, and therefore they teach

---

* Cialdini, Robert, *Influence*, New York: HarperCollins Publishers, © 1988.

us how to feel and what to do. However, there are different levels of beliefs that have different levels of impact on the quality of our lives. Some are very specific. For example, the beliefs you have about a particular friend will determine how you think and feel about his behavior, and the meaning that you'll link to anything that he does. If you "know" that he is loving, then even if he appears to be angry at the moment, you will not question his ultimate intent. This belief will guide all of your interactions with this person. But this will not necessarily affect the way you deal with a stranger. These beliefs impact you in only one specific area of your life: your interactions with this friend.

Some beliefs, however, have an expanded influence on your life; I call these **global beliefs.** These are the beliefs which have much further-reaching consequences. For example, the beliefs you have about *people in general* will affect not just the way you deal with your friend, but with everyone you meet. These beliefs will powerfully impact your career, your level of trust, your marriage, and so forth.

The global beliefs you have about the concepts of *scarcity and abundance,* for example, will determine your stress level and your generosity of time, money, energy, and spirit. If you believe we live in a world with scarce resources—where there's only so much money, so much time, so much love—then you'll constantly live in fear that you won't have enough. This stress will affect the way you think of your neighbors, your co-workers, your financial capabilities, and opportunities in general.

More powerful than any of these, though, is the core belief that is the ultimate filter to all of our perceptions. This belief directly controls the consistency of your life's decisions. These are the beliefs you have about your **identity**.

What we can or cannot do, what we consider possible or impossible, is rarely a function of our true capability. It is more likely a function of our beliefs about **who we are.** In fact, if you've ever found yourself unable to even *consider* doing something, where your response to someone is, "I could never do that" or "I'm just not that kind of person," then you've run up against the barriers of a limited identity. This isn't always bad, of course. Not perceiving yourself as a murderer is a very important distinction! Not perceiving yourself as someone who would take advantage of others is probably very useful. It's important to realize that we define ourselves not only by who we are, but by who we are not.

What exactly is identity? It is simply **the beliefs that we use to define our own individuality, what makes us unique—good, bad, or indifferent—from other individuals.** And our *sense of certainty* about who we are creates the boundaries and limits within which we live.

Your capability is constant, but how much of it you use depends upon the identity you have for yourself. For example, if you feel certain that you are an outgoing, outrageous person, you'll tap the resources of behavior that match your identity. Whether you see yourself as a "wimp" or a "wild man," a "winner" or a "wallflower," will instantly shape which capabilities you access. You may have read the book *Pygmalion in the Classroom,* which details the dramatic change in students' performance when they become convinced that they are gifted.

Time and again, researchers have shown that students' capabilities are powerfully impacted by the identities they develop for themselves as the result of teachers' belief in their level of intelligence. In one study, a group of teachers were told that certain students in their classes were truly gifted and to make sure that they challenged them to continue to expand. As can be expected, these children became the top achievers in their class. What makes this study significant is that these students had not actually demonstrated higher levels of intelligence—and, in fact, some had previously been labeled poor students. Yet it was their sense of certainty that they were superior (which had been instilled by a teacher's "false belief") that triggered their success.

The impact of this principle is not limited to students. **The kind of person other people perceive you to be controls their responses to you.** Often this has nothing to do with your true character. For example, if a person sees you as a crook, even if you're an honest person and do good things, this person will search for the sinister motive behind your acts. What's worse is that, after making a positive change, we often allow others in our environment who have not changed their image of us to anchor our own emotions and beliefs back into our old behaviors and identities. We all need to remember that we have tremendous power to influence the identities of those we care about most.

This is the power that Marva Collins commands when she influences her students to believe that they are the masters of their destinies, that they are as talented as any human being who has walked on earth.

> *"The best effect of fine persons is felt after we have left their presence."*
> —RALPH WALDO EMERSON

We all will act consistently with our views of who we truly are, whether that view is accurate or not. The reason is that **one of the strongest forces in the human organism is the need for consistency.**

Throughout our lives, we've been socialized to link massive pain to inconsistency and pleasure to being consistent. Think about it. What labels do we attach to people who say one thing and then do another, who claim to be one way and then behave another? We call them hypocritical, fickle, unstable, unreliable, wishy-washy, scatterbrained, flaky, untrustworthy. Would *you* like to have these labels attached to you? Would you even like to *think* of yourself in this way? The answer is obvious: a resounding no! As a result, whenever we take a stand—especially a public stand—and state what we believe, who we are, or what we're about, we experience intense pressure to remain consistent with that stand, regardless of what that inflexibility may cost us in the future.

Conversely, there are tremendous rewards for remaining consistent with our stated identities. What do we call people who are consistent? We use words like trustworthy, loyal, steady, solid, intelligent, stable, rational, true-blue. How would you like to have people consistently use these labels to describe you? How would it feel to think of yourself in this way? Again, the answer is obvious: most people would love it. Thus, the need to remain consistent becomes irrevocably tied to your ability to avoid pain and gain pleasure.

> *"A foolish consistency is the hobgoblin*
> *of small minds."*
> —RALPH WALDO EMERSON

The Pygmalion effect also works in reverse. If you feel certain that you are "learning-disabled," it becomes a self-fulfilling prophecy. This is quite different from believing that your current strategy for learning is ineffective. The ability to change one's strategy is perceived by most of us to be a simple and achievable task, as long as we have the right teacher. However, changing *ourselves*—changing the essence of who we are—is perceived by most to be next to impossible. The common response, "I'm just this way," is a phrase that murders dreams. It carries with it the sentence of an unchangeable and permanent problem.

A person who believes they have *developed a drug addiction* can clearly change. It will be difficult, but a change can be made, and it can last. Conversely, a person who believes himself to *be a drug addict* will usually return to the use of drugs even after weeks or months of abstinence. Why? It's because he believes that this is *who he is.* He doesn't have a drug addiction; he *is* a drug addict. Remember from Chapter 4 that once a person has a conviction about anything, he will ignore and even defend against any evidence that's contrary to his belief. Unconsciously, this person will not believe that he can change long-term, and this will control his behavior.

In addition, there's often a secondary gain involved in the process of maintaining this negative behavior. After all, this man can blame his addiction on something he can't control—it's simply "who he is"—instead of facing the reality that taking drugs is a conscious decision. This will be augmented by the need within the human nervous system for consistency, and he will return to this destructive pattern again and again. Surrendering his identity would be even more painful than the clearly destructive effects of the drugs themselves.

Why? Because **we all have a need for a sense of certainty. Most people have tremendous fear of the unknown. Uncertainty implies the potential of having pain strike us,** and we'd rather deal with the pain we already know about than deal with the pain of the unknown. Thus, living in an ever-changing world—one in which we are constantly surrounded by the flux of new relationships, redefined job roles, changing environments, and a steady stream of new information—the one thing that we all count on to be constant is our sense of identity. If we begin to question who we are, then there is no foundation for all of the understandings upon which we've built our lives.

If you don't know who you are, then how can you decide what to do? How can you formulate values, adopt beliefs, or establish rules? How can you judge whether something is good, bad, or indifferent? The biggest challenge for someone who perceives his identity as a drug addict is: what does he change his identity to? To a "recovering drug addict"? This doesn't change his identity; it merely describes the state he's in currently. "Drug-free" doesn't do it either, because most see it as a temporary state—and it still focuses on drugs as one of the ways of defining oneself. When this person develops the conviction that he is absolutely clean, that he's now a "Christian," "Muslim," "Jew," or "Buddhist," or now that he's a "leader"—or anything else other than a "drug addict"—*that's when his behavior changes.* **As we develop new beliefs about who we are, our behavior will change to support the new identity.**

The same thing happens with a person who has excess weight whose identity is, "I'm a fat person." This individual may diet and lose weight in the short term, but he will always gain it back because his sense of certainty about who he is will guide all his behaviors until they are once again consistent with his identity. We all must maintain the integrity of our convictions of who we are, even when they are destructive and disempowering.

The only way to create lasting change for an individual who's been using drugs is to change his conviction from "I am a drug addict" to "I'm a health nut" or "I'm a living example that no problem is permanent" or "Now I'm _____." Whatever the new identity, it must be one that would never even consider the use of drugs. If drugs are offered again, his immediate response is not to evaluate whether he should use them or not, but to simply state with absolute certainty, "I'm not that kind of person. That's who I *used* to be."

Those with excess weight must transform their identity from a fat person to a vital, healthy, and athletic human being. This identity change will shift all their behaviors, from their diet to their exercise, and allow them to create the long-term physiological changes that are consistent with their new identity. This shift may sound like it's merely a semantic manipulation, but in truth it is a much deeper and more *profound* transformation of personal reality.

In fact, **one shift in identity can cause a shift of your entire Master System**. Think about it. Doesn't a drug addict have a completely different system of evaluation—the **states** he consistently experiences, the **questions** he asks, the **values** that guide his actions, and the **references** he organizes into **beliefs**—than does someone who considers himself to be a leader, a lover, an athlete, or a contributor? While it's true that not all identity shifts are as complete as others, some are indeed so far reaching that one Master System is literally replaced in a moment by another.

If you've repeatedly attempted to make a particular change in your life, only to continually fall short, invariably the challenge is that you were trying to create a behavioral or emotional shift that was inconsistent with your belief about who you are. Shifting, changing, or expanding *identity* can produce the most profound and rapid improvements in the quality of your life.

HOW YOUR IDENTITY IS FORMED

Why is it that during the Korean War more American POWs informed on their fellow prisoners than in any other war in modern history? The answer is that the Chinese Communists, unlike their allies, the North Koreans, understood **the power of identity to instantaneously change not only their long-held beliefs and values, but their actions, in an instant.** Rather than brutalize the prisoners, they doggedly pursued their own ingenious form of psychological warfare designed not merely to extract information or create compliance, but rather to convert the American fighting man to their political philosophy. They knew that if they could lead him into a new set of beliefs and values, then he would see his country's role in the war as futile and destructive, and therefore assist them in any way they requested. And they succeeded. Understanding what they did can help you understand how you've arrived at your current identity and how you can expand your identity, and therefore your entire life, in a matter of moments.

The task before the Chinese Communists was formidable indeed. How can you change someone's entire identity without the threat of death or the promise of freedom? Especially knowing that the American soldier has been trained to give only his name, rank, and serial number? Their plan was very simple: start small, and build. The Chinese understood that **the way we identify anyone is by their actions.** For example, how do you know who your friend really is? Isn't it by the way he or she acts, the way he or she treats people?

The Communists' real secret, though, was that they understood that we determine who we are—our own identities—by judging our own actions as well. **In other words, we look at what we do to determine who we are.** The Chinese realized that in order to achieve their broader objective of changing the prisoner's beliefs about his identity, all they had to do was get the prisoner to do things that a collaborator or a Communist would do.

Again, this is not a simple task, but they realized it could be done if they simply could wear the American POW down through conversation that lasted twelve to twenty hours, and then make a minor request: get him to say something like "The United States is not perfect" or "It's true in a Communist country that unemployment is not a problem." Having established this footing, the Chinese would simply start small and build. They understood our need for consistency. Once we make a statement that we say we believe, we have to be willing to back it up.

They would merely ask the POW to write down some of the ways in which America is not perfect. In his exhausted state, the GI was then asked, "What other social benefits are there to communism?" Within a short period of time, the GI would have sitting in front of him a document not only attacking his own nation, but also promoting Communism with all the reasons written in his own handwriting. He now had to justify to himself why he'd done this. He'd not been beaten, nor had he been offered special rewards. He'd simply made small statements in his need to stay consistent with the ones he'd already written, and now he'd even signed the document. How could he explain his "willingness" to do this? Later he would be asked to read his list in a discussion group with other prisoners or even to write an entire essay about it.

When the Chinese broadcast these essays, along with the names of the prisoners who had written them, suddenly the prisoner would find himself publicly identified as an enemy "collaborator." When fellow prisoners asked him why he did it, he couldn't defend himself by saying he'd been tortured. He had to justify his acts to himself in order to maintain his own sense of integrity. *In an instant, he would state that he wrote it because it was true! In that moment, his identity shifted.* He now perceived himself as pro-Communist, and all those around him also labeled him as such. They would reinforce his new identity by treating him the same way they treated the Communist guards.

Soon his new identity would cause him to openly denounce his country and, in order to maintain consistency between his statements and his new label, he would often collaborate even more extensively with his captors. This was one of the most brilliant facets of the Chinese strategy: once a prisoner had written something down, he couldn't later pretend to himself that it had never happened. There it was in black and white, in his own handwriting, for anyone to see—something which drove him "to make his beliefs and his self-image consistent with what he had undeniably done."*

Before we judge our POWs harshly, however, we should take a good look at ourselves. Did you consciously choose *your* identity, or is it the result of what other people have told you, significant events in your life, and other factors that occurred without your awareness or approval? What consistent behaviors have you adopted that now help to form the basis of your identity?

Would you be willing to undergo a painful bone-marrow extraction to help a stranger? Most people's first response would be, "Absolutely not!" Yet in a study done in 1970, researchers found that if a person was led to believe that the consistency of their identity relied upon it, many would commit to just such a selfless act.

The study showed that when the subjects were asked to make small commitments first, and followed up with two simple acts which made not volunteering seem "out of character," many began to develop a new identity. They began to see themselves as "donors," as a person who unconditionally commits to help those in need through personal sacrifice. Once this occurred, when the request for the bone marrow was made, these people felt compelled by the force of their new identity to follow through regardless of the time, money, or physical pain involved. **Their view of themselves as donors became a reflection of who they were. There is no more potent leverage in shaping human behavior than identity.**

You might ask, **"Isn't my identity limited by my experience?" No, it's limited by *your interpretation* of your experience. Your identity is nothing but the decisions you've made about who you are, what you've decided to *fuse* yourself with. You become the labels you've given yourself. The way you define your identity defines your life.**

* Cialdini, *Influence*.

THE ULTIMATE PAIN—SEEDS OF AN IDENTITY CRISIS

People who act inconsistently with who they believe they are set the stage for the societal cliché of an "identity crisis." When the crisis hits, they are immediately disoriented, questioning their previous convictions. Their whole world is turned upside down, and they experience an intense fear of pain. This is what happens to so many people having a "midlife crisis." Often these people identify themselves as being young, and some environmental stimulant—turning a certain age, comments from friends, graying hair—causes them to dread their approaching years and the new, less desirable identity that they expect to experience with it. Thus, in a desperate effort to maintain their identity, they do things to prove they're still young: buy fast cars, change their hairstyles, divorce their spouses, change jobs.

If these people had a solid grasp of their true identities, would they experience this crisis at all? I suspect not. Having an identity that is specifically linked to your age or how you look would definitely set you up for pain because these things *will* change. If we have a broader sense of who we are, our identity never becomes threatened.

Even businesses can have identity crises. Years ago, photocopying giant Xerox Corporation underwent an interesting shift in its image. When personal computing emerged as "the wave of the future," Xerox wanted to use their technological power to enter this exciting new market. They put their research and development staff on it and, after spending approximately $2 billion, they came up with a number of innovative advances, including the precursor to what we now call a "mouse."

Why, then, isn't Xerox in the competitive computer race, running neck and neck with Apple and IBM? One reason surely is that in the beginning, its identity didn't really allow for the company to head in this direction. Even its "graphic" identity, which used a roly-poly monk, confined its capacity to be identified as the epitome of cutting-edge computing technology. While the monk symbolized the exacting nature of manuscript copying, he was hardly appropriate for this new venture into high technology, where speed was one of the most highly valued criteria. On the consumer side, the identity Xerox had established as the world's leading copier company did not instill a high confidence in the company's efforts to market computers. Compound this with a graphic identity that had little to do with how to process information rapidly, and you begin to see where some of Xerox's problems originated.

Marketing and graphic-design experts alike will tell you that corporate image is a huge filter through which consumers process buying information—they must know who you are, what you stand for, and when they're investing large sums of money, they usually want to buy from a company that exemplifies their product. As Xerox grappled with incorporating this facet of computerization into its existing identity, other companies zoomed to the forefront, overtaking the marketplace. At this point, Xerox decided that, rather than try to change its identity, it would utilize it. It would *computerize its photocopiers* and concentrate its R & D dollars on improving what it already knew how to do best.

Today, Xerox is beginning the process of transformation by producing new "Xerox images"—airing commercials featuring fast-paced imagery of plotters, hardware, software, communication networks—and completing the visual message with the words, "Xerox . . . the Document Company." This expanded identity must be conditioned within the culture for Xerox to expand its market, and it is using every opportunity to do so.

> *"When written in Chinese, the word 'crisis' is composed of two characters—one represents danger, and the other represents opportunity."*
> —JOHN F. KENNEDY

It doesn't take a crisis for most of us to understand that we can change our behavior, but the prospect of changing our identity seems threatening or impossible to most. Breaking away from our core beliefs about who we are gives us the most intense pain, and some people would even go so far as to kill themselves to preserve those beliefs. This was dramatically illustrated in Victor Hugo's masterpiece *Les Misérables*. When the hero Jean Valjean is released from his prison work crew, he is frustrated and alone. Although in the many years he's spent in the custody of the French police he has never accepted his label of "criminal" (he'd merely stolen a loaf of bread to feed his starving family and was sentenced to many years of hard labor), once released, he discovers that he can't get an honest day's work. He is scorned and rebuffed because of his status as an ex-convict.

Finally, in a state of helplessness, he begins to accept the identity that his societal label has imposed. He now *is* a criminal and begins to act as such. In fact, when a kind priest takes him in, feeds him, and gives him shelter for the night, he fulfills his criminal identity by stealing his benefactor's humble silver setting. When the police stop Valjean on a routine check, they discover not only that he is an ex-convict, but also that he is carrying the priest's most valuable possessions—a crime punishable by a life of hard labor.

Valjean is brought back to face the priest, and upon presentation of the facts, the priest insists that the silver was a gift and reminds Valjean that he's forgotten the two remaining silver candlesticks. To Valjean's further surprise, the priest subsequently makes his generous falsehood a truth and sends him away with the silver to start a new life.

Valjean has to deal with the priest's actions. Why would he believe in him? Why didn't he send him away in chains? The priest told him that he was his brother, that Valjean no longer belonged to evil, that he was an honest man and a child of God. This massive pattern interrupt changes Valjean's identity. He tears up his prison papers, moves to another city, and assumes a new identity. As he does, all of his behaviors change. He becomes a leader and helps those in his community.

However, a policemen, Monsieur Javert, makes it his life's crusade to find Valjean and bring him to justice. He "knows" Valjean is evil and defines himself as one who brings evil to justice. When Javert finally catches up with him, Valjean has the opportunity to eliminate his nemesis—but he magnanimously spares his life. After a lifetime of pursuit, Javert discovers that Valjean is a good man—perhaps a better man than he—and he cannot deal with the potential of realizing that maybe he was the one who was cruel and evil. As a result, he throws himself into the rapids of the river Seine.

"His supreme agony was the disappearance of certainty, and he felt himself uprooted . . . Oh! what a frightful thing! The man projectile, no longer knowing his road, and recoiling!"
—VICTOR HUGO, *LES MISÉRABLES*

WHO ARE YOU, ANYWAY?

What does all of this really mean? This can all seem very esoteric unless we start to actually define ourselves. **So take a moment to identify who you are. Who are you?** There are so many ways in which we define ourselves. We may describe ourselves as our emotions (I'm a lover, I'm peaceful, I'm intense), our professions (I'm an attorney, I'm a doctor, I'm a priest), our titles (I'm Executive Vice-President), our incomes (I'm a millionaire), our roles (I'm a mother, I'm the eldest of five girls), our behaviors (I'm a gambler), our possessions (I'm a "Beemer" owner), our metaphors (I'm king of the hill, I'm low man on the totem pole), our feedback (I'm worthless, I'm special), our spiritual beliefs (I'm Jewish), our looks (I'm beautiful, I'm ugly, I'm old), our accomplishments (I'm the 1960

Spring Valley High Homecoming Queen), our past (I'm a failure), and even what we're not (I'm not a quitter).

The identity that our friends and peers have tends to affect us as well. Take a good look at your friends. Who you believe they are is often a reflection of who you believe *you* are. If your friends are very loving and sensitive, there's a great chance that you see yourself in a similar vein. The time frame you use to define your identity is very powerful as well. Do you look to your past, your present, or the future to define who you truly are? Years ago my present and past weren't terribly exciting, so I consciously fused my identity with the vision I had of who I knew I would become. I didn't have to wait; I began to live as this man *now*.

It's very important, when you are answering this question, to be in the right state. You need to feel relaxed, safe, and curious. If you're just powering through this book, scanning and reading rapidly, or if you have many distractions, you're not going to get the answers you need.

Take a nice, deep breath in; relax the breath out. Let your mind be curious—not fearful, not concerned, not looking for perfection or for anything in particular. Just ask yourself, *"Who am I?"* Write down the answer, and then ask it again. Each time you ask it, write down whatever surfaces, and keep probing deeper and deeper. Continue to ask until you find the description of yourself that you have the strongest conviction about. How do you define yourself? What is the essence of who you are? What metaphors do you use to describe yourself? What roles do you play?

Often, if you don't create this safe and curious state, all of the fears and hesitations about identity will keep giving you inadequate answers. In fact, often if you just ask this question up front of somebody, blurting out, *"Who are you?"* without putting them in the right state, you'll get one of two responses:

1) A blank stare. This type of question throws many people into a tailspin because they have never been called upon to seriously ponder what their answer is.

2) A surface-level answer. This is a first-attempt evasion technique. This response can be defined as the "Popeye Principle," where a person will simply insist, "I am what I am, and that's all that I am." Often, what I find is that when you ask someone a question, especially an emotional one, they won't answer you until they've answered two questions of their own.

First they ask themselves, "Can I answer this question?" If a person's not sure who he is, often he'll say, "I don't know" or give you the first surface answer. Sometimes people are afraid to ask the question for fear of realizing that they lack clarity in this critical area of their lives. And the second question they ask themselves before answering is: "What's in it for me? If I answer this question, how will this benefit me personally?"

Let me offer you the answer to these two questions. First, you *do* know who you are. Yes, you can come up with the answer if you take a moment to brainstorm a bit right now. But you've got to trust yourself to let whatever answers come out of you just flow, and write them down. Second, the benefit to knowing who you are is the ability to instantaneously shape all of your behaviors.

If you take the time to get in the right state, you'll come up with . . .

A thoughtful answer. I hope this is the kind of answer you're searching for right now!

> ### *"I think, therefore I am."*
> —RENÉ DESCARTES

So take a moment right now to answer a question pondered by philosophers through the ages, from Socrates to Sartre. Put yourself in that safe, curious state. Take a deep breath and release it. Ask, *"Who am I?"*

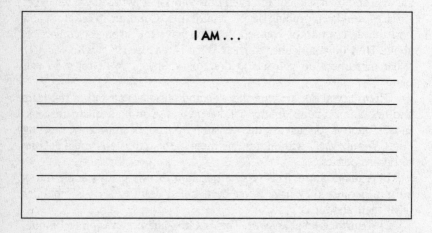

To assist you in defining yourself, remember that identity is simply what distinguishes you from everyone else. Here are a couple of exercises I think you will enjoy.

1) If you were to look in the dictionary under your name, what would it say? Would three words just about cover it, or would your epic narrative consume page after page, or demand a volume of its own? Right now, write down the definition you would find if you were to look up your name in a dictionary.

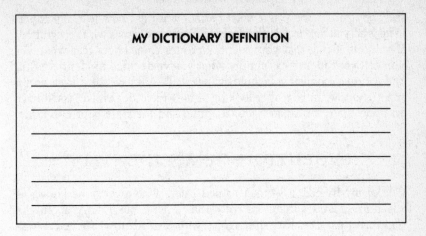

MY DICTIONARY DEFINITION

Take a moment, and let your answers sink in. When you're ready, move to the next exercise.

2) If you were to create an ID card that would represent who you *truly* are, what would be on it—and what would you leave off? Would it include a picture or not? Would you list your vital statistics? Your physical description? Your accomplishments? Your emotions? Your beliefs? Your affiliations? Your aspirations? Your motto? Your abilities? Take a moment to describe what would be on this identity card and what would be left off in order to show someone who you *really* are.

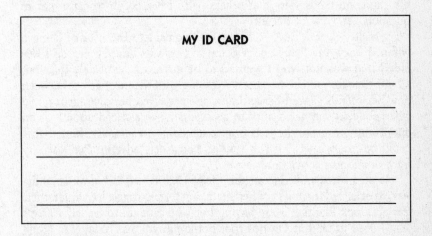

MY ID CARD

Now, take a look at what you've written down, at the descriptions you have of your identity—in essence, the story of your life. How do you feel about it? I hope you're taking a moment right now to really appreciate who you are, to feel the deep emotion that comes with recognition. If you're noticing that your identity creates pain, know that **whatever you call your identity is simply what you've decided to identify with**, and that in a moment you could change it all. You have the power within you right now. In fact, after looking at how identities evolve, you'll have an opportunity to expand your identity, and therefore your entire life.

EVOLUTION OF AN IDENTITY

One of my friends, a woman named Debra whom everyone knows as adventurous and vibrant, recently shared with me a story about the transformation she had undergone with her identity. "When I was growing up," she said, "I was always a *wimp*. I wouldn't do anything physical, or anything that had any potential of my getting hurt." After attending some of my seminars and having new experiences (scuba diving, firewalking, and skydiving), she began to see that she *could* do these things—if she *forced* herself. But these references were not yet organized into a new belief about who she is. She now merely saw herself as "a wimp who'd skydived." The transformation had not yet taken place, but unbeknownst to her, it had been *set in motion*. She reports that other people were envious of her accomplishments, saying things like, "I wish I had the guts to do what you did. You're so adventurous!" She was genuinely taken by surprise by their comments, but the continuous view that others had of her began to cause her to question her view of herself.

"Finally," Debra said, "I began to link pain to the idea of being a wimp. I knew my belief about being wimpy was limiting me, so **I decided that was not who I wanted to be anymore**." Not only that, but all this time her psyche had been wrestling with the incongruity between how her friends viewed her and how she perceived her own identity. So when she had another chance to go skydiving, she seized upon it as an opportunity to make the leap from potentiality to actuality, from "what could be" to "what is." It was time to boost her "adventurous" identity from opinion to conviction.

As the plane climbed to an altitude of 12,500 feet, Debra watched the less experienced members of her skydiving team struggle to contain their fear and look like they were having fun. She thought to herself, "That's who I used to be, but **I'm not that person anymore**. Today, I'm going to have fun!" She used their apprehension as contrast with the new person she had decided to become. She thought to herself, "That's how

I *used* to respond"—and was startled to realize that she had just made a major shift. She was no longer a wimp, but an adventurous, powerful woman about to have the time of her life.

She was the first jumper to leave the plane, and all the way down she whooped with delight, joy, and exhilaration. She had never before felt such intense levels of pure physical energy and excitement. One key element that may have pushed her over the edge in instantly adopting her new identity was her deep level of commitment to setting an example for the other jumpers in her role as team leader. She told me, "It's like what you do, Tony. If you did a whole seminar about breaking through fear and limitation, but refused to do the Firewalk, it just wouldn't work. You have to *walk your talk.*"

Debra's transformation was complete. She gained new references that started to chip away at her old identity, made a decision to identify with greater possibilities, and when the right moment came, contrasted her new identity with what she no longer wanted to be. This was the final leverage she needed to bring about the transformation. Her evolution was simple yet powerful. This complete identity change now impacts her kids, her business, and everything else she's involved in. Today, she's truly an adventurous leader.

Of course, you can always *decide* to redefine yourself. Think of the wondrous imagination that suffuses the heart and soul of every child. One day he's Zorro, the masked avenger. The next he's Hercules, the Olympian hero. And today, he's Grandpa, his own real-life hero. Identity shifts can be among the most joyous, magical and liberating experiences of life. Why do adults look forward all year to Halloween or New Orleans's Mardi Gras? One reason, I'm sure, is that these celebrations give us *permission* to step outside ourselves and assume an alter ego. We may do things in these new identities that we wouldn't normally do; we may do things we *want* to do all the time but see as inconsistent with our identities.

The reality is that we could do this any day of the year! We could completely redefine ourselves, or we could simply decide to let our "real selves" shine through. Like mild-mannered Clark Kent shedding his spectacles and business suit to reveal the mighty Superman, we may uncover a giant identity that is more than our behaviors, more than our past, more than any label we've been giving ourselves.

THE POWER TO REINVENT YOURSELF

Now, let's expand!

If your identity isn't everything you want it to be, then make it that way. Start by taking the following four steps to reinvent yourself.

1. **Make a list right now of all the elements of your identity you want to have.** As you make the list, revel in the power you have right now to change simply by *deciding to*. Who are some people who have these characteristics you aspire to having? Can they serve as role models? Imagine yourself *fusing* with this new identity. Imagine how you'd breathe. How would you walk? How would you talk? How would you think? How would you feel?

---

2. **If you'd truly like to expand your identity and your life, then, right now, consciously decide who you want to be. Get excited, be like a kid again, and describe in detail who you've decided**

you are today. Take a moment now to write down your expanded list.

---

3. **Now develop a plan of action you could take that would cause you to know that you're truly living consistently with your new identity.** In developing this plan, pay special attention to the friends you're choosing to spend time with. Will they reinforce or destroy the identity you're creating?

There's nothing quite as pleasurable as seeing someone expand their identity. One of the greatest joys I've experienced in recent years was watching the transformation of my eldest son, Tyler, as he went from a neophyte interested in flying helicopters with me, to a master jet pilot, to a commercial helicopter pilot.

What a change in self-esteem as he began to realize that he'd become one of the few who do versus the many who talk—that he had mastered the skies and created for himself the unlimited freedom that few would ever hope to experience!

4. **The final step is to commit to your new identity by broadcasting it to everyone around you.** The most important broadcast, however, is to yourself. Use your new label to describe yourself every single day, and it will become conditioned within you.

THE FUTURE OF YOUR IDENTITY

Even after completing this exercise, you'll want to continue to refine your identity, expand it, or create better rules for it. We live in a dynamic world where our identities must continually expand in order to enjoy a greater quality of life. You need to become aware of things that may influence your identity, notice whether they are empowering or disempowering you, and take control of the whole process. Otherwise you become a prisoner of your own past. I'm curious: **Are you now the same person you were when you picked up this book?**

I am continually redefining myself, and people often wonder at my level of confidence in pursuing new ventures. I'm often asked, "How have you accomplished so much in your life?" I think that a big part of it is that I look at things in a different way than most: **while most people have to establish competence before they feel confident, I decide to feel confident, and that provides the sense of certainty to persist until I *am* competent.** That's why my identity is not limited by my past references.

If you were to ask me who I am today (and I might decide to change tomorrow!), I would say that I am a creator of possibility, an instigator of joy, a catalyst for growth, a builder of people, and a producer of passion. I am *not* a motivator, a preacher, or a guru. I *am* one of the nation's experts in the psychology of change. I *am* a coach, an entrepreneur, a husband, a father, a lover, a friend, an entertainer, a television personality, a nationally best-selling author, one of the most impactful speakers in the nation, a black belt, a jet helicopter pilot, an international businessman, a health expert, an advocate for the homeless, a philanthropist, a teacher, a person who makes a difference, a force for good, a healer, a challenger . . . and a fun, outrageous, and *humble* kind o' guy! I identify with the highest elements of my self, and I view those facets of me that are not yet perfect as an opportunity for growth rather than as character flaws.

You and I need to expand our view of who we are. We need to make certain that the labels we put upon ourselves are not limits but enhancements, that we add to all that's already good within us—for whatever you and I begin to identify with, we will become. This is the power of belief.

> *"If we all did the things we are capable of doing, we would literally astound ourselves."*
> —THOMAS A. EDISON

Because of my commitment to constantly expand my capacity to appreciate all aspects of life, I'm always pursuing unique references. Years ago, I decided to visit the Bellevue morgue, and I experienced a major life transformation. I went there because my friend, Dr. Fred Covan, who is Chief Psychologist of Bellevue Hospital in New York, convinced me that in order to understand life you've got to understand death. Becky and I arrived at his office with a great deal of apprehension. Fred sat us down and cautioned us not to say a word during the experience. "Just let it happen," he said. "Notice what feelings come up, and then we'll talk about it later."

Not knowing what to expect, we nervously followed the doctor as he descended the stairs. He led us to the section for unclaimed bodies, where most of the remains were from the indigent street population. As he pulled out the first metal drawer and unzipped the body bag, I felt a shudder ripple through my body. Here was this "person" there with me, yet I was instantly struck by the feeling of emptiness. Becky was shaken when she thought she saw the body move. Fred later pointed out that Becky's experience was common, that we all have a difficult time dealing with bodies that don't move, that are devoid of the pulse of life.

As he opened each successive drawer, the emotion hit me again and again: there's no one here. The body is here, but there is no *person*. Moments after death, these people weighed the same amount as they did when they were alive, but whatever they were—the essence of who they truly were—was no longer there. **We are not our bodies.** When we pass on, there's no question that what's missing is the intangible, weightless identity, that essence of life some call spirit. I believe that it's equally important for us to remember that while *we're* alive, we're not our bodies. **Neither are we our past, nor our behaviors in the moment.**

This experience gave me an incredible sense of gratitude for the blessed gift of life. Suddenly I looked at people who had major physical challenges and thought, "Boy, do they look healthy." There's nothing like a little contrast to remind us of how fortunate we all are!

Recently, my feelings were put into words when I had the opportunity to visit with author Wayne Dyer. He said something that day that typifies my feelings. He told me, "We are not human beings having a spiritual experience. *We are spiritual beings having a human experience.*" Our identity is the cornerstone of that experience. **I believe that our *true* identity is something that's indefinable and greater than anything that's describable.** We are soul; we are spirit. Remembering who we really are puts everything into perspective, doesn't it? Once we act with the knowledge that we're spiritual beings, we won't get caught up in all the little games that separate us from one another. We'll know with deep conviction that we are truly connected with all of creation.

> *"Each of us inevitable;*
> *Each of us limitless—each of us with his or her*
> *right upon the earth;*
> *Each of us allow'd the eternal purports of the earth;*
> *Each of us here as divinely as any is here."*
> —WALT WHITMAN

The next time you catch yourself saying, "I could never do that," or "That's just not me," take a moment to consider the impact of what you're saying. Have you limited your concept of self? If so, take advantage of every opportunity to expand your identity. Get yourself to do those things you don't think you can do, and use your new actions as a reference that gives you a sense of certainty that you're more than you thought.

Begin to ask yourself, "What more *can* I be? What more *will* I be? Who am I becoming *now*?" Think about your values and dream list, and commit to yourself that, regardless of the environment, "I *will* consistently act as a person who is already achieving these goals. I will breathe this way. I will move this way. I will respond to people this way. I will treat people with the kind of dignity, respect, compassion, and love that this person would." If we decide to think, feel, and act as the kind of person we want to be, we will become that person. We won't just be behaving "like" that person; we will *be* that person.

You are now at a crossroads. This is your opportunity to make the most important decision you will ever make. **Forget your past. Who are you now?** Who have you decided you really are now? Don't think about who you *have* been. Who are you *now*? Who have you decided to *become*? Make this decision consciously. Make it carefully. Make it powerfully.

As we now leave our study of the Master System, just remember this: you don't have to make all of the changes we've talked about here in order to transform the quality of your life. If you change any *one* of the five areas of the system, your whole life will change. A change in your habitual **questions** alone will change your focus and change your life. Making shifts in your **values** hierarchies will immediately change the direction of your life. Cultivating powerful, resourceful **states** in your physiology will change the way you think and the way you feel. This alone could change your identity. So could changing some of your **global**

beliefs. Pursuing additional **references** will provide the raw materials for assembling a new experience of who you are. And certainly, **deciding to expand your identity** could transform virtually everything.

I know that you'll want to return to these pages again and again throughout your life as you begin to reinvent yourself and define who you truly want to be now versus who you've been in the past. Be playful! Have fun! Discover the adventure that comes with an ever-expanding sense that who you are is something more each and every day that you're alive.

Now let's have some fun by beginning a seven-day challenge where each day I'll give you a brief exercise to use what you've been learning and give you an opportunity to start reaping the rewards of some of the strategies and tools to which you've been exposed. Let's begin with . . .

PART • THREE

THE SEVEN DAYS TO SHAPE YOUR LIFE

19
EMOTIONAL DESTINY: THE ONLY TRUE SUCCESS

DAY ONE

Your Outcome: *Take control of your consistent emotions and begin to consciously and deliberately reshape your daily experience of life.*

There is no true success without emotional success, yet, of the more than 3,000 emotions that we have words to describe, the average person experiences only about a dozen different ones in the course of an average week. We must remember that this does not reflect our emotional capacity, but rather the limitations of our present patterns of focus and physiology.

Throughout this book, we've continually studied the mastery of emotion, and you've developed a broad spectrum of tools to powerfully and rapidly change any emotion you desire. You now realize that changing how you feel is the motivation behind virtually all of your behaviors. Thus, it's time that you develop a proactive plan for dealing with the negative emotional patterns that you habitually experience. It's equally important to give yourself the gift of expanding the amount and quality of time that you spend in positive emotional states. The arsenal of skills you have for changing your emotional states includes:

- ▶ physiology
- ▶ focus
- ▶ questions
- ▶ submodalities
- ▶ Transformational Vocabulary
- ▶ metaphors
- ▶ Neuro-Associative Conditioning

- ▶ beliefs
- ▶ compelling future
- ▶ values
- ▶ rules
- ▶ references
- ▶ identity

The purpose of today's exercise is simply to make you aware of your present emotional patterns and get you to utilize as many of the above-listed skills as necessary to guarantee that you shape your own emotional destiny daily.

> *"Seeing's believing, but feeling's the truth."*
> —THOMAS FULLER, M.D.

Today's Assignment:

1. Write down all the emotions that you experience in an average week.

2. List the events or situations you use to trigger these emotions.

3. Come up with an antidote for each negative emotion, and employ one of the appropriate tools for responding to the Action Signal. Do you need to change the words you use to describe this experience? Do you need to change what you believe about this emotional state? Do you need to ask yourself a new question? Be sure to consistently focus on solutions instead of problems.

Commit throughout this day to replacing the old, limiting emotion with a new, empowering emotion, and condition this new pattern until it's consistent. With our emotions well in hand, we'll begin tomorrow to master our . . .

20
PHYSICAL
DESTINY:
PRISON OF PAIN
OR PALACE
OF PLEASURE

DAY TWO

Your Outcome: *Just as you've learned to condition your nervous system to produce the behaviors that will give you the results you want, the physical destiny you experience depends on how you condition your metabolism and muscles to produce the levels of energy and fitness you desire.*

His goal was to break a world record. For eleven straight days, he had been running twenty-one hours a day and sleeping a mere three hours a night. The mental challenge was as great as the physical challenge: he had to travel from the everyday world he'd lived in his entire life into one where his primary objective was the next step. He devoted years of training not only to his body, but also to his mind. His objective? To demonstrate the unlimited physical potential that lies locked within us all. By breaking the previous record and running over 1,000 miles in eleven days and nineteen hours, at an average of eighty-four miles per day, Stu Mittleman demonstrated that by understanding how to condition both the mind and body, one can produce results far beyond anything society would consider possible. He has proven by his example that the human capacity is incredible, and that we can adapt to anything if we make the right demands upon ourselves *incrementally*. The purpose of this chapter is to share with you the fundamental secrets that empowered Stu Mittleman to train himself to accomplish this unparalleled task.

For years I have pursued those I've considered to be masters in their areas of expertise, and physical fitness and health have been a major focus in my life for over a decade. When I first began my research in this area, I became confused by the maelstrom of conflicting viewpoints expressed by experts all supposedly equally qualified. For negotiating my way through the maze of opinions, my number-one criterion was results. Those who consistently produced quality results were the ones I emulated and learned from. Just as I had a hard time giving credence to a doctor who was counseling patients about health but who himself was forty pounds overweight, so, too, did I question the validity of so-called fitness experts who appeared emaciated and had a host of injuries and low energy levels.

When I first heard about Stu Mittleman and his accomplishments, I became fascinated, particularly when I heard further that all those who had witnessed his amazing feat said he looked *better* at the end of his 1,000-mile run than he did when he left the starting line! He experienced no injuries—not even a blister! What gave him the incredible capacity to stretch his body to its limits and still maximize his potential *without injuring it?*

Certainly, Stu was well-prepared for his run. He has master's degrees in sports psychology, sociology, and social psychology, and is working toward a doctorate in exercise physiology at Columbia University. But the knowledge that proved most invaluable to him was the distinction that **health and fitness are not the same.** This is a distinction that Jim Fixx, the famous running-book author, did not have. He was clearly fit, but also unhealthy.

The failure of most individuals to grasp the difference between fitness and health is what causes them to experience the frustration of working out religiously and still having the same five to ten pounds stubbornly clinging to their midsection. Talk about learned helplessness! Worse than that is the plight of those who make exercise the centerpiece of their lives and believe that their actions are making them healthier, yet each and every day they are pushing themselves one step further toward fatigue, disease, and emotional upheaval.

What exactly do I mean by the difference between health and fitness? **Fitness is "the physical ability to perform athletic activity." Health, however, is defined as "the state where all the systems of the body— nervous, muscular, skeletal, circulatory, digestive, lymphatic, hormonal, etc.—are working in an optimal way . . . ."** Most people think that fitness implies health, but the truth is that they don't necessarily go hand in hand. It's ideal to have both health and fitness, but by putting

* Maffetone, Dr. Philip, *Everyone Is an Athlete,* New York: David Barmore Publishers, 1990.

health first, you will always enjoy tremendous benefits in your life. If you achieve fitness at the expense of health, you may not live long enough to enjoy your spectacular physique.

The optimum balance of health *and* fitness is achieved by **training your metabolism**. Just as we train our minds, and just as we train our muscles, Stu and one of his trainers, Dr. Philip Maffetone, have proven that we can in fact train our metabolism. Stu's results definitely bear this out: while he was on his 1,000-mile run, he certainly should have "hit the wall." Yet he *never* experienced this in spite of running eighty-four miles a day. Understanding the simple yet profound distinctions that Stu used can change not only how you look, but also your level of energy, the quality of your life, and ultimately the physical destiny you set in motion.

The biggest difference between health and fitness comes down to understanding the distinction between *aerobic* and *anaerobic* exercise, between *endurance* and *power*. **Aerobic** means, literally, "with oxygen," and refers to **moderate exercise sustained over a period of time**. Your aerobic system is your system for endurance, and encompasses the heart, lungs, blood vessels, and aerobic muscles. If you activate your aerobic system with proper diet and exercise, you burn *fat* as your primary fuel.

On the other hand, **anaerobic** means, literally, "without oxygen," and refers to **exercises that produce short bursts of power**. Anaerobic exercise burns *glycogen* as its primary fuel, while **causing the body to store fat**. Genetics plays a part in your body's ability to burn fat and, in fact, some people are born with a highly aerobic system already in place. These are the people we envy who seemingly can eat anything and not gain an ounce.

> Most types of exercise can be *either* aerobic or anaerobic. **The level of intensity determines whether you are using your aerobic or anaerobic system**. Walking, jogging, running, biking, swimming, dancing, etc., can provide either benefit. **Lower heart rates make these activities aerobic, and *higher* heart rates make them anaerobic**. . . . Usually, tennis, racquetball, basketball, and similar sports are anaerobic.*

Most Americans today have a lifestyle that causes them to live in a constantly anaerobic state, inundated with stress and demands, compounding it with the way they choose to exercise. As a result, they train

---

* Maffetone, Dr. Philip, "The 1,000-Mile Race of Life: How to Be Healthy *and* Fit," *Robbins Research Report,* Fall 1990, San Diego: Robbins Research International, Inc.

their metabolism to continuously be anaerobic, i.e., burn glycogen as a primary source of energy. When levels of glycogen become excessively low, the anaerobically trained metabolism turns to blood sugar as its secondary source of fuel. This immediately disrupts your level of health and vitality.

As your anaerobic demands rob your body of blood sugar you could be using for other tasks, you immediately begin to feel the negative effects. Since **your nervous system demands the use of two-thirds of your blood sugar**, the deficit created by anaerobic exercise can cause neuromuscular problems like headaches or disorientation. Here is a list of some telltale symptoms directly related to excessive anaerobic training of your metabolism: **fatigue, recurrent exercise injuries, low blood sugar patterns, depression and anxiety, fat metabolism problems, premenstrual syndrome, or circulation problems and stiff joints.**

We live in a society that is anaerobic-excessive and aerobic-deficient, and it's negatively impacting the quality of health across the nation. In modern, industrialized society, people become less physically active. Only a few decades ago, most people accomplished their daily chores in a physical way. Today, though, we have designed active demands for our bodies to replace the inactivity that our day-to-day life no longer creates. This forced activity we call exercise. Unfortunately, many people with positive intentions, including skilled athletes, are becoming less healthy with exercise. Out of our drive to produce the greatest results in the shortest period of time, most of us create an improper balance between health and fitness, and suffer the consequences.

The solution, however, is simple. Stu Mittleman's secret is that he understands that **health and fitness must go together**. According to Dr. Maffetone, this is accomplished by understanding that:

> . . . **all exercise programs require that you begin by building an aerobic base**—a period of time during which your entire exercise program is exclusively based upon aerobic activity without any anaerobic exercise at all. This base period may last from a minimum of two to a maximum of about eight months, during which your aerobic system is developed and maximized. This base period is then followed by anaerobic workouts of one, two, or sometimes three per week. **Properly developing your aerobic system will not only make you a better athlete, [but] it will also burn off the extra fat from your hips, improve your immune system, give you more energy,** and keep you relatively injury-free. In other words, it's

a way to build your total health and fitness through both the proper conditioning of your metabolism for aerobic and, when appropriate, anaerobic training.*

By creating an aerobic base, you'll also create a tremendous amount of energy and endurance. Remember, by expanding your aerobic capacity, you're expanding your body's ability to deliver oxygen (the source of energy and health) to every organ and system of the body.

The problem is that most people try to push themselves beyond their ideal heart rates, and they spend all their time exercising in an anaerobic state. If you have not yet built an aerobic base, then all of your anaerobic exercise is at the expense of endurance. Many people, out of their desire to "whip" themselves into a state of fitness, try to exercise at their maximum heart rates. Traditionally, the formula for maximum heart rate is 220 minus your age. For a thirty-year-old, this would mean aiming for a heart rate of 190. Surely exercising at this intensity for long periods of time is one of the most destructive things you can do to your body: it may make you "fit," but it will do so at the cost of your health.

By the way, guess who was guilty of this for several years. I pushed myself to "achieve" maximum heart rate: I would jump onto my Stair-Master and crank it up to the highest level, and go for twenty minutes. Or, after not having run in several weeks, I would go out and run five miles with absolutely no warm-up. I wouldn't be able to walk for several days afterward, but I believed that through this "no-pain, no-gain" discipline I was making myself more healthy! All I was doing was establishing a love-hate relationship with exercise. My mixed associations of pain and pleasure made me put it off as long as my conscience would allow, then try to make up for lost time in just one session.

Since then I've learned that **when you begin to work out at a pace which immediately throws your body into anaerobic capacity, a very dangerous thing can occur.** In order to supply the immediate demand for blood that anaerobic exercise requires for the muscles that need it most, your body shunts blood from critical organs like your liver and kidneys. As a result, these organs lose a large amount of oxygen, which significantly impairs their vitality and health. Continually doing this results in their weakness, damage, or destruction.

The key is to **train your metabolism to consistently operate in aerobic fashion. Your body won't burn fat unless you specifically *train* it to do so.** Thus, **if you want to lose that persistent layer of fat around your midsection, you must train your body to burn *fat*, not**

---

* Maffetone, "The 1,000-Mile Race of Life."

sugar. Remember that both Stu's and Phil's criterion for aerobic function is the burning of fat. One of the biggest benefits of aerobic exercise is that it prevents the clogging of arteries that leads to heart disease, the top cause of death in the United States (responsible for killing one out of every two people).*

Some individuals, in their zeal to eliminate *all* fat from their diet, actually induce their body to enter an "emergency" mode in which it begins to store fat even more efficiently. They compound the mistake by starving themselves, and when they inevitably return to old eating patterns, even more fat is stored from the same amount of food they had been eating before the diet—and they gain back more weight than they lost! This is why our culture is so obsessed with losing "those last ten pounds."

When people tell me they want to lose ten pounds, I ask them, "Ten pounds of *what?*" Most often they're exercising in a way that causes them to lose water or muscle, not fat. You can weigh the same amount today as you weighed ten years ago but be much less healthy because your muscle has been replaced with fat. Muscle weighs more than fat, so if you weigh the same as you did ten years ago and your body is made up of even more fat, you're in deep trouble!

While it's true we want to limit our fat intake so it's not excessive (20 percent to 30 percent of your caloric intake), nothing can compare with aerobic exercise for training your metabolism to burn fat. **There is no one "right" percentage of fat intake for all individuals; it depends on how you metabolize the fat you do ingest.**† Wouldn't you love to have the same capacity that you envy in others who seem to be blessed with metabolisms that burn fat? You can! It's all a matter of conditioning.

So how do you train your metabolism to burn fat so that you have the energy, endurance, and vitality to put into practice everything you've learned in this book and live life to the fullest? I have some good news and some bad news. First the good news: you can accomplish this through some simple steps each day. Now the bad news: you won't be able to use the traditional American method of filling the bathtub, pulling the plug, and fighting the current! Neither will driving a golf cart from hole to hole do the trick. These are not forms of aerobic exercise. Throwing your pendulum to the other extreme won't work, either. Wind sprints are an anaerobic exercise. They create an immediate oxygen deficit in the

---

* For additional distinctions on diet, please read the chapter "Energy: The Fuel of Excellence" in my first book, *Unlimited Power*.

† There is a principle of physiology called the **Law of Mass Action** that governs how your body uses the fuel you give it. If you give your body sufficient fat, it will use it as fuel; if you starve your body of fat, it will store it. In other words, your body will use what you feed it. Of course, this equation is incomplete without the factor of exercise to actually burn the fat you consume.

*"You need more exercise. Go and
get me a cheeseburger with onions."*

cells and begin to cause you to train your metabolism to burn glycogen
and/or blood sugar; thus, the fat continues to be stored.

Probably the most important element to one's health is *oxygen*. Every
day, we breathe approximately 2,500 gallons of air in order to supply our
tissues with oxygen. Without it, cells become weakened and die. There
are about 75 trillion cells in your body, and they provide you with
adenosine triphosphate (ATP), the basic energy for everything that your
body does, whether it's breathing, dreaming, eating, or exercising. In
order to survive, cells *must* have oxygen in order to burn glucose and
create ATP for continued growth.

The point is that you don't want to deplete oxygen during exercise.
If you want to know whether you've moved beyond aerobic into anaerobic, here's a simple test: **when you're exercising, can you talk** (aerobic)? Or are you too winded (anaerobic)? **Your breathing should be
steady and audible, but not labored.** What does it feel like when you're
working out? If you're exercising aerobically, it should be **pleasurable
though tiring.** If you're exercising anaerobically, you definitely feel
pushed. On a scale from 0 to 10, with 0 being minimum exertion and 10
being the most intense, what's your score? **If you've exceeded 7, then
you've gone beyond aerobic into anaerobic; ideally, you'll evaluate
yourself between 6 and 7.**

Tapping your aerobic capacity requires a very specific form of training. **First, it's advisable to wear a heart-rate monitor. Then warm up
gradually to reach your optimum aerobic training zone.** (See box
below.)

Your warm-up will accomplish at least two things: 1) You will be gradually mobilizing the fatty acids stored throughout your body to your bloodstream so that you can use your fat instead of your vital blood sugar. This is critical. If you don't warm up, you may exercise aerobically, i.e., with oxygen in the cells, but not *burn the fat*. During warm-up, you should count your heart rate at 50 percent of the maximum using the standard method of calculation (see footnote for the heart rate box). 2) You will prevent cramping. **This warm-up period should take about fifteen minutes.** This allows your body to *gradually* distribute blood to those areas that need it rather than immediately diverting it from vital organs—a critical distinction to make sure that your workouts build health and fitness without injuring your system.

Second, exercise within your aerobic training zone for at least twenty minutes, ideally working up to thirty to forty-five minutes.

The best way to find your optimal training heart rate is to apply the following formula:

COMPUTING YOUR IDEAL HEART RATE*

180 – your age = your ideal heart rate (the rate at which you can exercise aerobically before going anaerobic).

If you are recovering from a major illness or are on medication, subtract an additional 10 points.

If you have not exercised before, or have an injury or are gearing down in your training, or if you often get colds or flu or have allergies, subtract 5 points.

If you have been exercising for up to two years without any real problems, and have not had colds or flu more than once or twice per year, keep your score the same.

If you have been exercising for more than two years without any problems, while making progress in competition without injury, add 5 points.

Before beginning any program of physical exercise, consult your physician.

Third, take twelve to fifteen minutes to cool down appropriately by walking or some other form of mild movement. In this way you prevent your blood from pooling in your working muscles. If

---

* The traditional calculation for your training zone is: 220 − Your Age = Maximum Heart Rate; Maximum Heart Rate × 65% − 85% = Training Zone. The formula in the text above is from Stu Mittleman and Dr. Philip Maffetone.

you abruptly stop movement after exercise, there is no way for the blood to be returned for cleansing, reoxygenation and redistribution. It will stay in the muscle, engorging it, and increasing toxicity in the bloodstream.

People are often reluctant to commit to a workout because they link too much pain to it, either physical pain or the pain of not having enough time. But if you just give it a try, you'll make two pleasant discoveries: 1) You'll love working out this way because it produces pleasure and no pain. 2) You'll experience a level of physical vitality you've never felt before.

If you're concerned about the amount of time it takes, think of ways in which you can maximize your time. For instance, while you're warming up you can listen to tapes, read, watch the news, do your Morning or Evening Power Questions, read your values and rules hierarchy, and make other productive uses of your time. When I asked Stu Mittleman what he recommends as a workout schedule, he suggested starting out with at least three sessions a week, with fifteen minutes of warm-up, twenty minutes at your aerobic training zone, and fifteen minutes of cool-down. Then graduate to longer sessions as you see fit.

Am I suggesting to you that aerobic training is the only type of exercise worth doing? Of course not. Having health *and* fitness is the goal; we want to enhance performance as well as endurance. (Just remember that any time you work out at an anaerobic pace, you do so at the expense of your endurance.) So as you begin to develop your aerobic capacity, once you reach a plateau (somewhere in your second to fourth month of exercise), you can build power by adding anaerobic exercise to your regimen, such as by fast repetitions with weights. This differs from person to person, and the best test is to just listen to your body. If you're running on the beach, and suddenly feel like sprinting, do it! Develop body wisdom; learn to notice your body's ability to handle more challenging physical tasks.

In fact, Stu assures us that we can maintain and improve endurance into our golden years. We do not have to be frail in our old age! Chronology is not so much the arbiter of our health as is our commitment to a health-enhancing lifestyle. Even though some people are born with a predisposition to burn fat, or are blessed with a gift of speed or power, **anyone can achieve endurance and vitality by consciously deciding to condition their body's chemistry.**

> *"We are not limited by our old age; we are liberated by it."*
> —STU MITTLEMAN

The most exciting news of all is that, like all patterns that give us pleasure, **exercise can become a positive addiction.** As much as you may
currently avoid exercise, you will probably be more powerfully drawn to
it once you discover how pleasurable it is to work out *properly*. Research
has shown that if you exercise consistently for over a twelve-month
period of time, you will form this positive addiction for a lifetime. Even
if you get off track for a period of time, you'll always return to a consistent
exercise regimen throughout your life. Your body will be driven to the
pleasure of health, to the natural high of maximizing your physical potential. Why is this? You will have trained your nervous system by conditioning your metabolism to *thrive* on this experience. We all deserve
the physical vitality that can transform the quality of our lives. Your
physical destiny is intimately related to your mental, emotional, financial,
and relationship destinies. In fact, it will determine whether you have a
destiny at all!

THE FOUNTAIN OF YOUTH

An undeniably powerful totem in our culture is youth and physical
vitality. Think of the old men and women who got a new lease on life in
the movie *Cocoon*. So many people chase after whatever they think will
prolong their "youth," while the real fountain of youth already exists
within them. It's known as human growth hormone (HGH). HGH stimulates tissue growth, increases muscle tone and lean mass, enhances
flexibility, thickens muscles, stimulates the growth of bones and organs,
and helps maintain healthy tissues. From the time you're born to approximately the age of thirty, HGH is naturally released into the bloodstream about an hour and a half after you go to sleep and also once before
you wake up in the morning. (I just turned thirty-one this year, so I don't
buy that time schedule!) High levels of HGH naturally drop over time. By
age sixty, about 30 percent of men produce little or none of the substance. It is conjectured that women continue to secrete growth hormone
into their old age, and that's one of the reasons they live longer.

   **We also receive human growth hormone bursts after heavy exer-
cise and/or after a serious injury because HGH is a healing substance. HGH is now being synthesized in laboratories and
administered to children who have dwarfism to stimulate their
growth. But how can you enhance your own natural abilities to
release HGH into your system? The one way to trigger it instantly
and continuously is through explosive exercise.** This means performing repetitions of an activity which you can maintain for thirty-five to
forty-five seconds only, such as heavy weight lifting. Laboratory tests in

Miami, Florida, have produced exciting results. People in their sixties who've gone at least ten to fifteen years without any muscle tone are learning to lift weights and create muscle mass equivalent to that of twenty-one-year-olds, with energy levels to match.

What does all of this mean? It means that *you can be as strong in your seventies and eighties as you were in your twenties and thirties!* Not only can you continue to build your endurance factor with aerobic exercise, as we've already discussed, but you can continue to boost your power with short, explosive bursts of anaerobic exercise. Just remember the other factor in the equation: give your body the nutrients it needs. Make sure you aren't poisoning your body with excess sugar, fats, salt, or meat. All of this is great news, since as we enter the twenty-first century, estimates are that 24 percent of the American population is expected to be over the age of sixty-five. If we take control of our bodies now, one out of every four Americans will not be a drain on society, but a strong and vital member who makes valuable contributions and enjoys life to the utmost!

> *"The human body is the best picture*
> *of the human soul."*
> —LUDWIG WITTGENSTEIN

Today's Assignment:

1. Make the distinction between fitness and health. You've done this already.

2. Decide to become healthy. I hope you've done this already, too.

3. Know where you are. Are you currently exercising aerobically or anaerobically? Are you burning fat or glycogen? Either visit somebody who can test you, or answer the following questions:

Do you wake up in the morning feeling tired?

Do you feel famished after working out?

Do you experience wild mood swings after working out?

Does that same layer of fat hang in there despite your most diligent efforts?

Do you feel aches and pains after exercising?

If you answered yes to these questions, chances are that you're exercising anaerobically.

4. Purchase a portable heart-rate monitor (they cost in the range of $175 to $200). It's one of the best investments you'll ever make.

5. Develop a plan. Condition your metabolism to burn fat and produce consistent levels of energy by beginning a ten-day program of

aerobic exercise according to the guidelines I outlined above. Begin *immediately*.

6. Part of your ten-day challenge, if you want to extend it, is to read the chapter "Energy: The Fuel of Excellence" in my first book, *Unlimited Power*.

7. Decide to make exercise part of your identity. It is only through a long-term, lifelong commitment to exercise that we can truly reap the rewards that life has to offer us.

Now, let's hold ourselves to a higher standard by increasing the quality of our . . .

21
RELATIONSHIP DESTINY: THE PLACE TO SHARE AND CARE

DAY THREE

Your Outcome: *Measurably enhance the quality of your personal relationships, and deepen your emotional connection with the people you care about most by reviewing the six fundamentals of successful relationships.*

Success is worthless if we don't have someone to share it with; indeed, our most desired human emotion is that of connection with other souls. Throughout this book we've talked consistently about the impact of relationships on shaping character, values, beliefs, and the quality of our lives. Specifically, today's exercise is designed simply to remind you of six key points that are valuable to any relationship. Let's briefly review them before I give you your assignment for today:

1. **If you don't know the values and rules of the people with whom you share a relationship, you should prepare for pain.** People can love each other, but if for whatever reason they consistently break the rules of someone they care about, there are going to be upsets and stress in this relationship. Remember, every upset you've ever had with another human being has been a rules upset, and when people become intimately involved, it's inevitable that some of their rules will clash. By knowing a person's rules, you can head off these challenges in advance.

2. Some of the biggest challenges in relationships come from the fact that most people enter a relationship in order to get something: they're trying to find someone who's going to make them feel good. **In reality, the only way a relationship will last is if you see your relationship as a place that you go to give, and not a place that you go to take.**

3. Like anything else in life, in order for a relationship to be nurtured,

there are certain things to look for—and to look out for. There are certain warning signals within your relationship that can flag you that you need to tackle a problem immediately before it gets out of hand. In her book *How to Make Love All the Time,* my friend Dr. Barbara DeAngelis identifies four pernicious phases that can kill a relationship. By identifying them, we can immediately intervene and eliminate problems before they balloon into destructive patterns that threaten the relationship itself.

Stage One, Resistance: The first phase of challenges in a relationship is when you begin to feel **resistance**. Virtually anyone who's ever been in a relationship has had times when they felt resistance toward something their partner said or did. Resistance occurs when you take exception or feel annoyed or a bit separate from this person. Maybe at a party they tell a joke that bothers you and you wish they hadn't. The challenge, of course, is that most people don't communicate when they're feeling a sense of resistance, and as a result, this emotion continues to grow until it becomes . . .

Stage Two, Resentment: If resistance is not handled, it grows into resentment. Now you're not just annoyed; you're *angry* with your partner. You begin to separate yourself from them and erect an emotional barrier. Resentment destroys the emotion of intimacy, and this is a destructive pattern within a relationship that, if unchecked, will only gain speed. If it is not transformed or communicated, it turns into . . .

Stage Three, Rejection: This is the point when you have so much resentment built up that you find yourself looking for ways to make your partner wrong, to verbally or nonverbally attack them. In this phase, you begin to see everything they do as irritating or annoying. It's here that not only emotional separation occurs, but also physical separation as well. If rejection is allowed to continue, to lessen our pain, we move to . . .

Stage Four, Repression: When you are tired of coping with the anger that comes with the rejection phase, you try to reduce your pain by creating emotional numbness. You avoid feeling any pain, but you also avoid passion and excitement. This is the most dangerous phase of a relationship because this is the point at which lovers become *roommates*—no one else knows the couple has any problems because they never fight, but there's no relationship left.

What's the key to preventing these "Four R's"? The answer is simple: **communicate clearly up front.** Make sure your rules are known and can be met. To avoid blowing things out of proportion, use Transformational Vocabulary. Talk in terms of preferences: instead of saying, "I can't *stand* it when you do that!," say, "I'd *prefer* it if you did this instead." Develop pattern interrupts to prevent the type of argument where you can't even remember what it's about anymore, only that you've got to win.

4. **Make your relationships one of the highest priorities in your**

life; otherwise they will take a back seat to any or all of the other things that are more urgent that happen during your day. Gradually, the level of emotional intensity and passion will drift away. We don't want to lose the power of our relationships simply because we got caught up in the law of familiarity, or we let neglect habituate us to the intense excitement and passion we have for a person.

5. One of the most important patterns that Becky and I discovered early that is critical to making our relationship last is to **focus each day on making it better**, rather than focusing on what might happen if it ended. We must remember that whatever we focus on we'll experience. If we constantly focus on our fear of a relationship being over, we'll begin to do things unconsciously to sabotage it so that we can extract ourselves before we get too entwined and true pain results.

A corollary to this principle is that **if you want your relationship to last, never, never, never, ever, ever threaten the relationship itself.** In other words, don't ever say, "If you do that, then I'm leaving." Just making this statement alone creates the possibility. It also induces a destabilizing fear in both partners. Every couple that I've ever interviewed with a lasting relationship has made it their rule, no matter how angry or hurt they felt, never to question whether or not the relationship would last and never to threaten to leave it. Just remember the racing school metaphor of the skid car and the wall. You want to focus on where you want to go in a relationship, not on what you fear.

6. **Each day, *reassociate* to what you love about this person you're in a relationship with. Reinforce your feelings of connection and renew your feelings of intimacy and attraction** by consistently asking the question, "How did I get so lucky to have you in my life?" Become fully associated to the privilege of sharing your life with this person; feel the pleasure intensely, and continuously anchor it into your nervous system. Engage in a never-ending quest to find new ways to surprise each other. If you don't, habituation will set in, and you will take each other for granted. So find and create those special moments that can make your relationship a role model—one that's legendary!

> *"In a full heart there is room for everything, and in an empty heart there is room for nothing."*
> —ANTONIO PORCHIA

Today's Assignment:

1. Take the time today to talk with your significant other and **find out what's most important to each of you in your relationship. What**

are your highest values in a relationship together, and what has to happen for you to feel like those values are being fulfilled?

2. **Decide that it's more important for you to be in love than to be right.** If you should ever find yourself in the position of insisting that you're right, break your own pattern. Stop immediately and come back to the discussion later when you're in a better state to resolve your conflicts.

3. **Develop a pattern interrupt that you both agree to use when things become most heated.** In this way, no matter how mad you are, for at least a moment you can smile and let go of the upset. To make it easier for both of you, use the most bizarre or humorous pattern interrupt you can devise. Make it a private joke that can serve as your personal anchor.

4. When you feel resistance, communicate it with softeners such as, "I know it's only my idiosyncrasy, but when you do that, it makes me a tad peckish."

5. Plan regular date nights together, preferably once a week, or at the minimum, two times a month. Take turns surprising your partner and dreaming up the most romantic and fun things to do.

6. Make sure you get a good,180-second wet kiss every day!

These are your only assignments for today! Act upon them and enjoy them. I can promise you, the rewards are immeasurable. To make sure that we commit to constant and never-ending improvement, **CANI!**, on a daily basis, let's develop an enjoyable plan by creating your . . .

22
FINANCIAL DESTINY: SMALL STEPS TO A SMALL (OR LARGE) FORTUNE

DAY FOUR

Your Outcome: *Take control of your financial future by learning the five foundational elements for establishing wealth.*

Money! It's one of the most emotionally charged issues of our lives. Most people are willing to give up things that are much more valuable than money in order to get more of it: they'll push themselves far beyond their past limitations, give up time with their family and friends, or even destroy their health. Money is a potent source associated to both pain and pleasure within our society. Too often it's used to measure the difference in the quality of lives, to magnify the separation of the haves and have-nots.

Some people try to deal with money by pretending it doesn't matter, but financial pressure is something that affects us all every day of our lives. For the elderly especially, a lack of money often translates into a lack of critical resources. For some people, money holds mystery. For others, it is the source of desire, pride, envy, and even contempt. Which is it, really? Is it the maker of dreams or the root of all evil? Is it a tool or a weapon? A source of freedom, power, security? Or merely a means to an end?

You and I know, intellectually, that money is merely a medium of exchange. It allows us to simplify the process of creating, transferring, and sharing value within a society. It's a convenience that together we've created in order to allow ourselves the freedom to specialize in our life's work without having to be concerned as to whether others will find our work worthy of barter.

We have learned to associate some of our most debilitating emotions to a scarcity of this commodity: anxiety, frustration, fear, insecurity, worry, anger, humiliation, and being overwhelmed, to name but a few. As we are now witnessing in Eastern Europe, political systems have been toppled by the pressure associated to financial deprivation. Can you think of any country, any corporation, or anyone's personal life that has not been touched by the experience of financial stress?

Many people make the mistake of thinking that all the challenges in their lives would dissipate if they just had enough money. Nothing could be further from the truth. Earning more money, in and of itself, rarely frees people. It's equally ridiculous to tell yourself that greater financial freedom and mastery of your finances would not offer you greater opportunities to expand, share, and create value for yourself and others.

So why do so many people fail to achieve financial abundance in a nation where economic opportunity surrounds us? We live in a country where people can create net worths in the hundreds of millions starting with a little idea for a computer that they first built in their garage! All around us there are role models of unbelievable possibility, people who know how to create wealth and maintain it. What is it that keeps us from getting wealth in the first place? How can it be, living in a capitalist country where our forefathers died for our right to life, liberty, and the pursuit of happiness, where economic reform was a major stimulus for independence, that 95 percent of the American population by age sixty-five, after a lifetime of work, cannot support themselves without help from government or family?

As I've pursued the keys to building lasting wealth, one thing becomes clear: creating wealth is simple. Yet most people never build it because *they have holes in their financial foundations.* These can be found in the form of internal value and belief conflicts, as well as poor plans that virtually guarantee financial failure. This chapter will not provide you with everything you need to know to master your entire financial life. It would certainly take more than a chapter to do that! But it *is* designed to give you some simple fundamentals that you can use to **take immediate control of this critically important area.**

Let's begin by remembering the power that our beliefs have to control our behaviors. The most common reason most people do not become financially successful is that **they have mixed associations** to what it would *take* to have more money, as well as what it would *mean* to have excess money, i.e., money beyond what they need to support their current lifestyle. As you learned in Chapter 5, your brain knows what to do only when it has a clear association about what it needs to avoid and what it needs to move toward. For money, we often send mixed signals—and so we get *mixed results.* We tell ourselves that money will provide us freedom, a chance to give to those we love, a chance to do all those things we've always dreamed about, a chance to free up our time. Yet simultaneously we may believe that in order to accumulate an abundance of money, we'd have to work so much harder, and spend so much more time that we'd probably be too old and tired to enjoy it. Or we may believe that if we have excess money, we won't be spiritual, or we'll be judged, or someone will swindle us out of it anyway, so why even try?

These negative associations are not limited to ourselves. Some people resent anyone who is doing well financially, and often they assume that if someone has made a lot of money, he or she must have done something to take advantage of others. If you find yourself resenting someone who is wealthy, what message does that send your brain? It's probably something like "Having excess money is bad." If you harbor these feelings for others, you're subconsciously teaching your mind that for you to do well would make you a "bad" person. By resenting others' success, you condition yourself to avoid the very financial abundance that you need and desire.

The second most common reason why so many people never master money is simply that **they think it's too complex.** They want an "expert" to handle it for them. While it's very valuable to get expert coaching (which is why we created our own financial company, Destiny Financial Services™), we all must be trained to understand the consequences of our financial decisions. If you exclusively depend upon someone else, no matter how competent they are, you'll always have them to blame for what occurs. But if you take responsibility for understanding your finances, you can begin to direct your own destiny.

Everything in this book is based upon the idea that we have the power to understand how our minds, bodies, and emotions work, and because of this, we have the capacity to exert a great deal of control over our destinies. Our financial world is no different. We must understand it and not limit ourselves by beliefs about the complexity of finances. Once you understand the fundamentals, mastering money is a fairly simple matter. So the first task I would give you in taking control of your financial world is to utilize the NAC (Neuro-Associative Conditioning) technology to condition yourself for financial success. Become clearly associated with all the great things you could do for your family and the peace of mind you'd feel if you had true economic abundance.

The third major belief that keeps people from succeeding financially and creates tremendous stress is the **concept of scarcity**. Most people believe they live in a world where everything is limited: there's only so much available land, so much oil, so many quality homes, so many opportunities, so much time. With this philosophy of life, in order for you to win, somebody else has to lose. It's a zero-sum game. If you believe this, the only way to become financially successful is to follow the approach of the robber barons of the early 1900s and corner the market on a particular product so that you get 95 percent of something while everyone else has to split the remaining 5 percent.

The truth of the matter, however, is that cornering a scarce supply no longer guarantees lasting wealth. A good friend of mine is economist Paul Pilzer, a Wharton Business School graduate who has become quite famous for his economic theory of **alchemy**. Paul has recently written a book that I highly recommend—the title itself reflects his core belief and the evidence he has to back it up: we live in a *resource-rich* environment. He calls it *Unlimited Wealth*. Paul points out that we are in a unique time in human history, where the traditional idea of obtaining scarce physical resources is no longer the primary arbiter of wealth. **Today, technology determines the value of a physical resource and how large a supply of it actually exists.**

When I interviewed him for my PowerTalk audio-magazine, Paul gave me a great example demonstrating how the value of resources and their availability is completely controlled by technology, and that technology thus determines the price and value of any product or service. In the seventies, everyone was certain that we were running out of oil. By 1973, people were spending hours in gas lines, and after sophisticated computerized analysis, the best experts in the world were predicting that we had approximately 700 billion barrels of oil left in the entire world, which, at our then-current rate of consumption, would last thirty-five to forty years. Paul said that if these experts were correct, then by 1988 we should have seen our oil reserves dwindle to 500 billion barrels. Yet by 1987, we had nearly 30 percent *more* oil than we had fifteen years earlier! In 1988, estimates indicated that we had *900* billion barrels, counting only our proven reserves. This didn't include the nearly 2,000 billion additional barrels of oil that researchers now believe our new discovery-and-recovery techniques may be able to tap.

What made this radical change in the amount of oil that was available? Two things: certainly our ability to *find* oil has been enhanced by technology, and technology has also powerfully impacted our ability to *utilize* oil more efficiently. Who would have thought back in 1973 that someone would come up with the idea for computerized fuel injectors that would be installed in virtually every automobile in the United States and instantly double the fuel efficiency of our cars? What's more, this computer chip cost $25 and replaced a $300 carburetor!

The minute this technology was developed, it instantly doubled the effective supply of gasoline and changed the relative scarcity of oil overnight. In fact, the price of oil today, adjusted for inflation and based upon the distance it will now take you with today's more fuel-efficient cars, actually costs you *less* per mile than at any time in the history of the automobile. In addition, we live in a world where, when companies or individuals begin to experience too much economic pain, they immediately look for alternative sources to produce the results they're after. Scientists all over the world are finding alternatives to the use of petroleum for the powering of factories, automobiles, and even airplanes.

Paul said that what happened to the Hunt brothers of Texas is a powerful example that the old strategy of cornering the market on some commodities just doesn't work anymore. When the Hunts attempted to take complete control of the silver market, they went broke. Why? One major reason is that the largest user of silver in the world was Kodak Corporation, which utilized silver in the developing process. Motivated by the pain of increased prices, Kodak began to find *alternative* ways of processing photographs, and as a result less silver was needed. Instantly, silver prices plunged, and the Hunts were wiped out.

This is a common mistake made by some of the most powerful people in today's society who continue to operate using the old formula for creating wealth. You and I need to realize that the value of anything is purely dependent upon technology. Technology can turn a waste product into an invaluable resource. After all, there was a time when having oil on your land was a curse, but technology turned it into a source of wealth.

True wealth, Paul says, comes from the ability to practice what he calls "economic alchemy," which is the **ability to take something that has very little value and convert it into something of significantly greater value**. In medieval times, those who practiced alchemy were trying to convert lead into gold. They failed. But in attempting this process, they laid the foundation for the science of chemistry. Those who are wealthy today are truly modern-day alchemists. They have learned to transform something common into something precious and have reaped the economic rewards that come with this transformation. When you think about it, doesn't the magnificent processing speed of a computer really reduce down to dirt? After all, silicon comes from sand. Those who've taken ideas—mere thoughts—and turned them into products and services are certainly practicing alchemy. **All wealth begins in the mind!**

Modern alchemy has been the source of financial success for the wealthiest people in the world today, whether it is Bill Gates, Ross Perot, Sam Walton or Steven Jobs. All of these individuals found ways to take items of hidden value—ideas, information, systems—and organize them in a way that would enable more people to use them. As they added this value, they began to create tremendous economic empires.

Let's review the five fundamental lessons for creating lasting wealth. And then I'll immediately put you to work on beginning to take control of your financial destiny.

1. **The first key is the ability to earn more income than ever before, the ability to <u>create wealth</u>.** I have a simple question for you. Can you earn twice as much money as you do now in the same amount of time? Can you earn three times as much money? Ten times? Is it possible that you could earn *1,000 times* the amount of money you do now *in the same amount of time?* Absolutely!—if you find a way to be *worth* 1,000 times more to your company or your fellow man.

The key to wealth is to be more valuable. If you have more skills, more ability, more intelligence, specialized knowledge, a capacity to do things few others can do, or if you just think creatively and contribute on a massive scale, you can earn more than you ever thought possible. The single most important and potent way to expand your income is to **devise a way to consistently add real value to people's lives, and you will prosper.** For example, why is a doctor paid more than a doorman? The answer is simple: the doctor adds more value. He has worked harder and developed himself so that he is worth more in terms of his capacity to add measurable value to people's lives. Anyone can open a door. A doctor opens the doors of life.

Why are successful entrepreneurs so well rewarded financially in our culture? It's because they add more value than virtually anyone around them. There are two primary benefits that entrepreneurs create. First, they obviously add value to their customers by increasing the quality of their lives through the use of their product. This, by the way, is critical for any company to prosper. So often, companies forget that their *real* purpose for being is not just to make a profit. While a profit is an absolute must for a company to survive and flourish—like eating or sleeping, a necessity—it's not the real purpose. **The true purpose of any corporation is to create products and services that increase the quality of life for all the customers they serve.** If this is achieved on a consistent basis, then profit is absolutely assured. However, a company can profit in the short term and not be here in the long term if it doesn't *continually* add value to people's lives. This holds true for corporations as much as individuals.

The second thing that entrepreneurs do is that, in creating their products, they create jobs. Because of these jobs, the employees' children can go on to higher education and become doctors, lawyers, teachers, social workers, and add more value to society as a whole—not to mention the fact that these families spend the money that they earn with other vendors. The chain of value is never-ending. When Ross Perot was asked for the secret of his wealth, he said, "What I can do for this country is create jobs. I'm pretty good at that, and Lord knows we need them."* The more value you contribute, the more you will earn if you put yourself in the position to do so.

The lesson is simple. You don't have to be an entrepreneur to add more value. But what you must do every day is to continually expand your knowledge, your skill, and your ability to give more. This is why self-education is so critical. I became a very wealthy man at an extremely young age for one reason: I mastered skills and abilities that could instantaneously increase the quality of life for virtually anyone. Then I figured out a way to share that information and those skills with a huge number of people in a short period of time. As a result, I have prospered not only emotionally, but financially as well.

If you want to earn more money where you are today, one of the simplest ways to do so is to ask yourself, *"How can I be worth more to this company?* How can I help it to achieve more in less time? How could I add a tremendous amount of value to it? Are there some ways that I could help cut costs and increase quality? What new system could I develop? What new technology could I use that would allow the company to produce its products and services more effectively?" If we can help people to do more with less, then we truly are empowering others, and we will be empowered economically as well, as long as we put ourselves in a position to do so.

In our Financial Destiny seminars, participants brainstorm ways they can add more value and therefore increase their income. We ask them to consider whether they have resources they've been failing to use. The key question to ask yourself is: How could I help touch more lives? How could I do it at a deeper level? How could I give a better quality of product or service? Inevitably, some people will say, "There's no way that I could add more value; I'm already working sixteen hours a day as it is!" Remember, I didn't suggest you work harder or even that you need to work smarter. What I'm asking is what new resources could you employ that could add more value to other people?

For example, I remember a massage therapist who was one of the most successful in his field in the San Diego area, and he wanted to know how he could increase his earnings when he was booked solid. He couldn't see one more person a day, and he was already charging the

---

* Perot, Ross, Speech to the National Press Club, December 6, 1990.

Financial security is on the way. You'll be feeling
safe very soon now.

highest rates in his field. As he began to brainstorm new ideas, focusing on how he could take the resources he had to help his patients and others, he began to realize that if he could team up with someone who owned a physical-therapy unit, and refer his patients who needed help, he could receive a referral fee. His income is now almost double, working the same number of hours a day. All he did was find a way to add more value to both his doctors and his clients. Since he knew the doctors well, and they understood his form of therapy, there was a greater consistency of care between them, and he benefited financially in the process.

In Phoenix, Arizona, one of the top radio salespersons is a woman whose primary marketing strategy is not merely to sell radio time, but to constantly look for opportunities to help local companies prosper. For example, the minute she hears that a new shopping center is going to be built, she contacts potential vendors for the shopping center and lets them know about the opportunity, allowing them to get a jump on the market. She then contacts the developer, and introduces herself as a radio-station representative who works with people in their industry all the time. Would the developer like to see a list of the top vendors in their fields?

Out of this strategy, several things result. She's adding value beyond the radio time people would purchase to promote their companies. She's found a way to give them much more than anyone else around, so they usually buy a significant portion, if not all, of their radio time from her. This motivates them to reciprocate value for value. This does not require a great deal of her time, but it makes her more valuable to her customers than any other radio salesperson in the region, and her income reflects it.

Even if you work in a large corporation, you can add more value. I remember a woman who was a claims processor for a hospital. She saw how slowly things were going and, knowing that claims processing was the economic lifeline of the hospital, she discovered that she could be much more efficient and potentially process four to five times as many claims as she had previously. She asked her supervisors, if she could do the work of five people, would they increase her salary by 50 percent? They said that if she proved she could consistently produce results over a period of time, they would do so. Since then, not only has she increased job efficiency and her income, she has a newfound sense of pride.

The key to increasing your income with your company is remembering that you can't just increase the quality of what you're doing by 50 percent and expect a 50 percent increase in income. A company must profit. The question to ask yourself is, *"How can I increase the value of what I do by ten to fifteen times?"* If you do this, in most cases you'll have no trouble increasing your income.

THE DISTRIBUTION WAVE OF THE FUTURE

One of the most powerful ways of adding value in the nineties and beyond is understanding that **in today's society, wealth is created by distribution.** Products and services are changing constantly, but those who've figured a way to take something of tremendous value and deliver it to a mass number of people will prosper. This has been the secret of the richest man in the United States, Sam Walton. He became wealthy by creating a distribution system. Ross Perot did the same thing with information at EDS. If you can figure out how to take something that already has great value and distribute it to people, or distribute it at a lower cost, then you've found another way of adding value. Adding value is not just *creating* products; it's *finding a way to make sure that more people experience an increase in the quality of life.*

But of course, if we really think about it, you and I know why people don't do well financially. Yes, they have limiting beliefs. But more importantly, there's a core belief that most people have: they should get something for nothing. Most people, for example, expect their income to grow each and every year, whether they've increased their contribution to their company or not.

Raises should be tied to increased value, and we can easily increase our value as long as we educate ourselves and expand our repertoire of skills. Any company that continually gives people raises without its employees finding ways to add more value is a company that's going deeper in the hole and will eventually find itself economically troubled or destroyed. If you're asking for a raise, you've got to find a way to add at least ten times more value than what you're asking for in return.

Companies, too, must realize that as they're looking to invest in equipment, equipment gives a limited return. As Paul Pilzer says, *labor is capital.* If someone makes $50,000 a year and can generate $500,000 in value, why not take this person and increase their skill, ability, talent, attitude, and education, so that they can add a *million* dollars in value? A $50,000 investment that brings a $1 million return is a very, very valuable asset. There is no better investment that companies can make than in the education and development of their own people.

> ## "Wealth is the product of man's capacity to think."
> —AYN RAND

For years I helped people throughout the nation increase the quality of their lives by taking ideas that were valuable and delivering them in a way that people could truly utilize them. By creating a technology for change and delivering it in an impactful way, I prospered. But my prosperity exploded when one day I asked myself, "How can I reach more people than ever before? How can I reach people *while I sleep?*" As a result of those empowering questions, I discovered a way to expand my influence in a way that I had never even considered before: by offering my audio-tapes through television.

That was two years ago. Since that time, we've now distributed over 7 million audiotapes of my *Personal Power* program around the world, sharing ideas and information that continue to impact people twenty-four hours a day! My partners at Cassette Productions estimate that, in the last twenty-four months, the amount of tape that's been used to carry my message is enough to circle the earth twenty times at the equator! In the process, I've had the joy of knowing that we not only impact the quality of life for all those who have used our tapes, but we've also provided about 75,000 hours of employment in the manufacturing process. This does not include all the hours that other vendors have spent as well.

You've heard many examples of how adding value creates wealth. The formula is simple and powerful. Ask yourself, **"How can I add more value to *any* environment I'm in?"** In your work environment, ask yourself the question, "How have I made or saved my company money in the last twelve months?" **True contribution makes life richer, so don't limit yourself to adding value strictly for personal gain**. How can you add more value in your home, in your church, in your school, in your community? If you can figure out a way to add at least ten times more value than what you're looking for, you'll always feel fulfilled. Imagine what life would be like if everyone followed your example.

   2. The second key is to <u>maintain your wealth</u>. Once you have an effective strategy for accumulating wealth, for earning large sums of money, how do you maintain it? Contrary to popular opinion, you can't maintain wealth simply by continuing to earn money. We've all heard of the famous people who've made fortunes and lost them overnight: the athletes whose talent allowed them to make huge sums but who have created lifestyles that depleted it the moment their income changed. When their income dropped, they often had tremendous demands that they couldn't possibly meet, and they lost it all.

   There's only one way to maintain your wealth, and that is simply this: **spend less than you earn, and invest the difference**. Without question, although this is not a very sexy principle, it is the *only* way to secure wealth over the long term. What never ceases to amaze me, though, is to see that no matter how much money people earn, they seem to find a way to spend it. The annual incomes of people who attend our Financial Destiny seminars range from $30,000 up to $2 million, with the average being around $100,000. People from even the highest-earning categories are often "broke." Why? Because they make all their economic decisions based on the *short term* rather than the *long term*. **They have no clear-cut spending plan, much less an investment plan**. They're on a course for Niagara Falls.

   The *only* possible way to build wealth is to **pick a specific percentage of your income that you will invest each year up front**. Now, many people know this; we've all heard about the virtues of saving a minimum of 10 percent and investing it. But very few people do it—and, interestingly enough, very few people are wealthy! The best way to insure that you'll be able to maintain your wealth is to have 10 percent taken out of your paycheck and invested before you even see it.

   To maintain your wealth, you must take control of your spending. **But don't develop a budget; develop a spending plan**. How's that for Transformational Vocabulary? Truly, if a budget is done effectively, it *is* a spending plan. It's a means for you—or if you're married, you and your spouse—to decide what you *want* to spend money on in advance rather than get caught up in the moment. Too often opportunities come up and out of a sense of urgency we make decisions that later on we regret. I can also tell you that if you and your spouse get a clear plan for how much you need to spend each month in each category of your life, you can save yourself a lot of arguments.

Unfortunately, most Americans live far beyond their means. In 1980, Americans owed over $54 billion on credit cards. By the end of 1988, the total had more than tripled to over $172 billion! This is a system that guarantees financial disaster. Be intelligent: spend less than you earn, and you will maintain your wealth.

You may ask, "But won't my investments cause me to grow?" Yes, but you'll also have to deal with inflation. You must go to the third step of creating lasting wealth.

3. The third key is to increase your wealth. How do you accomplish this? You add another simple yet powerful factor to the equation I just explained. In order to become wealthy, **you must spend less than you earn, invest the difference, and reinvest your returns for compounded growth**.

Most people have heard about the exponential power of compounding, but very few understand it. Compounding allows you to put yourself in a position where your money goes to work for you. Most of us work our entire lives to fuel the machines of our lifestyles. Those who succeed financially are those who set aside a certain percentage of their money, invest it, and continue to reinvest their profits until they produce a source of income that is large enough to provide for all their needs without ever having to work again. We call this accumulation of capital that frees you from the necessity of work **critical mass**. The pace at which you achieve your financial independence is in direct proportion to your willingness to reinvest—*not spend*—the profits of your past investments. In this way, the "offspring" of your dollars will grow and multiply until you have a solid economic base.

Let me offer you a simple and dramatic example of the power of compounding. If you fold a cloth napkin (⅟₃₂ of an inch thick) upon itself once, how thick is it? Obviously, it is ⅟₁₆ of an inch. Folded upon itself a second time, its thickness measures ⅛ of an inch. On the third fold, it equals ¼ of an inch. On the fourth, ½ of an inch, and by the fifth fold, the thickness equals 1 inch. Here's my question for you: How many times would you need to fold this napkin upon itself (compound it) before its thickness would touch the moon? Here's a clue: the moon is 237,305 miles away. Amazingly, you'd reach the moon on the thirty-ninth fold. By your fiftieth fold, theoretically, the thickness of your napkin would be enough to go to the moon and back 1,179 times! This is the power of compounding. Most people don't realize that a small amount of money compounded through time can be worth a fortune.

You might say, "This is wonderful. I'd love to begin compounding my investments, but how do I know what to invest in?"

There is no simple answer to this question. You must first decide what your financial goals are. What do you want to accomplish, and in what period of time? What's your **risk tolerance**, the amount of risk that you're comfortable with? Without a clear understanding of your desires, your needs, and your potential concerns, what to invest in is not clear. Often, would-be investors allow financial experts to advise them even though these experts frequently have no idea what their clients' true needs are.

The most important thing you'll ever do in your financial life is to decide to truly understand the various types of investments and what their potential risks and returns are. Responsible advisors will make certain that all of their clients thoroughly understand the kinds of investments that are available and that they take part in the development of their own **financial plans. Without a clear-cut investment plan, you will eventually fail financially.** According to financial newsletter editor Dick Fabian, "Evidence shows that investors—investors in anything—make no money over a ten-year period. There are several reasons for this tragic statistic, including:

1) Not setting a goal;
2) Chasing after trendy investments;
3) Relying on reports from the financial press;
4) Blindly taking advice from brokers or financial planners;
5) Making emotional mistakes, and so on."*

Fortunately, the answers to your financial questions are easily accessible. They're available in books from the masters, from the Peter Lynches to the Robert Prechters to the Warren Buffets, and there are effective financial coaches who can assist you in developing a plan that will help you to meet your lifelong financial needs. Make certain, since finances play such a large role in the amount of pain or pleasure you have in your life, that you model the best financial people. If you don't, you're going to experience pain. If you do, you can have a level of financial abundance that's far beyond what you've ever dreamed of before.

Now that you've really begun to create and expand your wealth, you're ready for the fourth key element to financial success.

4. The fourth key is to protect your wealth. So many people who have wealth are equally or more insecure today with an abundance of money than they were when they had none. People often feel less secure when they think they have more to lose. Why? It's because they know that in any moment, someone could sue them for completely unfair or unjust reasons, and decimate their assets.

Would you like to know how bad the current climate is in the United

---

* Fabian, Dick, *How to Be Your Own Investment Counselor.*

States? According to an article in the *London Financial Times,* June 22, 1991, of all the lawsuits that were filed around the world in 1988 and 1989, a staggering *94 percent* were filed in the United States alone. There are 18 million lawsuits filed per year; in fact, current statistics from the American Bar Association show that if you live in California and make more than $50,000 a year, there is almost a one-in-four chance that you will be sued.

From the European perspective, it seems that Americans are always looking for someone to blame when anything goes wrong, and this is the genesis of this incredible number of lawsuits. These are harsh words, but, unfortunately, they're true. This attitude is not found anywhere else in the world, and it is destroying our nation economically, tying up our time, capital, and energy in wasteful and nonproductive ways. For example, as recently reported in *The Wall Street Journal,* a man who was driving his vehicle while drunk tried to move the shotgun on the seat next to him, and it accidentally discharged and killed him. His widow, rather than acknowledge her husband's inebriated state, sued the shotgun manufacturer for $4 million on the grounds that the gun did not have safety devices for drunk drivers, and won!

Knowing that the wealth that they've spent years of intense work to create could be claimed by people who have no right to it understandably makes most people feel edgy. It makes them wary of the liability of business and often impacts their follow-through on investment decisions. However, the good news is that **there are legal avenues for protecting your assets as long as you're not currently involved in a lawsuit.** This philosophy of protecting your assets is not one of trying to avoid your legitimate debts, but simply to protect yourself from frivolous attacks. People with dishonest motives will sue you for only one of two reasons: because they want a share of your insurance, or they want to seize your assets. If there are no assets to touch, it's much more difficult for them to retain an attorney based merely on a contingency fee. If you act judiciously in advance, you can protect your assets, and the guidelines for doing so are very clear and concise.

In my quest to understand finances, I began to study the John Templetons of the world and began to gain distinctions on how they structure their finances in a way that protects their assets from illegitimate claims. As in any situation in life, it's important to find out what the "big players" are doing, and model their evaluation procedures and strategies. I spent two years pursuing and understanding the best asset-protection systems available in the United States for the doctor clientele of my Fortune Management company. One common misperception is that asset protection involves mystery and deceit. The reality is that honesty is the best policy. Your assets do not need to be hidden, just protected. If asset protection is not a major concern for you today, it will be as you begin to build your wealth. Just know that there are many things you can do to make changes in this area.*

5. The fifth key is to enjoy your wealth. So many people have gone through the first four stages. They've figured out how to earn wealth by adding real value. They've discovered how to maintain it by spending less than they were earning. They've mastered the art of investing and are experiencing the benefits of compounded interest. And they now know how to protect their assets, but they're still not happy; they feel empty. The reason is that they have not yet realized that **money is not the end; it's only a means.** You and I must make sure that we find a way to share its positive impact with the people we care about, or the money will have no value. When you discover ways to contribute that are proportionate to your income, you will tap into one of the greatest joys in life.

I can tell you that unless you link a certain level of pleasure to creating value and earning money, you'll never keep it long term. Most people wait until they've accumulated a certain amount of money to start enjoying themselves. This is a great way to teach your brain to link pain to wealth creation. Instead, reward yourself emotionally along the way. Occasionally, you need to give yourself a jackpot (as we talked about in Chapter 6), where you give yourself a financial surprise so that your brain is taught that earning money is enjoyable and rewarding.

Also, remember the power and value of tithing. I can tell you that my financial world began to turn around the day I gave a little more than twenty dollars to someone when I really didn't have the twenty dollars to give. That day, I felt so good about myself that the feelings alone transformed my performance and my capacity to earn even more. Most people say, "I'll tithe when I have more money." But which do you think would be more difficult to do: to give a dime out of a dollar or to give $100,000 out of a million? The answer is obvious, isn't it? I'm not suggesting that 10 percent is a figure that should be etched in stone, but do make a commitment to consistently take a portion of what you earn and give it in a way that gives you joy. The beauty of tithing is that by giving away a portion of what you earn, you are teaching your brain that you have more than enough. You'll be beyond scarcity, and that belief system alone will change your life.

True wealth is an emotion: it's a sense of absolute abundance. Our heritage alone makes us wealthy. We have the privilege of enjoying great works of art that we didn't paint, music we didn't compose, great educational institutions we didn't build. Feel the wealth of the nation's

* For more information on asset protection, contact Destiny Financial Services at (619) 453-6330.

parks that you own. Know that you're a wealthy person now, and enjoy that wealth. Realize that this is a part of your abundance, and this feeling of gratitude will allow you to create even more.

Let me simply say this to you in closing: changing your beliefs and mastering your finances can be an incredibly rewarding experience in personal development. Commit yourself now to begin the process.

> *"Charity and personal force are the only investments."*
> —WALT WHITMAN

Today's Assignment:

1. Take a look at your beliefs, see if there are any that are out of alignment, and change them with NAC.

2. Institute a process for adding more value in your place of employment, on a major scale, whether you're paid for it or not. Add ten times more value than you do currently and prepare for the processional effects of your actions.

3. Commit to save a minimum of 10 percent, and have it deducted from your check and invested in your planned portfolio.

4. Get some good coaching. Whether you contact our Financial Destiny Group professionals, or your own local financial "coach," make certain that whoever works with you helps you to develop a detailed financial plan that you understand. Pick up some great financial books. There are many that can teach you how to make intelligent, informed investment decisions.

5. If you're concerned about your assets being under attack, take action to develop an asset-protection plan.

6. Create a small jackpot to start the process of linking pleasure to financial success. Who could you do something special for? What could you do for yourself as reinforcement for getting started today?

Now you're ready to . . .

23

BE IMPECCABLE: YOUR CODE OF CONDUCT

DAY FIVE

Your Outcome: *Is it possible to have great values, to have all your rules aligned to support them, to be asking yourself the right questions, and not to be living your values in the moment? If you're being honest with yourself, you know the answer is yes. All of us at one time or another have let events control us, instead of controlling our states or our decisions as to what those events mean. We need a clear-cut way to ensure that we consistently live the values to which we've committed ourselves, and a way of <u>measuring</u> whether or not we're actually achieving that value on a daily basis.*

The young man had achieved enormous success by the time he was twenty-seven years old. He was very bright, well-read, and he felt like he had the world by the tail. But one day he realized something: he wasn't very *happy!* Many people disliked him because they perceived him as haughty and overbearing. He felt that he was no longer in command of his life's direction, much less his ultimate destiny.

He decided that he would take control of his life by setting a higher standard for himself, developing a strategy to achieve that higher standard, and creating a system so that he could measure his results *daily.* He began by selecting twelve "virtues"—twelve states that he wanted to experience every day—that he felt would take his life in the direction he wanted. Then he took out his journal and wrote down all twelve states, and next to this list he created a grid of all the days of the month. "Every time I violate any one of these virtues," he said, "I will put a small black dot next to that value for that day. My goal is to have no black dots on my chart. Then I will know I am truly living these virtues."

He was so proud of his idea that he showed his journal and explained his system to a friend. His friend said, "Great! Only I think you should add humility to your list of virtues." And Benjamin Franklin laughed and added the 13th virtue to his list.

I remember reading this story from Ben Franklin's autobiography in a beat-up hotel room in Milwaukee. I was on an intense schedule, facing the prospect of doing several radio and television talk shows, a book signing, and a free guest event. The night before meeting all these obligations I decided, "Okay, you're here, so make the best of it. At least you can feed your mind."

I had very recently come up with the idea of values and their hierarchies, and I had created what I thought was a great list of values for myself, one that I felt good about living. But as I reflected upon Ben's list of virtues, I told myself, "Yes, you have love as a value, but are you being *loving* right now? Contribution is one of your top values, but are you *contributing* in this moment?" And the answer was no. I had great values, but I wasn't *measuring* whether or not I was truly living them on a moment-to-moment basis. I knew I was a loving person, but as I looked back, I saw a lot of moments when I wasn't *being* loving!

I sat down and asked myself, **"What states would I be in if I were my highest and best? What states will I commit to being every single day, no matter what?** Regardless of the environment, regardless of whatever challenges break loose around me, **I will be these states at least once every day!"** The states to which I committed myself included being friendly, happy, loving, outgoing, playful, powerful, generous, outrageous, passionate, and fun. Some of these states were the same as my values, and some of them weren't. But I knew that if I truly lived each of these states every day, I would be living my values continually. As you can imagine, it was a pretty exciting process!

The next day, as I appeared on the radio and TV talk shows, I deliberately put myself into these states. I was happy, loving, powerful, funny, and I felt that what I said and did made a contribution, not only to my hosts, but to the people who were listening and watching. Then I went down to the local shopping mall for a book signing. When I got there, the manager approached me with a distressed expression and said, "There's a slight problem, Mr. Robbins . . . the announcement that you're going to be here signing books is coming out in *tomorrow's* paper!"

Now, if this had happened before I'd read about Ben Franklin's list, I might have reacted in a rather unique way. But with my new list in mind I thought, "I'm committed to living in these states *no matter what.* What a great test to see if I'm truly living my personal code every day!" So I walked over to the book-signing table and looked around. Nobody was there; only a few people were strolling through the mall. How could I create excitement where none seemed to exist?

The first thing that popped into my mind was *outrageousness.* After all, one of the states on my list was to be outrageous. So I picked up a copy of my book, *Unlimited Power*, and started reading it and making all kinds of interesting noises: "Ooooh! Aaaah! Wow, is that true?"

Soon a woman walked by, was attracted by my enthusiasm for what clearly had to be a brilliant book, and stopped to see what I was reading. I raved to her about this incredible book, and pointed out all of the best stories and techniques. Someone else stopped to see what all the hubbub was about, then a few other folks joined us, and within around twenty minutes, about twenty-five to thirty people were crowding around me to hear about the great book I had found.

Finally, I said, "And you know the best thing of all? I happen to be *a good friend of the author!*" The first woman's eyes lit up: "Really?" I held up the book jacket with my picture on the back and said, "Look familiar?" She gasped, and laughed, and so did all the other people. I sat down and started signing books.

That afternoon turned out to be a terrific success, and all of us had fun. Instead of letting events control my actions and perceptions, I had consciously chosen to live by what I now call my **Code of Conduct**. I also had the tremendous sense of satisfaction of knowing that by living in these states—by *being who I truly am*—I was meeting my values in the moment.

"Go put your creed into your deed."
—RALPH WALDO EMERSON

Ben Franklin and I aren't the only people who have Codes of Conduct. What do you think the Ten Commandments are all about? Or the Boy Scouts' Oath? Or the American Serviceman's Code of Conduct? How about the Optimists' Club Creed?

One way to create your own code is to review codes of conduct that already exist. . . .

OPTIMISTS' CLUB CREED

Promise yourself . . .

To be so strong that nothing can disturb your peace of mind.

To talk health, happiness, prosperity to every person you meet.

To make all your friends feel that there is something of value in them.

To look at the sunny side of everything and make your optimism come true.

To think only the best, to work only for the best, and to expect the best.

To be just as enthusiastic about the success of others as you are about your own.

To forget the mistakes of the past and press on to the greater achievements of the future.

To wear a cheerful countenance at all times and give every living creature you meet a smile.

To give so much time to the improvement of yourself that you have no time to criticize others.

To be too large for worry, too noble for anger, too strong for fear, and too happy to permit presence of trouble.

When John Wooden, the great UCLA basketball coach, graduated from grade school at age twelve, his father gave him a seven-point creed. John says this creed has been one of the most powerful influences on his entire life and career. It's a creed he still lives by every single day:

JOHN WOODEN'S SEVEN-POINT CREED: "MAKING THE MOST OF ONESELF"

1. Be true to yourself.
2. Make each day your masterpiece.
3. Help others.
4. Drink deeply from good books.
5. Make friendship a fine art.
6. Build a shelter against a rainy day.
7. Pray for guidance and give thanks for your blessings every day.

"You can preach a better sermon with your life than with your lips."
—OLIVER GOLDSMITH

Today's Assignment:

1. Make a list of the states you are committed to experiencing every day in order to live in accordance with your highest principles and values. Make sure the list is long enough to give your life the richness and variety you deserve, yet short enough that you can truly be in these states *every day!* Most people find that anywhere from seven to ten is optimum. What states would you like to be in on a consistent basis? Happy? Dynamic? Friendly? Connected? Cheerful? Grateful? Passionate? Balanced? Adventurous? Amusing? Outrageous? Generous? Elegant? Some of these states might be the same as some of your moving-toward values; and some of them might be things that you feel will lead you toward living your values every day.

2. After you have compiled your list, write a sentence next to each one describing how you will know you are doing it—in other words, your rules for these states; for example: "I am being cheerful when I smile at people"; "I am being outrageous when I do something totally unexpected and fun"; "I am being grateful when I remember all the good things I have in my life."

3. Make the commitment to yourself to genuinely experience each of these states at least once a day. You might want to write your Code of Conduct on a piece of paper and put it in your wallet or on your desk at work or by your bed. Every now and then, during the course of the day, take a look at your list and ask yourself, "Which of these states have I already experienced today? Which of them haven't I had yet, and how am I going to accomplish it by the end of the day?"

If you truly commit to your Code of Conduct, imagine how incredible you will feel! You'll no longer be controlled by events; you'll know that, no matter what happens around you, you can maintain your sense of yourself and live up to the vision you've created. There is a tremendous pride that comes with holding yourself to a higher standard and knowing that each day you alone will determine how you feel, that you will conduct yourself only at the highest level.

Wayne Dyer recently shared a great metaphor with me relating to how people blame the way they behave on the pressure they're feeling. He said, "Pressure doesn't create negative behavior. Think of yourself as an orange. If an orange is squeezed, if all this pressure is being applied from the outside, what happens? Juice comes out, right? But the only thing that comes out when the pressure is applied is *what's already inside the orange.*"

I believe that *you* decide what's on the inside by holding yourself to a higher standard. So when the pressure's on, what's going to come out is the "good stuff." After all, you cannot always count on easy sailing. It's up to you to live by your Code of Conduct and commit yourself to the principle of **CANI!** in order to keep a true bearing on your course. Remember, it's who you are every day—the small actions as well as the most grandiose—that build your character and form your identity.

One of the most important actions you can take is to learn to . . .

24

MASTER YOUR TIME AND YOUR LIFE

DAY SIX

Your Outcome: *Learn how to use time to your advantage rather than allowing it to rule your levels of satisfaction and stress.*

If you've ever felt stress —and who hasn't?—chances are excellent that it's because you felt you just didn't have enough time to do what you wanted to at the level of quality to which you were committed. You could be feeling this frustration, for example, because you're focusing exclusively on the demands of the moment: present requests, present challenges, present events. In this stressed and overloaded state, your effectiveness is rapidly diminished. The solution is simple: **Take control of the time frame you're focusing upon**. If the present is stressful, then become more resourceful in dealing with your challenges by focusing on the future and the successful completion or resolution of the tasks before you. This new focus will instantly change your state and give you the very resources you need to turn things around in the present.

Stress is so often the result of feeling "stuck" in a particular time frame. One example of this is when a person keeps thinking of their future in disempowering ways. You can help this person or yourself by getting them to refocus on what they *can* control in the present. Or some people, when they're called upon to take on a challenge, begin to focus exclusively on their past poor performance. As they remain in the past, their stress increases. A shift to the present, or an anticipation of a positive future, could instantly change their emotional state. Our emotions, then, are powerfully impacted by the time frame in which we're operating at the moment.

So often we forget that time is a mental construct, that it is completely relative, and that our experience of time is almost exclu-

sively the result of our mental focus. How long is a long time, for example? It all depends upon the situation, doesn't it? Standing in line for more than 10 minutes can seem like an eternity, while an hour of making love can pass all too quickly.

Our beliefs also filter our perception of time. For some people, regardless of the situation, twenty minutes is a lifetime. For others, a long time is a century. Can you imagine how these people walk differently, talk differently, look at their goals differently, and how stressed they might be if they were trying to deal with one another while operating out of completely different frames of reference? This is why time mastery is a life skill. The ability to flex your experience of time is the ability to shape your experience of life.

For today's exercises, let's briefly review and apply three "time-saving" tips.

I. THE ABILITY TO DISTORT TIME

After you've mastered the ability to change time frames by changing your focus, you're ready to move on to the second major skill of time mastery, and that is **the ability to distort time so that a minute feels like an hour, or an hour like a minute.** Haven't you noticed that when you become totally engrossed in something, you lose track of time? Why? Because you no longer focus upon it. You make fewer measurements of it. You're focused on something enjoyable and, therefore, time passes more rapidly. Remember that you're in control. Direct your focus and consciously choose how to measure your time. If you are constantly checking your watch, then time seems to crawl. Once again, your experience of time is controlled by your focus. How do you define your *use* of time? Are you spending it, wasting it, or killing it? It's been said that "killing time is not murder; it's suicide."

II. A MATTER OF IMPORTANCE

The third, and perhaps the most critical distinction of all, is an understanding of how *urgency* and *importance* control your decisions about what to do with your time, and therefore your level of personal fulfillment. What do I mean? Let me ask you this: **Have you ever worked your tail off, completed every single thing on your "to do" list, but at the end of the day still felt unfulfilled? That's because you did everything that was urgent and demanded your attention in the moment, but you didn't do what was *important*—**the things that would make a difference long-term. Conversely, have you ever had days when you got only a few things done but at the end felt that this was a day that had really mattered? These are the days when you've focused on what's important rather than what urgently needed your attention.

Urgency seems to control our lives. The phone rings, and we're doing something important, but we "have to" pick it up. After all, what if we missed out on something? This is a classic example of handling what's urgent—after all, you might miss out on a high-powered phone conversation with a computerized surveyor! On the other hand, we buy a book that we know can make a difference in our lives, yet put off reading it time and again because we "just can't squeeze it in" between opening the mail, filling the gas tank, and watching the news on TV. The only way to truly master your time is to organize your schedule each day to spend the majority of it doing things that are important rather than urgent.*

III. SAVE YOURSELF YEARS

The most powerful way I've learned to compress time is to learn through other people's experience. We can never truly master time as long as our primary strategy for learning and mastering our world is based upon trial and error. Modeling those who've already succeeded can save you years of pain. This is why I'm a voracious reader and a committed student of tapes and seminars. I've always seen these experiences as necessities, not accessories, and they have given me the wisdom of decades of experience and the success that results from it. I challenge you to learn from other people's experiences as often as you can, and to utilize whatever you learn.

"We have time enough if we will but use it aright."
—JOHANN WOLFGANG VON GOETHE

Today's Assignment:

1. Throughout this day, begin to **explore changing time frames**. Whenever you're feeling the pressures of the present, stop and think about the future in ways that are empowering. For example, think of

* I've developed a Time Mastery system designed to help you organize your time based on your values and core beliefs about what's most important in your life. For information, contact Robbins Research International, Inc. at 1-800-445-8183.

goals that compel you, and become fully associated to them. Visualize the image, listen to it, step into it and notice how it feels. Put yourself back into the midst of a treasured memory: your first kiss, the birth of your child, a special moment with a friend. The more you develop your capability to quickly change time frames, the greater your level of freedom and the range of emotions you will be able to create within yourself at a moment's notice. Do this enough until you truly know you can use this change in focus to instantly change your state.

2. **Learn to deliberately distort time.** For something that normally seems to take a long time to complete, add another component that will not only speed up your perception of time, but allow you to accomplish two things at once. For example, when I'm running, I'll don a pair of headphones and listen to my favorite music. Or I'll watch the news or make phone calls while I'm on my StairMaster. This means I'll never have an excuse not to exercise, not to do what's important: working out *and* returning my calls.

3. Write a "to do" list that **prioritizes according to importance** instead of urgency. Instead of writing down zillions of things to do and feeling like a failure at the end of the day, focus on what's *most* important for you to accomplish. If you do this, I can promise you that you'll feel a sense of satisfaction and accomplishment few experience.

Of course, we must always take time to . . .

25

REST AND PLAY: EVEN GOD TOOK ONE DAY OFF!

DAY SEVEN

Your Outcome: *Achieve some balance.*

You've worked hard and you've played hard. Take a day off to have some fun! Be spontaneous, be outrageous, do something that takes you outside yourself. What would create the most excitement for you?

> *"The great man is he*
> *that does not lose his child's-heart."*
> —MENCIUS

Today's Assignment:

1. Either plan something fun and stick to it, or do something on the spur of the moment. Whatever it is, enjoy it!

Tomorrow, you'll be ready to explore . . .

PART · FOUR

A LESSON IN DESTINY

26

THE ULTIMATE
CHALLENGE:
WHAT ONE
PERSON CAN DO

"A mighty flame followeth a tiny spark."
—DANTE

He knew he must stop them. With a mere $800 in his pocket, Sam LaBudde drove across the Mexican border, stood on the fishing docks of Ensenada, and waited for his opportunity. Toting a video camera to get some "home movies" of his excursion, he posed as a naive American tourist and offered his services as a deckhand or engineer to each captain who docked his boat in the harbor.

He was hired on the *Maria Luisa* as a temporary crew member, and as the Panamanian tuna boat pulled away from the Mexican coast, LaBudde began to secretly film the activities of the crew. He knew that if he were discovered his life would be in jeopardy.

Finally it happened: they were surrounded. A whole school of dolphins, known to many as "water people," began jumping and chattering near the *Maria Luisa*. Their friendly nature had drawn them to the boat; little did they know that they were also being drawn to their death. The fishermen trailed the dolphins because they knew that yellowfin tuna usually swim below the playful creatures. With cold-blooded calculation, they lay their nets in the path of the dolphins, not noticing or even caring what happened to them.

Over the course of five hours, LaBudde's video recorded the horror. One after another, dolphins became entangled in the nets, unable to free themselves and come to the surface for the oxygen they needed to stay alive.

At one point the captain bellowed, "How many in the net!?"* As LaBudde swung to capture the slaughter on video, he heard a crew member yell, "About fifty!" The captain ordered the crew to haul in their catch. Numerous dolphins lay strangled and lifeless on the slippery deck as the crew separated them from the tuna and discarded their sleek, gray bodies. Eventually, the corpses of these magnificent animals were tossed overboard as casually as sacks of garbage.

LaBudde's footage gave clear-cut evidence of what others had claimed for years: that hundreds of dolphins were regularly being killed in a single day's fishing expedition. Estimates are that over six million dolphins have been killed in the last ten years alone. Edited down to an eleven-minute format, LaBudde's video stunned viewers with the heart-wrenching reality of what we were doing to these intelligent and affectionate beings with whom we share our planet. One by one, outraged consumers across the nation stopped buying tuna, launching a boycott that only gained speed as media attention became more pointed.

Just four years after LaBudde first captured the tragedy on film, in 1991 the world's largest tuna canner, Starkist, announced that it would no longer pack tuna caught in purse seine nets. Chicken of the Sea and Bumblebee Seafoods followed suit, issuing similar statements just hours later. While the fight is not over—unregulated foreign tuna boats still kill six times as many dolphins as did the U.S. boats—LaBudde's day on the *Maria Luisa* has served as a catalyst for major reform in the American tuna industry, saving countless dolphin lives and undoubtedly helping to restore some balance to the marine ecosystem.

> *"Every man is an impossibility until he is born."*
> —RALPH WALDO EMERSON

So many people feel powerless and insignificant when it comes to social issues and world events, thinking that even if they did everything right in their own personal lives, their welfare would still be at the mercy of the actions of others. They feel beset by the proliferation of gang warfare and violent crime, perplexed by massive government deficits and the S&L crisis, saddened by homelessness and illiteracy, and overwhelmed by global warming and the relentless extinction of the other species who live on this planet. Such people fall into the mindset of thinking, "Even if I get my own life and the lives of my family in order, what good will it do? Some nut in a position of power could accidentally push the button and

---

* Reed, Susan, and Lorenzo Benet, "A Filmmaker Crusades to Make the Seas Safe for Dolphins," *People* magazine, August 6, 1990.

blow us all up anyway!" This kind of belief system fosters the feeling of being out of control and impotent to create change at any significant level, and naturally leads to the learned helplessness typified by the phrase, *"Why even try?"*

Nothing could be more crippling to a person's ability to take action than learned helplessness; it is the primary obstacle that prevents us from changing our lives or taking action to help other people change theirs. If you've come this far in the book, you know without a doubt my central message: **you have the power right now to control how you think, how you feel, and what you do.** Perhaps for the first time you are empowered to take control of the Master System that has unconsciously guided you until this point. With the strategies and distinctions you've gained from reading and doing the exercises in this book, you have awakened to the conviction that you are truly the master of your fate, the director of your destiny.

Together we've discovered the giant power that shapes destiny—**decision**—and that our decisions about what to focus on, what things mean, and what to do are the decisions that will determine the quality of our present and future.

Now it's time to address the power of **joint decisions** to shape the destiny of our community, our country, and our world. What will determine the quality of life for generations to come will be the collective decisions we make *today* about how to deal with such current challenges as widespread drug abuse, the imbalance of trade, ineffective public education, and the shortcomings of our prison system.

By fixating on everything that's *not* working, we limit our focus to effects, and we neglect the *causes* of these problems. We fail to recognize that **it is the small decisions you and I make every day that create our destinies.** Remember that all decisions are followed by consequences. If we make our decisions unconsciously—that is, let other people or other factors in our environment do the thinking for us—and act without at least anticipating the potential effects, then we may be unwittingly perpetuating the problems we dread most. By trying to avoid pain in the short term, we often end up making decisions that create pain in the long term, and when we arrive further down the river we tell ourselves that the problems are permanent and unchangeable, that they come with the territory.

Probably the most pervasive false belief most of us harbor is the fallacy that only some superhuman act would have the power to turn our problems around. Nothing could be further from the truth. *Life is cumulative.* Whatever results we're experiencing in our lives are the accumulation of a host of small decisions we've made as individuals, as a family, as a community, as a society, and as a species. The success or failure of our lives is usually not the result of one cataclysmic event or earth-shaking decision, although sometimes it may look that way. Rather, success or failure is determined by the decisions we make and the actions we take every day.

By the same token, then, it is the daily decisions and actions of *each one of us,* taking responsibility on an individual level, that will truly make the difference in such matters as whether we are able to take care of our disadvantaged and whether we can learn to live in harmony with our environment. In order to bring about massive and far-reaching changes, both in our individual and joint destinies, it is necessary to commit ourselves to constant and never-ending improvement, to the discipline of **CANI!** Only in that way can we truly make a difference that will last in the long term.

THE ULTIMATE SOLUTION

What do you suppose is the one common element in all the problems facing us today as a nation and as a world? From soaring numbers of homeless people to escalating crime rates to huge budget deficits to the slow strangulation of our ecosystem, the answer is that **every single one of these problems was caused or set in motion by human behavior. Therefore, the solution to every one of these problems is to change our behavior.** (This requires changing the way we evaluate or make decisions, which is what this entire book is about.) We don't have a drug problem; we have a behavior problem. Teenage pregnancy is not the result of a virus. It is the consequence of specific behavior. Gang warfare is a behavioral problem. Even nuclear war is ultimately a behavioral problem! Our decisions built the bombs, and our decisions will eliminate them. **All of these problems are the result of actions that people have chosen to take.**

For example, when an individual becomes a gang member, that single decision sets in motion a whole series of behaviors and problems. With this new gang identity, he will hold himself to a very specific code of behavior which places utmost value on such things as loyalty to the group, and out of that flows a whole system of characteristic rules and behaviors. A global example of the long-term effects of our decisions is the chronic famines and food shortages that take the lives of so many around the world. The World Health Organization has proven that it is possible to feed every man, woman, and child on this earth, yet *every day,*

<u>*40,000 children die of starvation.*</u>* Why? Obviously we have the resources, but something has gone terribly awry, not only with the way food is distributed, but with the way our resources are used.

What's great about all of this? The good news is that once we realize that the root of all problems is behavior (and the decision-making process we use to initiate it), then we know that *we* are the ones who can change it! As you've learned in this book, **the one thing we have absolute control over is our internal world—***we* **decide what things mean and what to do about them**—and as a result of our decisions, we take actions that impact our external environment. There are actions each and every one of us can take in our own homes, our own businesses, and our own communities that will initiate a chain of specific positive consequences. **With our actions, we communicate our most deeply held values and beliefs,** and through the global influence of our mass media, even the simplest actions we take have the power to influence and move people of all nations.

While this sounds encouraging for the human race, you may be asking yourself, "What can one person do to truly make a difference in the world?" *Virtually anything!* **The only limit to your impact is your imagination and commitment.** The history of the world is simply the chronicle of what has happened because of the deeds of a small number of ordinary people who had extraordinary levels of commitment to making a difference. These individuals did little things extraordinarily well. They decided that something *must* change, that *they* must be the ones to do it, and that they *could* do it—and then they summoned the courage to persist until they found a way to make it work. These are the men and women we call **heroes**.

I believe that you and I—and everyone we'll ever meet—has the inborn capacity to be heroic, to take daring, courageous, and noble steps to make life better for others, even when in the short term it seems to be at our own expense. The capacity to do the right thing, to dare to take a stand and make a difference, is within you now. The question is: **When the moment arrives, will you remember you're a hero and selflessly respond in support of those in need?**

> ### "It was involuntary; they sank my boat."
> —JOHN F. KENNEDY, when asked how he'd become a hero

So many people want to avoid any hint of a problem or challenge, yet **surmounting difficulty is the crucible that forms character.** Many

---

* Institute for Food and Development Policy. See John Robbins, *Diet for a New America,* Walpole, New Hampshire: Stillpoint Publishing, © 1987, p. 352.

people don't discover their heroic nature until a major difficulty or life-threatening situation occurs and they must rise to the occasion because there is no other choice. The next time you find yourself in a tough spot, decide to make a difference in that situation and take action, no matter how small it seems at the time. Who knows what consequences you will set in motion? Identify yourself as a *hero* so that you can act as one.

Many people look at a person like Mother Teresa and assume that she was born to heroism. They claim that she's just an incredibly spiritual woman and that she's always been set apart by her commitment and selfless contribution to the poor. While it is true that she is a woman of extraordinary courage and compassion, it is also true that Mother Teresa had some crucial moments that defined her role as one of the great contributors of our time. Mother Teresa did not set out to help the poor. In fact, for over twenty years she taught the wealthiest children in Calcutta, India. Every day she overlooked the impoverished slums that surrounded the well-to-do neighborhood in which she worked, never venturing outside her tiny sphere of influence.

One night, as she was walking down the street, she heard a woman crying out for help. It was in the moment that this dying woman fell into her arms that Mother Teresa's life changed forever.

Realizing the seriousness of the woman's condition, Mother rushed her to the hospital, where she was told to sit and wait. She knew the woman would die without immediate attention, so she took her to another hospital. Again, she was told to wait; the woman's social caste made her less important than the others being treated. Finally, in desperation, Mother Teresa took the woman home. Later that night, she died in the comfort of Mother Teresa's loving arms.

Mother Teresa's "defining moment" had transpired: the moment when she decided that *this would never happen again to anyone within her reach*. From that moment on she decided that she would devote her life to easing the pain of those who suffered around her and that, whether they lived or died, they would do so *with dignity*. She would personally do everything in her power to see that they would be treated better than they had ever been treated their entire lives, with the love and respect that all people deserve.

> *"Let the word go forth from this time and place, to friend and foe alike, that the torch has been passed to a new generation of Americans, born in this century, tempered by war, disciplined by a hard and bitter peace, proud of our ancient heritage, and unwilling to witness or permit the slow undoing of*

*those human rights to which this nation has always
been committed, and to which we are committed
today, at home, and around the world.
Let every nation know, whether it wishes us well or
ill, that we shall pay any price, bear any burden,
meet any hardship, support any friend, oppose any
foe, to assure the survival and the success of liberty."*
—JOHN F. KENNEDY

Many people today seem to shy away from the very idea of being a hero, perhaps avoiding the responsibility they feel it would entail. Besides, aren't such aspirations egotistical? Isn't all heroism false anyway? After all, no one's *perfect*. Today we live in a society where we not only overlook potential heroes, but we denigrate the ones we have. With morbid fascination, we scrutinize their private lives, digging for some chink in their armor, and eventually we find it—or fabricate one. In every campaign race, people complain about the caliber of the candidates, yet they systematically pursue evidence of even the slightest indiscretions of a candidate's past behavior, even to the extent of focusing on the fact that a potential Supreme Court Justice once smoked a marijuana cigarette decades ago!

If we held the great heroes of our past to the same unbending criteria by which we judge our present-day heroes, *we wouldn't have any heroes!* The Kennedys and the Kings would have had difficulty withstanding today's tabloid mentality. It seems that we're so afraid of being let down that we try to find something wrong to begin with—just so we're not disappointed later. As long as we operate from the frame that all heroes have feet of clay, then clearly we must believe that there is something wrong with all of us, that none of us has what it takes or is "good enough" to be a hero.

How do I define a hero? A hero is a person who courageously contributes under even the most trying circumstances; a hero is an individual who acts unselfishly and who demands more from himself or herself than others would expect; a hero is a man or woman who defies adversity by doing what he or she believes is right in spite of fear. A hero moves beyond the "common sense" of the promoters of the *status quo*. A hero is anyone who aims to contribute, anyone who is willing to set an example, anyone who lives by the truth of his or her convictions. A hero develops strategies to assure his outcome, and persists until it becomes a reality, changing his approach as necessary and understanding the importance of small actions consistently taken. A hero is not someone who is "perfect," because none of us is perfect. We all make mistakes, but that doesn't invalidate the contributions we make in the course of our lives. **Perfection is not heroism; humanity is.**

THE CHALLENGE OF HOMELESSNESS

Knowing that within each of us flickers the spark of heroism, just waiting to be fanned into a mighty flame, how can we tackle a giant social issue such as the plight of our country's homeless population? The first key to changing this situation is to **hold ourselves to a higher standard**. We must *decide* that, as the richest country on earth, we are *no longer willing to settle* for having so many of our men, women, and children cast out on the streets like human refuse.

What percentage of our population is homeless? At this writing the results of the 1990 census on the homeless have not been fully tabulated. In fact, by the very nature of homelessness—the people involved have no address—exact figures are difficult to obtain. The most commonly cited statistics estimate that at least 3 million of our citizens are homeless, or roughly one in every 100 people live on the streets or in shelters.[*]

The second key to addressing this problem is to **change our beliefs**. We must stop believing that these problems are a permanent malaise pervading our country and that there is nothing that any individual can do to truly make a difference. The way to break free of learned helplessness is to adopt the belief that, as an individual, you *can* make a difference, and that in fact all great reform movements have been carried out by committed individuals.

Another belief we must change is that the homeless are in their current situation because they are all "mentally deranged." Again, statistics cannot be precise, but it is estimated that between 16 percent and 22 percent of the homeless suffer some form of mental illness.[†] In order to really help these people, we must break through our stereotypes. Generalizing about the homeless does not empower us to help them, and beyond a shadow of a doubt, many *can* be helped.

What causes homelessness in the first place? Besides the already-mentioned mental illness, other reasons commonly cited include the spiraling cost of housing coupled with diminishing income, drug or alcohol abuse, and the breakdown of the traditional American family. The truth is

---

[*] Snyder, Mitch, and Mary Ellen Hombs, "Homelessness Is Serious," David L. Bender, ed., *The Homeless: Opposing Viewpoints,* Greenhaven Press, © 1990.
[†] Ibid.

that all of these are legitimate reasons. Yet underlying them all are belief systems. After all, there are plenty of people who have also survived the ravages of drug and alcohol abuse, who have lost their homes or can't even earn enough to pay the rent, and who have never experienced a stable family life—yet these people never became homeless.

What's the difference? **It all comes down to the basic beliefs, values, and identity of each individual.** Many who are on the streets may see themselves as "homeless" people; but others may see themselves as being "temporarily without a home." Thus they pursue solutions and will find a way back into the traditional lifestyle. **To create long-term change for a homeless individual, there must be a change in *identity*.** This is the only way to produce a consistent change in their behavior.

Since 1984, I have worked with homeless organizations in the South Bronx, Brooklyn, Hawaii, and San Diego, assisting people in making the transformation from "homeless person" to "societal contributor." Each year in my Mastery programs, participants spend an evening with several homeless people to facilitate change and help them turn their lives around. The results of these one-hour interactions are often astounding.

One terrific example of this is a young man named T. J. We first met him two years ago, when we brought him in off the street and invited him to have dinner with us if he'd share a little bit of his life story. At the time, he says, he was "high as a kite." He had been living on the street for over ten years, addicted to cocaine, methadone, and amphetamines. After spending a mere hour with him, the seminar participants I had trained were able to help him make huge shifts in his beliefs and assist him in developing strategies to support his new identity.

Today, T. J. is not only off the street and off drugs, but he is also a major contributor to society—he is a fireman in Texas. In fact, for the last two years he has returned to our program to help us recruit and assist others who are in the same position he was in only a couple of years ago.

In interviewing homeless people, I've found that many of them are just like T. J. They have drug or alcohol problems, or they have lost their homes and don't know how to cope with the situation. Most of their challenges are not unlike many other people's. They have neuro-associations that limit them; they have values that preclude a change; some of their rules keep them from moving forward; their identity ties them to their limiting circumstances. Since freedom tends to be one of their highest values, they feel happy in spite of their dissatisfaction with their physical environment. After all, they don't have to play by society's rules, and they avoid the pressures they associate with those rules. Besides, they've built up a whole community of friends, and they often see themselves as being "strong" because they survive by their wits. Often they think it builds character. I've even met people who used to be homeless and now have homes, yet they spend time in shelters because they still identify so completely with their homeless persona.

Through our friendship and caring, you and I can be the bridge between the harsh reality of homelessness and the challenge of personal responsibility that rejoining society requires. We all act upon what we feel is compelling. What would happen if you cultivated a friendship with a homeless person and offered this individual some new reference experiences, like a visit to the spa or the theater? New references provide the fabric for new beliefs and new identities. Remember, small efforts can make a big difference.

THE CHALLENGES FACING OUR PRISON SYSTEM

We have equally disturbing challenges in our prisons. It doesn't take a genius to see that our current incarceration system is ineffective, with a recidivism rate of 82 percent. Of all federal and state inmates in 1986, 60 percent had been in prison two or more times, 45 percent three or more times, and 20 percent six or more times.*

In the last five years, our prison population has swollen in size, creating the stresses that come with massive overcrowding. To relieve the pressure, many inmates are abruptly released with $200 in their pockets, sent away from a system they hate yet have learned to rely upon for a sense of certainty and security.

Clearly they have not learned how to change their system of decision making. Living in an environment where you must pay someone just so you won't be physically harmed or sexually abused, where you must steal or join a gang to survive, does not enhance your view of yourself or your world. Inmates are driven to maintain their criminal identity in order to survive in the prison society, where acknowledgment and prestige are earned by a savage set of rules.

As one ex-convict shared with me, "As soon as I was released, I started thinking about going back. After all, I knew no one on the outside. In the joint I had respect. I had guys that would kill for me. On the outside, I was just a worthless ex-con." Sent out into a world where they know no one, thinking that they have no way to control their own environment, these men and women often do things—consciously or unconsciously—to ensure return to their "home."

* Wright, John W., ed., *The Universal Almanac,* Andrews and McMeel, © 1989.

Can this cycle of criminality be interrupted? Of course it can—**if there is enough pain linked to being in prison, and enough pleasure to being outside of it.** If we could train people effectively, the combination of these factors would be amazing. Recently, I interviewed a man who had just been released after serving eight years for attempted murder. When I asked him if he'd shoot someone again, he smiled and said, "In a heartbeat—if anyone tried to take my drugs." I asked, "Don't you want to avoid going back to prison?" He said, "No! Prison's not so bad. There, I didn't have to worry about my next meal. And I got to watch TV. And I really had things wired; I knew how to deal with all the other guys, so I never really had to worry." Prison is not a deterrent to his sociopathic behavior. He simply doesn't associate pain to incarceration.

Now contrast this with the experiences of Frank Abagnale, author of the book *Catch Me If You Can*. He is world famous for his antics as "the great imposter," traveling around the world posing as a Pan Am airline pilot, a hospital administrator, an aide to the attorney general of Louisiana, among other guises, and conning people out of millions of dollars. Today, Frank is one of the foremost experts in bank security systems and a contributor to his community.

What turned him around? *Pain.* As the result of one of his escapades, he was arrested and incarcerated in a French prison. No one threatened him with physical or sexual abuse, but the pain was incredibly intense. First, he spent his entire sentence in a dark cell and totally isolated from all contact with the outside world: no television, no newspapers, no radio, no conversation with other inmates or guards. Second, they gave him *absolutely no idea when he'd be released.* He didn't have a clue whether he'd be held there for sixty days or sixty *years.*

The pain of not knowing—the sense of uncertainty—was the severest form of punishment imaginable, and Frank linked so much pain to this "hell on earth" that he vowed he'd never return. And you know what? He's not alone. Not surprisingly, French prisons have a recidivism rate of 1 percent and spend about $200 on each prisoner annually (an even more astounding figure when you consider that Americans spend about $30,000 a year on our prisoners, and perpetuate an 82 percent recidivism rate!).

Am I suggesting that we duplicate the French penal system? No, all I'm saying is that the system we have in place is obviously not working and that it's time to try something else. We must provide our prisoners with an environment in which they don't have to constantly worry about being beaten or attacked by cellmates, yet at the same time we cannot make prison the home they never had. I'm suggesting that prison terms should be *undesirable—uncomfortable*—and that during a prison term, people should be shown ways to make the outside world an experience that they can be in control of, one of pleasure and possibility, so that when they're released, it's something they pursue rather than fear. They must link pain to being in prison, and pleasure to changing. Otherwise, the behavior that landed them in jail will never be modified long-term.

Above all, a prisoner must know that someone *cares* about him and is committed to offering him strategies that will steer his life in a new direction. Not all prisoners are ready for change, but those who are clearly deserve our support.

> *"While there is a lower class I am in it; while there is a criminal element I am of it; while there is a soul in prison, I am not free."*
> —EUGENE VICTOR DEBS

What can *you* do? One simple yet profound action would be to commit once a month to visiting a prisoner who has truly decided to change the quality of his life. Become a loving, supportive friend and show him or her the choices available. I'll never forget the relationship I developed as a result of volunteering to visit with an inmate of the Chino, California prison. Through my assistance and encouragement, he began running up to three miles a day, reading inspirational and instructional books, and beginning the transition from "prisoner" to "valued person." When he was released two years later, the sense of connection and contribution we shared was one of the more rewarding experiences of my life.

THE CHALLENGE OF GANG VIOLENCE

While adult crime is a demanding problem indeed, we also need to address the question of how we can stem the flow of our youth into the juvenile penal system. What about the senseless murders that are being committed every day by young gang members in the inner cities? The unrelenting savagery of two gangs that originated in Los Angeles and then spread across the nation—the Crips and the Bloods—has taken an unfathomable toll on the cities in which they live, and most of us are at a loss as to how to address this frightening problem. I'm certain, however, that one of the first things that must happen is to get gang members to rethink their rules. Remember, all of our actions stem from our core beliefs about what we must and must never do or be.

I recently read a *Rolling Stone* article excerpting a book focusing on the day-to-day life of gang members.* This "slice of life" details a gang class held at a juvenile hall called Camp Kilpatrick. When the students (gang members) were asked why they would kill someone, they rapidly fired off a list of *thirty-seven reasons*. These are a few of those I found most shocking: *if someone looks at me funny, if someone asks me where I'm from, for a nickel, if someone walks funny, if someone touches my food (for example, takes a french fry), for fun, if someone gives me a bad haircut.*

With such aberrant rules—rules that almost no one else in the society shares—it is no surprise how volatile these young men and women are. They have more reasons to kill than virtually anyone, and thus they act in accordance with their rules. What was encouraging to me, though, was to see that the facilitator understood the power of questions to weaken even the most strongly held beliefs. He asked, "For which of these things would you be willing to *die?*" In other words, if you knew that by killing someone for a bad haircut you would also die, would you still do it?

By asking this question, he got them to reevaluate their rules and to reconsider the importance of those things for which they'd previously been willing to murder. By the time he was done with this questioning process, these gang members had radically changed their rules. Instead of thirty-seven reasons to kill, they now had only three: *self-defense, for family, and for association (gang)*. The latter remained only because one young man persisted in believing that this was perhaps the *most* important thing in his life. Whenever any of the other kids tried to dissuade him, he simply insisted, "Y'all don't know me." His identity was a conviction, one so tied to his gang that surrendering it would mean surrendering his whole sense of self—probably the only thing constant in this young man's life.

By pursuing this method of asking and answering questions, this "school" is getting through to many of the kids who take the course. It is weakening the reference legs of destructive beliefs until these kids no longer feel certain about them. **Remember, all behaviors can be changed by changing beliefs, values, rules, and identity.** Obviously the conditions that produce the gangs in the first place need to be addressed—ultimately, this too can be handled through modifying behavior at the level where it counts, case by case.

* Bing, Léon, "Do or Die," *Rolling Stone,* September 1991.

THE CHALLENGES FACING OUR ENVIRONMENT

The environment is no longer just a rallying cause for the counterculture, but has come to the forefront as a major national and international concern. After four of the hottest consecutive years ever recorded in history, people have become extremely concerned about global warming—the phenomenon caused by excess carbon dioxide that is trapped by the ozone layer, resulting in rising temperatures. What are the major sources? One of them is the fluorocarbons found in air conditioners and spray bottles. Another major source of the global-warming effect is the wanton destruction and burning of our Central and South American rainforests. **Rainforests account for an astounding 80 percent of the earth's vegetation, and are critical to our ecosystem.** *

Trees absorb the toxic gases of excess carbon dioxide that we release into the atmosphere, and convert it to breathable oxygen. **Trees are our ultimate rejuvenators: without them, life on earth as we know it could not exist.** Rainforest trees also provide an environment for the largest diversity of animal and insect species in the world. **By burning our rainforests, not only do we destroy the oxygen-producing vegetation and the environment in which the animals and plants live, but we release huge amounts of carbon dioxide into the atmosphere and hasten the deleterious global-warming effect.**

With all their importance, why are the rainforests being cleared so relentlessly? The answer is a simple matter of pain and pleasure: economics. Huge tax breaks have been given in these countries as incentives for ranchers to clear the land. Is it to make room for more housing? Of course not. It's to clear *grazing land for cattle to be exported as beef to the United States.* This nation imports 10 percent of its beef from Central and South America.† In order to meet this need, **rainforests are being eliminated at a pace of one acre every five seconds.‡**

The inefficiency of the use of this land for grazing is one of the most destructive, short-term decisions that man can make. We're bulldozing the source of our survival. Do you realize that every time you buy a quarter-pound hamburger using rainforest beef, it represents the destruction of fifty-five square feet of tropical rainforest?** Once destroyed, *it can never be replaced.* Further, **the current rate of species extinction is**

* Robbins, John, *Diet for a New America.*
† "Acres, USA," vol 15 #6, June 1985, cited in J. Robbins.
‡ Robbins, John, *Diet for a New America.*
** "The Fate of Our Planet," *Robbins Research Report,* Fall 1990, Robbins Research International, Inc. © 1991.

1,000 per year due to the destruction of the rainforests—an unimaginable assault on our ecosystem.

What's the point of it all? It's solely for the purpose of cycling more meat through our bodies, which medical science has already established is directly related to the top killers in this nation: heart disease and cancer. The shocking statistic is that one out of two Americans dies of some form of heart disease—Russian roulette gives you better odds of survival than following the standard American diet! **Ultimately, we cannot destroy the external environment without destroying our own internal environment.**

Do you want to stop the destruction of our rainforests? Do you want to help restore the delicate balance of our ecosystem? In addition to sending your financial support to environmental organizations like Greenpeace, the most powerful thing you can do is to link pain to any of your personal behaviors that perpetuate the ill use of our planet. Clearly, one step would be to reduce or eliminate your consumption of hamburger meat. A boycott worked with the tuna industry, and it can work here as well. We're not just talking about dollars and cents. The earth itself is at stake. **Know that the decisions you make about what to put on your dinner plate determine, in a small yet undeniable way, such things as how much carbon dioxide is released into our atmosphere and how many plant and animal species will die each day.**

Now let's look at the impact of your dietary decisions on a local level. Perhaps you live in a state, like I do, that is experiencing a severe water shortage. In fact, it's been said that in the twenty-first century water will be the gold of the future, one of our most valuable and scarce resources. How can this be true, on a planet that is predominantly covered with water? The reason can be found in our incredibly poor management of this vital resource. Specifically, it's related to the meat industry. Consider this: **the amount of water that is used to raise one single steer is enough to float an American destroyer!*** In California, we're all working hard to conserve water, taking steps such as not watering our lawns and installing flow restrictors in our toilets and shower heads. All of these actions are important, but did you know that it takes 5,214 gallons of water to produce one pound of California beef?† This means that **you can save more water by not eating one pound of beef than you could by skipping showers for an entire year!**‡ According to Cornell economist David Fields and his associate Robin Hur, "Every dollar that state

---

* "The Browning of America," *Newsweek*, February 22, 1981, cited in J. Robbins.

† "The Fate of Our Planet," Robbins Research Report.

‡ This figure assumes a total of 5,200 gallons of water used by a person taking 5 showers a week, 5 minutes per shower, with a flow rate of 4 gallons per minute. Robbins, John, *Diet for a New America*.

governments dole out to livestock producers, in the form of irrigation subsidies, actually costs taxpayers over seven dollars in lost wages, higher living costs, and reduced business income."* What can one person do to save more water? The answer seems obvious to me: cut your meat consumption.

Here's something else for you to chew on. Did you know that **more energy is consumed by the beef industry than any other single industry in the United States?**† The percentage of all raw materials that the United States devotes to the production of livestock is a staggering one-third of all energy consumption, and **the fossil fuel required to produce one pound of beef is roughly thirty-nine times that required to produce the equivalent protein value in soybeans.** If you wanted to save energy, it would be wiser to drive your car to the restaurant down the block than if you walked there, fueled by the calories you consumed from a quarter-pound of beef or chicken raised by the energy-inefficient standard of the industry.

Are you concerned about nuclear power plants? **If we were to reduce by 50 percent our meat consumption, we could totally eliminate our reliance on nuclear power throughout the United States, as well as significantly or completely reduce our reliance on foreign oil imports.**‡

One final issue we're all concerned about is world hunger. With 60 million people dying every year of starvation, clearly it's time for us to examine just how efficiently we're utilizing our resources. Remember, all decisions have consequences, and unless we have some understanding of the long-term impact on our planet, we will make poor decisions.

The amount of food produced on any prime acre of land is *markedly* reduced when that food is beef. **The same acre of land that would produce 250 pounds of beef would produce 40,000 pounds of potatoes—roughly the difference between feeding one person, and 160 persons!**** The same resources that are used to produce one pound of beef can produce sixteen pounds of grain.†† **The land required to feed one meat-eater for a year is three and a quarter acres; for a lacto-ovo-vegetarian, one-half acre; and one complete vegetarian, one-sixth acre.**‡‡ In other words, **one acre can feed twenty times as**

---

* Fields, David, and Robin Hur "America's Appetite for Meat Is Ruining Our Water," *Vegetarian Times,* January 1985.
† Spencer, Vivian, "Raw Materials in the United States Economy 1900–1977," Technical Paper 47, Dept. of Commerce, Dept. of Interior, Bureau of Mines, cited in J. Robbins.
‡ Robbins, John. *Diet for a New America.*
** Department of Agriculture, cited in J. Robbins.
†† Robbins, John, *Diet for a New America.*
‡‡ Lappe, Frances Moore, *Diet for a Small Planet.* Ballantine Books. © 1982, cited in J. Robbins.

many people if they eat a vegetarian diet! Forty-thousand children starve every day, yet we clearly have the ability to feed them if we just manage our resources more effectively. What's more, if every American were to reduce his or her meat intake by just 10 percent, the number of people who could be fed using the resources that would be freed from growing livestock would be 100 million!* This is enough food to feed every single starving man, woman, and child on earth—and have a surplus. Obviously, we'd still have to deal with the political challenge of distribution, but the food would certainly be available. Finally, one of the most important natural resources that we are depleting as a result of our meat habit is our topsoil. It takes nature 500 years to create one inch of topsoil, and we're currently losing one inch every 16 years! Two hundred years ago, our country had twenty-one inches of topsoil, and now we have only six inches.† The amount of topsoil loss that is directly related to livestock production is 85 percent.‡ Without adequate topsoil, our food chain collapses, and with it our ability to exist.

My initial exposure to most of the above statistics and the devastating impact of meat eating on our environment was through my good friend John Robbins (who is not related to me by birth, yet we truly are brothers in our commitment to making a difference). John wrote a book, *Diet for a New America,* that was nominated for a Pulitzer Prize. I believe this book has a place in the home of every American who wants to be aware of the effects of their daily decisions and actions.

As John makes clear, the decision about what to put on your dinner plate tonight is one that has profound processional effects. It sets in motion a whole series of events and activities that are shaping the quality of life on earth. You may ask, **"How can one person hope to turn the tide of such an enormous challenge?"** John maintains that this battle will be won not on Capitol Hill or in the boardrooms, but by individuals: "the shopper in the supermarket stopping at the meat counter, picking up that chuck steak marked $3.98 a pound, and realizing that they're holding in their hand a very costly illusion. Behind that little price sticker hides the forests that have been cut down, our children's food and water supply, our children's topsoil, their future environment. And we have to look at that steak and say, '*That costs too much.*' **Real power lies in the**

---

* Lester Brown of the Worldwatch Institute, cited by Resenberger, UNICEF, "State of the World's Children," adjusted using 1988 figures from the USDA, *Agricultural Statistics 1989,* cited in J. Robbins.
† Harnack, Curtis, "In Plymouth County, Iowa, the Rich Topsoil's Going Fast, Alas," *New York Times,* July 11, 1980, cited in J. Robbins.
‡ Hur, Robbin, Soil and Water Resources Conservation Act—Summary of Appraisal, USDA Review Draft, 1980, cited in J. Robbins.

decisions you make in the supermarket and in restaurants and in your kitchen."*

TAKE A STAND

By taking a stand, you not only stop participating in the misuse of our resources, but you send a clear message to big businesses whose lifeblood is tied to hamburger. In recent years, food-service companies like McDonald's and Carl's Jr. (Carl Karcher Enterprises) have begun to respond to changes in consumer tastes by featuring salad bars and other alternative foods. McDonald's also recently stopped using polystyrene containers for its foods, and as a result estimates that it reduced its production of hydrocarbons by 25 percent, making a measurable difference toward an improved environment. As a consumer, use the skills that you've learned in this book to bring about positive change: know what you want, **use your buying power as leverage to interrupt destructive patterns, cause the companies to look for alternatives, and then reinforce them for the desired behaviors by patronizing their products and services.**

TEACH YOUR CHILDREN WELL—LEAD BY EXAMPLE

As with any challenge, our environmental issues require education and action to create change. Unfortunately, most people's idea of education is tied to being in school, and they stop learning as soon as they graduate—or even before they graduate! So many teachers who start out with a vision of making a difference have fallen into the trap of learned helplessness as a result of trying to cope with numbing administrative policies and not being prepared to deal with the personalities and real-life issues confronting their students.

Yet throughout this book you've been exposed to many models of excellence from whom we can learn. So how can you and I make a difference? We can each take an active role in determining the quality of our children's education. Could your children's teacher benefit by understanding the power of questions, global metaphors, Transformational Vocabulary, values, rules, and conditioning? Share what you've learned, and you can truly make a difference in this area.

* "The Fate of Our Planet," *Robbins Research Report.*

Most important, we must teach our children the consequences of their actions. We must make them aware of the impact they have on an individual or local level and, by extension, their collective impact on the global level. **Don't let them ever fall into the trap of thinking that their actions don't make a difference**—if there's anything I've tried to convey in this book, it's that even **small decisions and small actions, consistently made, have far-reaching consequences**.

One of the best ways to ensure that your child grows up with a healthy sense of self-esteem is to *show* them that their decisions and actions, consistently made, make a major difference. How can you do that? **Demonstrate what's possible by being an example.** Demonstrate to your kids the effect of asking empowering questions, living according to values and rules you've consciously chosen, and using all the other strategies you've learned thus far.

There are so many ways that you and I could contribute. We don't need to wait until we have a grandiose master plan to make a difference. We can have impact in a moment, in doing the smallest things, making what often seem like insignificant decisions. It's true that most of our heroes are hidden behind what seem like small acts done consistently. Look around you. There are heroes everywhere, but we don't acknowledge them with the accolades they deserve for doing their jobs every day. The men and women who work day in and day out as police officers are clearly heroes. They protect us, they create for us a sense of security, yet many of us see them as our enemy. Firemen are heroes, yet we generally don't see them in that light unless we find ourselves in an emergency situation. The same principle holds true for ambulance drivers, 911 emergency dispatchers, crisis-intervention counselors, and a whole host of other unsung heroes.

Just being prepared can make all the difference. For example, how would you feel if someone had a heart attack in your presence, but you were CPR-certified and knew what to do? What if your concerted efforts to keep their blood circulating, despite the apparent absence of any signs of life, actually resulted in saving a life? I can promise you one thing: the feeling of contribution you would get from that experience would give you a greater sense of fulfillment and joy than anything you've ever felt in your life—greater than any acknowledgment anyone could possibly give you, greater than any amount of money you could possibly earn, greater than any achievement you could possibly have.

These are just some of the most dramatic examples. Are there other ways in which you could contribute? You bet! You can be a hero by simply being *a people-builder,* that is, by noticing people around you and giving them support, encouragement, or a reminder of who they really are. What if you were walking through a grocery store, and instead of meandering aimlessly from the artichokes to the zucchinis, you actually noticed and *acknowledged* each person you passed with a cheerful grin? What if you gave a sincere compliment to a stranger? Could you, in that moment, change their emotional state enough so that they could pass on the smile or the compliment to the next person *they* saw as well? Perhaps to their children? Could there be a processional effect set in motion by that one action?

There are so many simple ways to make a difference. We don't have to go out and save somebody's life. But maybe getting them to smile *is* saving their life, or at least getting them to enjoy the life that they already have. What are some other simple ways you could make a difference today? On your way home from work, what if you decided to stop at a senior citizens' home, walk in, and strike up a conversation? How would it make them feel if you were to ask, "What are some of the most important lessons you've learned in your life?" I'll bet they'd have plenty to tell you! What if you stopped at your community hospital, visited a patient and helped brighten their afternoon? Even if you did nothing but *listen* to the person, you'd be a hero.

Why are so many people afraid to take such small steps to help others? One of the most common reasons is that they are just embarrassed to be doing something they're uncertain about. They're afraid of being rejected or appearing foolish. But you know what? **If you want to play the game and *win*, you've got to play "full out." You've got to be willing to feel stupid, and you've got to be willing to try things that might not work—and if they don't work, be willing to change your approach.** Otherwise, how could you innovate, how could you grow, how could you discover who you really are?

> *"You can't live a perfect day without doing something for someone who will never be able to repay you."*
> —JOHN WOODEN

If we want to change the quality of life in our country, then we clearly have to affect the value systems of a mass number of people. Our future is in the hands of our youth. Their values will one day be society's. As I write these words, President Bush has recently signed a document that offers a unique opportunity for us if we maximize its use. It's called the National and Community Service Act of 1990 and is intended to provide program funds, training, and technical assistance to enable communities to develop and expand service opportunities. While the bill encourages all citizens to give of their time, talents, and energy, it is aimed specifically at involving young people in a variety of worthwhile projects.*

Consider the sense of contribution these young people will experience by helping the aged, physically disadvantaged, cancer patients, functionally illiterate, and others. Through the daily experience of contributing, their identities and destinies will be profoundly affected. **Once touched by the gratitude of a fellow human being, a life transforms forever.** Can you imagine the impact if the majority of our young people share this experience?

Indeed, the most powerful processional effect you will ever set in motion will be your burgeoning sense of contribution. We all have a need to go beyond our base drives to avoid pain and gain pleasure. I believe that in the deepest part of ourselves, we all want to do what we believe is right, to go beyond ourselves, to commit our energy, time, emotion, and capital to a larger cause. We must meet our moral and spiritual needs even if it brings us pain in the short term. **We respond not just to our psychological needs, but to our moral imperative to do more and be more than anyone could expect. Nothing gives us a greater sense of personal satisfaction than contribution.** Giving unselfishly is the foundation of fulfillment.

The power of such programs is that by giving to others on an ongoing basis, we begin to reorient our values to the importance of contribution. As a country, if we embrace this one value, it could change the face of the nation and expand our influence in the world abroad. **Don't limit yourself to the structure of government-backed programs, however.** There are so many organizations that have a crying need for manpower and expertise, as well as financial and physical resources. Imagine the impact if, regardless of reward or lack thereof, Americans as a whole make contribution a must. Do you realize that **if everyone in the country** (except the very young and elderly) **were to contribute only three hours a week, our nation would reap the rewards of over 320 *million* hours of much-needed manpower dedicated to those causes that need it most? If we all were to contribute *five* hours, the figure would jump to half a *billion* hours with a monetary value in the *trillions*!** Do you think we could handle a few social challenges with this kind of commitment?

Contributing your time to any one of the following will definitely alter your perceptions of who you are and start you on the path of becoming a hero.

---

* For more information on National and Community Service, please contact your congressperson or The Commission on National and Community Service, The National Press Building, 529 14th Street NW, 4th Floor, Washington, DC 20004, tel. 202-724-0600.

JUST TO NAME A FEW . . .

Here are some of the ways you can help. A small amount of time can make a big difference. Consider the possibility of committing a few hours a week or a few hours a month in one of the following areas within your community:

Programs for the mentally and physically disadvantaged

Remedial tutoring in basic skills

Day care

Voter registration

Volunteer citizen patrols (Neighborhood Watch)

Library work—reshelving, cataloguing

Book distribution to bedridden

Energy conservation

Park maintenance

Community clean-up drives

Walk-a-thons

Drug education

Hotline counseling

Big Brother/Big Sister programs

International family adoption

Outreach programs

Emergency aid

Painting and building beautification

Orphanage programs

Arts and cultural museums

Hosting exchange students

Recycling programs

A GIFT OF POSSIBILITY: AN INVITATION TO CONTRIBUTE

How does one embrace the homeless, heal criminals, rejuvenate the aged, and mobilize the young? One exciting opportunity for you to contribute is to work in partnership with me through **The Anthony Robbins Foundation**. We are a nonprofit organization formed to create a coalition of caring professionals who have committed to consistently reach and assist people who are often forgotten by society. We are aggressively working to make a difference in the quality of life for children, the homeless, the prison population, and the elderly. The Foundation is dedicated to providing the finest resources for inspiration, education, training, and development for these important members of our society. I founded it as the result of my own life experience.

Years ago, I decided that **contribution is not an obligation; it's an opportunity to give something back.** When I was eleven years old, my family did not have enough money one year to afford a traditional Thanksgiving dinner, and a charitable organization delivered food to our door. Since then, helping the hungry and homeless has become one of the missions to which I've dedicated my life, and, every Thanksgiving since I was eighteen, I've made and delivered food baskets to needy families. It was also at the age of eighteen that I first joined the Chino prison support system. As a result of my community service, I formed an identity as a philanthropist, a person who would truly make a difference, someone who was committed. It increased my pride, my integrity, and my capacity to give more to other people as well. And it allowed me to inspire others to do the same.

Because of the massive exposure that my books, tapes, and television shows have produced, I daily receive letters from people from all over the world calling out for help. Some of the most profound and moving transformations I hear about have been made by prisoners and those who are no longer homeless. **As a result, the Foundation has made available a complimentary copy of my thirty-day audio library, *Personal Power*, as well as a copy of my first book, *Unlimited Power*, to every prison system in the United States.** As of this writing, we're in the process of contacting each homeless shelter in the country to make them the same offer. I've dedicated 10 percent of the royalties from this book to the Foundation in order to fund these tape distributions. In addition, Anthony Robbins & Associates,™ the franchisees who represent me with my video-based seminars across the United States, is committed to conducting up to two programs a year in its respective communities at no charge. These programs are held in prisons, homeless shelters, high schools, and senior citizen centers.

If you'd like to join forces with us, please contact the Foundation, and consider enrolling in our **Commit-2** program. It's a simple and balanced way to cause yourself to grow personally and to contribute in a way that truly makes a difference. Through Commit-2 you can give others the gift of possibility through a monthly commitment to briefly visit an assigned prisoner, elderly person, homeless adult or child, and be a true friend. You can also commit to help support one of our annual programs. We sponsor a **Youth Leadership Program**, the Thanksgiving **Basket Brigade**, prison seminars, and a project for the elderly, **Project Wisdom** (more information follows this chapter).

Certainly you're not limited to working with our Foundation to make a difference. There are organizations in your community right now that need your help. In fact, I've designed my Foundation to empower local organizations already in place to succeed. Our Foundation members are trained in how to make a measurable difference for the people they coach monthly. While a different coaching style is necessary for different challenges, there are some universal principles. We all need to raise our standards, change our beliefs, and develop new strategies for personal success. In helping people, we need to provide *profound knowledge*—simple, basic distinctions that can immediately increase the quality of their lives. Very often they need to break through learned helplessness and develop new identities. These are skills and strategies, obviously, that form the backbone of my technology, and therefore we want all those who are involved in this program to have mastery of these skills as well. If you're interested in finding out more, please contact us at 1-800-964-2200, ext. TR.

> *"Only those who have learned the power of sincere and selfless contribution experience life's deepest joy: true fulfillment."*
> —ANTHONY ROBBINS

If a simple Albanian nun, with no resources except her faith and commitment, can positively affect the lives of so many, then certainly you and I can deal with whatever challenges we have before us. If Ed Roberts can emerge from his iron lung each morning to figure out how to change an entire nation's attitudes toward the physically disadvantaged—and succeed—then maybe you and I can be heroes, too. If one person can single-handedly mobilize a nation through a videotape and an $800 investment to stop the murdering of dolphins, then maybe you and I can also set powerful effects in motion. Often we don't know where the chain of events will lead us. Trust your intuition and give of your heart; you'll be surprised at the miracles that will occur.

If you'll commit to giving an hour or two once a month, it will enhance your identity and you'll become certain that you are "the kind of person" who truly cares, who takes deliberate action to make a difference. You'll discover that you have *no problems* in your business, because you've seen what *real* problems are. The upsets you thought you had because your stock went down today tend to disappear when you carry a man with no legs to his bed, or when you cradle an AIDS baby in your arms.

> *"Verily, great grace may go with a little gift; and precious are all things that come from friends."*
> —THEOCRITUS

Once you've mastered the elements of this book, your ability to deal with your own challenges becomes a minor focus. What used to be difficult becomes easy. At this point, you'll find yourself redirecting your energies from concentrating primarily on yourself to improving what's happening in your family, your community, and possibly the world around you. The only way to do so with a lasting sense of fulfillment is through unselfish contribution. **So don't look for heroes; be one!** You don't have to be Mother Teresa (although you could, if you desired!).

However, make *balance* your watchword. **Strive for balance rather than perfection.** Most people live in a black-and-white world where they think that they're either a volunteer with no life of their own, or just a materialistic, achievement-oriented person who doesn't care to make a difference. Don't fall into this trap. Life is a balance between giving and receiving, between taking care of yourself and taking care of others. Yes, give some of your time, capital and energy to those who truly need it—but also be willing to give to *yourself*. And do so with joy, not with guilt. **You don't have to take the weight of the world on your shoulders. More people would contribute if they realized that they didn't have to give anything up to do so. So do a little, and know that it can mean a lot.** If everyone did this, fewer people would have to do so much, and more people would be helped!

The next time you see someone who's in trouble, instead of feeling guilty because you have so many blessings and they don't, feel a sense of *excitement* that you might be able to do just some little thing that could make them think about themselves in a new way or simply feel appreciated or loved. You don't have to commit your whole life to this. Just be sensitive; learn to ask people new questions that will empower them; touch them in a new way. Capture these moments of opportunity, and contribution will be a pleasure rather than a burden.

I often meet people who live in pain because they constantly focus on the injustices of life. After all, how could a child be born blind, without the chance to ever experience the wonder of a rainbow? How can a man who has never hurt anyone his entire life become a victim of a drive-by shooting? **The meaning and the purpose behind some events are unknowable. This is the ultimate test of our faith.** We must trust that everyone in life is here to learn different lessons at different times, that good and bad experiences are only the perceptions of man. After all, some of your worst experiences have truly been your best. They've sculpted you, trained you, developed within you a sensitivity and set you in a direction that reaches out to impact your ultimate destiny. Remember the adage, "When the student is ready, the teacher will appear." By the way, just when you think that *you're* the teacher, take another look—you're probably there to learn something from this person you're so busy teaching!

"Somebody should tell us, right at the start of our lives, that we are dying. Then we might live life to the limit, every minute of every day. Do it! I say. Whatever you want to do, do it <u>now!</u> There are only so many tomorrows."

—MICHAEL LANDON

What's the message? **Live life fully while you're here.** Experience everything. Take care of yourself and your friends. Have fun, be crazy, be weird. Go out and screw up! You're going to anyway, so you might as well enjoy the process! Take the opportunity to learn from your mistakes: find the cause of your problem and eliminate it. Don't try to be perfect; just be an excellent example of being *human.* Constantly find ways to improve yourself. Practice the discipline of **CANI!**; be a lifelong learner. Take the time now to set up your Master System so that the game of life is winnable. Let your humanity—your caring for yourself and others—be the guiding principle of your life, but don't treat life so seriously that you lose the power of spontaneity, the pleasure that comes from being silly and being a kid.

Eighty-six-year-old Nadine Stair said it best:

> "If I had my life to live over again, I'd dare to make more mistakes next time. I'd relax. I'd limber up. I'd be sillier than I've been this trip. I would take fewer things seriously. I would take more chances, I would take more trips, I would climb more mountains and swim more rivers. I would eat more ice cream and less beans. I would, perhaps, have more actual troubles but fewer imaginary ones. You see, I'm one of those people who was sensible and sane, hour after hour, day after day.
>
> Oh, I've had my moments. If I had it to do over again, I'd have more of them. In fact, I'd try to have nothing else—just moments, one after another, instead of living so many years ahead of each day. I've been one of those persons who never goes anywhere without a thermometer, a hot-water bottle, a raincoat, and a parachute. If I could do it again, I would travel lighter than I have.
>
> If I had my life to live over, I would start barefoot earlier in the spring and stay that way later in the fall. I would go to more dances, I would ride more merry-go-rounds, I would pick more daisies."
>
> —NADINE STAIR

How do *you* want to be remembered? As a giant among men? Start acting that way right now! Why wait to be memorable? Live each day as if it were one of the most important days of your life, and you'll experience joy at a whole new level. Some people try to conserve their energy so that they'll last longer. I don't know about you, but I believe that what's most important is not how long we live, but *how* we live. I'd rather wear out than rust out! Let's have the end find us climbing a new mountain.

I think one of the greatest gifts our Creator has given us is the gift of anticipation and suspense. How boring life would be if we knew how it would all turn out in advance! The truth is that in life, we *never* know what's going to happen next! In the next few moments, something could happen that could change the entire direction and quality of your life in an instant. We must learn to love change, for it is the only thing that is certain.

What can change your life? Many things: a moment of deep thought and a few decisions as you complete this book could change everything. So could a conversation with a friend, a tape, a seminar, a movie, or a big, fat, juicy "problem" that causes you to expand and become more. This is the awakening you seek. So live in an attitude of positive expectancy, knowing that everything that happens in your life benefits you in some way. **Know that you are guided along a path of never-ending growth and learning, and with it, the path of everlasting love.**

Finally, as I leave you now, I just want to tell you how much I respect and appreciate you as a person. We've never met, but it sure feels like it, doesn't it? While we may not have met face to face, we've certainly touched hearts. You've offered me a great gift in allowing me to share parts of my life and my skills with you, and my sincere hope is that some of what we've shared here has moved you in a special way. If you'll now use some of these strategies to increase the quality of your life, then I'll feel very lucky indeed.

I hope you'll stay in touch with me. I hope you'll write to me or that we'll have the privilege of meeting personally in a seminar, at a Foundation function, or by a "chance" crossing of our paths. Please be sure to introduce yourself. I look forward to meeting you and hearing the story of your life's success.

'Til then, remember to expect miracles . . . because you *are* one. Be a bearer of the light and a force for good. I now pass the torch on to you. Share your gifts; share your passion. And may God bless you.

"Someday, after we have mastered the winds, the waves, the tide and gravity, we shall harness for God the energies of love. Then, for the second time in the history of the world, man will have discovered fire."
—TEILHARD DE CHARDIN

The Anthony Robbins Foundation

The Anthony Robbins Foundation is a non-profit organization formed to create a coalition of caring professionals who have committed to consistently reach and assist people who are often forgotten by society.

Specifically, we are aggressively working to make a difference in the quality of life for children, the homeless, the prison population and the elderly.

The Anthony Robbins Foundation is dedicated to providing the finest resources for inspiration, education, training and development for these important members of our society.

A Vision Realized

The Foundation is a lifelong dream come true for Mr. Robbins. He has been a committed philanthropist since the age of 18 and has worked extensively with the Salvation Army in the South Bronx and Brooklyn as well as with the homeless in Hawaii and the San Diego area. Currently, we are offering a complimentary copy of his highly successful "Personal Power" audio library, as well as copies of his national bestseller, <u>Unlimited Power</u>, to every homeless shelter and federal prison. Your purchase of this book also contributes to the Foundation: 10% of all Anthony Robbins' royalties from <u>Awaken the Giant Within</u> will be donated to fund its efforts.

Support to Communities Across the U.S.A.

In addition, Anthony Robbins' nationwide force of franchise associates has committed to produce two complimentary video-based programs per year for interested prisons, high schools or homeless shelters within your community. With your help, and through the structure of this organization, we will be able to reach hundreds of thousands of people and give them a new sense of possibility. They'll know that someone out there truly cares about them and that there is a future worth pursuing.

Your Commitment

The Foundation's charter is expressed through the theme of Commit-2. It means that as a member of the Foundation you will commit to two projects, one from each of the following categories:

1. Monthly Commitment – As a member of the Foundation, you will be asked to make a one-year commitment to visit an assigned prisoner, elderly person, homeless individual or child on a monthly basis. Your visits will be designed so that as you listen to your partner and share your experiences with them you will ultimately, through your skill, caring and commitment, help them to increase the quality of their life.

2. Annual Commitment – As a member of the Foundation, you will also be asked to commit to help support, organize or sponsor at least one of the following programs once per year within your community.

OPPORTUNITY TO GIVE

EDUCATION

• **YOUTH LEADERSHIP PROGRAM:** This program takes place at various times throughout the year and involves helping to organize a regional conference in your area. At the conference, high school students are offered an opportunity to learn from the finest instructors in the country how to truly lead by example and master the principles and disciplines of **CANI!**™ (Constant And Never-Ending Improvement).

• **THE "BASKET BRIGADE":** This program takes place during Thanksgiving and involves making up food baskets and delivering them to the homeless, as well as the elderly and poor families who are not able to make it to a shelter or a soup kitchen.

HOMELESS

PRISONS

• **PRISON SEMINAR:** This program takes place at various times throughout the year and involves working with one of our local representatives to bring a video-based Anthony Robbins training seminar to a prison in your area.

• **NATIONAL WISDOM DAY:** This program takes place during the month of January and is designed to follow the holidays with a positive, compelling and impactful event for the elderly. It offers them an opportunity to share their wealth of knowledge with others. Your involvement includes the coordination of a visit from an elderly person to a local school, camp or other organization where this valued member of our culture will be able to share parts of their history and wisdom with the younger generation.

ELDERLY

"A Gift of Possibility: An Invitation to Contribute"

THE CHALLENGE

Life is a gift, and all of us who have the capacity must remember that we have the responsibility to give something back. Your contributions, both financial and physical, can truly make a difference. Please join us now and commit to helping those less fortunate enjoy a greater quality of life.

People interested in more information about the Foundation may write to the Anthony Robbins Foundation, 9191 Towne Centre Drive, Suite 600, San Diego, California 92122, or **call 1-800-554-0619.**

THE ANTHONY ROBBINS FOUNDATION

9191 Towne Centre Drive
Suite 600
San Diego, California 92122

ABOUT THE ANTHONY ROBBINS COMPANIES

The **Anthony Robbins Companies** (ARC) are a force of men and women who are driven to constantly improve the quality of life for everyone who desires it. Offering cutting-edge technologies for the management of human emotion and behavior, ARC is dedicated to empowering individuals not only to recognize but also to *utilize* their unlimited choices.

We believe there is only one way to succeed long term, and that is through commitment to the discipline of **CANI!**™, Constant and Never-ending Improvement. No corporation or individual is satisfied with achieving a certain level of success. True fulfillment occurs only through a sense that we are constantly growing and contributing. Profound growth is the direct result of continual improvement. By sharing the finest technologies for personal and corporate change, ARC's mission is to assist all those who are committed to taking their lives and companies to the next level through personal and professional mastery.

The Anthony Robbins Companies fulfill this promise by constantly pursuing **profound knowledge**—simple strategies, ideas, systems, and plans that are universally applicable and, the minute we understand them, can be used to increase the quality of our individual and corporate lives. We seek out excellence in all forums, modeling the strategies of its creation and sharing the steps that are required to produce lasting impact for change.

We believe that all change occurs through individuals, and ARC is committed to improving the world by teaching its citizens to improve themselves, for it is through the forging of each link that the mightiest chain is built.

Although we may never *exactly* duplicate the achievements of the world's greatest individuals, we *can* duplicate their excellence in our own lives. Each of us can use more effective tools to shape our personal, social, political, and corporate environments—and to enjoy our lives more in the process!

Listed below is a sampling of some of the Anthony Robbins Companies that can provide useful resources for you or your organization.

Robbins Research International, Inc.

This research and marketing arm of Anthony Robbins's personal development businesses conducts personal development, sales and corporate seminars that cover a wide range of topics, from mental conditioning and personal achievement systems to communication mastery.

Anthony Robbins & Associates™

The Anthony Robbins & Associates Franchise and Distributor Network brings video-based seminars to local communities and businesses worldwide.

Owning an Anthony Robbins & Associates franchise offers you the opportunity to be a source of positive impact and growth for the members of your community. Anthony Robbins & Associates provides its franchisees the training, visibility, and ongoing support to create a business that truly makes a difference in people's lives.

Robbins Success Systems™

Robbins Success Systems (RSS) provides Fortune 1000 corporations with state-of-the-art management systems, communication, and teamwork trainings. The RSS team combines thorough pre-training diagnostics, customized facilitation and training, and post-program evaluation and follow-up. Tailored to meet your individual needs, RSS is a catalyst for constant and never-ending improvement in the quality of life within corporations worldwide.

Destiny Financial Services™

Destiny Financial Services (DFS) provides clients with custom-designed plans based on the results and strategies of top financial planning strategists. The Financial Destiny Group™ offers insurance, mutual funds, pension plans, and asset protection and is a fully registered broker-dealer through the National Securities Dealer Association. For more information, please call (619) 453-6330.

Fortune Practice Management™

Fortune Management is a full-service professional practice-management company that provides healthcare professionals with vital strategies and support for increasing the quality and profitability of their practices. Fortune Management is committed to making a difference in the quality of healthcare and in the quality of life of its practitioners.

Tony Robbins Productions

Tony Robbins Productions is a television production company whose primary focus is the creation of the highest quality direct-marketing infomercials to be broadcast nationally. TRP has worked in joint venture to produce three of the most successful infomercials of the last five years. Based on sophisticated market analysis, TRP specializes in tailoring products and promotions to meet the unique needs of specific audiences.

Namale Plantation Resort

For over six years, Tony and Becky Robbins have escaped to Fiji, an incredibly beautiful land where the people's highest value is happiness. Now you can stay at the Robbins' private paradise, the famous Namale Plantation Resort—121 acres of tropical island with pristine beaches, magnificent coral reefs, blowholes, and waterfalls. You can snorkel, scuba-dive, water-ski, lie on the beach, ride horses, or play tennis, basketball, and volleyball. Or try bathing under a cool waterfall. Share the music, joy, and warmth of the wonderfully loving Fijian people.

Only 20 people at a time can enjoy this magnificent and private tropical hideaway. After staying at Namale, you'll never look at the world—or yourself—the same way again. If you'd like to visit Namale Plantation Resort, please telephone 011-679-850-435 or your local travel agent for information or reservations.

For a complete list of available services, please call **1-800-445-8183.**

ABOUT THE AUTHOR

A MILLIONAIRE by the age of twenty-four, Anthony Robbins is an entrepreneur—the founder of nine companies—and the best-selling author of *Unlimited Power,* a book now published in thirteen languages around the world. Considered the nation's leader in human development training, he is the founder and chairman of the board of Robbins Research International, Inc., the research and marketing arm of his personal development businesses.

Deeply committed to contribution and making a difference, he has established The Anthony Robbins Foundation as a philanthropic organization dedicated to assisting those individuals who would not otherwise be reached. By enabling our nation's youth, elderly, homeless, and prison population to tap their inner resources, the Foundation empowers these often-forgotten members of our society to become valuable contributors as well.

Since 1984, millions of people have enjoyed the warmth, humor, and dynamic presentation style of Mr. Robbins's corporate, sales, and personal development seminars. He has been a peak performance consultant to the executives of such organizations as IBM, AT&T, American Express, McDonnell-Douglas, and the United States Army, as well as professional sports teams, such as the Los Angeles Dodgers, Seattle Mariners, and gold medal-winning Olympic athletes.

Mr. Robbins is thirty-two years old and lives in Del Mar, California, with his wife and children.